The President's Words

The President's Words

Speeches and Speechwriting in the Modern White House

Edited by Michael Nelson and Russell L. Riley

University Press of Kansas

Published by the University Press of Kansas (Lawrence, Kansas 66045), which was organized by the Kansas Board of Regents and is operated and funded by Emporia State University, Fort Hays State University, Kansas State University, Pittsburg State University, the University of Kansas, and Wichita State University
Library of Congress Cataloging-in-Publication Data

The president's words : speeches and speechwriting in the modern White House / Michael Nelson and Russell L. Riley, editors
   p. cm
  Includes bibliographical references and index.
  ISBN 978-0-7006-1738-8 (cloth : alk. paper)
  ISBN 978-0-7006-1739-5 (pbk. : alk. paper)
  1. Presidents—United States—History—20th century. 2. Presidents—United States—History—21st century. 3. Presidents—United States—Language—History. 4. Speeches, addresses, etc., American—History and criticism. 5. Speechwriting—United States—History. 6. Speechwriters—United States. 7. Rhetoric—Political aspects—United States—History. 8. Political oratory—United States—History. 9. United States—Politics and government—20th century. 10. United States—Politics and government—2001–2009. I. Nelson, Michael, 1949– II. Riley, Russell L. (Russell Lynn), 1958–
  E176.1.P9725 2010
  973.932—dc22   2010011920

British Library Cataloguing-in-Publication Data is available.

Printed in the United States of America

10 9 8 7 6 5 4 3 2 1

Contents

Preface and Acknowledgments

The genesis of this volume was a two-day symposium on presidential speech-making hosted by the University of Virginia's Miller Center of Public Affairs in June 2008. Featured at the symposium were nine former speechwriters—four Democrats and five Republicans—who among them had worked for every president from Richard Nixon to Bill Clinton. These veterans of the political trenches were joined by a small group of scholars who were assembled to help probe the politics and crafting of presidential rhetoric. Four successive panels were convened, one each devoted to the convention acceptance speech; the inaugural address; the state of the union address; and other landmark speeches, such as those occasioned by crises or major presidential initiatives. The heart of this book consists of four pairs of chapters, each of them organized around a major form of presidential oratory. The first chapter of each pair is by a renowned presidential scholar: Martin J. Medhurst, Charles O. Jones, Kathryn Dunn Tenpas, and Andrew Rudalevige. The second is an annotated transcript of the related speechwriters' panel.

The symposium was organized as a group oral history by the Miller Center's Presidential Oral History Program, which has been conducting in-depth interview projects on every American president since Jimmy Carter. The program's core activity over these many years has been portraiture of individual presidencies, drawn in the words of those who knew each president best. Typically, senior officials from an administration have discussed their experiences in a tape-recorded conversation with the promise that it will not see the light of day for some years to come—maximizing prospects that the interviewee will speak candidly to history.

The group interview, however, offers two advantages over the program's standard fare. First, discussions with people who shared common duties in different presidencies provide enhanced opportunities for cross-administration analysis and reflection, with the contours of the institution more fully distinguished from what may be the idiosyncrasies of a single presidency. So, too, do the subtleties of institutional change more clearly emerge. Thus the great strong suit of the group interview is in providing data for contrast and comparison—both over time and across the partisan divide. To be sure, this volume is rich in wonderful character sketches of individual presidents—such as Jimmy Carter's attempt to tie his understanding of original sin to the practice of American politics—and splendid insights into the internal dynamics of particular White Houses—such as tales of internecine bloodletting under Ronald Reagan. But the most significant contributions these discussions make to our understanding of the contemporary presidency are in revealing the enduring and evolving features of the institution, and also in underscoring how the operating style and rhetorical manner of each president shapes the speechwriting process—and, accordingly, the broader policymaking process within the White House.

Second, the center's individual interviews are always conducted in private. But because this symposium took place as a public event, we are free to publish the proceedings immediately rather than having to wait out the protracted interval necessary for the release of confidential interviews. Admittedly, there may have been some attendant loss of candor at occasional points in the discussions, but that deficiency is more than offset by the accessibility of these sessions now to a wide audience of students and scholars. Readers of this volume will find a wealth of original, raw interview data to be exploited, as well as a set of essays, drafted by an accomplished group of scholars, that weave the first use of these materials into their own independent research and analysis concerning speechmaking and the modern White House. We disseminate the former as well as the latter as an open invitation for others interested in presidential politics to generate their own theories and arguments about the stuff of these deliberations.

THE UNCONVENTIONAL NATURE of this volume makes the editors especially indebted to others for its publication. First and foremost, our thanks go to those speechwriters and scholars who traveled to Charlottesville and offered their time and expertise to help us all understand better the presidency as they know it. Truly this book would have been impossible without their contributions. We appreciate Sidney M. Milkis's contribution of a concluding chapter based on the panels and essays, which neatly balances the introductory chapter by Michael Nelson. We are also grateful to the leadership of the

Miller Center of Public Affairs, its director Governor Gerald L. Baliles, and associate director Taylor Reveley IV for providing the funds and the institutional support necessary for bringing together this group of practitioners and academics.

The Oral History Program's administrator, Katrina Kuhn, did a marvelous job in helping to secure the attendance of all participants and in taking care of scores of logistical concerns during the course of the symposium. The Miller Center's support staff, especially Rob Canevari, Michael Greco, and Kevan Holdsworth, did yeoman's labor in handling the technical aspects of the symposium, which were splendidly complicated by the presence of C-SPAN television cameras. Jane Rafal Wilson's crack editorial staff provided us invaluable assistance after the symposium ended in beginning the move from the spoken to the written word with this book. And it is a testament to Fred Woodward's vision as director of the University Press of Kansas that he was enthusiastic about publishing a volume with such an unconventional frame.

On this final point, it should be noted that we have exercised much greater editorial license in producing the written text of the panel discussions than would be typical of a standard oral history interview, where the literal authenticity of the spoken word is usually considered inviolate. As anyone who has ever labored over a raw transcript will know, the clarity of spoken sentences, where physical gestures and tone communicate meaning, rarely survives transcription intact—without vigorous editing. While endeavoring to track as closely as possible to the original, informal tone of the spoken discussions, Russell Riley has taken as the primary aim in this book the convenience of the reader and has edited accordingly. Thus, anyone for whom the literal phrasing of a particular spoken passage might be crucial is encouraged to consult the video of the original proceedings, which can be accessed at http://millercenter.org/scripps/archive/conference/detail/4001.

Michael Nelson and Russell Riley

Chapter 1

Speeches, Speechwriters, and the American Presidency

Michael Nelson

The president of the United States is both chief of government and chief of state.[1] As chief of government, the president is called to act as a partisan political leader, in the manner of the British prime minister. The role is by its nature wonderfully divisive—wonderfully because democracy requires vigorous competition between political parties and ideas and divisive because people have different preferences.

In contrast, as chief of state the president is the equivalent of the British monarch: the ceremonial leader of the nation and the anthropomorphic symbol of national unity. Various icons, such as the White House, *Air Force One*, Mount Rushmore, and president-laden coins and currency, manifest this role in a superficial way, as do certain presidential actions: greeting championship teams, lighting the national Christmas tree, commissioning officers at the service academies, and so on. But the real power of the chief of state role is embedded in the public's emotions. Before they know anything about politics and government, small children already regard the president as an omnipotent, benevolent figure. When presidents die in office, the public responds with symptoms typical of grief at the death of a loved one. In Great Britain, children regard the monarch, not the prime minister, as powerful and good, and people grieve more deeply at the monarch's death than at their elected chief of government's.

At times, the president's chief of state role buttresses his effectiveness as chief of government, mainly during the honeymoon period that greets a new president, when millions of voters put aside their partisan opposition, and in times of crisis, when the public "rallies-round-the-flag" in the person of the president. But often the two roles are in tension. As Thomas Cronin has noted, Americans impose wildly contradictory expectations on the president, whom they want to be "gentle and decent but forceful and decisive,"

1

"open and caring but courageous and independent," "a common man who gives an uncommon performance," and so on.[2] Most of these contradictions are really one: Americans want the president to be a chief of state who unites them and a chief of government who leads and thus divides them. Without knowing they were doing so, the framers of the Constitution created this tension when they made the presidency a unitary office.

Much of the tension between the president's roles as chief of government and chief of state is manifested in the speeches presidents give. Speechmaking has become a major presidential activity, and as a result speechwriters have become important political actors. The first part of this chapter reviews the origins and development of presidential speechwriting. The second part assesses the four major kinds of speeches that presidents make, each of which is the subject of two chapters later in the book: one by a scholar, the other the transcript of a discussion by former White House speechwriters. The acceptance speeches that presidential candidates, including reelection-seeking presidents, make to the party's national convention display the chief of government role in strongest form. Next in the order that they are delivered, but opposite in character, are inaugural addresses, which powerfully manifest the president's role as chief of state. State of the union addresses are an interesting hybrid: they invoke unifying, chief of state–style symbols to buttress the president's effectiveness as chief of government. Finally, crisis speeches and other landmark addresses, unlike the regularly scheduled acceptance, inaugural, and state of the union addresses, often arise out of unpredictable circumstances and thus are less predictable in character.

Presidential Speechwriting: Origins and Development

For more than a century, presidents seldom gave speeches and never employed speechwriters. It was not unheard of for a president occasionally to call on literate, trusted, and politically experienced aides and allies for help in drafting speeches, as George Washington sometimes did with James Madison and Alexander Hamilton, Andrew Jackson did with Amos Kendall, and both James K. Polk and Andrew Johnson did with George Bancroft. But not until the twentieth century did speechmaking and, consequently, speechwriters become a familiar part of the presidency. Presidential speechwriting has evolved through three eras: the rise of the rhetorical presidency and the professional speechwriter (1901–1933), the era of the speechwriter-adviser

(1933–1969), and the current era of the speechwriting specialist, which began in 1969.

The Rise of the Rhetorical Presidency and the Professional Speechwriter: 1901–1933

In his classic 1987 book *The Rhetorical Presidency*, Jeffrey Tulis described the early twentieth-century transformation of the presidency from an office in which the use of popular rhetoric was proscribed into one in which it is prescribed. "Popular or mass rhetoric has become a principal tool of presidential governance," Tulis argued, so much so that "it is taken for granted that presidents have a duty constantly to defend themselves publicly, to promote policy initiatives nationwide, and to inspirit the population." Theodore Roosevelt was the first president "to successfully appeal 'over the heads' of Congress," but "he did so in a way that preserved, and did not preempt, Congress' deliberative capacities."[3] (Specifically, TR campaigned for a railroad regulation bill, the Hepburn Act, but not while Congress was debating it.) Woodrow Wilson's approach to popular rhetoric was bolder: "to prescribe it always."[4] On April 8, 1913, five weeks after taking office, Wilson shattered the precedent against presidents speaking to Congress by urging the assembled legislators to pass his tariff bill. He began by saying: "I am very glad indeed to have this opportunity to address the two Houses directly and to verify for myself the impression that the President of the United States is a person, not a mere department of Government hailing Congress from some isolated island of jealous power, sending messages, not speaking naturally with his own voice."

Wilson was a graceful, lucid, and rapid writer who personally crafted the many speeches on behalf of his policies that he believed it was the president's duty to deliver. His successor, Warren G. Harding, was not and did not. Of Harding's inaugural address, H. L. Mencken wrote: "It reminds me of a string of wet sponges; . . . of stale bean soup; of college yells; of dogs barking idiotically through endless nights. It is so bad that a sort of grandeur creeps into it."[5] To meet new public expectations that the president speak frequently, Harding became the first president to employ a professional speechwriter. Judson P. Welliver, who after Harding died returned to write for Herbert Hoover, served on the White House staff with the title of Literary Clerk.

The Era of the Speechwriter-Adviser: 1933–1969

Welliver was the first presidential speechwriter but not until decades later, near the end of the second speechwriting era, would he have been a typical one. Speechwriters in administrations from Franklin D. Roosevelt to John F. Kennedy and, for a time, Lyndon B. Johnson were more than literary clerks; they were close Presidential advisers on matters of substance as well as rhetorical style. These speechwriter-advisers often held a title such as "Special Counsel to the President" and their office was in the White House. Typically, they were lawyers or scholars rather than journalists, as Welliver had been and as most writers in the third era would be. Because their duties were greater, because the powers of the presidency were expanding, and because, in an era of trains and then airplanes, radio and then television, presidents found it easier to give many addresses (and were expected to do so), the number of staff members involved in writing speeches grew. Ironically, the rising importance of speechwriting during the second era eventually triggered a decline in status for speechwriters.

During Roosevelt's twelve years as president he employed a series of talented speechwriter-advisers, including Rexford Tugwell, Raymond Moley, Benjamin Cohen, Thomas Corcoran, Samuel Rosenman, Robert Sherwood, and Harry Hopkins. Yet the president's speaking style remained remarkably consistent throughout his tenure. One reason was that FDR edited speech drafts thoroughly, until he was comfortable with how they sounded. Another was that all of his writers learned to write in his voice. Harry S. Truman's writer-advisers, Clark Clifford and George Elsey, learned from close and frequent contact with the president that although he did poorly with texts (he would keep his face buried in them and read as fast as he could), he did well with notes or an outline from which he could extemporize. Kennedy's relationship with Theodore Sorensen was so close that consistency of voice was never a problem. "Whatever success I achieved as a speechwriter for Kennedy arose from knowing the man so well," wrote Sorensen. In addition, Sorensen was a key participant in most of the decisions he wrote about in his speeches ("I *was* the senior staff member"), and Kennedy trusted him completely.[6]

Even in the second era of presidential speechwriting, not all presidents enjoyed a close relationship with their writers. For example, although Dwight D. Eisenhower's speechwriters were involved in policy discussions and had frequent access to the Oval Office, Ike thought his first writer, Emmett John

Hughes, wrote in too flowery a style and that his second, Bryce Harlow, was too bluntly partisan. He finally brought in Kevin McCann, who had written for him when he was a general and was thoroughly familiar with the plain, even-tempered speaking style that Ike preferred.[7] In any event, once a draft was written, Eisenhower "would fully immerse himself in the project, revising speech texts virtually to the moment of their delivery."[8] Johnson spent less time with his writers and did not work as hard on his speeches. But he knew what he wanted: four-letter words, four-word sentences, and four-sentence paragraphs, all marshaled in the service of an unadorned, straightforward argument. On one occasion LBJ reportedly scratched out an attribution to Socrates and substituted "my granddaddy."[9]

Johnson also insisted that every one of his speeches make news by launching an initiative. Speeches thus became action-forcing events. Johnson's budget director, Charles Schultze, complained: "You damned speechwriters spend more money than all the rest of the executive branch put together."[10] In January 1964, LBJ declared "unconditional war on poverty" and, from that point on, the administration's "primary problem was to fashion a program that fit Johnson's rhetoric."[11] Even in foreign policy, former secretary of state Dean Acheson complained, speechwriting is "often where policy is made, regardless of where it is supposed to be made."[12] This was because writing a presidential speech forces an administration to clarify and perhaps even determine its position on an issue well enough to explain and defend it. On the fourth day of the 1962 Cuban Missile Crisis, for example, Sorensen was asked to draft a speech announcing a naval quarantine to keep Soviet vessels from reaching Cuba. He discovered that he had too many questions about how the quarantine would work to write anything useful, and by bringing those questions to the president and his advisers he usefully clarified the discussion.[13]

During the second era of presidential speechwriting, radio (by the early 1930s) and television (by the early 1960s) spread to nearly every American home. No longer was the sound or sight of the president limited to those who were physically present—far from it. FDR knew, and taught his writers, that the audience for radio speeches was as intimate as it was vast: although it consisted of many millions of people, they were gathered in groups of three or four in their homes. His solution was the "fireside chat," an informal talk with homey illustrations in which Roosevelt explained a situation or a course of action to the American people. Knowing that "individual psychology cannot . . . be attuned for long periods of time to a constant repetition of the highest note in the scale," FDR gave only two or three fireside chats per year.[14] Presidents in the television age have heeded that advice. As Samuel Kernell found, the number of "major" presidential speeches—that is, those delivered on network radio or television—has increased very little from the days of Herbert Hoover.[15]

In contrast, "minor" addresses delivered to what Kernell calls "special constituencies" in Washington and around the country have skyrocketed. Kennedy and Johnson averaged about four times as many minor speeches per year as Truman and Roosevelt, an upward trend that has accelerated ever since.[16] Johnson initially relied on close advisers such as Bill Moyers, Richard Goodwin, Jack Valenti, and Harry McPherson to do most of his writing. But the steeply increasing volume of minor presidential speeches—many of them "Rose Garden rubbish," in Moyers's caustic phrase—led Johnson to hire a number of speechwriting specialists, whom he spent little time with and generally regarded as mere wordsmiths.[17] Serving as a substantive presidential adviser in the Johnson White House became one thing, writing speeches another. According to Martin Medhurst, the president believed that aides could "develop the policy in one part of the White House, then ship it across the street to the Old Executive Office Building where the speechwriters could put some 'language' in it."[18] In a final indignity, Johnson relocated his speechwriters from the White House to the OEOB, a powerful symbol of their reduced status.

The Era of the Speechwriting Specialist: 1969–

Richard Nixon institutionalized the late Johnson-era practice of housing presidential speechwriters in their own unit, outside the policy development process. He first created a writing and research department because, as Nixon speechwriter Ray Price observes, "Most of his speeches were not written. Most of our writing was not speeches."[19] This unit was placed in the White House communications office, a Nixon innovation that along with the new office of public liason, manifested the high value the administration placed on speeches and public relations.[20] If anything, Nixon believed too strongly in the efficacy of presidential rhetoric, says speechwriter Lee Huebner. The success of his prime-time televised "Checkers" address in 1952 deluded him into thinking he could readily "turn around public opinion with that kind of speech."

Nixon's personal involvement in writing his speeches exceeded that of any other modern president and, along with the remarkably high caliber of

Price, William Safire, Pat Buchanan, and Nixon's other writers, concealed the extent of the institutional downgrading that speechwriting received when it was reduced to a unit in the communications office. That decline became more apparent under Gerald Ford, whose chief of staff, Donald Rumsfeld, inaugurated the practice of systematically vetting the speechwriters' drafts with all interested parties in the White House and executive branch. Rumsfeld's reasons were varied: partly to avoid further surprises such as Ford's endorsement of a labor-related program that no one in the budget bureau or the labor department knew about, and partly to undermine Robert Hartman, the staff member who controlled speechwriting and Rumsfeld's main rival for influence with the president.[21] The enduring effect of Rumsfeld's vetting rule was to undermine the writers' say about the style and coherence of the president's remarks.

Jimmy Carter was a boon to speechwriters in one way: he was the first of a series of political outsiders to be elected president and one of the first to serve in a Washington marked, in Kernell's terms, less by "institutionalized pluralism" than "individualized pluralism." Presidents from Truman to Ford, Kernell argues, were Washington insiders who preferred to work within the capital's institutional structure and served at a time when its political institutions were strong. Carter and nearly all of his successors climbed the political ladder by rousing grassroots support and, once in office, continued to bring public pressure to bear on a Washington whose institutions, since the mid-1970s, have been much less resistant to such pressure. These presidents, operating in an increasingly porous governing environment, readily "go public" as a matter of course.[22]

Carter's eagerness to give speeches proved less than a boon to his speechwriters, however, because he "resented using someone else's words."[23] He had never employed a speechwriter before running for president and preferred logical lists of points to stirring rhetorical flourishes, which he associated with southern demagogues like Georgia's Eugene Talmadge and Tom Watson.[24] Carter also liked to ad-lib his remarks, a tendency he reined in only after speechwriter James Fallows told him that the best way to communicate a clear message to the public was to read speeches whose text was circulated and explained to reporters in advance.[25] Carter "did not have time for his speechwriters," says writer Walter Shapiro, "because, after all, they were merely a technical, little, appendix-like necessity in being president." Nor did he know where to place them organizationally: at various times his speechwriters reported to Press Secretary Jody Powell, Communications

Director Gerald Rafshoon, or Administrative Aide Al McDonald. The "one constant," says writer Hendrik Hertzberg, was that "there was surprisingly little personal contact between us and the man we were writing for."[26]

Reagan, in contrast, was a speechwriter's delight. For thirty years before becoming president he had written and delivered thousands of speeches and commentaries to audiences in person, on television, and on the radio. Most important, perhaps, as a successful Hollywood actor in the 1940s, Reagan had learned to deliver scripted lines in ways that effectively connected with viewers through the camera lens—and he valued those who wrote the lines. Reagan had developed a rhetorical voice so consistent and political views so distinctive that his writers could work with confidence that they knew what he would say and how he would say it if he were writing the speech. Speech-writer Peggy Noonan, for example, was able to draft one of Reagan's best speeches—his 1984 D-day address in Normandy—without ever having talked with the president about that or any other speech. As with FDR, no matter who wrote the speech, it sounded like Reagan.

To be sure, Reagan's writers still resided far down the organization chart, remote from the Oval Office. But divisions within the administration sometimes elevated their importance. As speechwriter Peter Robinson recalls, "One reason why the speeches tended to be fought over so often, and frankly so viciously . . . was that the speeches were an occasion for making policy." Robinson tells of being assigned to write an education speech, discovering "we had no policy," and using the speech to craft one. "And it was up to the speechwriters not only to do, so to speak, the first draft writing but the first draft thinking for the president. If you were the president, what would you say in such a circumstance?"[27] The fight would begin when the speech draft was circulated throughout the administration for comment, but by then the writers had already framed the debate.

George H. W. Bush was generally inattentive to the importance of speech-making, something he lamented after leaving the White House "because part of being seen as a visionary is being able to have flowing rhetoric."[28] The same could not be said of Bush's successor. Like Carter, Bill Clinton had never had a speechwriter while serving as governor. When speechwriter Don Baer asked the president what he wanted from his writers, Clinton replied, "I have no idea." Perhaps for this reason, National Security Adviser Anthony Lake was able to seize a piece of turf that some of his predecessors had reached for unsuccessfully. At the outset of the Clinton presidency, Lake's staff took charge of writing national security speeches and of collaborating with the regular speechwriters on state of the union addresses. Yet what seemed like a power grab was consistent with Clinton's general desire to reclaim at least in part the tradition of the speechwriter-adviser. Clinton liked writers who also worked on public policy, such as Bruce Reed, Gene Sperling, and Michael Waldman. Consequently, the separate tracks that had developed between policy and rhetoric were merged to some extent under Clinton.

The era of the specialized speechwriter continues. George W. Bush and Barack Obama, like nearly all their recent predecessors, were political outsiders who rose to the presidency by rallying grassroots support. (Bush in particular learned from his father's bad examples that time spent preparing speeches was time well spent.) The Washington in which they have governed is still riddled with centrifugal forces that outsider presidents are especially inclined to think rhetoric can overcome. Kernell found that the number of speeches the president delivers per year has continued to accelerate, increasing by about 250 percent from Reagan to George W. Bush.[29] Other innovations of the specialized speechwriter era also remain in place. Speechwriters are still housed in the White House communications office, speech drafts are still vetted throughout the administration, and the National Security Council staff still write national security speeches.

Chief of Government, Chief of State

Although the American executive has been transformed since its creation by developments such as the rise of the rhetorical presidency and the expansion of the White House staff, the office has changed very little in certain fundamental ways. To be sure, presidents make more speeches than in the past, in greater variety, and with the assistance of a writing staff that started small and has grown large. But like all presidents since the early republic, Barack Obama and his successors face the challenge of being both a partisan, substantive chief of government and a unifying, symbolic chief of state. Speeches have become one of their primary devices for negotiating these sometimes reinforcing, often conflicting roles. With insights and arguments borrowed from the scholars' and speechwriters' chapters that constitute the rest of this book, I assess four major forms of presidential speechmaking: the convention acceptance address, the inaugural address, the state of the union address, and the crisis speech and other landmark addresses.

The Convention Acceptance Address

Of all the major forms of presidential speechmaking, the acceptance address that candidates for president deliver at their parties' nominating conventions is the newest.[30] During the 1830s and 1840s, when national conventions first were held, candidates were notified of their nomination at home and in writing, and they accepted with a brief, formal, and usually content-free letter. By the 1850s, candidates had begun to use the acceptance letter to enumerate their positions on the issues, and since they now were being notified of their nomination in person, they made a brief acceptance speech to accompany the letter. In 1892 the Democratic nominee for president, Grover Cleveland, transformed the acceptance speech by delivering his at a rally at New York City's Madison Square Garden. By 1900 every nominee gave an acceptance speech, which usually was long and detailed because the real audience was the millions who would read the speech rather than the thousands who would hear it.

Not until 1932, however, when Franklin Roosevelt decided to surprise the Democratic convention that nominated him by immediately flying from Albany to Chicago to accept the nomination in person, was the modern acceptance speech born. Not only are modern acceptance speeches delivered to the delegates, they have become the climax of every convention. And because the era of the modern acceptance speech corresponds to the modern era of live radio and television, these speeches are much more widely seen and heard than read; consequently, they are as a rule shorter and simpler than in the past.

Every president since FDR has given an acceptance speech when running for reelection, as has every challenger since Republican Thomas E. Dewey in 1944. Whether the speech is delivered by an incumbent or an aspiring president, however, the speaker rhetorically assumes the presidential role of chief of government in its least alloyed form. Acceptance speeches are "purely political," notes Medhurst in Chapter 2. That is by design: as Cleveland, giving the first acceptance speech to a mass rally, declared, "The tone of partisanship befits the occasion."[31] To the extent that achieving unity is a major goal of the speech, it involves unifying the party rather than the nation as a whole. Such unity is typically sought by repeatedly reminding the party why it is good and the other party is bad. Thus, Medhurst finds, acceptance speeches are full of dialectical opposites that carry a "moral valence": light vs. darkness, strength vs. weakness, safety vs. danger, honor vs. disgrace.

Because acceptance speeches are meant to unify and motivate the party, most candidates feel obligated to canvass widely for suggestions among other party leaders. When trying to win these leaders' enthusiastic support, candidates may find it hard to turn them down. This can make coherence difficult to achieve. According to Patrick Anderson, who was Carter's chief speechwriter during the 1976 campaign, when Adam Walinsky, with assistance from other speechwriters associated with the Kennedys, tried to rewrite Carter's speech, "its style [became] too ornate and its substance too conventionally liberal for Carter."[32] The day before the speech Carter had to fend off party groups and leaders besieging him with one or another line that they wanted him to include—according to Anderson, Carter "told me if you started that you never stopped."[33] The hybrid nature of many acceptance speeches may help to explain why so few are memorable. Of the top 100 American speeches of the twentieth century identified in a scholarly survey by Medhurst and Stephen Lucas, twelve were delivered at national conventions but only two were acceptance speeches.[34]

Reagan speechwriter Ken Khachigian notes an additional challenge that presidential candidates face, this one born of the fact that "frankly, what's more important is that audience out there on television, not the audience in front of you." Reagan's 1984 acceptance speech "reads much better by the eye than it does by the ear" because, wanting to include a lyrical passage about the journey of the Olympic torch across America that summer, the candidate necessarily mentioned a number of states. Serial eruptions of applause arose from the convention floor. "Don't ever mention states in a convention speech," Khachigian learned; "it will be interrupted throughout."

Doubts about the excellence of the acceptance speech do not extend to its importance. As Anderson points out, "You could blow your inaugural—you were safely elected by then—but you couldn't blow the acceptance speech without risking disaster."[35] As a result, candidates work closely with their writers. Although Nixon "would sometimes have a thought and he'd want you to develop it . . . to see if it worked," recalls Ray Price, Nixon mostly wrote his 1968 and 1972 acceptance speeches himself. A similar collaboration took place between Carter and Anderson in 1976. When Carter drafted the line "I see no reason why big-shot crooks should go to country clubs and the poor ones go to jail," Anderson persuaded him that the meaning of "go to country clubs" was much less clear than "go free" would be. In the end, it was "probably the most popular line in the speech." In 1988 George H. W. Bush took his speechwriters' reference to a "kinder nation" and memorably inserted the word "gentler."[36] Harry Truman's triumphant acceptance speech in 1948 was the result of his speechwriters figuring out that he spoke much better when they gave him an outline and encouraged him to improvise than when they gave him a text and expected him to read it.[37]

Although it is the rhetorical form that expresses most strongly the president's role as chief of government, the acceptance speech is not immune to the public's expectation that every would-be president will also strive to unify them as chief of state. Starting with Nixon in 1968, candidates have used the speech to weave their own lives into the ongoing life of the nation. In Nixon's peroration, he spoke of his time as "a child . . . [who] hears the train go by at night and he dreams of faraway places where he'd like to go." He is helped by many others along the way:

A father who had to go to work before he finished the sixth grade, sacrificed everything he had so that his sons could go to college.
A gentle, Quaker mother, with a passionate concern for peace, quietly wept when he went to war but she understood why he had to go.
A great teacher, a remarkable football coach, an inspirational minister encouraged him on his way.
A courageous wife and loyal children stood by him in victory and also defeat.
And in his chosen profession of politics, first there were scores, then hundreds, then thousands, and finally millions who worked for his success.
And tonight he stands before you—nominated for President of the United States of America.
You can see why I believe so deeply in the American Dream.

The Inaugural Address

Just as the acceptance address is the newest genre of major presidential speeches, so is the inaugural address the oldest. The first president's first significant act after taking the oath of office in 1789 was to make the first inaugural address. The address is also the rarest and most precisely scheduled presidential speech, delivered only once every fourth January 20 during the noon hour. Having won the office as the nominee of one party by defeating the nominee of the other party, the new chief executive is at last able to speak to the nation as president of all the people. As Anderson observes, "In your acceptance speech you introduce yourself as a candidate; in your inaugural you introduce yourself as president."

Similarly, just as the acceptance speech manifests the president's role as chief of government in its strongest form, so does the inaugural address most powerfully manifest the president as chief of state. According to Price, the address is "uniquely sacramental" in marking "the peaceful transfer of power," a sentiment that Nixon invoked at the start of his 1969 inaugural: "In the orderly transfer of power, we celebrate the unity that makes us free." Scholars Karlyn Kohrs Campbell and Kathleen Hall Jamieson point out that nearly all inaugural addresses have served as "an essential element in a ritual of transition in which the covenant between the citizenry and their leaders is renewed."[38]

As part of this sacramental ceremony, Don Baer says, the inaugural address is meant to "remind the nation more of what we have in common than of what divides us." The precedent for this approach was firmly established in 1801, when for the first time the opposition party candidate (Republican Thomas Jefferson) defeated the candidate of the party in power (Federalist John Adams), who was also the incumbent president. In his address Jefferson declared, "We have called by different names brethren of the same principle. We are all Republicans, we are all Federalists." In like spirit Carter began his 1977 address by turning to President Ford, his defeated Republican opponent, and saying: "For myself and for our Nation, I want to thank my predecessor for all he has done to heal our land." Most of Carter's successors have, in their own way, followed his example. In the second sentence of his 2009 inaugural address, for example, Obama said: "I thank President Bush for his service to our nation as well as the generosity and cooperation he has shown throughout this transition."

The unifying, chief of state character of the inaugural address involves more than the words the president offers. Because tens of millions of viewers watch the president speak, even "the people who are on the stand behind you," many of them leaders of Congress, the Supreme Court, and the outgoing administration, are important elements of the address, according to Price. They "represent part of the continuity that the inauguration symbolizes." In 1981 Reagan moved the inauguration to the east side of the Capitol and thus was able to refer to (and television cameras could show) powerful symbols of the American political tradition: the Washington Monument, the Jefferson and Lincoln memorials, and Arlington National Cemetery. So important is the inaugural address in marking the peaceful transfer of power and celebrating national unity that all but one of the nine vice presidents who succeeded to the presidency when the president died or resigned made an inaugural-style speech pledging continuity with the nation's best traditions and fealty to the departed president's legacy.[39] Lyndon Johnson even relied on John Kennedy's friend and speechwriter, Theodore Sorensen, to write most of his post-assassination remarks, although he deleted Sorensen's line "I who cannot fill his shoes must occupy his desk."[40]

The inaugural address is one element of a ceremony that, aside from the constitutional requirement that the president take the oath of office stated in Article II, is embedded in tradition, not law. Much of this tradition originated with the first inauguration. Washington took the oath in an outdoor setting before an exuberant crowd. Observing the oath-taking custom of the time, he placed his left hand on the Bible, raised his right hand heavenward, and appended the words "so help me God" to the official language of the oath. The first president then went inside to the Senate chamber to deliver an inaugural address.

Washington's address deployed formal, elevated language in the service of two themes that have been echoed in the inaugural addresses of most of his successors. First, he spoke of national unity grounded in common values and a shared dedication to the Constitution. Second, he paid "homage to the Great Author of every public and private good," noting the benign workings of "providential agency" in the birth of the United States and urging Congress and the American people to earn "the propitious smiles of Heaven" by acting with justice and magnanimity. Invoking God as the nation's guide and protector became a largely uncontroversial element of most subsequent inaugural addresses. But invoking Christ or dwelling on religion, which would risk division, did not. Aides pleaded with Carter not to quote 2 Chronicles 7:14, in which God urges "my people [to] . . . humble themselves, and pray, and seek my face, and turn from their wicked ways." As Anderson told him, "It could be interpreted as you suggesting that the American people humble themselves and turn from their wicked ways and their sins. But you've been arguing all along that the government was bad and that the people were good." Carter resented this advice, quoted the Old Testament passage at a National Prayer Breakfast soon after, and told the audience that he was still mad at his staff. But he took it out of his inaugural address.[41]

Washington also set a precedent in his inaugural address by declaring what he would not do—namely, use the occasion to exercise his constitutional authority as chief of government to make "recommendation of particular measures" to Congress. In preparation for his first inauguration in 1829, Andrew Jackson drafted an address that dealt specifically with legislative issues such as the tariff, but a team of advisers reworked it to fit Washington's less controversial mold.[42] Reelected modern presidents, knowing that they will deliver a state of the union–style speech soon after the inauguration, sometimes choose, as Truman did in 1949 and George W. Bush did in 2004, to devote the inaugural address to unifying themes of foreign policy and save intrinsically more controversial domestic policies for the subsequent speech to Congress.

Presidents work hard on their inaugural addresses and some, such as FDR and Kennedy, even strive to create the false impression that they wrote it without any assistance.[43] But effort is no guarantor of success. In Chapter 4, Charles O. Jones judges only six inaugural addresses to have been great, the most recent of which—and the only one of the six delivered in the absence of a national crisis—was Kennedy's in 1961, a half-century ago. JFK's address was a model of the genre in its elevated language, general reference to God, stirring evocation of national traditions and values, and above all its unifying character. According to Sorensen, who helped to write it, Kennedy "wanted the speech to focus on foreign policy, in part because domestic policy was more partisan and divisive." The address's most famous line—"Ask not what your country can do for you. Ask what you can do for your country"—was broadly appealing. It "resonated with liberals who shared Kennedy's belief in public service, and with conservatives who were weary of government handouts."[44]

Part of the problem presidents have with the inaugural address is that it is the only speech of its kind that most of them ever give. It's "in a big open-air setting," Baer notes, "as large a one as any human being ever speaks at. . . . They are used to speaking to large crowds of people who give them back the love. You don't get that at an inaugural, because you cannot hear any of the applause." Even the fact that the inauguration is in January and "it's cold, so everybody is wearing gloves," is problematic, says Khachigian, because "when they clap, it's always muffled." Add to that the length of time required for the president's words to travel as much as two miles up the National Mall and for the applause to trickle back and, not surprisingly, he is liable to lose his customary rhetorical rhythm. (Wait for applause and risk seeming arrogant or, if it doesn't come, forlorn? Charge ahead and be out of synch with the sound of the crowd?) Although second-term presidents know what to expect, they face an additional challenge, which Baer describes as "unifying or trying to persuade the nation that it is one nation" after four years of political controversy. Nonetheless, second-term addresses are uniquely important because they reaffirm that every presidential term is a gift from the people.

The State of the Union Address

The Constitution states that the president "shall from time to time give to the Congress Information of the State of the Union, and recommend to their Consideration such Measures as he shall judge necessary and expedient." Nothing is said concerning the form, frequency, or setting in which the president is to fulfill these responsibilities; nor is any guidance given about the weight properly assigned to the reporting and recommending duties. In practice, the first two presidents, Washington and Adams, and every president since Wilson have reported on the state of the union annually in the form of a speech to Congress delivered in the chamber of the House of Representatives.[45] But for more than a century, presidents from Jefferson to William Howard Taft did so in writing, in an annual message. When the state of the union provision was being considered at the Constitutional Convention, the delegates replaced "may" with "shall" so that, instead of being an option, recommending measures to Congress would be "the *duty* of the President" and therefore legislators could not take "umbrage or cavil at his doing it."[46] In truth, presidents nearly always devote much more time and attention in the state of the union address to recommending than to reporting.

The modern state of the union is the most important annual speech the president gives. Visually, it is almost as rich as the inaugural address in symbolism that affirms the president's unifying role as chief of state. The president enters the House chamber to a prolonged bipartisan ovation and proceeds up a center aisle bordered by legislators of both parties clamoring for handshakes and autographs. The audience includes not just senators and representatives but also cabinet members, justices of the Supreme Court, members of the Joint Chiefs of Staff, foreign ambassadors, and, in an innovation introduced by Reagan and emulated by all of his successors, heroic figures whose recent exploits the president recounts near the end of the speech, ranging from British prime minister Tony Blair to plane crash victim rescuer Lenny Skutnik. Watching a state of the union address on television with the sound off, someone generally uninformed about the American system might readily conclude that the president is the government and that everyone else works for him.[47]

In contrast to the setting, however, the address itself shines the national spotlight on the president as chief of government. The words the president speaks from the well of the House consist largely of legislative recommendations, most of them politically controversial, which he wants Congress to enact. Members of the president's party invariably cheer these recommendations and members of the opposition party typically cross their arms, look bored, and occasionally boo or hiss. What Clinton speechwriter Terry Edmonds celebrates as the "Super Bowl" of speeches, in which you "put [Congress] on notice that this is something you're going to fight for," is decried by Ken Khachigian as "a spectacle of partisanship, where they jump up and do standing ovations on one side and sit on their hands or stand up on the other side." Good or bad, modern state of the union addresses are written and delivered as a series of applause lines for the president's party, so much so in the case of George W. Bush that his addresses included twenty-nine seconds of applause, nearly all of it from Republicans, for every sixty seconds that he spoke.[48]

Not only is the state of the union address an annual event, but a considerable portion of each year is spent preparing it. As early as the July preceding the January or February speech, and no later than the early fall, the call goes out to all the executive departments and agencies for information and proposals that might be included. Apart from gathering raw material for the speech, the process of deciding which of these contending, sometimes conflicting proposals will be included "plays a useful role in disciplining the government," says Lee Huebner. After the address is delivered, "it is combed over for signals hidden or not as to what the president's agenda is in terms of [the departments'] own responsibilities." Clark Judge says that in the Reagan administration—a "coalition government" of conservative Republicans, liberal Republicans, and "Scoop Jackson Democrats"—writing the speech was a process of "mediation and negotiation" that, difficult and even stormy as it was, had the good effect of imposing coherence on the various factions. But presidents are not confined to the menu of ideas offered by the departments. In 1949, for example, Truman added the Point 4 foreign aid program to his state of the union address without consulting the state department or budget bureau. "I'll announce it and then they can catch up with me!" he said.[49]

Presidents also instruct their speechwriters to seek advice widely from a list that, according to Kathryn Dunn Tenpas in Chapter 6, includes "pollsters, members of Congress, business leaders, economists, historians, authors, and others." The danger posed by what Edmonds calls the "excruciatingly collaborative" process of speech drafting is that the speech itself may become so densely packed with proposals as to lose all coherence. In 1979, for example, when Carter's congenital fondness for lists of ideas melded completely with the departments' penchant for supplying such lists, the president's own communications director judged his address to be a "just horrendous . . . laundry list."[50]

Once the contents of the state of the union address are at least roughly determined and assembled, the first of two "rollouts" begins, both of them innovations of the Clinton White House. First, during the late November and December preceding the speech, with Congress out of session and not crowding the media spotlight, the president and other administration officials preview proposals that they think will be especially popular, always being sure to save at least a couple of surprises for the speech itself. Then, after the address, the president takes to the road to promote the agenda it outlined. "The state of the union address is no longer conceived of as a single event," Dunn Tenpas concludes, "but rather as part of a broader strategy to promote a president's agenda."

Different circumstances may call for different emphases. A rhythm often marks each presidential term so that offering new proposals becomes the theme of first- and third-year state of the union addresses, while showcasing accomplishments dominates the addresses of the second and fourth years when elections are scheduled. Huebner notes that Nixon's 1970 address, for example, was designed to "challenge the Democrats and set the stage for the fall campaign." What to do in a time of scandal poses its own challenge. Although Nixon mentioned Watergate in his 1974 address and Reagan admitted in 1987 that "serious mistakes were made" in the Iran-Contra affair, Clinton told Don Baer after the Monica Lewinsky scandal broke just days before the 1998 address: "We're not going to say anything about this. My job is to stand up there and tell the country what I'm going to do as president and to show them that I'm going to perform the job every day that they hired me to do." That strategy imposed a special burden on the writers to comb the speech for anything remotely resembling a double entendre. Among those they found were a reference to people "twenty years old" ("Do you want it replayed on David Letterman, over and over?" asked writer Michael Waldman) and a mention of the word "abroad" ("We can't say 'abroad,'" said political adviser Paul Begala. "Say 'around the world.'").[51] Clinton's address, by showing how focused he was on public policy, saved his presidency. During the eight days bracketing his speech, CBS News polls showed, Clinton's approval rating rose by 17 percentage points.[52]

As with acceptance and inaugural addresses, effort does not always translate into political success. The president may hope that the chief of state–style setting of the state of the union will buttress his effectiveness as chief of government in persuading Congress to enact his agenda into law, but the speech's densely packed and thus weakly thematic character usually impedes this goal. After leaving office Nixon asked Huebner to edit a book consisting of thirty speeches spanning Nixon's career: none of them was a state of the union address. The address is "one of the central mysteries of modern American life," says Peter Robinson. "The president doesn't want to give it, Congress doesn't want to listen to it, the networks don't want to cover it, and every year the damn thing happens all the same." Dunn Tenpas reports that of the fifty-one state of the union addresses since 1953 for which polling data are available, only three raised the president's approval rating by at least 6 percentage points. Forty addresses had no significant effect at all and eight actually prompted a loss of 6 points or more.

Can state of the union addresses be made more consistently effective? Working against them, as well as against most of the landmark speeches discussed in the chapter's next section, is the declining, albeit still large, audience for such events. The spread of cable and satellite television, the rapid increase in the number of channels, and the proliferation of home video players mean that viewers have many more choices. As recently as the 1960s and 1970s, most televisions received only three or four channels—if the president was speaking, viewers had little choice but to watch. The audience is also growing more partisan: in 1984, for example, about the same percentage of Republicans and Democrats watched Reagan's speech, but in 2006 the percentage of Republicans watching Bush was about twice as high as the percentage of Democrats.[53] Nonetheless, Baer is optimistic. He describes the state of the union as "that one communal moment a year when the country comes together." As attested by the size of Clinton's audience, which sometimes grew larger the longer he spoke, this "is one of the reasons why the length of these speeches doesn't matter anymore. The country actually craves it." Add to the mix older innovations, notably Johnson's decision to move the address from noon to prime time, and recent adaptations such as the pre- and post-address rollouts, Baer suggests, and the state of the union address has adapted well to the new challenges.

The Crisis Speech and Other Landmark Addresses

Andrew Rudalevige defines landmark presidential addresses to include both speeches that are "prompted by a crisis" and speeches that are about "a particular issue that the president wants to elevate to a major part of his national agenda." Crises, which almost by definition are unexpected and unsettling, rattle the country's sense of safety and identity. All ears—and eyes, because crisis speeches nearly always are televised—turn to the president as chief of state to speak the unifying words of resolve and reassurance that the crisis will be met. When the president is called on to give a crisis speech, little time is available for the usual background research and circulation of drafts that a scheduled speech allows. Out of necessity the speechwriter comes to the fore, often working much more closely and directly with the president than usual.

On June 11, 1963, for example, after Governor George C. Wallace famously stood in the "schoolhouse door" of the University of Alabama to force a confrontation with justice department officials over the enrollment of two African American students, Kennedy turned to Sorensen and said, "I think we'd better give that speech tonight." "What speech?" wondered Sorensen, whose own preference was to wait until the administration's civil rights bill was ready to present to Congress. Kennedy overruled his speechwriter-adviser and, together, they worked until moments before airtime on what turned out to be one of Kennedy's most effective speeches. "We are confronted primarily with a moral issue," the president declared. "It is as old as the scriptures and is as clear as the American Constitution."[54]

Disastrous events such as the explosion of the *Challenger* space shuttle on January 28, 1986, and the bombing of the Oklahoma City federal building on April 19, 1995, pose unusual challenges and create unusual opportunities for presidents and their writers. Peggy Noonan recalls that after hearing about the shuttle explosion she immediately started typing a speech for President Reagan, concluding her draft with a quotation from John Gillespie Magee's poem "High Flight," in which a pilot is portrayed as having "slipped the surly bonds of Earth . . . and touched the face of God." Overruling a staff member who wanted to insert the telephone company slogan "reach out and touch someone" into the passage, Reagan used the poet's line to powerful, memorable effect in his peroration.[55] Because Clinton's remarks after the Oklahoma City bombing were so moving, notes Michael Waldman, they marked "the first time Clinton had been a reassuring figure rather than an unsettling one."[56]

Nothing guarantees that the president will immediately rise to the occasion, however. As Rudalevige points out in Chapter 8, Bush's early remarks after the September 11, 2001, terrorist attacks were disappointing: "On the evening of the attacks, Bush had given a less-than-reassuring brief talk from the White House, followed by several days of meandering bellicosity." Not until September 20, with his speech to Congress, did Bush hit his rhetorical stride. But he lost it again when addressing the nation from the Oval Office about the financial crisis seven years later, on September 24, 2008. Frustrated when told that the speech had him recommending a complicated bailout proposal that was the opposite of what he thought it was, Bush reportedly "threw up his hands in frustration. 'Why did I sign on to this proposal if I don't understand what it does?' he asked." Perhaps as a consequence, Bush's delivery of the speech struck speechwriter Matt Latimer as being "uncomfortable, . . . stony and tense." In short order, the House of Representatives rejected the president's plan.[57]

The noncrisis form of landmark address involves the president as chief of government, speaking to draw attention to an issue of particular importance, striving to rally support for his approach—and succeeding. (That's what makes it a landmark address instead of a failed attempt at one.) Because these speeches usually have longer lead times than crisis speeches, they allow more opportunity for research and circulation among other White House and executive branch officials. This is a decidedly mixed blessing in the minds of speechwriters, every one of whom has a tale to tell about cabinet officers or staff members doing their utmost to ruin a great speech. Peter Robinson's account of how everyone from Secretary of State George Shultz to National Security Adviser Colin Powell tried and failed to persuade Reagan to delete "Mr. Gorbachev, tear down this wall" from his 1987 Berlin speech is a classic of the genre.[58] But forging consensus within an administration, even at the expense of rhetorical brilliance, may justify all the trouble it takes if it increases the likelihood that a policy will be implemented effectively. In December 1950, for example, drafts of a speech that Truman planned to give about the Korean War circulated throughout the government to good effect. "It's funny," the president said, "how a pending speech will clear the air on policies," making it much more likely that the various departments and agencies will coordinate efforts to make them succeed.

Because such landmark speeches are especially important to the president, however, they resemble crisis speeches in commanding his personal attention throughout the drafting process. So important did Nixon regard his November 3, 1969, speech on Vietnam that he wrote it himself. The phrase that Nixon used in his successful appeal for public support—the "silent majority"—caught on even though he did not capitalize on or otherwise draw attention to it. In contrast, the phrase he later hoped would catch on from his 1971 state of the union address—the "New American Revolution"—did not. In like manner, "new deal" was plucked from FDR's 1932 acceptance speech and "fair deal" from Truman's 1949 state of the union address and took root in ways that various Carter and Clinton efforts, such as "Beloved Community" and "New Foundation" (Carter) and "New Promise" (Clinton) never did.[59]

Ironically, Carter's most famous speech came in the aftermath of a canceled address.[60] Convinced that the viewing audience would be embarrassingly small for a scheduled prime-time speech about energy policy (his fifth) on July 5, 1979, Carter withdrew his request for airtime thirty hours before the speech was to be delivered. Then, determined to figure out what was wrong with the country, which seemed convinced that there was no real crisis, just shady oil companies and an incompetent president, Carter immediately began a nine-day retreat at Camp David. Much of this time was spent meeting with groups of governors, congressional leaders, average families, religious thinkers, journalists, and other prominent citizens—one of whom, former Truman writer Clark Clifford, told a reporter that the president was worried about a national "malaise." Eventually speechwriters Hendrik Hertzberg and Gordon Stewart gathered all of Carter's advisers around a table and goaded them to help formulate a speech tracing the nation's energy crisis to a more general "crisis of confidence" among the American people that they could begin to solve by first solving the energy crisis.[61] More than 100 million viewers watched the July 15 speech on television and, initially, most responded favorably. But Carter surrendered his newfound public support when, two days later and for reasons not foreshadowed in the speech, he fired five members of his cabinet. As speechwriter Walter Shapiro recalls, "The markets were totally roiled. Europe reacted like the government was going to fall because that's what happened in traditional European settings."

Conclusion

Presidents have given inaugural addresses from the very beginning. As candidates they introduced the acceptance address in the 1890s and developed it into a live, nationally broadcast speech in the 1930s. State of the union addresses, regularly delivered in person to Congress, took root in the early twentieth century. With the rise of the rhetorical presidency, the crisis speech and other landmark addresses became expected elements of each administration, their importance vastly amplified by the immediacy of radio, television, and the Internet. In addition, a rapid increase in the number of presidential speeches to narrower audiences has occurred in recent years.

As speechmaking has increased, so has the need for speechwriters. Diana Carlin has aptly summarized the job of the presidential speechwriter: to "frame a message that is consistent with the administration's broad goals and specific policy initiatives. The message must reflect the president's personality and language—and even the strengths and weaknesses of the president's delivery. The message must satisfy audience expectations and conventions of form, be supported by research, respond to opponents and critics, and be written with the knowledge that the world will listen and the media will dissect every word."[62] Malcolm Moos, a Johns Hopkins University political scientist and an Eisenhower speechwriter, defined the job more simply: "to try to find out what the president wants to say, and help him say it in the best way."[63]

Speechwriters have never been more important than during the thirty-six-year period that began with FDR and ended with (and to a large extent because of) LBJ. Speechwriters of this era did more than write; they also were close and wide-ranging presidential advisers. Tellingly, Sorensen titled the memoir of his years with Kennedy *Counselor*, something few speechwriters since him would have been able to do convincingly.

But to say that recent speechwriters are less important than in their golden age is not to say that they are unimportant—far from it. Speeches are the primary form of presidential communication, not just to the American people but also to the rest of the executive branch, which pores over them for guidance about what the president expects to be done. And if not the primary form, they are still a major form of presidential communication with Congress, with interest groups, with other countries, and, in significant ways, with history. Speechwriters do not have the last word about what presidents say, but in most cases they have the first word, writing the drafts that, however much they may be rewritten by others, set the terms of the debates that follow.

Notes

1. For a fuller discussion of the president as chief of government and chief of state, see Erwin C. Hargrove and Michael Nelson, *Presidents, Politics, and Policy* (Baltimore: Johns Hopkins University Press, 1984), ch. 2; and Michael Nelson, "Evaluating the Presidency,"

in *The Presidency and the Political System*, 8th ed., ed. Michael Nelson (Washington, D.C.: CQ Press, 2006), 1–27.

2. Thomas E. Cronin, "The Presidency and Its Paradoxes," in *The Presidency Reappraised*, 2nd ed., eds. Thomas Cronin and Rexford Tugwell (New York: Praeger, 1977), 69–85.

3. Jeffrey K. Tulis, *The Rhetorical Presidency* (Princeton, N.J.: Princeton University Press, 1987), 4, 106.

4. Ibid., 203.

5. Robert Schlesinger, *White House Ghosts: Presidents and Their Speechwriters* (New York: Simon & Schuster, 2008), 3.

6. Ted Sorensen, *Counselor: A Life at the Edge of History* (New York: Harper, 2008), 131, 133.

7. None of Eisenhower's speechwriters held the title of Special Counsel.

8. Charles J. G. Griffin, "Dwight D. Eisenhower: The 1954 State of the Union Address as a Case Study in Presidential Speechwriting," in *Presidential Speechwriting: From the New Deal to the Reagan Revolution and Beyond*, eds. Kurt Ritter and Martin J. Medhurst (College Station: Texas A&M Press, 2003), 82.

9. Sorensen, *Counselor*, 140.

10. Schlesinger, *White House Ghosts*, 173.

11. Tulis, *Rhetorical Presidency*, 166.

12. Charles E. Walcott and Karen M. Hult, *Governing the White House: From Hoover Through LBJ* (Lawrence: University Press of Kansas, 1995), 211.

13. Sorensen, *Counselor*, 293.

14. Stephen Hess, *Organizing the Presidency*, 3rd ed. (Washington, D.C.: Brookings Institution Press, 2002), 28.

15. Samuel Kernell, *Going Public: New Strategies of Presidential Leadership*, 4th ed. (Washington, D.C.: CQ Press, 2007), 121–123.

16. Calculated from data in ibid., 122.

17. Schlesinger, *White House Ghosts*, 165.

18. Martin J. Medhurst, "Presidential Speechwriting: Ten Myths That Plague Modern Scholarship," in *Presidential Speechwriting*, eds. Ritter and Medhurst, 6.

19. Unless otherwise noted, all quotations from speechwriters are from the transcripts of the Miller Center symposium reported in Chapters 3, 5, 7, and 9.

20. On the rise of the White House communications office, see John Anthony Maltese, *Spin Control: The White House Office of Communications and the Management of Presidential News* (Chapel Hill: University of North Carolina Press, 1992).

21. Schlesinger, *White House Ghosts*, 237, 242.

22. Kernell, *Going Public*, passim.

23. Patrick Anderson, *Electing Jimmy Carter: The Campaign of 1976* (Baton Rouge: Louisiana State University Press, 1994), 32.

24. Kevin Mattson, *"What the Heck Are You Up to, Mr. President?"*: Jimmy Carter, America's

"Malaise," and the Speech That Should Have Changed the Country (New York: Bloomsbury USA, 2009), 64.

25. Schlesinger, *White House Ghosts*, 278.

26. John H. Patton, "Jimmy Carter: The Language of Politics and the Politics of Integrity," in *Presidential Speechwriting*, eds. Ritter and Medhurst, 169.

27. Elvin T. Lim, *The Anti-Intellectual Presidency: The Decline of Presidential Rhetoric from George Washington to George W. Bush* (New York: Oxford University Press, 2008), 94.

28. Schlesinger, *White House Ghosts*, 400.

29. Kernell, *Going Public*, 122.

30. Richard J. Ellis, "Accepting the Nomination: From Martin Van Buren to Franklin Delano Roosevelt," in *Speaking to the People: The Rhetorical Presidency in Historical Perspective*, ed. Richard J. Ellis (Amherst: University of Massachusetts Press, 1998), 112–133.

31. Ibid., 119.

32. Anderson, *Electing Jimmy Carter*, 56.

33. Ibid., 62.

34. Stephen E. Lucas and Martin J. Medhurst, eds., *Words of a Century: The Top 100 American Speeches, 1900–1999* (New York: Oxford University Press, 2009).

35. Anderson, *Electing Jimmy Carter*, 57.

36. Schlesinger, *White House Ghosts*, 362.

37. Ibid., 51–53.

38. Karlyn Kohrs Campbell and Kathleen Hall Jamieson, *Deeds Done in Words: Presidential Rhetoric and the Genres of Governance* (Chicago: University of Chicago Press, 1990), 14.

39. Ibid., 37, 47. The exception was Calvin Coolidge. Gerald Ford, who succeeded to the presidency after Nixon resigned in disgrace in 1974, pledged fealty to the constitutional system rather than Nixon.

40. Sorensen, *Counselor*, 382.

41. Anderson, *Electing Jimmy Carter*, 157–158, 166.

42. Richard J. Ellis and Stephen Kirk, "Jefferson, Jackson, and the Origins of the Presidential Mandate," in *Speaking to the People*, ed. Ellis, 42.

43. Schlesinger, *White House Ghosts*, 11, 110.

44. Sorensen, *Counselor*, 221, 224.

45. Wilson and his successors occasionally followed the long tradition of sending a written message to Congress. Franklin D. Roosevelt set the pattern for the modern presidency: delivering the speech in person and referring to it as the state of the union address rather than the "annual message." Schlesinger, *White House Ghosts*, 16, 59.

46. See Sidney M. Milkis and Michael Nelson, *The American Presidency: Origins and Development, 1776–2007* (Washington, D.C.: CQ Press, 2008), 49.

47. In this I differ strongly from Campbell and Jamieson, who argue on page 52 of *Deeds Done in Words*: "The setting ritualistically reaffirms the existence of the three branches of government and that each is playing its constitutionally ordained role." In truth, the

setting—the president standing and speaking, Congress and the Supreme Court sitting below him and listening—seems to affirm that the president is their boss.

48. Lim, *Anti-Intellectual Presidency*, 64.

49. Schlesinger, *White House Ghosts*, 62.

50. Patton, "Jimmy Carter," in *Presidential Speechwriting*, eds. Ritter and Medhurst, 171.

51. Michael Waldman, *POTUS Speaks: Finding the Words That Defined the Clinton Presidency* (New York: Simon & Schuster, 2000), 212, 214.

52. Kernell, *Going Public*, 112–113.

53. Ibid., 142.

54. Sorensen, *Counselor*, 278–282.

55. Schlesinger, *White House Ghosts*, 348–349.

56. Waldman, *POTUS*, 82.

57. Matt Latimer, *Speech-Less: Tales of a White House Survivor* (New York: Crown, 2009), introduction and ch. 11.

58. For Robinson's riveting account of how the speech came to be written, see Chapter 9 of this book and Schlesinger, *White House Ghosts*, 354–358.

59. Taylor Branch describes the frantic efforts of Clinton and his speechwriters to invent a phrase for his administration that would catch on. New Freedom, New Balance, and Age of Possibility were rejected in favor of New Promise, which never caught on. Branch, *The Clinton Tapes: Wrestling History with the President* (New York: Simon & Schuster, 2009), 415–420.

60. In addition to the accounts in Chapters 8 and 9 of this book, see Mattson, *"What the Heck Are You Up to, Mr. President?"* passim.

61. Gordon Stewart, "Carter's Speech Therapy," *New York Times*, July 14, 2009.

62. Diana B. Carlin, "Harry S. Truman: From Whistle-Stops to the Halls of Congress," in *Presidential Speechwriting*, eds. Ritter and Medhurst, 42.

63. Griffin, "Dwight D. Eisenhower," in ibid., 78.

Chapter 2

The Acceptance Address: Presidential Speechwriting, 1932–2008

Martin J. Medhurst

In December 1999, Stephen E. Lucas and I released the results of a nationwide survey that identified and ranked the top 100 American speeches of the twentieth century. Speeches delivered at national nominating conventions were well represented, starting with Hubert Humphrey's speech supporting the minority report on civil rights at the 1948 Democratic convention. Also on the list were speeches by Adlai Stevenson (1952), Barry Goldwater (1964), Barbara Jordan (1976), Edward Kennedy (1980), Mario Cuomo (1984), Geraldine Ferraro (1984), Ann Richards (1988), Jesse Jackson (1984 and 1988), Mary Fisher (1992), and Elizabeth Glaser (1992). Yet of the twelve convention speeches on the list, only two were presidential nomination acceptance addresses, and both of those were by the losing candidate.[1] Indeed, one could make the case that the speeches by Stevenson in 1952 and Goldwater in 1964, whatever their other merits may be, were paradigm cases of how *not* to construct a nomination acceptance address. Such a claim would presuppose that one can know what a good acceptance address should be and do. I believe that we can.

Starting with Franklin D. Roosevelt's acceptance address at the 1932 Democratic National Convention in Chicago, I surveyed twenty-two acceptance addresses across eight decades, focusing on those candidates who went on to win the presidency in each election. In addition to FDR's 1932 speech, I examined his 1936, 1940, and 1944 acceptance addresses, along with the acceptance addresses of Truman (1948), Eisenhower (1952 and 1956), Nixon (1968 and 1972), Carter (1976), Reagan (1980 and 1984), George H. W. Bush (1988), Clinton (1992 and 1996), George W. Bush (2000 and 2004), and Obama (2008). The only speeches I examined by candidates who lost the general election were those of Stevenson in 1952 and Goldwater in

1964, and those only because scholars clearly found enough merit in them to vote them into the top 100 speeches of the century.[2]

What emerged from this sampling of acceptance addresses were both some general observations and some specific practices. By focusing on these observations and understanding how they were enacted through specific rhetorical performances, I want to show how the practice of presidential speechwriting has shaped the acceptance address into a distinctive genre, one whose requirements, problems, and strategies make it unique among the varieties of political rhetoric.[3]

Four General Observations

The first general observation about acceptance addresses is that they are purely political. They are part of an ongoing political campaign and have as their ultimate purpose success in the November general election. Therefore, everything that happens in an acceptance address happens for a reason—a political reason. As Nixon speechwriter Ray Price notes, "The voter has to make that choice [between the major-party nominees] and you want to help the voter to make the right choice as you see it." The acceptance address offers reasons "to make the right choice."

The second general observation is that all acceptance addresses are contextually driven; that is, the political context of the moment drives the rhetorical action. Thus, even though the acceptance address is a distinct genre of discourse, it is a genre that is far more sensitive to political context than, say, an inaugural address or a state of the union speech, because the exigencies to which the acceptance speech must respond are more complex.[4] As Carter speechwriter Patrick Anderson notes, the acceptance address "is a tremendously rhetorical speech. . . . you're trying to inspire people and move people," among several other goals.

The third general observation is that the acceptance address is a rhetorical representation of the candidate as much as, and in more recent years considerably more than, a representation of the political party to which he belongs. There is an element of personality in acceptance addresses that is more prominent than in other genres of political rhetoric. Clark Judge, who wrote speeches for Ronald Reagan, points to this personal element when he posits that "a part of the challenge of not just an acceptance speech but . . . the whole convention within which the speech occurs, is not just to fit the polls and not just to fit what the political advisors say, it also has to fit what you are, and what you're advocating, and what your record is." The acceptance address is a representation of the person, not just the party.

The fourth and final observation is that acceptance addresses serve different functions for different audiences. Although all acceptance addresses serve the general functions of unifying disparate elements of the party and positioning the candidate for the fall election, some acceptance addresses target specific segments of the electorate that campaign strategists have deemed necessary for electoral success. Patrick Anderson, reflecting on his drafting of Carter's 1976 acceptance speech, recalls: "Some people were pushing us to do more for the Catholics, so we started off with a quote from [John F.] Kennedy and we talked about families." Nixon's 1972 acceptance address targeted the youth vote and senior citizens. Internal polling often points speechwriters to particular audiences in need of rhetorical attention.[5]

Functions and Purposes of the Acceptance Address

Unification and positioning are the two axes around which the other functions of a presidential acceptance address revolve. Two of the reasons that the Goldwater and Stevenson addresses were not successful are that they failed to unify the party and they failed to position the candidate properly for the fall campaign, among many other rhetorical and strategic errors. It is difficult to overstate the rhetorical and political failures of these two speeches, because each violates the most basic axioms of the acceptance address. Instead of moving to unify an ideologically ruptured Republican convention, Goldwater used his acceptance address to underscore his creed of individual liberty and self-reliance. Instead of trying to position himself for the fall election, Goldwater excoriated the Democrats—all Democrats—and charged them with having "a fundamentally and absolutely wrong view of man, his nature, and his destiny." Instead of seeking a middle ground or at least trying to invite conservative Democrats to his cause, Goldwater declared that "it's been during Democratic years that our strength to deter war has stood still, and even gone into a planned decline." By condemning the entire Democratic Party and failing to make any appeal to moderate or independent voters, even those who usually voted Republican, Goldwater ensured that his address would be a failure even before he got to the part about "extremism in the defense of liberty is no vice." The speech, which was drafted by Harry Jaffa, neither unified the party nor strategically positioned Goldwater for the fall election.[6]

Adlai Stevenson's acceptance address of 1952 was equally ill conceived. One of the primary functions of an acceptance address is to get the party—and through the mass media, the nation—to rally behind the candidate selected by the convention. Yet, Stevenson opened his address with not one but seven distinct statements that undermined his ethos and status as party leader:

"I should have preferred to hear those words uttered by a stronger, a wiser, a
  better man than myself."
"I have not sought the honor you have done me."
"I would not seek your nomination for the presidency. . . ."
"I have not sought this nomination. . . ."
"I could not seek it [the nomination] in good conscience. . . ."
"I would not seek it in honest self-appraisal. . . ."
"Better men than I were at hand for this mighty task. . . ."

Humility is one thing, but saying that he had not wanted the nomination and that others were better qualified was not the way to rally the troops or to inspire confidence that they had selected the right man. Likewise, comparing one's situation to the agony of Christ in the Garden ("I have asked the Merciful Father—the Father of us all—to let this cup pass from me") seems not only a bit over the top, but bordering on the sacrilegious as well. Instead of accentuating the positive, Stevenson assured his listeners that "our troubles are all ahead of us." Add to these miscues the elevated literary language ("Its potential for good or evil, now and in the years of our lives, smothers exultation and converts vanity into prayer") and a sentence that ran on for some sixty-six words, and one finds the perfect example of how not to write an acceptance address.[7]

Whatever criteria scholars used to select the Stevenson and Goldwater efforts as among the top 100 speeches of the twentieth century, they were not criteria derived from study of acceptance addresses. Close study of successful presidential nomination acceptance addresses reveals that they fulfill nine specific purposes or functions. Not all such speeches fulfill all nine functions, but those speeches that have fulfilled most of these functions are the ones that history has judged to have been most politically effective. These nine functions or purposes are as follows:

- to unify the party
- to strategically position the candidate for the fall election campaign

- to build a presidential ethos
- to set forth a vision or agenda
- to negatively characterize the opposition's words, actions, or policies
- to positively characterize one's own words, actions, and policies
- to motivate both those in the convention hall and those watching at home to work on behalf of and to vote for the ticket
- to inspire confidence in party and opinion leaders that victory will be won
- to launch efforts to preempt perceived weaknesses in one's own record

These nine functions or purposes are activated within a unique constellation of contextual factors. Although the factors themselves remain constant, the ways in which they combine to form specific constellations of concern vary with each new election and according to the following:

whether the candidate or party is an incumbent or a challenger
the state of intraparty relations at the time of the convention (unified or splintered)
national economic conditions (depression, recession, or prosperity)
national security conditions (peace, war, cold war)
national sociocultural conditions (culture wars)
popularity of the incumbent administration (public opinion polls)
public views about the candidates (strengths and weaknesses)
public views about the parties (strengths and weaknesses)
mood of the electorate (fearful, angry, bored, turned-off, confused, etc.)

How the speechwriter matches the functions or purposes he or she wishes to achieve with the reigning contextual constellation is a matter of campaign strategy. The overall strategy dictates the speech; the speech does not dictate the strategy. The speech is written in a specific way, using specific inventions and techniques, precisely to achieve certain campaign goals. Kenneth Khachigian, who wrote Reagan's 1984 acceptance address, recalls,

> In the case of 1984, it was clearly our strategy to frame Mondale as far over to the left. If you remember, the Democratic convention was in San Francisco that year, and Jeane Kirkpatrick came up with that wonderful line, "San Francisco Democrats," which was a metaphor for the party that year. Mondale, who was not hard to put on the left—he grew to politics on the left—his convention was not only in San Francisco, the heart of left-wing America, but he promised that he would raise taxes and all the things that played into our hands. The goal was to keep him over on the left—the party on the left—and to show that Reagan had brought America back, which was the

theme of the campaign: "Morning Again in America." That was thematic—and then we put meat on the bones.

No modern speechwriter would try to write an acceptance address without thoroughly understanding the campaign strategy being pursued. The strategy is the blueprint for victory in November; the acceptance address is one of the initial tactical moves in the campaign to realize that strategy.

Rhetorical Invention and Acceptance Addresses

The inventions and techniques of acceptance addresses have become standardized since the 1932 address of Franklin D. Roosevelt.[8] That address, written by Raymond Moley and Samuel Rosenman, was historic in many ways. In addition to being the first acceptance speech delivered in person by the nominee to a national convention, it began the use of certain rhetorical inventions and techniques that have been emulated and expanded ever since. The term "rhetorical invention" refers to that process by which a speechwriter discovers or "invents" content for the speech.[9] Where can speechwriters go to "discover" what a candidate can say in an acceptance address? According to my investigation, they can go to eighteen different places:

- the candidate's own stump speeches
- the opponent's stump speeches
- the platform of one's own party
- the platform of the opponent's party
- the deeds and words of the Founding Fathers
- American myth and history, especially heroes and wars
- the candidate's personal and family background
- legislative action or inaction
- judicial action or inaction
- the deeds and words of former presidents
- the rhetoric of popular culture
- the nature and destiny of America and Americans
- patriotic lyrics, poetry, or prose
- scriptural reference, quotation, or allusion
- the nature of the presidential office
- current domestic policies
- current foreign policies
- the past record, in word and deed, of the opposition candidate and party

When speechwriters turn to these sources of rhetorical invention, they inevitably find a plethora of information that could be used in an acceptance address. The tough part, however, is to decide what, out of all this material, should be used. This is where the campaign strategy comes in.

The Democratic campaign of 1948 offers a case in point. Once the Truman team made the decision to run against the "do-nothing 80th Congress" rather than against Republican nominee Thomas Dewey, many of the decisions about what to include in Truman's acceptance address became clear. Indeed, after asking for unity at the beginning of the speech, Truman spent only 495 words on the record of his own party, while devoting the rest of the speech—more than 1,800 words—to attacking the Republican Congress and calling that Congress into special session to enact into law many of the promises contained in the Republican platform. This was a brilliant move that Truman calculated would result in exactly nothing happening, thereby demonstrating the truth of his convention claims and strategically positioning him for the fall campaign.

Truman's entire speech pivoted on a common topic of political discourse—right and wrong. As Truman said at the outset: "Senator Barkley and I will win this election and make these Republicans like it—don't you forget that!! We will do that because they are wrong and we are right." The topos of "right vs. wrong" is one of a large number of dialectical topics, or opposites, that speechwriters regularly call upon to help structure their speeches. Sometimes, as in the Truman case, the dialectical topos sets the structure for the rest of the speech. In other instances, the use of dialectical opposites serves a different purpose. After going through a lengthy discussion of the depression and various financial issues of 1932, Roosevelt concluded his discussion: "At last our eyes are open. At last the American people are ready to acknowledge that Republican leadership was wrong and the Democracy is right." Here the topos of right and wrong is used to secure a conclusion rather than to announce a structure. Dialectical opposites can be used in many different ways, but the advantage that often accrues from their use is moral clarity. Note how most of these dialectical topoi have a moral valence:

- up vs. down
- light vs. darkness
- new vs. old
- more vs. less

- strength vs. weakness
- safety vs. danger
- clarity vs. confusion
- honor vs. disgrace
- forward vs. backward
- advance vs. retreat
- top vs. bottom
- honest vs. crooked
- remembered vs. forgotten

Roosevelt used the topos of "remembered vs. forgotten" in his 1932 acceptance: "The consumer was forgotten. Very little of it went into increased wages; the worker was forgotten; and by no means an adequate proportion was even paid out in dividends—the stockholder was forgotten." Here the topos is used enthymematically—that is, it leaves part of the argument unspoken because it already exists in the mind of the hearer.[10] By reminding the audience about who has been forgotten, the speechwriter sets Roosevelt and the Democrats up as the party that will remember "the forgotten man," a topic that Roosevelt had developed earlier in his famous speech of April 7, 1932. By using the eighteen inventional locations and the numerous dialectical topics at their disposal, speechwriters are able to discover and deploy ideas and arguments that help the candidate to put the campaign strategy into rhetorical action.

Dispositional Deployment

After inventing the discourse, the speechwriter needs to decide how to arrange and deploy it in the most effective manner. There are many ways in which speeches can be arranged for maximum effect. Common patterns of arrangement include topical patterns, problem/solution patterns, chronological patterns, cause/effect patterns, sequential patterns, spatial patterns, pro/con patterns, and patterns of residual argumentation.[11] There is no single pattern that all presidential nomination acceptance addresses follow. In the speeches I surveyed, at least five different organizational schemes are represented. Some of the speeches, including those of Stevenson and Goldwater, almost defy classification. What is common to these acceptance addresses—or at least very widespread—is a series of recurring parts. Most of them include the following, though not necessarily in this order:

- acceptance of the nomination
- acknowledgment of the defeated primary candidates and/or the vice presidential nominee
- humorous references or wordplay, often self-directed
- content drawn from the nominee's stump speeches
- introduction of memorable slogans or catchphrases
- a strong signal to the base
- quotations from the opponent
- a call-and-response sequence
- direct appeal or reference to God, religion, or the Bible
- a historical portrait or vignette of the American people
- a poignant story that carries a value-laden message

Here is how these parts were ordered in George W. Bush's 2000 acceptance address:

Acceptance of nomination: "Mr. Chairman, delegates, and my fellow citizens. . . . I accept your nomination. Thank you for this honor."

Humorous reference: "Our founders first defined that purpose here in Philadelphia. . . . Benjamin Franklin was here. Thomas Jefferson. And, of course, George Washington—or, as his friends called him, George W."

Acknowledgment of defeated primary candidates and vice presidential nominee: "I am proud to have Dick Cheney by my side. He is a man of integrity and sound judgment, who has proven that public service can be noble service. . . . I am grateful for John McCain and the other candidates who sought this nomination. Their convictions strengthen our party."

Historical portrait or vignette of the American people: "My father was the last president of a great generation. A generation of Americans who stormed beaches, liberated concentration camps and delivered us from evil. Some never came home. Those who did put their medals in drawers, went to work, and built on a heroic scale . . . highways and universities, suburbs and factories, great cities and grand alliances—the strong foundations of an American Century."

Content drawn from stump speeches: "Seven of ten fourth-graders in our highest poverty schools cannot read a simple children's book. . . . millions are trapped in schools where violence is common and learning is rare."

Poignant story that carries a value-laden message: "Greatness is found when American character and American courage overcome American challenges. When Lewis Morris of New York was about to sign the Declaration of Independence, his brother advised against it, warning that he would lose all his property. Morris, a plain-spoken founder, replied . . . 'Damn the consequences, give me the pen.' That is the eloquence of American action. We heard it during World War II, when General Eisenhower told paratroopers on D-day morning not to worry—and one replied, 'We're not worried, General. . . . It's Hitler's turn to worry now.' We heard it in the civil rights movement, when brave men and women did not say . . . 'We shall cope,' or 'We shall see.' They said 'We shall overcome.' An American president must call upon that character."

Content drawn from stump speeches: "We will strengthen Social Security and Medicare for the greatest generation, and for generations to come. Medicare does more than meet the needs of our elderly, it reflects the values of our society. We will set it on firm financial ground, and make prescription drugs available and affordable for every senior who needs them."

Quotations from the opponent: "Every one of the proposals I've talked about tonight, he has called a 'risky scheme,' over and over again. It is the sum of his message—the politics of the roadblock, the philosophy of the stop sign. If my opponent had been there at the moon launch, it would have been a 'risky rocket scheme.' If he'd been there when Edison was testing the light bulb, it would have been a 'risky anti-candle scheme.' And if he'd been there when the Internet was invented, well . . . I understand he actually was there for that. He now leads the party of Franklin D. Roosevelt. But the only thing he has to offer is fear itself."

Introduction of memorable slogans or catchphrases: "Don't mess with Texas."

A strong signal to the base: "I will lead our nation toward a culture that values life—the life of the elderly and the sick, the life of the young, and the life of the unborn. I know good people disagree on this issue, but surely we can agree on ways to value life by promoting adoption and parental notification, and when Congress sends me a bill against partial-birth abortion, I will sign it into law."

A direct appeal to God, religion, or the Bible: "I believe in tolerance, not in spite of my faith, but because of it. I believe in a God who calls us, not to judge our neighbors, but to love them. I believe in grace, because I have seen it . . . in peace, because I have felt it . . . in forgiveness, because I have needed it."

A call-and-response sequence: "After all of the bitterness and broken faith, we can begin again. The wait has been long, but *it won't be long now*. A prosperous nation is ready to renew its purpose and unite behind great goals . . . and *it won't be long now*. Our nation must renew the hopes of that boy I talked with in jail, and so many like him . . . and *it won't be long now*. Our country is ready for high standards and new leaders . . . and *it won't be long now*. An era of tarnished ideals is giving way to a responsibility era . . . and *it won't be long now*."

These eleven parts of a presidential nomination acceptance address appear across party and across time. Not all eleven parts are found in every acceptance address, but every acceptance address draws upon these parts to a greater or lesser degree. The parts are clearly identifiable, yet extraordinarily flexible as well. Different parts have played central roles in different addresses.

Roosevelt's 1932 address is best remembered for his introduction of the slogan "a new deal," but he also acknowledged his nomination, drew from his earlier speeches, made a brief allusion to American history, referenced the Bible, and, without quoting his opponent directly, alluded to his opponent's views. Truman's 1948 address accepted the nomination, recognized his vice presidential running mate, Alben Barkley, rehearsed themes from the primary season, alluded to the positions of his opponent by citing the Republican platform, and repeated a biblical allusion made by Roosevelt. Eisenhower followed a similar pattern in 1956. He accepted the nomination, praised the selection of Richard Nixon as vice presidential candidate, made a historical allusion to Lincoln, sounded the primary season campaign themes of prosperity and progress, used the catchphrase "out of many—one," and quoted the Bible. Although acceptance addresses of the 1930s and 1940s used only four or five of the standard elements, by the 1980s and 1990s most of the eleven elements appeared regularly. In 2008, Barack Obama used nine of the standard elements in his acceptance address.

The Style of Accepting

In addition to calling upon standard sources of rhetorical invention, dialectical topics, and recognized parts, speechwriters employ a distinctive style of rhetorical discourse when composing acceptance addresses. Three kinds of stylistic tokens stand out: rhetorical figures, controlling terms and rhetorical forms, and appeals to principles and common sense.

Rhetorical Figures. There are so many different kinds of rhetorical figures and tropes that entire books have been written to try to define and distinguish them from one another.[12] With Greek names, Latin names, and English names for each figure, the picture can quickly become confused. But speechwriters seem to have reduced this confusion by relying heavily on seven specific figures: anaphora, alliteration, chiasmus, antithesis, antistrophe, analogy, and rhetorical question.

When a candidate begins successive statements with the same word or phrase, he is using anaphora. In 1968, Nixon used anaphora when he said: "They are not racist or sick; they are not guilty of the crime that plagues the land. They are black and they are white—they're native born and foreign born—they're young and they're old. They work in America's factories. They run America's businesses. They serve in government. They provide most of the soldiers who died to keep us free. They give drive to the spirit of America. They give lift to the American Dream. They give steel to the backbone of America." Usually the use of a rhetorical device such as anaphora is a sign that a professional speechwriter has been practicing his craft. In the case of Nixon's 1968 acceptance address it seems that the stylistic devices may actually have originated with the president, who often wrote long sections of his own speeches. Nixon's chief speechwriter in 1968, Ray Price, recalls:

> [O]ne thing about Nixon [and] his '68 acceptance speech: Unlike probably most others, we speechwriters did not write that. He wrote that himself. A few of us gathered out at the east end of Long Island, Montauk Point, for several days before the convention. He had his own cabin. We had others there. He would keep sending out questions. We'd send stuff in. He was putting it together himself. None of us on the writing staff knew what he was going to say until we heard it at the convention.

Unlike Nixon, Bill Clinton did use his speechwriter, David Kusnet, to structure an appeal using anaphora at the 1992 Democratic convention: "for too long politicians have told the most of us that are doing all right that what's really wrong with America is the rest of us—them. Them, the minorities. Them, the liberals. Them, the poor. Them, the homeless. Them, the people with disabilities. Them, the gays. We've gotten to the point where we've nearly them'd ourselves to death. Them, and them, and them." Anaphora underscores through repetition of both sound and sense.

Alliteration achieves a somewhat different effect by stringing words together that begin with the same sound. In 1976, Jimmy Carter spoke of "idealists without illusions"; in 1980, Reagan warned of when "tyrants are tempted" and lauded the "prospects of peace"; in 1988, George H. W. Bush, through the pen of Peggy Noonan, noted that "they promise—we perform," and spoke of change that "risks retreat"; in 2004, George W. Bush offered a "compassionate conservative" philosophy and promised to extend the "frontiers of freedom." Alliteration is a powerful stylistic tool, but there is always the temptation to overuse, as when Goldwater, in 1964, referred to "rules without responsibility, and regimentation without recourse." The first phrase was immediately understandable; the second was not. Alliteration, to be effective, must be both clear and sensible. The best alliteration calls attention to ideas, not to the words themselves.

Chiasmus is probably the most familiar use of rhetoric in presidential discourse. When Theodore Sorensen wrote John Kennedy's statement, "Ask not what your country can do for you; ask what you can do for your country," he was employing chiasmus. Based on the Greek letter chi (χ), the figure is named for the crossing pattern represented in the letter. There are very few perfect chiasmuses in presidential acceptance addresses, but there are many that aspire to perfection. The only perfect chiasmus in the acceptance addresses I surveyed is Nixon's 1972 statement: "here in America a person should get what he works for and work for what he gets." Clinton's 1996 speechwriters, led by Michael Waldman, were clearly trying to think in terms of the chiasmus when they wrote: "He took the richest country in the world and brought it down. We took the poorest state in America and lifted it up." It was not a true chiasmus, but it was a striking image nevertheless.

All chiasmuses employ antithesis, but not all antitheses are chiasmuses. Antithesis simply means opposite. Any use of the dialectical topoi would, by definition, be an antithesis. In 1988, George H. W. Bush held that "strength and clarity lead to peace—weakness and ambivalence lead to war." This is, in fact, a double antithesis, since strength and weakness are opposites and peace and war are opposites. In 2004, George W. Bush proclaimed: "Here buildings fell. Here a nation rose." And in 1992, Clinton contended that "the rest of the world will not look down on us with pity but up to us with respect again." Speechwriters love antitheses because they draw sharp contrasts that help to make clear the differences between the candidates and the parties.

Antistrophe is the counterpart to anaphora. But instead of a series of repetitions that begin a thought, antistrophe is a series of repetitions that end a thought. In 1948, Truman used antistrophe when he said he was going to call Congress back into special session. "At the same time," said Truman, "I shall ask them to act upon other vitally needed measures such as aid to education, which they say they are for; a national health program, which they say they are for; civil rights legislation, which they say they are for." By repeating this statement, Truman's speechwriters, Samuel Rosenman and Clark Clifford, were underscoring his larger point that what the Republicans say and what they do are two different things. This particular usage married ridicule with antistrophe to achieve its effect. In 1984, Reagan employed antistrophe when he said: "We promised that we'd reduce the growth of the Federal Government, and we have. We said we intended to reduce interest rates and inflation, and we have. We said we would reduce taxes to provide incentives for individuals and business to get our economy moving again, and we have." Reagan used antistrophe to underscore promises kept, thus reinforcing his credibility. In his 2000 acceptance address, George W. Bush also used antistrophe when he ended a series of charges against the Clinton-Gore administration with the refrain "They have not led. We will."

Analogy is the figure that compares one thing to another. In his 1960 acceptance address, drafted by Theodore Sorensen, John F. Kennedy used historical analogy when he observed, "For just as historians tell us that Richard I was not fit to fill the shoes of bold Henry II—and that Richard Cromwell was not fit to wear the mantle of his uncle—they might add in future years that Richard Nixon did not measure to the footsteps of Dwight D. Eisenhower." In his 1980 acceptance address, Reagan compared the economy to a bad stew: "First, we must overcome something the present administration has cooked up: a new and altogether indigestible economic stew, one part inflation, one part high unemployment, one part recession, one part runaway taxes, one part deficit spending and seasoned by an energy crisis. It's an economic stew that has turned the national stomach." In 1988, Bush offered another analogy, comparing the economy before Reagan-Bush to a sick patient in a hospital: "My friends, eight years ago this economy was flat on its back—intensive care. We came in and gave it emergency treatment: got the temperature down by lowering regulation, got the blood pressure down when we lowered taxes. Pretty soon the patient was up, back on his feet, and stronger than ever." By discussing one (often complex) thing in terms of another (often simple or everyday) thing, analogy helps a candidate to connect with a mass audience.

Rhetorical questions are questions introduced for effect, because everyone already knows the answers to them. In an acceptance address, a speechwriter can use a series of rhetorical questions to get the audience involved and to underscore an attitude, often a negative attitude, toward the opposition. In 1980, Reagan asked: "Can anyone look at the record of this administration and say, 'Well done'? Can anyone compare the state of our economy when the Carter Administration took office with where we are today and say, 'Keep up the good work'? Can anyone look at our reduced standing in the world today and say, 'Let's have four more years of this'?" The answer is, of course, implied in the question. In 1988, Bush combined rhetorical question with antithesis to form a powerful appeal: "Should public school teachers be required to lead our children in the pledge of allegiance? My opponent says no—but I say yes. Should society be allowed to impose the death penalty on those who commit crimes of extraordinary cruelty and violence? My opponent says no—but I say yes. Should our children have the right to say a voluntary prayer, or even observe a moment of silence in the schools? My opponent says no—but I say yes. Should free men and women have the right to own a gun to protect their home? My opponent says no—but I say yes." As this example illustrates, rhetorical figures can be combined in many different ways to form powerful appeals.

Anaphora, alliteration, chiasmus, antithesis, antistrophe, analogy, and rhetorical questions are just seven of the many rhetorical figures available to speechwriters. Certainly other figures have been employed from time to time—a syndeton (the omission of conjunctions between words, phrases, or clauses), catachresis (the intentional misuse or misapplication of a name or term), irony (expressing a meaning that is the opposite of that intended), polysyndeton (use of a conjunction between clauses), significatio (to imply more than one says), synecdoche (substitution of part for whole or whole for part), apodioxis (rejecting an argument indignantly as being false), apostrophe (breaking off the discourse to address directly some present or absent person or thing), and accumulatio (heaping up praise or accusation), among others. Presidential speechwriters may not know the technical names for each of the figures they employ, but they have a sensitivity to language and an acute understanding of how audiences react to particular linguistic formations.

Controlling Terms and Rhetorical Forms. Figures of speech are just one stylistic resource. Controlling terms and rhetorical forms are another. The specific words and rhetorical forms used in presidential acceptance addresses are not simply matters of taste or personal style, whether that of the speechwriter or of the candidate. Terms and forms are chosen to advance the persuasive strategies of the speech. Some acceptance addresses are built around specific terms, because those terms carry a particular kind of weight or significance to the listening audience that will help to advance the campaign strategy.

In 1956, for example, Eisenhower was running as an incumbent on the theme of "peace, prosperity, and progress." The main strategy of the fall campaign was to keep the focus on the good economic times and on the nation's forward movement across a range of fields and concerns. The Republican Party, Ike said, was the "party of the future." To underscore that perspective, Eisenhower's speechwriter, Arthur Larson, had Ike repeat the word "future" twenty-two times and featured terms such as "forward-looking" and "tomorrow" five more times. The strategy was also to emphasize Eisenhower's ethos, perhaps his strongest quality, by picturing him as a man of "principle," a term that occurred thirteen times in the address. The image that emerged was that of a principled leader, presiding over an era of peace and prosperity, and committed to a bright and progressive future.

In 2000, Bush chose a different kind of strategy, running against the behavior rather than the record of the Clinton-Gore administration. The strategy was to make Bush appear to be the better leader by portraying himself as an agent of change and by reminding the audience of the president's character problems. To do this, the speechwriter, Michael Gerson, emphasized Bush's stands on high-profile, controversial issues such as military readiness, education reform, Social Security, Medicare, and the tax code, while simultaneously reminding listeners of Clinton's character problems. When discussing education, for example, Bush concluded by saying: "But when the moment for leadership came, this administration did not teach our children, it disillusioned them." The "disillusion" was an indirect but rhetorically effective reminder of the Monica Lewinsky scandal. This was "education" of a different sort, and the Bush forces exploited it unmercifully. The term "character" appeared nine times in the speech, along with related terms such as "integrity," "responsibility," and "dignity."

Not all acceptance speeches pivot on a key term or set of terms, but many of them use a rhetorical form based on the Puritan jeremiad. This secularized jeremiad calls on the audience to (1) remember the "promise" of America, (2) lament the "fall" brought on by the "sins" of the incumbent administration, and (3) join in the "renewal of the promise"—portrayed as a compact between the president and the people rather than a covenant between the people and God. Kurt Ritter goes so far as to claim that all acceptance addresses are secular jeremiads.[13] Although the jeremiadic form cannot account for all the elements found in acceptance addresses, the three movements of the jeremiadic form often do form an important part of the style of accepting. This jeremiadic form manifests itself stylistically in the repeated use of terms—terms for the promise, terms for the fall, and especially terms for the renewal.

The terms for the "promise" are the most frequently used words in acceptance addresses—liberty, freedom, democracy, equality, and justice. They embody in the constitutional and political orders what grace, charity, repentance, judgment, and mercy embody in the divine order. They are, in the words of Kenneth Burke, the "god terms" of American politics.[14] They occur, in one form or another, in every acceptance address. In 2004, Bush managed to include all five of these god terms in a single paragraph: "The wisest use of American strength is to advance *freedom*. As the citizens of

Afghanistan and Iraq seize the moment, their example will send a message of hope throughout a vital region. Palestinians will hear the message that *democracy* and reform are within their reach, and so is peace with our good friend Israel. Young women across the Middle East will hear the message that their day of *equality* and *justice* is coming. Young men will hear the message that national progress and dignity are found in *liberty*, not tyranny and terror." It would be difficult, if not impossible, to write an acceptance address that did not include at least one of these five god terms.

The terminology of the "fall" is presented in images of descent and decline. References to the "valley," the "desert," "shadows," and "falling" mark this part of the jeremiadic form. Words such as uncertainty, weakness, drift, tragedy, failure, decay, torment, confusion, crisis, disgrace, chaos, oppression, waste, struggle, anguish, calamity, destruction, suffer, demoralize, deprive, betray, abandoned, vacillate, indecision, flounder, paralysis, despair, privation, and disease are the markers of the descent. As Barack Obama put it in 2008, "These challenges are not all of government's making. But the *failure* to respond is the direct result of a *broken* politics in Washington and the *failed* policies of George W. Bush." It is because of this "fallen" state that candidates and their speechwriters can conjure an answering rhetoric of renewal.

The rhetoric of renewal includes such terms as renew, reform, rebirth, recover, redeem, recapture, restore, recall, reconstruct, resume, reconstitute, reawaken, reconsecrate, rediscover, reignite, remold, rebuild, and revitalize, among others. Of the twenty-two acceptance addresses surveyed for this chapter, all but five repeatedly employed one or more of these terms. Reagan's 1980 acceptance address used rebirth (four times), restore, reaffirm, reestablish, renewed (three times), redeem, and recapture. The 1980 Reagan speechwriters, led by Peter Hannaford, used the jeremiadic form and style to structure the entire speech. A large portion of Obama's 2008 acceptance address, drafted by Jon Favreau, also employed the jeremiadic form and featured such terms of renewal as recover, restore (three times), rebuild (twice), and renew.

Closely related to the style of renewing the promise are images of ascent—rising, climbing, scaling, growing, reaching, lifting, or building. Examples are not hard to find:

> *Roosevelt, 1932*: "Out of every crisis, every tribulation, every disaster, mankind *rises* with some share of greater knowledge, of *higher* decency, of purer purpose. . . . To return to *higher* standards we must abandon the false prophets and seek new leaders of our own choosing. . . . they have failed in national vision, because in disaster they

have held out no hope, they have pointed out no path for the people below to *climb back* to places of security."

Eisenhower, 1956: "Our economic power, as everyone knows, is displaying a capacity for *growth* which is both rapid and sound, even while supporting record military budgets. We must keep it *growing*."

Nixon, 1968: "The time has come for us to leave the valley of despair and *climb the mountain* so that we may see the glory of the dawn."

Carter, 1976: "The hope of a laborer to *build* a better life for us all. . . . an America that *lives up* to our Constitution."

Reagan, 1984: "Isn't our choice really not one of left or right, but of *up* or down? Down through the welfare state to statism, to more and more government largesse accompanied always by more government authority, less individual liberty and, ultimately, totalitarianism, always advanced as for our own good. The alternative is the dream conceived by our Founding Fathers, *up* to the ultimate in individual freedom consistent with an orderly society.

Bush, 1988: "I seek the presidency to *build* a better America. . . . How do we complete [the mission]? We *build* it. . . . America is not a decline. America is a *rising* nation."

Clinton, 1992: "When I am your President, the rest of the world will not look down on us with pity but *up* to us with respect again. . . . we must plow back every dollar of defense cuts into *building* American jobs right here at home. . . . a country that once again *lifts* its people."

Bush, 2000: "America's way is the *rising* road."

Bush, 2004: "Since 2001, Americans have been given hills to *climb* and found the strength to *climb* them. . . . Now, because we have faced challenges with resolve, we have historic goals within our *reach* and greatness in our future. We will *build* a safer world."

Obama, 2008: "That's the promise of America, the idea that we are responsible for ourselves, but that we also *rise* or fall as one nation, the fundamental belief that I am my brother's keeper, I am my sister's keeper."

Images of ascent are part of the jeremiadic form, which was, in its Puritan iteration, a striving for transcendence, a reaching up to God in an effort to restore the harmonious relationship that had been severed. Today, presidential speechwriters, by using images of ascent, portray the president and/or the people as striving to enact political ideals, thus renewing the right relationship between the people and their leaders.

Appeals to Principle and Common Sense. American audiences respect leaders of principle who exhibit old-fashioned common sense. Rather than take the chance that the electorate might miss these desirable qualities in their candidate, speechwriters have repeatedly included appeals to principle and common sense in their acceptance addresses. Eisenhower's 1956 address was built around portraying him as a man of principle, but appeals to principle occur in most acceptance addresses.

Roosevelt referred to the 1932 Democratic platform as a "declaration of principles" and said that his own program was based on a "simple moral principle." In 1956, Eisenhower said that he would "reject expediency in favor of principle." Reagan pledged to "campaign on behalf of the principles of our party" in 1984. Four years later Bush referred to "the principles that we hold dear," and later said, "We weren't saints—but we lived by standards." In 2000, George W. Bush said: "I will act on principle" and then proceeded to use the phrase "on principle" three times to describe his beliefs. Four years later, Bush promised "principled leadership." The appeal to or from principle arises from the inventional place of establishing a presidential ethos. One way to establish such an ethos is to portray oneself as a defender of principle.

Alongside the appeal to principle is the appeal to common sense. Roosevelt identified with his audience in 1932 by describing both himself and them as "common-sense citizens." Later, he said, "Let us use common sense and business sense." In 1976, Carter promised to govern "not by confusion and crisis, but with grace and imagination and common sense." Four years later, Reagan promised the same thing, saying, "We will simply apply to government the common sense we all use in our daily lives." Although presidential speechwriters clearly value "principle" as a rhetorical marker of honesty, straightforwardness, and righteousness, they must not let such high-mindedness spill over into idealism, self-righteousness, and being perceived as so dedicated to principle that the candidate loses touch with the electorate. Excessive dedication to principles and ideals marred the Stevenson and Goldwater acceptance addresses, so much so that the former came off as a hopeless idealist and the latter appeared to be consumed by ideology. It is precisely to prevent these sorts of problems that candidates appeal to common sense. Because the voters want candidates who are both principled and in possession of common sense, speechwriters often include both kinds of appeals in the acceptance addresses.[15]

Conclusion

Writing a presidential nomination acceptance address is a daunting task. The best acceptance addresses have been written by political professionals who clearly understood the interrelated generic, strategic, and contextual dimensions of their assignment. The worst ones were by writers or candidates who lost sight of one or more of these dimensions. By understanding the inventional storehouse, the dispositional expectations, and the stylistic possibilities available to presidential speechwriters, one can begin to understand the scope of the art required to fashion such a speech.

Presidential speechwriting is a practical art, not a fine art. Those who have penned successful nomination acceptance addresses have been masters not only of language, but of history, politics, and audience psychology as well. They have learned to craft their speeches in light of the exigencies of the moment. Although many misperceptions about presidential speechwriters persist, by better understanding the compositional possibilities of a standard genre such as the acceptance address, scholars can acquire a rich analytical perspective by which to evaluate presidential discourse.[16]

Notes

1. The list of top 100 speeches was picked up by a wide range of media outlets. *USA Today* ran a long story on the rankings. See Dru Sefton, "'I Have a Dream': In a Century of Speeches, Certain Words Still Soar," *USA Today*, December 30, 1999, 8D. Nine years later, we released the authenticated texts of these speeches. See Stephen E. Lucas and Martin J. Medhurst, eds., *Words of a Century: The Top 100 American Speeches, 1900–1999* (New York: Oxford University Press, 2009). Also on the list was William Jennings Bryan's acceptance of the Democratic nomination in 1900, but that speech was not delivered to a national nominating convention.

2. All quotations from presidential nomination acceptance addresses come from the archive at The American Presidency Project, University of California, Santa Barbara, online at http://www.presidency.ucsb.edu. I have added all of the italics appearing in the quotations of presidential nomination acceptance addresses.

3. There is a large literature on presidential nomination acceptance addresses that stretches from the 1920s to the present. Among the more helpful studies are E.L.H. [Everett Lee Hunt], "Contemporary Speeches," *Quarterly Journal of Speech* 14 (1928): 601–604; Robert T. Oliver, "The Speech That Established Roosevelt's Reputation," *Quarterly Journal of Speech* 31 (1945): 274–282; Craig R. Smith, "Richard Nixon's 1968 Acceptance Speech as a Model of Dual Audience Adaptation," *Today's Speech* 19 (1971): 15–22; David B. Valley, "Significant Characteristics of Democratic Presidential Nomination Acceptance Speeches," *Central States Speech Journal* 25 (1974): 56–62; Kurt W. Ritter, "American Political Rhetoric and the Jeremiad Tradition: Presidential Nomination Acceptance Addresses, 1960–1976," *Central States Speech Journal* 31 (1980): 153–171; Keith V. Erickson, "Jimmy Carter: The Rhetoric of Private and Civic Piety," *Western Journal of Speech Communication* 44 (1980): 221–235; William E. Wiethoff, "'I Accept Your Nomination':

Carter, Reagan, and Classical Obscurantism," *Indiana Speech Journal* 16 (1981): 33-40; Henry Z. Scheele, "Ronald Reagan's 1980 Acceptance Address: A Focus on American Values," *Western Journal of Speech Communication* 48 (1984): 51-61; C. Thomas Preston, Jr., "Reagan's 'New Beginning': Is It the 'New Deal' of the Eighties?" *Southern Speech Communication Journal* 49 (1984): 198-211; Nancy L. Miller and William B. Stiles, "Verbal Familiarity in American Presidential Nomination Acceptance Speeches and Inaugural Addresses (1920-1981)," *Social Psychology Quarterly* 49 (1986): 72-81; J. Justin Gustainis and William L. Benoit, "Analogic Analysis of the Presidential Candidates' Acceptance Speeches at the 1980 National Nominating Conventions," *Speaker and Gavel* 25 (1988): 14-23; Kevin W. Dean, "Bill Clinton's 'New Covenant': Re-visioning an Old Vision," *National Forensic Journal* 10 (Fall 1992): 101-110; Mary Ann Renz, "The Stories in George Bush's Acceptance Speech," *National Forensic Journal* 10 (1992): 123-134; Wayne Fields, *Union of Words: A History of Presidential Eloquence* (New York: Free Press, 1996), 71-112; Ray D. Dearin, "The American Dream as Depicted in Robert J. Dole's 1996 Presidential Nomination Acceptance Speech," *Presidential Studies Quarterly* 27 (1997): 698-713; Davis W. Houck, "Reading the Body in the Text: FDR's 1932 Speech to the Democratic National Convention," *Southern Communication Journal* 63 (1997): 20-36; William L. Benoit, "Acclaiming, Attacking, and Defending in Presidential Nomination Acceptance Addresses, 1960-1996," *Quarterly Journal of Speech* 85 (1999): 247-267; Sharon E. Jarvis, "Campaigning Alone: Partisan versus Personal Language in the Presidential Nominating Convention Acceptance Addresses, 1948-2000," *American Behavioral Scientist* 44 (2001): 2152-2171; William L. Benoit, "Framing through Temporal Metaphor: The 'Bridges' of Bob Dole and Bill Clinton in Their 1996 Acceptance Addresses," *Communication Studies* 52 (2001): 70-84; William L. Benoit et al., *Campaign 2000: A Functional Analysis of Presidential Campaign Discourse* (Lanham, Md.: Rowman and Littlefield, 2003), 145-154; William L. Benoit, Kevin A. Stein, and Glenn J. Hansen, "How Newspapers Cover Presidential Nomination Acceptance Addresses," *Newspaper Research Journal* 25 (Summer 2004): 83-89; and Sharon E. Jarvis and Emily Balanoff Jones, "Party Labels in Presidential Acceptance Addresses: 1948-2000," in *In the Public Domain: Presidents and the Challenges of Public Leadership*, eds. Lori Cox Han and Diane J. Heith (Albany: State University of New York Press, 2005), 29-48; Judith S. Trent and Robert V. Friedenberg, *Political Campaign Communication: Principles and Practices*, 6th ed. (Lanham, Md.: Rowman and Littlefield, 2007), 238-253.

4. On the idea of rhetorical exigency as applied to presidential discourse, see Martin J. Medhurst, "Rhetorical Leadership and the Presidency: A Situational Taxonomy," in *The Values of Presidential Leadership*, eds. Terry L. Price and J. Thomas Wren (New York: Palgrave/Macmillan, 2007), 59-84.

5. Wynton C. Hall, "The Invention of 'Quantifiably Safe Rhetoric': Richard Wirthlin and Ronald Reagan's Instrumental Use of Public Opinion Research in Presidential Discourse," *Western Journal of Communication* 66 (2002): 319-347; Wynton C. Hall, "'Reflections of Yesterday': George H. W. Bush's Instrumental Use of Public Opinion Research

in Presidential Discourse," *Presidential Studies Quarterly* 32 (2002): 531–558; Dick Wirthlin with Wynton C. Hall, *The Greatest Communicator: What Ronald Reagan Taught Me about Politics, Leadership, and Life* (New York: John Wiley and Sons, 2004), 48–64.

6. There has been very little rhetorical analysis of Goldwater's speech. For the best treatment, see John C. Hammerback, "Barry Goldwater's Rhetorical Legacy," *Southern Communication Journal* 64 (1999): 323–332; H. E. Knepprath and G. P. Mohrmann, "Buncombe Re-visited: The 1964 Republican Convention," *Central States Speech Journal* 16 (1965): 28–34. For the best historical treatment of how the speech came to be written, see Lee Edwards, *Goldwater: The Man Who Made a Revolution* (Washington, D.C.: Regnery, 1995), 248–280. For an accurate text of the speech with headnote and annotations, see Lucas and Medhurst, *Words of a Century*, 409–415.

7. Stevenson's 1952 nomination acceptance address appeared in multiple speech anthologies from the 1950s through the present. Strangely, it has seldom been the focus of sustained rhetorical analysis. See Russel Windes, Jr., and James A. Robinson, "Public Address in the Career of Adlai E. Stevenson," *Quarterly Journal of Speech* 42 (1956): 225–233; Alvin R. Kaiser, "Style and Personal Appeal of Adlai E. Stevenson," *Western Speech* 18 (1954): 181–185; Malcolm O. Sillars, "The Presidential Campaign of 1952," *Western Speech* 22 (1958): 94–99; John M. Murphy, "Civic Republicanism in the Modern Age: Adlai Stevenson in the 1952 Presidential Campaign," *Quarterly Journal of Speech* 80 (1994): 313–329. For an accurate text of the speech with headnote and annotations, see Lucas and Medhurst, *Words of a Century*, 306–309.

8. This chapter begins with Roosevelt's 1932 speech for several reasons. FDR was the first president to deliver a nomination acceptance speech in person to a national convention. Prior to 1932, presidential nominees were officially notified of their nomination weeks after the convention in person by a nomination committee. The nominee then gave a response—sometimes a full speech, sometimes just a few remarks, and sometimes a letter—accepting the nomination. FDR was also the first president to use a stable of speechwriters. Harding, Coolidge, and Hoover each had a single White House speechwriter, but Roosevelt often had six or more people helping him with speech drafts, thus professionalizing the craft. Finally, Roosevelt's 1932 address clearly became a model that other presidents tried to emulate. Even Ronald Reagan, in his 1980 acceptance speech, drew from FDR's 1932 address. Roosevelt's speech was not, however, the first acceptance address to be broadcast by radio. That distinction went to Democratic presidential nominee John W. Davis in 1924. On August 11, 1924, Davis said: "I indict the Republican Party in its organized capacity for having shaken public confidence to its very foundations. . . . I charge it with having exhibited deeper and more widespread corruption than any that this generation of Americans has been called upon to witness.

"I charge it with complacency in the face of that corruption, and with ill-will toward the efforts of honest men to expose it. I charge it with gross favoritism to the privileged, and with utter disregard of the unprivileged. I charge it with indifference to world peace, and with timidity in the conduct of our foreign affairs."

Three days later, on August 14, the Republican nominee, President Calvin Coolidge, gave his nomination acceptance address, thus becoming the first president to have his nomination acceptance speech broadcast over the radio. See "50,000 at the Notification—Candidate Scores Corruption and 'Gross Favoritism' in Office," New York Times, August 12, 1924, 1; "Notification Hall Filled—The Restricted Accommodation Permits Only 2,000 to Attend," New York Times, August 15, 1924, 1.

9. For more on how presidential speechwriters "invent" discourse, see Martin J. Medhurst, "Ghostwriting: Ethics Isn't the Only Lesson," Communication Education 36 (1987): 241–249. For other studies of presidential discourse that focus on the inventional processes of speechwriters, see Halford Ross Ryan, "Roosevelt's First Inaugural: A Study of Technique," Quarterly Journal of Speech 65 (1979): 137–149; Halford Ross Ryan, "Roosevelt's Fourth Inaugural Address: A Study of Its Composition," Quarterly Journal of Speech 67 (1981): 157–166; Laura Crowell, "Building the 'Four Freedoms' Speech," Speech Monographs 22 (1955): 266–283; Davis W. Houck, FDR and Fear Itself: The First Inaugural Address (College Station: Texas A&M University Press, 2002).

10. By allowing the listener to "fill in" the missing part of the argument, the form allows for a sort of self-persuasion. The term "enthymeme" originated with Aristotle in his book On Rhetoric. See Aristotle, On Rhetoric, trans. George A. Kennedy (New York: Oxford University Press, 1990), esp. 45–47, 186–190. Also, Christopher Lyle Johnstone, "Enthymeme," in The Encyclopedia of Rhetoric, ed. Thomas O. Sloane (New York: Oxford University Press, 2001), 247–250.

11. Topical patterns organize a speech by topic or issue, as when a speaker says that he'll be talking about economic policy, military policy, and health policy. Problem/solution patterns organize a speech by first introducing a problem, such as the cost of prescription medicines, and then proposing a specific solution to the problem. A chronological pattern organizes the speech by time, usually starting at the point when something began and moving forward in time to the present. Cause/effect (or effect/cause) patterns organize a speech by dealing first with the cause or causes of a specific problem and then moving to what the effect or effects are that follow logically from the cause. Sequential patterns are useful when the issue at hand has a particular sequence that needs to be understood and followed, as in making a cake or conducting an experiment. Spatial patterns use place as an organizing scheme, with the geographical or spatial locale being the organizing principle of the speech, as when describing the rooms in a new house. Pro/con patterns can be used to organize a speech if there are arguments to be considered on both sides of the issue. The need for a military draft would be an example. The speaker would first introduce the arguments in favor of a draft and then follow with the arguments opposed to a draft. Residual argumentation is a pattern used when the speaker wants to consider several options but end with only one preferred option. Arguments are considered and then dismissed until only one perspective remains. For a good treatment of organizational patterns in public speeches, see Stephen E. Lucas, The Art of Public Speaking, 9th ed. (New York: McGraw-Hill, 2006).

12. See, for example, Richard A. Lanham, *A Handlist of Rhetorical Terms* (Berkeley: University of California Press, 1991).

13. See Ritter, "American Political Rhetoric and the Jeremiad Tradition"; Kurt Ritter, "The Presidential Nomination Acceptance Address since 1980: An Evolving American Jeremiad," in *Generic Criticism of American Public Address*, ed. Dennis D. Cali (Dubuque, Iowa: Kendall/Hunt Publishing, 1996), 201–210.

14. Kenneth Burke, *A Grammar of Motives* (1945; rpt. Berkeley: University of California Press, 1969), 355–356.

15. This balancing of principle with common sense parallels what Sharon Jarvis found concerning the use of partisan labels in acceptance addresses. She writes: "candidates who are more likely than their opponents to include partisan labels in their speeches are likely to lose in the general election. Although it is important to avoid causal language here, the relationship is perhaps suggestive. Because candidates must appeal to their loyal base as well as to undecided voters to win in most elections, a highly partisan style may simply restrict the base of voters and be a short-sighted strategy given patterns of dealignment in the electorate." See Jarvis, "Campaigning Alone."

16. On misperceptions about presidential speechwriting, see Martin J. Medhurst, "Presidential Speechwriting: Ten Myths That Plague Modern Scholarship," in *Presidential Speechwriting: From the New Deal to the Reagan Revolution and Beyond*, eds. Kurt Ritter and Martin J. Medhurst (College Station: Texas A&M University Press, 2003), 3–19. For the standard rhetorical treatment of presidential genres of discourse, see Karlyn Kohrs Campbell and Kathleen Hall Jamieson, *Presidents Creating the Presidency: Deeds Done in Words* (Chicago: University of Chicago Press, 2008).

Chapter 3

Speechwriters on the Acceptance Address

Patrick Anderson, Kenneth Khachigian, Raymond Price

This session of the symposium featured Patrick Anderson, speechwriter for Jimmy Carter; Kenneth Khachigian, speechwriter for Ronald Reagan; and Raymond Price, speechwriter for Richard Nixon. The discussions were moderated by Martin Medhurst, Distinguished Professor of Rhetoric and Communications at Baylor University.

Medhurst: On this panel, we're going to talk about acceptance addresses. I want you to start, though, by talking a little more generally about how you first met the president for whom you worked, and what was the first speech that you wrote for him. Ray?

Price: I had met Nixon once at a Gridiron Dinner in Washington to shake his hand.[1] I had never met him otherwise until he called me on Washington's birthday, 1967, at home, when I had one of the worst hangovers of my life—which, having been at Yale, in the Navy, and on a New York newspaper, was saying a lot. Nixon wanted to see if I might come talk to him about helping with what *might* be a campaign for '68. I did. We had lunch that day, which was a holiday, at his home on tray tables in his study. We talked for three hours about everything under the sun. I had always been an active Republican. I had never been anti-Nixon, unlike other Republicans. I actually had favored Nixon over [Nelson] Rockefeller for the nomination in '60, as well as over [John] Kennedy for the general election.[2] I hadn't even thought about who my candidate would be for '68, much less whether I'd want to get involved.

After three hours of discussing everything—people and personalities and a campaign, the work, the nation, and everything else—I found him vastly more impressive than I'd expected, even though I'd been writing about him for years. At the end of the conversation, he asked me to work for him and to give him an answer in a week. I researched it intensively. By about the fifth day, I found, to my surprise, that he was my candidate. The toughest

51

thing in these circumstances is, do you face down everybody and give up everything else? I felt I should, so I called his office on the seventh day. He was then a lawyer in New York. People forget that he was elected president from New York, not from California.[3] He asked me to come down to the office. I went down. He introduced me to some people. He had an office ready for me there, and I started work that day. That's how it happened.

Medhurst: What was the first speech you wrote for Nixon?

Price: I don't remember. He hadn't even decided whether to run. We were preparing for what might or might not be a campaign. The first extensive thing I did with him was go with him on a three-week study tour through Asia. It was a good introduction to him and an introduction to the way he operated.

One thing also on acceptance speeches: he wrote his own acceptance speech for '68.[4] If we want to, I'll get into the rather unusual process for this. But having run the writing staff in his White House—this is an educated guess—about one out of twenty speeches, even as president, was written by the writing staff; nineteen out of twenty were not. And he never used notes. We did not call ourselves a speechwriting department. We called it "writing and research." Most of his speeches were not written. Most of our writing was not speeches.

Medhurst: Okay, let's go to Pat.

Anderson: Carter announced in January of '75 that he was going to run for president. I knew almost nothing about him. I happened to meet socially Peter Bourne and Mary King, who had been very close to him in Georgia and who continued to work on his campaign.[5] They talked to me about him, and they made him sound like a very interesting and progressive man. In those days, I was writing a lot for the *New York Times Magazine*. The magazine called me in the summer and said, "We'd like for you to do a campaign piece." I said, "Okay, but I think I'd like to write about this fellow Carter. I hear that he's interesting."

So in August of '75 I traveled with Carter in Florida, where he was campaigning very hard in anticipation of knocking off [George] Wallace the following spring.[6] My article on Carter appeared in December of '75, a cover piece in the *Times Magazine*.[7] It had a few little quibbles, but it was generally favorable. He was not taken very seriously at that point, but I thought he was an impressive campaigner. He was smart. The campaign had a plan. It turned out that their plan worked out very well.

I went my way, and then in the spring, in March, I had a book come out that did very well.[8] And suddenly I could do what I wanted to do. Like a fool, I called up Jody Powell and said, "Do you need a speechwriter?"[9] As it happened, they had already hired Bob Shrum, whom most of you probably know.[10] Shrum lasted ten days, at which point he resigned in anger and wrote an article saying that Carter was not a real liberal. Of course the rest of us already knew that, and that's why we were supporting him. We had supported a real liberal in '72, and you know what happened.[11] They then called me back and said, "Yes—can you come in?" And I did.

I think the reason they hired me was because Carter didn't know any writers. He didn't know anybody in Washington. He had a couple of staff people, not writers. I think they hired me because it looked like he had secured the nomination, but he was losing some primaries to Jerry Brown, and they were getting very nervous.[12] They didn't know what to change except possibly the rhetoric, so they thought maybe I could help with that.

The first speech I wrote for him—I wrote what you'd call a peroration, to close the speech. "I see an America with education; I see an America with justice; I see an America with opportunity," and so forth. I considered it somewhat Kennedy-esque rhetoric, if you will.[13] We used that in a speech at the Martin Luther King Hospital in Los Angeles, on June 1, in which he praised King and kind of volunteered himself as the keeper of the flame. He then closed with, "I see an America   ." It got very nice press. The *New York Times* said it was the best speech he'd ever delivered and so forth.[14] I think that was when they decided that perhaps I was useful. After all the grumbling in the press that he didn't know how to deliver a speech, suddenly he delivered a rather nice one. So that was the first thing I did for him, and it set me up a month later to work on the acceptance speech.

Medhurst: Ken, you've worked for two presidents. Tell us about that.

Khachigian: I started out as a second-year law student at Columbia University, in New York. I read an article in the *New York Times Magazine* about Ray and some of these other fellows who were helping the "New Nixon," and that he was going to run for president. This was in the fall of '67.[15] I was a political junkie, and I thought I'd like to get involved. I repeatedly wrote letters to his law office to see if I could get an interview. I finally called and they said, "We never got your letter." My wife was working then as an assistant on Wall Street, so she hand-delivered one, giving them no excuse.

I finally got a letter back from Pat Buchanan, who was Ray's colleague, and it said, "Why don't you come on in for an interview?"[16] It was a terrible interview. He thought I was a Rockefeller spy, since I was a Columbia Law student. I may or may not have had a beard at the time. I started out answering correspondence for the candidate and looking for ways I could get the attention of Ray and Marty Anderson and Pat Buchanan and others.[17] Somehow I did, and that summer I was hired. Alan Greenspan, the domestic policy advisor, was my boss.[18] I was a utility infielder. I did anything that anybody asked of me. After finishing law school, I got a job in the Nixon White House.

Medhurst: Very good. Let's move directly into talking about acceptance addresses specifically. Since Franklin Roosevelt flew to Chicago to accept the nomination in person in 1932, there have been thirty-eight such addresses by candidates of the two major parties. Some have been successful; some haven't been so successful. What must a good acceptance address do? What must it accomplish? Pat, let's start with you.

Anderson: Well, it's obviously the most important speech you will have made at that point in your campaign. Carter started out speaking to twenty people in somebody's living room, and then got up to a thousand, and suddenly he had the unique opportunity to speak to 40 or 50 million people for half an hour or more. Carter was relatively unknown, so it was a chance to introduce himself, to identify himself, to reach out to a lot of audiences, to reach out in a lot of directions, and to get his campaign off to a strong start, which, I think, fortunately he was able to do.

Medhurst: Ray?

Price: I think a lot of it depends on the candidate and on the times and circumstances. In Nixon's case, of course, he was well-known to the Republican Party. He had been vice president for eight years; he had lost by a hair's breadth in what a lot of us think was a stolen election in 1960;[19] and he'd been campaigning for Republican candidates all over the country for years. So when he finally decided to run—and incidentally, he didn't make the go, no-go decision on whether to run until New Year's weekend 1967-68—then he began to prepare. He announced his candidacy in New Hampshire, I think, on the first or second of March 1968. That's when he officially became a candidate for the nomination for '68.[20]

In his case, a lot of people had images of an old Nixon in their minds. For the convention, he had to present the Nixon of 1968. With other candidates, it was a different kind of thing. At the time we arrived in Miami for the convention in '68, we did not have the nomination in the bag. It was during the convention that John Mitchell, who was then the campaign manager, who had been Nixon's law partner, finally won South Carolina away from Reagan, so we got over the top.[21] Had he not managed that, Reagan would have been the nominee in '68. [Nelson] Rockefeller never had a chance.

Nixon had to present himself to the convention and to the world as the Nixon of '68. So it was a speech that would have to be global in scope, national in scope, but also show some of the personal depth and so forth of what you needed in a candidate.

Medhurst: How do you do that, Ken? How do you show the depth of the candidate, the character of the person, in an acceptance address?

Khachigian: In the case of Ronald Reagan's second acceptance speech—I wasn't involved in the first—he was an incumbent, so he wasn't introducing himself again.[22] At this point his job was to frame the issues in the campaign. The way he did it was just to be himself, which meant having clarity about his values. That's what always guided Reagan anyway, so in this case it was pretty easy. Walter Mondale wanted to raise taxes and announced that he would.[23] Reagan, being one who cut taxes, was able to leap on that right away. That speech was a reflection of his own history, going back to when he started giving speeches in the '40s as an activist, a political figure. The speeches he gave throughout the presidency were all reflective of what he thought throughout those years. And he was a showman. I don't think he was shy about any of that. He had a solid ego, though it didn't come out. I think he liked the idea of being up there.

We framed the campaign in that speech. We framed the issues in that campaign. It was going to be about strong foreign policy and strong national defense, and it was going to be about the economy. That was probably the strongest suit going. As Patrick will remember, there was something called the "misery index" in the 1976 election.[24] It came back as somewhat more miserable in 1980. Then by 1984, when the economy had started coming back, Reagan had some bragging rights. He wanted to get that news out. There was a lot going on that year. The Olympics were in Los Angeles, so we had some metaphorical advantages that year as well.

Price: If I could just inject one other thing about Nixon's '68 acceptance speech. Unlike probably most others, we speechwriters did not write that. He wrote that himself. A few of us gathered out at the east end of Long Island, Montauk Point, for several days before the convention. He had his own cabin. We had others there. He would keep sending out questions to us. We'd send stuff in. He was putting it together himself. None of us on the writing staff knew what he was going to say until we heard it at the convention.

Nelson: Ray, in '72, when Nixon was running for reelection, was it a different kind of process, a different kind of challenge?

Price: Yes, in reelections it's a different challenge. I'm quite sure he did that one himself also. He was riding high in '72. I'm not sure what was going on in his mind about the main things he thought he had to do, but we were trying to gear him up and trying to mobilize the party for the campaign.

Medhurst: Ken, in the 1984 acceptance address, you clearly see elements of what has become known as "The Speech," the speech that Reagan gave starting in, well, depending on how far back you want to go, maybe even to the '50s, all the way through.[25] Clearly one source of content for acceptance addresses is the things that the candidate has said previously. What are some of the other places you look to to find content for an acceptance address?

Khachigian: In this particular case what I did was come up with a number of ideas and thoughts before I put pen to paper, which meant doing a lot of research—in this case, economic research about the economy between 1980 and 1984. Clearly I'd been working for the president since the 1980 campaign. Working on his inaugural address in 1981, I read through all of his major speeches of the past. Then I had another advantage: I had access to his 3-by-5 index cards going back to the 1950s. His thought process and his writing style were in there. Basically I grabbed on to anything I could because this was a big platform. It was a big forum. You had tens of millions of people. You were setting the stage for the campaign.

After I gathered ideas and concepts, I'd sit down with him before anything was written and talk with him about it. I'd show him what I had in mind and then listen to him. My role was to take notes for as long as I could, for as long as he was willing to talk. After that, I'd go back and look at that empty page in the typewriter. We didn't have word processors in 1984.

Medhurst: Pat, how does that compare to how you worked with Carter?

Anderson: Carter certainly understood how important the speech was. He delivered it on July 15. I was working on a draft certainly by the first of July.[26] I was with him on, I think, the third of July in Plains, and I had a draft. We talked about it, went back and forth. Ultimately we got to New York. About two or three days before the speech, I think, he had a meeting of himself, his son Chip [James Earl Carter III], Jody Powell, Jerry [Gerald] Rafshoon the television man, Pat Caddell the pollster, myself, and Greg Schneiders.[27] We were kind of the hard core.

He said, "I'm going to go through this line by line. You interrupt me, and let's talk about everything you want to talk about." We went through it, and we argued, and we fought out certain points. He had never done this before. As far as I know, he never did it again. I think it ultimately paid off. If you know the speech as I know it, I could go through and show you: this is my line; this is Carter's line; this I picked up from Ted Sorensen;[28] this came out of his Georgia inaugural. Overwhelmingly it is Carter's, but there's other input. There was a point in here where he said, "I have spoken a lot of times this year about love," and then he'd written in the margin, "but love must be aggressively translated into simple justice." I said, "Governor, I think that's a beautiful line about translating love into justice." He said, "It should be. It's [Reinhold] Niebuhr."[29] But that was him too, because he knows a lot about Niebuhr. We quoted Kennedy. We quoted Bob Dylan.[30]

He had run as an outsider, but we knew it was time to pay tribute to the Democratic Party when you accept its nomination, so we said something about Roosevelt, [Harry] Truman, Kennedy, Johnson. Here's an example of the sort of thing you go through. Some people were pushing us to do more to appeal to the Catholics, so we started out with a quote from Kennedy, and we talked about families and so forth. But we started out mentioning Al Smith in this litany of great Democrats.[31] Then somebody said, "Wait a minute—leaving aside the question of who remembers Al Smith—he lost and all these other guys won. If you're going to mention Smith, what about [Adlai] Stevenson? What about [Hubert] Humphrey?[32] What about [George] McGovern and other candidates?" We went back and forth, and finally I said, "Governor, look, Smith lost. Let's just kill all the losers." He said, "Now you're speaking my language." That was it for Al Smith. Anyway there are a lot of very personal things in here. In this case I think it worked. Pat Caddell's polling afterward said it was an extremely popular speech.

Khachigian: I'd like to comment on the process because I could never imagine using a committee with Reagan, who loathed committees. With a lot of people in the room like that, he would not be responsive at all. He would have the most blank look on his face you could imagine. He wouldn't even have participated.

There were times when the speeches went through drafts and he thought it was done, then somebody would come back through and try to edit it. He asked me once, "Did the darn committee get a hold of this again?" My goal, frankly, was to keep others' fingers off of it. There were a couple of people, specifically in the White House, whom I won't mention, who liked to tinker with his speeches as much as they could and as secretly as they could. It finally got to where I'd try to be the last one to see him before he went on. That was my goal.

Medhurst: Pat raised the issue of pollsters. What is the relationship of polling and speechwriting?[33]

Anderson: We had Pat Caddell, and he often had opinions such as, "We need to talk more about the economy or talk more about justice," or whatever, and Carter listened to him. I never paid much attention to him. My interests were more rhetorical and not what the polls had to say.

Medhurst: When you say that Carter paid attention to him, did that translate into Carter saying, "We need to say more about this topic in our speeches"?

Anderson: I didn't see much of that. Carter listened to Caddell, but I always thought that what he was saying was pretty obvious to begin with.

Khachigian: I think polling, in terms of rhetoric, was a paint-by-numbers kind of thing that was not very helpful. Because the campaign would want me to talk to our pollster, I'd talk to him, but I almost uniformly ignored him, because it was this percentage of that and that percentage of this. One thing our old boss, Nixon, used to say is, "Politics is not about prose. It's about poetry." Polls don't show poetry. It's numbers and words that don't fit into the process. The last time I listened to our pollster was in the '82 midterm elections when he said that "Stay the course" was the line. I did it because I was told what the line was, and it was a very bad mistake. "Stay the course" means status quo, which is about the worst thing you can do if you're trying to motivate the public.[34]

Medhurst: Ray, you mentioned that Nixon wrote his own acceptance addresses in '68 and '72 but that you provided some input.

Price: A number of us sent in suggestions. He would send out memos asking us to try something and so forth, but he was putting it all together.

Medhurst: What sorts of input were they? Were they language? Were they themes? Were they metaphors?

Price: I don't have any specific recollections of it, but he would sometimes have a thought and he'd want you to develop it or something like that, to see if it worked. Things often seem as if they will work when you see them on paper, but then they don't work when spoken. It's better if you learn that sooner rather than later.

I don't recall polls having anything to do with what we wrote other than, perhaps, when it was a sophisticated kind of poll that wasn't just, "What do you like?" or, "What do you not like?" but "Why?" So it might indicate things that we had to educate the public on, to hit those objections.

Khachigian: There was one thing I remember about that '68 speech, Ray. I wasn't involved in it, but I learned about it later, quite obviously. He was not a senior speechwriter, but Bill Gavin,[35] who was part of the writing staff, had this notion of Nixon going back to the time of his youth when he heard the train whistle in the night at his home in Yorba Linda. That became thematic for the peroration. It became the thematic core of it. Nixon didn't use all the language he was given. He got an idea and maybe some of the language around it and then used it precisely to tell that story. That's one way he worked. He got ideas and then crafted in his head how he wanted to present them.

Medhurst: What is the importance of narrative, of storytelling, to speech-writing?

Price: I haven't thought of it in those terms. "Narrative" is a word that I never used to use, and it suddenly became the "in" word in recent years. We were just trying to frame an argument, essentially, rather than tell a story. Sometimes you would use a story to make a point, but I didn't think of that as narrative. You have to keep the audience awake. You need little things to wake them up as their eyelids are dropping. So you have to get little things in that will catch their imagination or attention, and sometimes little stories will help.

Medhurst: Reagan was famous for his storytelling. Did you all have anything to do with that, or was that just pure Reagan?

Khachigian: He was a born storyteller.[36] President Reagan was somewhat awkward sometimes with staff. When it was awkward and he didn't know who was around him or wasn't familiar with them, he'd start telling stories, usually about Hollywood. He'd talk about baseball all the time because he was an announcer at WHO in Des Moines.[37] But storytelling was the core of his craft. He was born to it. He loved it. He loved anecdotes. He loved illustrations. Some of them were apocryphal, and we had to convince him that we couldn't use all of them. Sometimes he overruled us and used them anyway.

Stories illustrated things for him. In speeches, you try to create word pictures. And if you go back to Reagan's time in radio, he had to create word pictures. Those of us who grew up with radio know that you'd listen and see things in your mind, whether colors or castles, princesses and princes. But he had a capability to spin yarns. That became a strong element of anything we did, and it would be a function of one of the other speeches we'll talk about later.

Anderson: You need flow. You need a speech that follows A, B, C, if possible. I think that Carter, who often had fascinating ideas, had an interesting mind, and he came up with interesting points. But in my experience he was not very good at putting things together in a logical way, which was part of what I did. He was good sometimes, like Nixon's train in the night in the acceptance speech. He talked about being a farm boy out in south Georgia. He'd been a Democrat all his life. He'd never met a Democratic president before, but he remembered as a boy that they would hook up the radio to the car battery and listen to the conventions from Chicago or New York or wherever they were in the '30s.[38] That was a nice story.

If you're in the audience of a speech, either in person or on television, you see the finished product, the polished version. One thing I'm very aware of, and I suspect that Ray and Ken are also, is that behind the scenes you see all the things that don't get in, that you have to fight over, the bad ideas that come with the good ideas. I'll give you an example. In our acceptance speech, Carter had agreed, or made a decision, that he was not going to mention [Gerald] Ford's pardon of Nixon. At the same time, we wanted to get into it indirectly at least. So that was the issue of equal justice under the law without getting specific. He told me to write something about equal justice. He said, "Make it be," so I gave him a line.

When he sent the draft back to me, after my statement on equal justice, he wrote in the margin, "I see no reason why big-shot crooks should go to country clubs and the poor ones go to jail." I thought that was classic Carter because I thought "big-shot crooks" was wonderful. I thought that was a great line. It was like earlier when he'd referred to [Henry] Kissinger's "Lone Ranger foreign policy."[39] It was good. But I thought, "go to country clubs"?—what was he saying there? Either it's the old right-wing notion that prisons are country clubs, which I don't agree with and didn't think he should say, or maybe he was saying literally that our country clubs are filled with unindicted felons, which may well be true, but I didn't think he should say that in an acceptance speech. So I persuaded him to change "go to country clubs" to just "go free." "I see no reason why big-shot crooks should go free and the poor ones go to jail." It was probably the most popular line in the speech.

Medhurst: One of the roles of a speechwriter, whether in an acceptance address or any other, is to do just that, to prevent the principal from saying something he shouldn't say. Can you think of instances in which you had that role of saying, "Maybe this is not the best way to say that"?

Price: The guy I worked with [Nixon] was pretty sensitive to that sort of thing, and I'm not sure that it would have been all that necessary with him. Ken may have some other recollections.

Khachigian: I don't have any Nixon stories in that regard, but I don't remember ever trying to talk Reagan out of anything except factual issues. We had to arm wrestle a few times. One big one was in the inaugural address of '81.[40] He was a good writer, and he knew what he wanted to say. I approached writing and working collaboratively with the president on the premise that I wasn't the president. I think the mistake of a lot of speechwriters is that they think that this is their opportunity to frame policy or to change the world and that they are in some cases smarter than the president or better than he, or someday she, is. I think that's a big mistake.

Reagan knew what he believed. He knew what he wanted. I worked hard. My first few speeches for him didn't fit in with his style. I listened to him very carefully, and once I got it down well enough, he would edit substantially, and then I'd go back and say, "I'm not going to mess with this." You did at your own peril, by the way, with Reagan.

Medhurst: One of the things that has happened over the last thirty years is the continuing decline of the amount of time television devotes to the conventions. What role did television play in the way you wrote an acceptance address? I remember, Ken, in the middle of the 1984 speech, Reagan said, "It's getting late," as a signal to the immediate audience to let him complete it in prime time.[41] So what effect does giving the address on national television have on the writing of the address?

Price: You know that attention spans are limited, and you want to take advantage of an audience while it's there. If you go on too long, you lose your audience. You don't try to be too curt, but you try to make each bit count.

Khachigian: You remember the famous McGovern acceptance speech in 1972. They debated in the hall for so long, the poor guy was giving his speech at 11 p.m.—prime time in Guam.[42]

I have a saying for people who give speeches: "Nobody ever walked out of church complaining that the sermon was too short." Brevity is the soul of wit, as they once said. In the case of 1984, Reagan was an incumbent president. He was popular. He was riding high. They had shown that convention documentary, which was just emotional, inspirational. He came on the stage, and the audience was so amped up, it interrupted the flow of the speech. That speech reads much better by the eye than it does by the ear because he was interrupted by "Four more years! Four more years!"

To all the beginning speechwriters I give this lesson. I made a big mistake in that speech, which I could never have known in advance. The Olympics were that year, so it was a great metaphor for the campaign to talk about the torch going through the U.S. If you read it, frankly, I think it is pretty poetic. He said, "It went through this state and that state." Every time he mentioned a state, that convention delegation would jump up and cheer. So all of a sudden, the flow of this wonderful poetry—"Billy the Kid's grave in Kansas" and "by the Golden Gate Bridge"—then the California delegation would get up—every state, they cheered. All of a sudden I thought, *Oh, my gosh. How could I have ever known that?* So don't ever mention states in a convention speech because it will be interrupted throughout.

Medhurst: But isn't that one of the unique aspects of an acceptance address, that you have not only the national television audience but you also have an immediate audience that feels as though they, too, are participants in the giving of this speech? Aren't there always going to be chants of "Four more years!" if it's an incumbent, or "USA!" or something like that? How does that affect the way you write the speech? Can you anticipate some of those? Indeed, can you provoke some of those by the way you write the speech?

Price: Actually, one of the problems of trying to do a good speech on television with a live audience is that you know that the commentators, at the end, are going to be evaluating it by how many times it was interrupted. If it was interrupted twenty times, it's fair; if it was thirty times, or forty, fifty. All that matters is the number—not the quality, but only the number of interruptions. So you put cheer lines in to provoke those numbers, so that the commentators afterward will have a high number to measure by. That's the main reason. It's not for the audience or anything else. It's just for the commentators.

Nelson: Pat, you were involved in writing Carter's '76 speech; you weren't involved in writing his '80 speech for reelection. I'm guessing you watched it in 1980 and had a professional perspective on that speech, which was generally regarded as unsuccessful. Do you remember what your thoughts were at the time, as somebody who had been so closely involved in writing the first one?

Anderson: That's a very good question. I have no answer for it because if I did watch it, I don't remember it. I obviously would not have thought it reached the great peaks of '76 [*laughter*], and obviously his circumstances had changed by then. I suspect it was a lesser speech, but I don't remember it.[43] You're talking about changes you make in speeches. I'll save it for now, but when we talk about the inaugurals, I'll tell you a story about a bitter fight with Carter, because he wanted to quote a biblical passage, which some of us thought was a very bad idea, and we had great difficulty.[44]

He often had trouble when he would start winging it. He once was before a room full of feminists. I'd written him a great speech and had him cheering for ERA [Equal Rights Amendment] and everything.[45] Finally he was trying to talk about ERA, that it would pass when the American people understood what it meant. He said, "The American people believe in justice." "Yeah, yeah!" "And the American people believe in fairness." "Yeah, yeah!" "The American people believe in brotherhood." "Boo!" [*laughter*] I couldn't believe it.

Khachigian: Bringing things up to the current era, if you watched Mr. [Barack] Obama's speech a couple of weeks ago, when he settled the nomination, you could see that he was annoyed at the reaction of the crowd, which was stepping on his lines. Sometimes they can be too exuberant. So a lesson for this era will be for them to moderate those crowds a little bit. Also, I probably would have fewer people standing behind the candidate, because that ambient noise gets picked up by the microphone. You could tell he had written a great speech. He is a good orator, but he was being interrupted.

Reagan was annoyed the night of his [1984] acceptance address. You could tell because he was doing this [*waving his hands downward*]. So it is a mixed blessing. But frankly, what's more important is that audience out there on television, not the audience in front of you.

Medhurst: Let's talk about the relationship of the acceptance address to the overall campaign strategy. Ken, you've been a campaign strategist in addition to being a chief speechwriter. How do you use the acceptance address as a vehicle to forward the campaign strategy?

Khachigian: Actually that's the easiest part of it. In the case of 1984, it was clearly our strategy to frame Mondale as far over to the left. If you remember, the Democratic convention was in San Francisco that year, and Jeane Kirk-patrick came up with that wonderful line, "San Francisco Democrats," which was a metaphor for the party that year.[46] Mondale, who was not hard to put on the left—he grew to politics on the left—his convention was not only in San Francisco, the heart of left-wing America, but he promised that he would raise taxes and all the things that played into our hands. The goal was to keep him over on the left, the party on the left, and to show that Reagan had brought America back, which was the theme of the campaign, "Morning Again in America." That was the thematic. And then we put meat on the bones. If you look at that '84 acceptance speech, it is full of statistics and data and numbers, which I found appalling last night as I looked at it. I couldn't believe I had stuffed that much in. I think that was probably part of our strategy as well.

Medhurst: Ray, could you talk a little bit about the strategy in '68 and how the speech spoke to that?

Price: Not really, since I didn't see the speech until I heard it delivered, just as nobody else did except the president. So I don't know what was in his mind in putting the pieces together the way he did, and I don't remember the speech that well. I can't tie the two together.

Khachigian: One thing in that '68 speech, clearly, was to plant the flag on Vietnam.

Price: Yes.

Khachigian: It was going to be a change in course from the Johnson admin-istration, and he wasn't specific about it, was relatively vague about it. But there was a clear sense that you had to have a departure on the war in Viet-nam, which was, for Johnson and for Humphrey, the opponent, a morass, at that time. That will be a lesson learned, by the way, for Obama and [John] McCain in their speeches this year.[47]

Medhurst: Pat and I were talking over lunch about people like [Hamilton] Ham Jordan and Jody Powell and so forth.[48] How do the speechwriters inter-face with the campaign strategists?

Anderson: I didn't have more than two conversations with Hamilton Jordan during the campaign. He and Jody divided up the world, and Jody worried about speeches and media, so I would work very closely with Jody on speeches. We agreed on things, and we worked together quite well.

As far as the strategy of the acceptance speech was concerned, it was certainly to introduce Carter and to reach out in a lot of directions and to make a lot of points that a lot of people would appreciate. I think it did the job, and I think we were way ahead in the polls at that point. Everything looked rosy. The problem came around September 1, when *Playboy* was published and the "lust in my heart" comments came out, offhand remarks. I understand what he was trying to say, but it was a very foolish thing to say. There were some other things said about Johnson that didn't help either.[49] That's what took us from being thirty points ahead to winning by 12,000 votes or whatever it was. That was, again, Carter trying to express himself but not doing a very good job of it.

Medhurst: Ken, is the relationship between the campaign-strategy people and the speechwriting people a close one, or should it be a close one?

Khachigian: It should be. Any good collaborator should be talking to a lot of people to get ideas. You can't shut everybody out or else you'll be making a big mistake. In the case of the Reagan reelection, the strategy was in the heads of a couple of people, mostly Stu Spencer, who was the campaign strategist.[50] There were a lot of people in the White House who also thought they were the strategists, and there were some in the polling community who thought they were the strategists. We'd listen collegially to that conversation, but basically it would be, at the end of the day, visiting with Stu and Bob Teeter, who was a big help in that campaign.[51] I can't imagine having to deal meaningfully with all these people, as I said. Reagan was so masterful at what he did that a lot of people wanted to get into the mix. It's not that I was precious about my words. It just made the process more difficult.

I'm trying to remember who our press secretary was in '84—Larry Speakes, I guess.[52] I didn't even talk to Larry or to the communications director. We sort of knew where it was going. Again, that was because you knew where Reagan was. It was self-evident. The main thing was to not hoke it up with a lot of stuff that he wouldn't buy off on.

Price: In the Nixon case, since Nixon was himself the campaign strategist, I don't think it was an issue.

Khachigian: I don't remember pollsters being much involved with the Nixon campaign.

Price: No, we brought in Roger Ailes to do ads and so forth, but that was separate from what we did.[53]

Anderson: I would say that the acceptance speech, for most of us, is a tremendously rhetorical speech. You mentioned not liking facts and figures; I didn't like them either. I think you're trying to inspire people and move people. There was a paragraph on peace, and the final sentence says, "We will pray for peace, and we will work for peace until we have removed from all nations for all time the threat of nuclear destruction." I wrote that. I believe it. I'd like to see it happen. Carter would like to see it happen. It didn't happen. It's pure rhetoric. He wasn't going to disarm or anything. But I think people like to hear that sort of inspirational ideal. There are a lot of lines in all the best speeches that are much more what you wish for than what is likely to happen.

Nelson: Did any of the presidents or candidates you wrote for feel guilty about having people write speeches for them, given the generation they came out of? There was an idea more prevalent at that time, I think, that a politician ought to be speaking his own words, or at least be giving the impression of speaking his own words. Did that generational issue figure into any of your relations with the candidates you served?

Khachigian: All I can say is that Reagan said on more than one occasion, "I used to do this myself." But I feel that I got into his head sufficiently that— and if I didn't, he edited heavily. Presidents don't have time to do their own speechwriting.

Ray worked on a lot of big addresses, like on the Vietnam War. Those were written texts that the president gave—one of the rare exceptions to the suggested-remarks rule. There, once again, in Nixon's case, I think he did a lot of the writing himself.

Anderson: I think that Carter had a problem with using other people's words. He was very proud of his writing abilities. When I first joined the campaign, I wrote, "I see an America that does this" and "I see an America that does that." Jody thought it was great, and we were at some union hall in

Ohio and he said to Carter, "You ought to use this. Try it." Carter made his basic remarks, and then he pulled out a piece of paper and said, "Now I'm going to read a statement that my staff has prepared." I was back there saying, "What? What is this man doing?" But then we used it again at the Martin Luther King speech when it got the praise from the newspapers. That's when I think he started thinking, *Maybe this system will work after all.*

Khachigian: I want to ask Pat a question about Carter being an engineer by training. Did that frame his linear thinking and limit his sense of poetry?

Anderson: I don't think so. He certainly has that engineering background, but he reads a lot, and he knows some poetry, and he was a Bob Dylan fan, and so forth. I think he appreciated poetry when somebody could come up with it.[54]

Medhurst: Pat raised the issue that used to be talked about under the heading of "a passion for anonymity."[55] It was said that the president's assistants, all of them, not just the speechwriters, were to have a passion for anonymity. It seems that over the course of the last thirty years or so that that has gone by the wayside, and now we have big print spreads on Michael Gerson and others who are very well-known.[56] What is your viewpoint about whether a speechwriter should be a public figure when they're working?

Price: I think it depends partly on the way he does it. I'm uncomfortable with speechwriters bragging about what they have done. I see too much of that these days. You just mentioned one who does that. It is not the sort of thing that I would do. I'll answer questions about speeches, but I don't do the "me, me, me." No, I think you lose something when you have too much of that.

It is always *his* speech. Actually, in Nixon's case, by the time it was done, it *was* his because we would go back and forth, seven or eight drafts, until he had what he wanted to say in the way he wanted to say it. I was simply helping him do it. I contributed some of it and so on. What the president says should be the president's, and should be seen as the president's, and should actually *be* the president's, no matter who else has helped him frame it.

Anderson: Yes, but at the same time, everybody knows what you're doing and why you're there. Throughout the '76 campaign, I spent a lot of time with reporters. We'd eat together and drink together, but I was off the record. Nothing I said was for the record, because I thought that was the safest way to get through a campaign. Otherwise, you'll say something foolish that will hurt you because it gets published, or your colleagues on the staff will say, "He's getting too full of himself." So I tried to keep a very low profile.

Price: I dealt with my friends in the press a lot when I was in the White House, but I was doing it on behalf of the president, not on my own behalf.

Medhurst: Ken, did you ever have problems like that?

Khachigian: Well, I came out of the Nixon White House, where anonymity in this regard was a virtue, believe me. I was a very junior member, so I didn't have that problem anyway. So about two or three weeks out from the '80 election, when we were pretty much getting on a roll, it was the first time I was ever mentioned in the press as a writer, and that was by Bob Novak in his column.[57] That came out, and I thought I'd get fired. I was very nervous about it. But the thing is, you're on the campaign plane. The reporters are five, ten feet away from you. They see you writing. They see somebody delivering paper to the candidate, so it's hard not to say that you participated in that process.

I think the main thing is, try not to go out of your way to draw attention. This became a bit of a problem in the Reagan White House. Because he was such a gifted communicator, people wanted to identify with him as much as they could. I didn't go out of my way to do it, but quite often reporters who run out of things to write about start writing about personalities. I can only remember one feature story written about me in the Reagan White House. That was by the *LA Times*, and there was a California angle to it. We have our views of some of those who were extravagant about the roles they made for themselves in the Reagan administration. We'll save that for another oral history.

Medhurst: We have around the table here a number of other scholars and a number of other presidential speechwriters. We're going to open the discussion to them and see what questions they may have.

Dunn Tenpas: You talked about the interaction between pollsters and speechwriters, but I was wondering if you could speak more generally about the interaction with other White House offices. For instance, did the speech-writers work frequently with those in domestic policy or in the NSC [National Security Council]? Can you talk a little bit about intra-White House operations?

Price: That was a central part of what we did. Nixon created a Domestic Council, first an Urban Affairs Council, under Pat Moynihan.[58] Then that morphed into the Domestic Council, under John Ehrlichman, when Pat left, as a counterpart to the National Security Council on domestic affairs.[59] As writers, we would work very closely with the Urban Affairs or Domestic Council people, and with the departments, to make sure that everything was coordinated and so forth. This was a large part of what we did in our writing, that kind of coordination. The whole White House structure was meant to encourage and enforce that kind of cooperation. So basically they were in charge of the policy, and we were in charge of the presentation. We made sure that the presentation followed the policy.

Judge: I'm Clark Judge. I also wrote for President Reagan. You've been talking about acceptance speeches. It strikes me that this year [2008] the acceptance speech is going to be a little different from past years, at least in status. There are two reasons—essentially because of the change in technology. First, we have cable television now, wall-to-wall coverage. Both of the major-party candidates have now given six or seven acceptance speeches to national audiences. Second, when Ken, Ray, Patrick, and I were serving in the White House, we were always looking for the sound bite, a way to game the reporting. Now it seems that that is almost ignored. You don't find the right phrasing that drives reporting nearly so much in candidate speeches now, I think, because the candidates have so much exposure, and they don't have to use it to drive reporting.

I'd like you guys to comment on how you see the rise of cable changing campaign speeches and acceptance speeches.

Anderson: I would hope that the acceptance speech would still be a major thing and that you would reach 30, or 40, or 50 million people. It might drop off, but that's still a lot of people who would tune in, settle back, and say, "Okay, I want to know what this guy is all about." I would hope that it would continue. Granted, the networks are cutting back everything they can, but I assume they'll still publish the acceptance speech. I certainly hope so.

Huebner: It might make the acceptance speech even more important in the sense that it gets recycled more often. Especially on YouTube, excerpts, for better or for worse, might get recycled.

Anderson: Certainly when I was working on the acceptance speech, I never thought in terms of sound bites. That might have been my weakness as a speechwriter, but I thought that there were a lot of great lines in there, and the press was going to focus on some of them—I probably couldn't guess which ones—and I was happy to give them the lines and let them figure it out.

Huebner: In 1968, if I remember right, Ray, the campaign commercials pulled passages out of the acceptance speech and ran them over and over again. So that could be done deliberately, to keep it in your control. It can also be under the control of those who don't want you to look good, but that's a new factor, and I think it's a big one.

Nelson: Ray, was that planned in advance to make commercials coming out of that speech?

Price: I don't know. Advertising was a separate operation from us. We brought in a top ad guy who was in charge of the ads. He had his own offices and everything else.

Khachigian: Talk about the change in circumstances: In '68, we did half-hour television shows, not just thirty-second ads. So that acceptance speech was recycled as a thirty-minute television show on the networks. We actually did three thirty-minute television speeches for the '80 campaign, probably the last time that's ever been done. And you'd try to roadblock them, which means you got all three networks at the same time. They'd never let you do that now.

I think, in a way, Lee, you just hit the nail—that it makes your sound bites *more* critical in terms of what they call "looping," over and over again. With the '84 acceptance speech, I worried less about television because I knew that the president would be compelling on television. I always wanted to know what that lead, and what that headline, was going to be in the major newspapers and the wire services. I was working toward that. The term I came up with, "Springtime of hope in America," I was hoping very much that that would be a headline in any newspaper that would write about the speech.

Price: You just reminded me of something I'd like to toss out here about our '68 campaign, which I thought was important. In '68 we reinvented radio as a political medium, and it worked. You could buy radio time for a minute fraction of what television time cost. We did practically all of our serious policy things—and they were serious policy speeches—on radio. This worked partly because we would buy fifteen- or twenty-five-minute radio slots. You could buy them for a couple thousand bucks. We could get an audience estimated at anywhere from half a million to two million, which is a lot more than you get at Madison Square Garden. And because it is an auditory medium, you're not distracted. You pay attention to the substance of it. We did practically all of our major, serious, policy things on radio, and it worked very well. We would buy nationwide, such as ABC or CBS radio, for that.

Jones: Is there a balance between defining yourself in an acceptance speech for who you *are* and defining yourself in terms of who you're running *against*?

Price: You pretty much have to do both, I think. The voter has to make that choice, and you want to help the voter make the right choice as you see it.

Edmonds: In an acceptance speech, which is probably the first time that a candidate speaks to the total nation, not just to his party, I think that the emphasis should be more on introducing yourself and your story and who you are rather than on contrasting yourself or attacking the other guy. I think this is the first chance to introduce more of a bipartisan quality to your campaign, because you're reaching out not just to people in your party but to people in the other party, and to independents as well.

Medhurst: That was one of the questions I wanted to ask, Terry. It seems to me like there are multiple functions for acceptance addresses, one of which is to unify the party. In some years that is more important than others. Another function is to reach out to independents and to, as Republicans would say, disaffected Democrats or discerning Democrats. But isn't there a sense in which those two goals in particular are sometimes in tension with one another? How do you unify and reach out at the same time?

Anderson: We agonized a lot about the high-road, low-road dispute. We settled for what we thought was a middle road. If you look at the speech, there is a lot of "We have been shaken by a tragic war abroad and scandals and broken promises at home." Watergate was mentioned specifically, etc. There was plenty of that. On the other hand, there was plenty of uplift. I remember discussing this issue with Ted Sorensen. He said, "Pat, you don't want to leave out all the negatives. People do vote against people sometimes." That was true.

Milkis: I would add a third consideration that sometimes comes into play, which is that sometimes you want to change your party. In fact, all three presidents that these gentlemen wrote for had some sense of redefining their party. I wonder, for example, Patrick, did you guys give a lot of thought to Carter's relationship to the liberal wing of the party and to his notions, also important to President Clinton, about the need for the party to change in order to be more successful nationally?

Anderson: I think a lot of what he said appealed to liberals. I certainly was writing things that I thought would appeal to liberals. On the other hand, there were other big issues, such as national defense. So I think you're trying to reach in both directions.

Jones: Could you talk a little bit about the coordination between what the vice president is going to say in his or her acceptance speech and the presidential nominee's acceptance speech?

Medhurst: Did you coordinate the speeches?

Price: I don't recall any coordination. That doesn't mean there wasn't any, because it was quite a while ago, and it might be that I don't remember or I wasn't aware of any. But [Spiro] Agnew had his own writers.[60] I don't recall any coordination.

Medhurst: When you were in the White House—and it's a good point, Ray—the vice president had his speechwriters; the president had a different set. Did they ever collaborate with one another?

Price: Pat Buchanan did a lot of campaign speeches for Agnew after he ceased doing any speeches for Nixon. Buchanan's last speech for Richard Nixon was in April 1970, the Cambodia speech, which was a disaster.[61] He just didn't write the kind of speech that Nixon wanted to give, but he was doing good, fiery campaign speeches for Agnew.

Anderson: We had a meeting with Mondale as soon as he was chosen. He came over and we shook hands, and he very nicely asked me to look over his speech. I thought it was fairly basic, liberal rhetoric. I didn't think it was a great speech at all, but on the other hand, I didn't want to start off with Mondale by being critical of the speech, so I made three rather minor suggestions, one of which became his biggest applause line. As far as I was concerned, we treated Mondale with kid gloves on. I'm going to read you a line from my account of it in my book. "In the next issue of the *New Yorker*, Richard Rovere praised Mondale's wit and intelligence, but complained that neither quality could be deduced from his acceptance speech, much of which had been drafted by Carter's writers so that it could be delivered by anyone the nominee chose." Not true. That's maybe what Mondale's people said. I don't know.[62]

Medhurst: One of Dwight Eisenhower's writers, Art Larson, who wrote Eisenhower's acceptance address in '56, was famous for arguing with Ike about what his speeches should say and what they shouldn't say.[63] When you feel strongly about a point, what is the line that you cannot go past?

Khachigian: As I told you, mine were always about facts, not about rhetoric. There was one occasion when the president wanted to put something in a speech that probably most everybody on the staff didn't think was a good idea. It was an extremely awkward situation, and I decided to go with the president on that one. If it had been really important, I suppose I would have stood up to him, but we were always in sync. Once it got to that final stage, he wasn't much interested in having someone mess with his prose. I don't know why you would, unless it was a policy error or something drastic.

   During the Iran-Contra situation, I was brought in for the state of the union speech.[64] He had written out something to put in the speech for the state of the union, which would not have fit very well at all. Luckily I didn't have to make that decision. The lawyers did. It didn't make it into the speech. Somewhere there is a scrap of paper that is very historical, I can tell you that.

Anderson: If you're going to work around the president or presidential candidate and you're going to last very long, I think you should probably be sensitive enough to figure out when he has his mind made up. Certainly with Carter, if he said no twice, I figured, *Okay, let's drop this and do it his way.*

Nelson: We have Terry Edmonds here. You uniquely may be able to address this one: What about when a president is speaking to a political convention at the end of his second term? Clinton's speech in 2000 was a big convention speech, but it wasn't for the purpose of getting himself reelected.[65] What was it like doing a speech like that?

Edmonds: That was one of the most difficult speeches I worked on for President Clinton because it was considered his last big political speech, and it was supposed to pass the torch to Al [Albert] Gore [Jr.]. We worked on that speech for weeks, right up to the last minute. I think the president had two purposes. One was, again, to pass the torch to Gore, but it was also to remind the country of how far we had come in the eight years of his presidency. There's a word that I think a lot of presidents don't like to use, which is "legacy." They don't like to talk about that, but I think it is in the back of every president's mind toward the end of his administration. What will I be remembered for? So I think it was a good chance to remind the country that it was in pretty good shape after eight years of Clinton.

Nelson: Was there some coordination between the writers for the Clinton and Gore campaigns about what would be said and how it would be said?

Edmonds: Not really, no. President Clinton worked on it pretty much by himself with his speechwriting team. We didn't coordinate that much with Gore.

Khachigian: There's another element of the modern acceptance speech, which can create a problem for a candidate, and that is the documentary that often precedes the speech. In Reagan's case, it was a no-brainer because "Morning Again in America," he could match that.[66] With Clinton, I think it was "The Man from Hope" that preceded his acceptance speech.[67] But you need to be careful if you're going to do a slick, wonderful documentary. The speech that follows it better match the quality of the documentary, because the documentaries are edited heavily. They're done in film, not in video. There's wonderful music underscoring it, and the audience is not screaming and yelling, "Four more years!"

Medhurst: Apart from the speech that each of you wrote or consulted on, what acceptance address over the course of American history stands out in your minds?

Anderson: Maybe Kennedy's, but I remember the inaugural much more than the acceptance speech.

Price: I don't remember any.

Medhurst: These are totally unmemorable addresses, huh?

Milkis: Did you read other acceptance speeches in preparing the ones you did?

Anderson: Carter had me reading other inaugural addresses, and he went back and read a lot of inaugural addresses before that, but I don't recall looking at anybody else's acceptance speech.

Medhurst: I did a study not too many years ago on the top 100 speeches in American history, two of which were nomination acceptance addresses, both by losing candidates, Stevenson and [Barry] Goldwater.[68] It is said that Goldwater's was the speech that lost the election for him. What was it about that acceptance address that didn't work?

Khachigian: "Extremism in the defense of liberty is no vice, and moderation in the defense of virtue—"[69] It is memorable because he had a clunker in there.

Price: Did he do it defiantly?

Khachigian: Yes, it was clear. I mean, I wasn't there, and I'm not close to Barry Goldwater, but clearly he was probably just angry and said, "I'm going to put in the words that I believe."

Price: Big mistake. [*laughter*]

Khachigian: Yes. I can't remember the name of the writer.

Price: It was some guy who went off and was a welder for a while or something, lived on a houseboat.

Nelson: Karl Hess had a lot to do with it. Harry Jaffa had a lot to do with it.[70]

Khachigian: It was Karl Hess.

Huebner: If you look at videotape of that speech, Goldwater uses the word "extremism" with great pleasure because that was the touchstone word of the convention, and he wanted to make that kind of point. Nixon had just introduced him as "the man who had been known as 'Mr. Conservative,' who as of today will be known as 'Mr. Republican,' and in November will be called 'Mr. President.'" It was a great introduction, I thought.

Nixon, when that "extremism" line came, carefully got into conversation with the person next to him and did not join in the applause—knowing how dangerous that line would appear to be later on.

Khachigian: I think the '68 address by Nixon was excellent. Everybody had a notion of Nixon of being the hard-line, right-wing conservative, anti-Communist loser from '60 and '62. He gave a pretty elegant address. I think he portrayed something that was a departure from who people thought he was, and he came out of that convention with a jump of at least ten points in the polls.[71] It was a good speech and was well done.

Price: And well received.

Khachigian: Yes, well received. He actually was a pretty skillful writer. He wrote over and over and over again. By the time he got up to speak, he knew his lines very well, just as Reagan did.

Price: I've often commented over the years that I was a professional writer before I went to work for Nixon, and I'd done a fair amount of speaking in parliamentary debating, but he taught me speechwriting as a form of art. He was a master at it.[72]

Huebner: I think each occasion defines the purpose and the challenge of the speech. On that occasion he had to do what Senator Obama probably will do this summer, and that is to tie the incumbent president to the nominee. It was an attack on failed leadership, as I remember that convention speech. It was a very strong attack on the Johnson/Humphrey record. Nixon was always at his best when he was attacking. He enjoyed the attack. Part of what made that speech soar, I think, was that it was a very vigorous, very specific attack on what Nixon thought were failures of the last four years.[73]

Judge: I'm thinking of the '88 campaign, and particularly of the Democratic convention, where they came out of the convention seventeen points ahead and we had caught back up by the time our convention opened.[74] [George H. W.] Bush was out of money and basically out of the game during that period, and it was Reagan who closed the gap. The Democrats had set themselves up—and this partly through their convention speech, through their whole convention—that they weren't going to be specific about policy. They didn't want anyone to brand them as liberal.

In our shop we looked at that and said, "That's a challenge. Why don't we take that challenge up?" It was taken up ultimately with the "L-word," the idea that they wouldn't speak this horrible word. We kept pounding on that until the middle of the campaign, when [Michael] Dukakis said, "Yes, I am a liberal."[75] But the point I'm making is that in writing acceptance speeches, in framing conventions, you have to have some core of authenticity. Their problem that year was that they were trying to distance themselves from what they were, and they didn't have an alternative story for what they were.

In fact, their story reinforced what they said they were not—or rather, it reinforced the idea that they were what they were disclaiming to be. So a part of the challenge of not just an acceptance speech but, as I say, the whole convention within which the speech occurs is not just to fit the polls and not just to fit what the political advisors say and what the strategy advisors say. It also has to fit what you are and what you're advocating and what your record is. If there are difficult points in your record, you have to be proud about it and out front, otherwise you set yourself up for the kind of thing that happened to Dukakis in '88.

Nelson: This has been a fascinating ninety minutes—with great thanks to Pat Anderson, Ray Price, Ken Khachigian, Marty Medhurst, and to all of you for your contributions.

Notes

1. Annual dinners hosted by the Gridiron Club, a Washington-based organization of journalists, have been a fixture of the capital's culture since the club's founding in 1885. The sitting president is usually expected to attend and perhaps to speak—and to allow himself to be the butt of the evening's humor. The dinner is an occasion for Washington's two antagonistic tribes—the journalists and the politicians—to set aside serious differences for a night of fun together.

2. Nelson A. Rockefeller (1908–1979) was Republican governor of New York from 1959 to 1973, and he served as Gerald Ford's vice president from 1974 to 1977. During the course of his political career he was constantly in the public spotlight as a prospective Republican presidential nominee, but he never won that nomination. He led the party's more liberal wing, placing him at odds with the followers of Barry Goldwater and Ronald Reagan.

3. Nixon left California after his failed bid for the governorship of that state in 1962.

4. The text of that speech can be found at http://www2.vcdh.virginia.edu/PVCC/mbase/docs/nixon.html.

5. Peter Bourne is an English-born physician who created Georgia's first drug treatment program, and later served as a health care advisor in the Carter White House. He held a senior position in the 1976 Carter campaign. Mary King, married to Bourne, is an academic and political activist. During Carter's initial presidential bid she served as national director of the Committee of 51.3%, so named because that figure represented the percentage of women in the U.S. population. She was later named by President Carter deputy director of ACTION, where her portfolio included oversight of the Peace Corps.

6. George C. Wallace (1919–1998) was a multiple-term governor of Alabama and a major conservative influence on American politics in the 1960s and 1970s. He ran for president four times, including 1976, although four years before he had been critically wounded by a would-be assassin while campaigning in Maryland—restricting him to a wheelchair for the rest of his life.

7. See Anderson's "Peanut Farmer for President," *New York Times Sunday Magazine*, December 14, 1975, 15+.

8. That book was *The President's Mistress* (New York: Simon & Schuster, 1976).

9. Joseph L. "Jody" Powell (1943–2009) was Governor Jimmy Carter's chief press aide in Georgia and during the 1976 campaign. He was White House press secretary during the entirety of Carter's presidential term.

10. Robert M. "Bob" Shrum is a Democratic political consultant, who as of this writing has never helped steer a winning presidential campaign.

11. The Democratic presidential nominee in 1972 was Senator George McGovern, whose electoral vote loss to Richard Nixon that year was 520 to 17.

12. Edmund G. "Jerry" Brown, son of former California governor Pat Brown, was a young California politician who had entered the governor's office himself there in January 1975.

13. Ironically, given the circumstances that brought Carter to the national stage, Richard Nixon had used that very same rhetorical device in his 1970 state of the union message: "I see a new America as we celebrate our 200th anniversary 6 years from now. I see an America in which we have abolished hunger, provided the means for every family in the Nation to obtain a minimum income, made enormous progress in providing better housing, faster transportation, improved health, and superior education. I see an

America in which we have checked inflation, and waged a winning war against crime. I see an America in which we have made great strides in stopping the pollution of our air, cleaning up our water, opening up our parks, continuing to explore in space. Most important, I see an America at peace with all the nations of the world."

14. Anderson seems to be referring to Charles Mohr, "Spanning the Spectrum: Carter Shows Rare Skill in Courting and Gaining a National Constituency," *New York Times*, June 5, 1976, 11.

15. Although the date is slightly off, Khachigian may be referring to Robert B. Semple, Jr., "It's Time Again for the Nixon Phenomenon," *New York Times Sunday Magazine*, January 21, 1968, 24+. This piece does not, however, mention Ray Price by name.

16. Patrick J. "Pat" Buchanan is a conservative author and commentator and has been a Republican political activist and presidential candidate. He was among the first people hired by Richard Nixon in preparation for the 1968 campaign, and he evidently traveled with Nixon extensively in the years leading up to that race. Buchanan later became a speechwriter in the Nixon White House.

17. Martin Anderson was the research director for the 1968 Nixon campaign and worked as a policy advisor in the Nixon White House. Anderson later became one of Ronald Reagan's senior-most advisors on domestic and economic policy.

18. The economist Alan Greenspan later served as chairman of the Council of Economic Advisors under President Gerald Ford, and from 1987 to 2006 was chairman of the U.S. Federal Reserve.

19. John F. Kennedy won the 1960 electoral vote by a margin of 303 to 219, but the popular vote totals were much closer: 49.7 percent to 49.6 percent. Moreover, charges have lingered since that election day that fraud in Texas—home of vice presidential candidate Lyndon Johnson—and Illinois—where the political machine of Richard Daley was in ascendance—secured the votes necessary for Kennedy to win. Had those two states gone Republican, the results of the race would have flipped in Richard Nixon's favor.

20. Nixon actually announced his candidacy in an open letter to the citizens of New Hampshire, dated January 31, 1968. See Robert B. Semple, Jr., "Nixon Announces for Presidency," *New York Times*, February 2, 1968, 1.

21. John N. Mitchell (1913–1988) was a Republican lawyer who first became associated with Nixon during his New York days. He managed both the 1968 and 1972 Nixon campaigns, and in between served as U.S. attorney general. He was later convicted of several felony offenses related to the Watergate scandal.

22. Reagan's speech was delivered before the Republican National Convention in Dallas, Texas, on August 23, 1984. The text is available at http://www.presidency.ucsb.edu/ws/index.php?pid=40290.

23. Reagan's Democratic opponent that year was former Minnesota senator and Vice President Walter Mondale. In Mondale's acceptance speech, delivered before the assembled Democrats in Chicago on July 19, he stated, "By the end of my first term, I will

reduce the Reagan budget deficit by two-thirds. Let's tell the truth. It must be done. . . . Mr. Reagan will raise taxes, and so will I. He won't tell you. I just did."

24. The invention of the misery index is generally credited to economist Arthur Okun (1928–1980), who had worked for President Lyndon Johnson. Okun's index was produced by the simple addition of the unemployment rate to the rate of inflation—giving a quick-and-easy measure of how much pain Americans were suffering economically. Carter made frequent use of the misery index as a rhetorical device in 1976. It came back to haunt him in 1980, when the index number had grown significantly greater than the one he had bludgeoned Gerald Ford with four years before.

25. On "The Speech," see Lou Cannon, *President Reagan: The Role of a Lifetime* (New York: Simon & Schuster, 1991), 88–94.

26. Carter's acceptance speech was delivered in New York City's Madison Square Garden. It can be read at http://www.4president.org/speeches/carter1976acceptance.htm.

27. Gerald M. Rafshoon directed all the media and advertising efforts for Carter's 1976 campaign, and he later went into the White House for a brief stint as communications director. Details of Rafshoon's work with Carter can be found in his oral history interview as a part of the Jimmy Carter Oral History Project with the University of Virginia's Miller Center of Public Affairs: http://web1.millercenter.org/poh/transcripts/ohp_1983_0408_rafshoon.pdf. Patrick H. Caddell was Jimmy Carter's pollster. Greg Schneiders also worked in Carter's communications shop with Rafshoon and for a time directed Carter's speechwriting office.

28. Theodore C. "Ted" Sorensen was a close confidant and speechwriter for President John F. Kennedy and has been consulted frequently by Democratic presidential candidates—and presidents—eager to channel Kennedy's legendary rhetorical powers.

29. Reinhold Niebuhr (1892–1971) was a Protestant theologian whose writings have influenced a number of prominent public officials, especially Democrats, interested in drawing on Niebuhr's philosophy about the proper role of Christian faith in public and international affairs.

30. Dylan (born Robert Allen Zimmerman) is an American songwriter and performer, most noted for his protest and folk songs of the 1960s. Carter quoted from Dylan in his campaign biography *Why Not the Best?* (New York: Bantam Books, 1976). Moreover, his first convention acceptance address included this line: "We have an America that, in Bob Dylan's phrase, is busy being born, not busy dying."

31. Alfred E. Smith (1873–1944) served several terms as governor of New York and was the Democrats' 1928 nominee for the presidency. He was the first Catholic nominee of a major U.S. political party, a factor that contributed to his lopsided loss in the general election to Republican Herbert Hoover.

32. Adlai E. Stevenson (1900–1965), U.S. senator from Illinois and later U.S. ambassador to the United Nations, was the Democratic nominee for president in 1952 and 1956, losing both times to Dwight D. Eisenhower. Hubert H. Humphrey (1911–1978), U.S.

senator from Minnesota and vice president with Lyndon B. Johnson, was the Democratic nominee in 1968, losing to Richard Nixon.

33. On the subject of speeches and polling, see Robert M. Eisinger, *The Evolution of Presidential Polling* (New York: Cambridge University Press, 2003); Wynton C. Hall, "The Invention of 'Quantifiably Safe Rhetoric': Richard Wirthlin and Ronald Reagan's Instrumental Use of Public Opinion Research in Presidential Discourse," *Western Journal of Communication* 66, no. 3 (Summer 2002): 319–346.

34. See Lou Cannon's chapter entitled "Staying the Course" in *President Reagan,* 232–279.

35. William F. Gavin was a member of the speechwriting staff for Richard Nixon from 1967 through 1970. He later wrote for Ronald Reagan. Gavin, who was unable to attend this symposium, has recorded many of his thoughts on presidential speechmaking in "Source Material: His Heart's Abundance: Notes of a Nixon Speechwriter," *Presidential Studies Quarterly* 31, no. 2 (June 2001): 358–368.

36. See the sections entitled "Reagan as Storyteller" and "Reagan's Humor" in Richard Jay Jensen, *Reagan at Bergen-Belsen and Bitburg* (College Station: Texas A&M University Press, 2007), 25–27.

37. Reagan reportedly broadcast Chicago Cubs and White Sox games in the 1930s, recreating the contest for listeners from nothing but telegraph reports. Reagan's controversial biographer Edmund Morris described the process this way: "Hastily typed slips shoved across the microphone table; dry codes flowering into vivid and voluble descriptions; red-headed kids leaping to catch fly balls, and enough blue shadows to fill the Intermontane Gap." *Dutch: A Memoir of Ronald Reagan* (New York: Random House, 1999), 122.

38. These two elements of his autobiography appear in Carter's 1976 acceptance address.

39. Henry A. Kissinger was both national security advisor and secretary of state for President Nixon (for a time simultaneously). As such, he drew intense criticism from the political opposition, especially among antiwar activists seeking American withdrawal from Vietnam.

40. Khachigian discusses this wrestling, over the story of Martin Treptow, in Chapter 5.

41. The text of Reagan's address on the Web site Wikisource includes multiple indications of audience interruptions, for everything from chants of "Four more years!" to booing of the Soviet Union and the Cambodian genocide. See http://en.wikisource.org/wiki/Ronald_Reagan's_Second_Presidential_Nomination_Acceptance_Speech.

42. McGovern would later recall that night: "I finished at 3:15 (a.m.). Probably the best speech I ever gave in my life. And it should have been the best I ever gave in my life," McGovern says. "But how many people saw it at 2:30 or 3 in the morning? I think my wife did. Maybe my mother if she didn't get too sleepy. . . . But a crowd of 90 million viewers at 9 o'clock . . . probably dwindled down to about 3 million." M. E. Sprengelmeyer, "George McGovern, Miami Beach 1972," *Rocky Mountain News*, August 12, 2008, at http://www .rockymountainnews.com/news/2008/aug/12/george-mcgovern-miami-beach-1972/.

43. The 1980 acceptance address was not one of President Carter's better moments. It included a painful blooper during a tribute to Minnesota's "Happy Warrior," whom he misidentified as "Hubert Horatio Hornblower."

44. Anderson's argument with Carter over the biblical quote is discussed in Chapter 5.

45. The Equal Rights Amendment, which would have formalized a prohibition against gender inequality within the U.S. Constitution, was a major civil rights issue during the 1970s. The amendment was only a few states shy of ratification when Carter left office, but the conservatism of the Reagan era swept the country in 1980, stalling any lingering momentum the ERA had.

46. Jeane J. Kirkpatrick (1926–2006) was a conservative foreign policy expert who left the Democratic Party after serving in the Reagan administration. From 1981 to 1985, she was U.S. ambassador to the United Nations. In her keynote address to the 1984 Republican convention, she claimed that she had grown disenchanted with the Democrats' "Blame America First" mentality.

47. John S. McCain III, U.S. senator from Arizona, was the Republican nominee for president in 2008.

48. Hamilton Jordan (1944–2008) was Jimmy Carter's chief political strategist in Georgia and during the 1976 campaign. He continued in this role in the Carter White House, eventually serving as White House chief of staff.

49. Carter decided during the course of the 1976 campaign to grant an interview to *Playboy*, during which he attempted to make the point that he was not the puritanical personality some believed him to be—inasmuch as he, too, had lusted in his heart for women other than his wife. Carter's interview appeared in the November 1976 issue of the magazine, and can be read at http://www.playboy.com/articles/jimmy-carter-interview/index.html. Anderson's point about Lyndon Johnson is unclear. Carter cited LBJ in two separate contexts in the interview: first, defending Johnson's motives for deepening American involvement in Vietnam; and second, for "lying, cheating and distorting the truth." The former, perhaps, would have offended the Democrats' liberal constituencies; the latter, its conservative ones.

50. Stuart K. Spencer is a Republican political strategist with a long association with Ronald Reagan, dating back to Reagan's pregubernatorial years in California. Spencer details his career in an oral history interview with the Miller Center of Public Affairs at the University of Virginia, available at http://web1.millercenter.org/poh/transcripts/ohp_2001_1115_spencer.pdf.

51. Robert M. Teeter (1939–2004) was a Republican pollster who worked closely with Presidents Ronald Reagan and George H. W. Bush. A brief survey of his career appears in Yvonne Shinhoster Lamb, "Robert M. Teeter, GOP Strategist and Public Opinion Pollster, Dies," *Washington Post*, June 15, 2004, B6.

52. From 1981 to 1987, Larry M. Speakes was acting White House spokesman for President Ronald Reagan. Although Speakes was effectively Reagan's press secretary, he did not formally hold that job title, which was reserved throughout the Reagan years for

James Brady, who was serving in that capacity when he was seriously injured by a would-be assassin's bullet in the same March 1981 incident that wounded the president.

53. Roger E. Ailes was a media consultant for Presidents Richard Nixon, Ronald Reagan, and George H. W. Bush. He later became head of the Fox News Channel.

54. Carter also was a fan of the work of Welsh poet Dylan Thomas (1914–1953), whom he frequently quoted.

55. This term is drawn from a study of White House staffing undertaken in 1937 by the President's Committee on Administrative Management, often called informally the Brownlow Committee after its chair, Louis Brownlow (1879–1963). The committee's final report famously asserted that "the President needs help" and recommended the creation of a more elaborate staff structure in the White House to assist the president in his work. It cautioned, however, that those hired to aid the president should be devoted to his service alone—they must have "a passion for anonymity."

56. Michael J. Gerson was chief speechwriter for President George W. Bush from 2001 to 2006. Gerson's work for Bush drew significant media attention—and occasioned critical backlash from others in Bush's orbit who asserted that Gerson's contributions were being overstated. See, for example, Matthew Scully, "Present at the Creation," *Atlantic Monthly*, September 2007, 76.

57. Robert Novak (1931–2009) was a conservative political columnist. The article Khachigian references here was coauthored with his longtime collaborator Rowland Evans, "It Could Have Been a Landslide," *Washington Post*, November 3, 1980, A21.

58. Daniel Patrick Moynihan (1927–2003) served as counselor to the president on urban affairs in the Nixon White House. He previously had worked for both Presidents John Kennedy and Lyndon Johnson and had done scholarly work on the question of poverty in America. He later went on to be U.S. ambassador to the United Nations under President Gerald Ford and was a U.S. senator from the state of New York from 1977 to 2001.

59. John D. Ehrlichman (1925–1999) was, successively, Richard Nixon's counsel and chief domestic policy advisor.

60. Spiro T. Agnew (1918–1996) served as governor of Maryland and was placed by Richard Nixon on the Republican ticket as vice president in 1968. He resigned in October 1973 after pleading no contest to a felony ethics charge.

61. Nixon's Cambodia incursion speech was delivered on April 30, 1970. The audio and text can be found at http://www.americanrhetoric.com/speeches/richardnixon cambodia.html.

62. See Richard Rovere, "Letter from the Garden," *New Yorker*, July 26, 1976, 64.

63. Lewis Arthur Larson (1910–1993) was the director of the U.S. Information Agency in 1956–1957 before becoming one of Eisenhower's chief speechwriters. For details on his life and career, see David L. Stebenne, *Modern Republican: Arthur Larson and the Eisenhower Years* (Bloomington: Indiana University Press, 2006). Larson provides his own assessment of the Eisenhower presidency in *Eisenhower: The President Nobody Knew* (New York: Charles Scribner's Sons, 1968).

64. The Iran-Contra affair was a foreign policy scandal that rocked the Reagan presidency in the middle of its second term. A number of White House national security specialists had taken on operational responsibility for a series of ploys to sell arms in the Middle East and to divert the proceeds to support anti-Communist insurgents in Latin America—in ways contrary to U.S. law and even in certain respects in violation of the president's own publicly announced policies. Several senior administration officials, including Reagan's national security advisor, Admiral John Poindexter, resigned in the wake of the scandal, and eleven officials were convicted of crimes associated with it. Documents extensively detailing the White House role in these events can be found in "The Iran-Contra Affair 20 Years On," on the Web site of the National Security Archive, at http://www.gwu.edu/~nsarchiv/NSAEBB/NSAEBB210/index.htm.

65. The text of Clinton's 2000 convention speech can be found at http://www.australianpolitics.com/usa/clinton/speeches/00-08-14dem-convention.shtml.

66. Video of the "Morning Again in America" ad is available at http://www.youtube.com/watch?v=EU-IBF8nwSY.

67. Video of the *Man from Hope* film is available at http://www.youtube.com/watch?v=6l_h9ltTZD0.

68. Barry M. Goldwater (1909–1998) was a U.S. senator from the state of Arizona and in 1964 was the Republican Party nominee for the presidency. The book referenced here is Stephen E. Lucas and Martin J. Medhurst, *Words of the Century: The Top 100 American Speeches, 1900–1999* (New York: Oxford University Press, 2008).

69. The correct phrasing is "Extremism in the defense of liberty is no vice. And let me remind you also that moderation in the pursuit of justice is no virtue."

70. Karl Hess (1923–1994) was a colorful author and speechwriter, whose own affinity for unconventional politics led him to embrace movements as varied as Goldwater Republicanism and back-to-the-land environmentalism. A film about him, *Karl Hess: Toward Liberty*, won the 1981 Academy Award for best short documentary. His memoir is *Mostly on the Edge: An Autobiography* (Amherst, N.Y.: Prometheus Books, 1999). Harry V. Jaffa is a conservative scholar, most noted for his work on Abraham Lincoln. Jaffa has written on the 1964 acceptance speech, in "Goldwater's Famous 'Gaffe'," *National Review*, August 10, 1984.

71. In Gallup polls conducted just after the convention, Nixon had extended his narrow 40 to 38 percent lead over Hubert Humphrey to 45 to 29. "Gallup Poll Shows Nixon Has Big Gain," *Chicago Tribune*, August 21, 1968, B26.

72. For an extended treatment of Nixon's methods, see Hal W. Bochin, *Richard Nixon: Rhetorical Strategist* (Westport, Conn.: Greenwood, 1990).

73. For example, Nixon said: "For five years hardly a day has gone by when we haven't read or heard a report of the American flag being spit on; an embassy being stoned; a library being burned; or an ambassador being insulted some place in the world. And each incident reduced respect for the United States until the ultimate insult inevitably occurred. And I say to you tonight that when respect for the United States of America

falls so low that a fourth-rate military power, like North Korea, will seize an American naval vessel on the high seas, it is time for new leadership to restore respect for the United States of America." Nixon's last reference was to the intelligence ship *Pueblo*, which had been taken captive in January 1968.

74. On the Dukakis convention bump up to seventeen points, see "Dukakis Lead Widens, According to New Poll," *New York Times*, July 26, 1988, A17.

75. On the 1988 debate about the "L-word," see Patrick M. Garry, *Liberalism and American Identity* (Kent, Ohio: Kent State University Press, 1992), ch. 1.

Chapter 4

The Inaugural Address: Ceremony of Transitions

Charles O. Jones

The inaugural address is the most exclusive of presidential speeches. It is delivered but once every four years by an elected president. Accordingly, thirty-nine of the forty-four presidents (counting Grover Cleveland's nonconsecutive terms as two) have delivered inaugural addresses, fifteen of them more than once (including Cleveland's nonconsecutive addresses and Franklin D. Roosevelt's four). Five takeover presidents—John Tyler, Millard Fillmore, Andrew Johnson, Chester Arthur, and Gerald Ford—were not subsequently elected to full terms but did deliver brief speeches after having been sworn in.[1] In three of these cases (Tyler, Johnson, and Arthur) the speeches were officially labeled "inaugural address."[2] Ford specifically noted that his remarks were "not an inaugural address."[3]

The address is an important part of a ceremonial occasion that also includes taking the oath of office, a parade, and inaugural balls. These activities mark two important transitions associated with the transfer of authority—one personal, the other constitutional. The personal is from campaigning to governing; the constitutional is from one presidency to the next. The more dramatic of these transitional exercises is the one occurring for a first-term president, involving as it does a change in who will occupy the White House.

This chapter briefly reviews the history of the inaugural address, denotes a few cases before and after the advent of speechwriters, evaluates these speeches by tests suggested by two prominent speechwriters, integrates observations by speechwriters in Chapter 5, and offers conclusions regarding the status and effectiveness of the addresses.

History

There is no provision for an inaugural address in the Constitution. The only speechmaking occasion specified in that document is that: "He shall from time to time give to Congress Information of the State of the Union, and to recommend to their Consideration such Measures as he shall judge necessary and expedient. . . ." (Art. II, Sec. 3). "From time to time" has come to mean an annual address, traditionally delivered early in the year before a joint session of Congress, with representatives of all three branches in attendance, along with representatives of the diplomatic corps and invited guests.

The oath of office is provided in Article II, Section 1: "I do solemnly swear (or affirm) that I will faithfully execute the Office of President of the United States, and will to the best of my Ability, preserve, protect and defend the Constitution of the United States." When George Washington first took the oath on April 30, 1789, on the balcony of the Senate Chamber, Federal Hall, New York City, he added the words "So help me God," an addendum repeated until this day.

Washington proceeded to deliver an address to a joint session of the House and Senate and a second tradition was born—the inaugural address. This first address by Washington hardly matched the magnitude of the moment. He spoke of his mixed feelings in accepting the new position, explaining that he "was summoned by my country, whose voice I can never hear but with veneration and love. . . ." Yet he heard this voice "from a retreat which I had chosen with the fondest predilection, and . . . with an immutable decision, as the asylum of my declining years. . . ." He appeared to be saying, in his elliptical style: "If it weren't for the honor, I'd sooner be at Mt. Vernon." And so he called on those who had chosen him to share the responsibilities of office, as well as invoking the blessings of the "Parent of the Human Race" on the work to be done.[4] The six-paragraph address was less inspirational than explanatory of Washington's personal circumstances and descriptive of the executive's role in the new government. Therefore, this first rendition was less a ceremony of transition than of creation. Washington was a reluctant candidate and he was the first to fill the post.

Washington's second inaugural address was even shorter than the first—a mere two paragraphs long, the shortest ever. And he delivered it at Congress Hall in Philadelphia to members of Congress, judges, foreign officials, and a small number of citizens. In this case, he delivered the address before taking the oath and mostly vowed to respect the obligations of its vows. However short and perfunctory it was, the fact that Washington spoke at all set another precedent—that of an address upon reelection to the presidency. One could imagine that a reaffirmation by the voters might have resulted in a less ceremonial oath-taking.

Table 4.1 lists the presidents delivering inaugural addresses, by year, in sequence, and whether or not they completed their term in office. Note that five presidents did not live to fulfill the promises of their first inaugural —William H. Harrison, Zachary Taylor, James Garfield, Warren Harding, and John Kennedy. Harrison, the first president to die in office, succumbed shortly after delivering the longest inaugural address in history. Three other presidents failed to complete their second terms—Abraham Lincoln, William McKinley, and Richard Nixon. FDR died at the very start of his fourth term. Note as well that none of the takeover presidents in the nineteenth century—Tyler, Fillmore, Andrew Johnson, or Arthur—won a full term. By contrast, four of the five takeover presidents in the twentieth century— Theodore Roosevelt, Calvin Coolidge, Harry S. Truman, and Lyndon Johnson—won full terms. Ford was the only loser in this set.

Tests of an Effective Address

Asked by the Online NewsHour to identify the goals of the inaugural address, Kennedy speechwriter Theodore Sorensen was cryptic: "Lofty, non-partisan, vision, basic principles." Asked the same question, Nixon speechwriter Ray Price was more expansively eloquent in placing the address in its institutional and constitutional context: "An inaugural is uniquely sacramental: the peaceful transfer of power it represents is one of the key elements that have made ours the oldest surviving democracy on earth." In that setting, Price judged, the address should both "heal the divisions of the past campaign, and set the directions for the new administration." It should be "uplifting" but "realistic" in what is promised. Quoting Lincoln's second address, Price advised, "it should speak to 'the better angels of our nature'" while "summoning us to those exertions required to make the future we seek achievable."[5]

A participant in the Miller Center symposium on the role of presidential speechwriters, Price commented further on these tests. He stressed the importance of the sacramental nature of the address: "I think the word 'sacramental' is key to it. It [the ceremony of transferring power] is one of the great sacraments of democracy." He then quoted from Nixon's first inaugural address, which he helped craft: "I ask you to share with me today the majesty

Table 4.1. Presidential Inaugural Addresses, 1789–2009

President	Year or Years	Completed Term(s)?
Washington	1789, 1793	Yes
Adams*	1797	Yes
Jefferson	1801, 1805	Yes
Madison	1809, 1813	Yes
Monroe	1817, 1821	Yes
J. Q. Adams*	1825	Yes
Jackson	1829, 1833	Yes
Van Buren*	1837	Yes
W. H. Harrison	1841	No—death; Tyler completed term
Polk	1845	Yes
Taylor	1849	No—death; Fillmore completed term
Pierce	1853	Yes
Buchanan	1857	Yes
Lincoln	1861, 1865	No—death; A. Johnson completed second term
Grant	1869, 1873	Yes
Hayes	1877	Yes
Garfield	1881	No—death; Arthur completed term
Cleveland*	1885	Yes
B. Harrison*	1889	Yes
Cleveland	1893	Yes
McKinley	1897, 1901	No—death; T. Roosevelt completed second term
T. Roosevelt	1905	Yes (first takeover president to win full term)
Taft*	1909	Yes
Wilson	1913, 1917	Yes
Harding	1921	No—death; Coolidge completed term
Coolidge	1925	Yes
Hoover*	1929	Yes
F. D. Roosevelt	1933, 1937, 1941, 1945	No—death; Truman completed fourth term
Truman	1949	Yes
Eisenhower	1953, 1957	Yes
Kennedy	1961	No—death; L. Johnson completed term
L. Johnson	1965	Yes
Nixon	1969, 1973	No—resignation; Ford completed second term
Carter*	1977	Yes
Reagan	1981, 1985	Yes
G. H. W. Bush*	1989	Yes
Clinton	1993, 1997	Yes
G. W. Bush	2001, 2005	Yes
Obama	2009	Pending

*Defeated for reelection.
Source: Compiled by the author.

of the moment. In the orderly transfer of power, we celebrate the unity that keeps us free."[6]

Other participants on the inaugural address panel agreed with Price's criteria, varying only in the adjectives used. For Patrick Anderson, a Carter speechwriter, the purpose of the nomination acceptance speech is to introduce oneself as the candidate, the inaugural address to introduce oneself as the president. The address should be "inspirational and personal." Donald Baer, a Clinton speechwriter, thought the address should be "elevating." Baer also observed a difference between the first and second inaugurals. Price agreed: "The first is more dramatic because it is the start of something new. The second is a continuation."

Truth be told, to the reader's eye relatively few inaugural addresses reach the heights suggested by speechwriters. In his book *What Do We Do Now? A Workbook for the President-Elect*, Stephen Hess cites former Nixon speechwriter William Safire as identifying just four great inaugural addresses: Lincoln's two, FDR's first, and Kennedy's. Hess, a speechwriter for Presidents Eisenhower and Nixon, notes that Jefferson's first and Wilson's second are also frequently mentioned. That makes a total of six of thirty-nine inaugural addresses.

Hess provides his own response to the question asked of Sorensen and Price: "What are the goals of an inaugural address?" He does so with advice regarding length, style, tone, and theme. I paraphrase his response:

> *Length*: Brevity is appreciated. Kennedy's was twelve minutes long—cited by Hess as the "gold standard." Even the normally prolix Bill Clinton limited himself to fourteen minutes.
>
> *Style*: Don't try to be Kennedy or any other past president; you are not, no point in trying. Clinton tried for Kennedy; mostly it didn't work.
>
> *Tone*: Sound like yourself. "George W. Bush gave a great speech—for some other president."
>
> *Theme*: Define your presidency, clarifying what should be expected from your assuming office.[7]

Hess's choice of topics reveals the changes that have occurred over the course of history. He is advising presidents in the era of electronic, even wireless, communication. His advice is primarily about presentation, understanding that what is said will be instantly transmitted to millions around the world. Even the thematic advice directs attention to "the one thought, even the one word, that best represents what you want your presidency to stand for."[8] Baer, too, emphasized themes: "To set a theme for the time and the moment we are in."

The difference in the immediate audience for an inaugural address coincides with the emergence of presidential speechwriters. The first person to hold the position was said to be Judson Welliver, a "literary clerk" working with Calvin Coolidge at the advent of radio.[9] Earlier presidents typically received help—Alexander Hamilton was said to have assisted George Washington— but Welliver is generally acknowledged to have held a position akin to a speechwriter. Accordingly, the following analysis of inaugural addresses is divided between two historical eras marked by the dramatic changes in communication pre- and post-1920s.

The Earlier Era

I sampled inaugural addresses from 1789 to 1925, reading accounts of the principal themes in a quest to identify those that met some or most of the criteria cited by Sorensen and Price, as reinforced by the panelists. It was a somewhat less-than-inspiring exercise, to be sure, though it is fair to state that most met Hess's criterion for tone. The addresses read like those who were speaking, at least judged by what we know of each president. I agree with Reagan speechwriter Ken Khachigian. Having read all inaugural addresses in preparation for working on Reagan's first, he concluded: "You could do sort of an historical time line of the United States by reading them. . . . The speech sort of told you what was on America's mind every four years."[10]

There were thirty-four inaugurals prior to 1925—twenty-five first and nine second addresses. I selected seven firsts and two seconds for special attention: Washington, Jefferson, Jackson, Lincoln first and second, Garfield, T. Roosevelt, and Wilson first and second.

I relied on several criteria in making my choices: historians' rankings of presidents, knowledgeable judgments about superior addresses, and "change points" in history. Five of the seven presidents I chose were ranked by historians in the top third in two recent surveys conducted by C-SPAN and the Federalist Society–*Wall Street Journal*:[11] Washington, Jefferson, Lincoln, Theodore Roosevelt, and Wilson. Jackson was so ranked in the *WSJ* survey, but not by C-SPAN. That leaves Garfield. His inclusion is explained by other criteria.

As noted earlier, Safire's list of great addresses is brief, including just two before 1925, both by Lincoln. Hess suggests two others before 1925,

Jefferson's first and Wilson's second. I agree with all these choices but include others based on the criterion of historical change points.

Change points refer to major happenings that demand notice and action by the president. Such events do not always coincide with the quadrennial election cycle. Thus, for example, our direct entry into World Wars I and II occurred after Wilson's and FDR's inaugurations in 1917 and 1941. More recently, the terrorists' attacks on 9/11 occurred in the eighth month of the George W. Bush administration, with the Iraq war to follow. Among the cases selected before 1925, certain events did coincide with the president's election: a first-ever president taking the oath (Washington), breaking from the founding generation (Jackson), secession (Lincoln), expanded world status (Theodore Roosevelt), and the collapse of the Republican majority (Wilson).

The change-point criterion explains Garfield's presence on the list despite his brief service. Post–Civil War integration of African Americans proceeded at a painfully slow pace over many decades. No pre-1925 inaugural address more cogently defined the issue of integration or articulately expressed the way forward than did that of the twentieth president. His untimely death early in his presidency prevented Garfield from leading at this change point in history. That tragedy should not obscure the importance of his important inaugural statement.

Table 4.2 portrays these nine inaugural addresses, relying on the Sorensen-Price goals and combining what appear to be similar intentions. As shown, the first few sets are more *thematic*, the next are more *programmatic*. This was a distinction made repeatedly in the panel discussion and was found to be useful here in distinguishing among the inaugural addresses selected for study.

Thematic
Lofty (Sorensen), Uplifting (Price)
Sacramental (Price)
Visionary (Sorensen), Appeal to better angels (Price)
Programmatic
Realistic, Summoning (Price)
Nonpartisan (Sorensen), Healing (Price)
Basic principles (Sorensen)

These goals are, for the most part, self-explanatory. Perhaps the least obvious is *sacramental*. Price associated it with the exceptionalism of the American

Table 4.2. Presidential Inaugural Addresses, 1789–1925:
Meeting the Goals in Selected Cases

President (date of inaugural)	Goals Achieved
Washington (April 30, 1789)	Lofty, Sacramental, Summoning, Nonpartisan
Jefferson (March 4, 1801)	Lofty, Sacramental, Visionary, Summoning, Healing, Basic principles
Jackson (March 4, 1829)	Summoning, Realistic, Nonpartisan, Basic principles
Lincoln 1 (March 4, 1861)	Summoning, Realistic, Basic principles (Legalistic), Appeal to better angels
Lincoln 2 (March 4, 1865)	Lofty, Sacramental, Summoning, Realistic, Healing, Appeal to better angels
Garfield (March 4, 1881)	Sacramental, Summoning, Realistic, Healing, Basic principles
T. Roosevelt (March 4, 1905)	Summoning, Realistic, Nonpartisan, Basic principles
Wilson 1 (March 4, 1913)	Summoning, Realistic (Presbyterian), Basic principles
Wilson 2 (March 5, 1917)	Lofty, Summoning, Realistic, Basic principles

Source: Compiled by the author, based on an analysis of inaugural addresses, relying on goals identified by Theodore Sorensen and Raymond Price (http://www.pbs.org/newshour/inauguration/speech4.html).

political system, featuring, among other characteristics, the peaceful transfer of power. Accordingly, I interpret it as expressing the rituals of American governance, with Jefferson's first inaugural address being a prime example. As used here, *sacramental* differs from *basic principles* as being more broadly descriptive of the governing system, less directly applied to policy issues.

As shown in Table 4.2, the addresses by Washington, Jefferson, Lincoln 2, and Wilson 2 were more thematic in content and style; those by Jackson, Lincoln 1, Garfield, Theodore Roosevelt, and Wilson 1 were more programmatic.

Individual attributes and careers, as well as the issues of the time, explain the differences within these groups. I mark Washington's first inaugural as lofty and sacramental because of who he was more than what he said. As noted earlier, the speech itself was self-effacing and did not really engage the issues facing the new government. But it would not have been possible at that time to have a loftier statesman assume leadership of the executive branch. Thus his taking the oath and addressing the assembled was by itself legitimizing and symbolically expressive.

Jefferson, by contrast, was an intellectual and a supreme wordsmith. He narrowly lost the presidency in 1796, then served as vice president to John

Adams, the man who defeated him. Running in 1800 against the president with whom he was serving, he eventually won in the House of Representatives after he and his presumptive running mate, Aaron Burr, had the same number of electoral votes. Accordingly his first inaugural address was an occasion for healing and for expressing his theories of governance. Truly, it is an address for which speechwriters would love to claim authorship.

Opening with a statement of humility in accepting the presidency (seemingly a requirement of the day), Jefferson summarized the greatness of the republic should it remain united. All views should be regarded as adding strength to the system. "But every difference of opinion is not a difference of principle. We have called by different names brethren of the same principle. We are all Republicans, we are all Federalists." This strength, he observed, is rooted in and guided by law. "I believe it the only [Government] where every man, at the call of the law, would fly to the standard of the law, and would meet invasions of the public order as his own personal concern."

These foundations led Jefferson to list "the essential principles of our Government." What he crafted in the fourth paragraph of his address remains a reliable summary of democratic goals, combining as it does the ideals of a republic and the time-honored agenda of its government.

The second inaugural addresses by Lincoln and Wilson were similar in one important respect. Each dealt with a contemporary crisis: the ending of a wrenching domestic struggle, the Civil War, for Lincoln; the beginning of American involvement in a world war for Wilson. The sequence in each case reversed the convention of a thematic first-term address (as suited to beginning a presidency) and a programmatic second-term address (as suited to the continuation of a presidency). The ending of the Civil War called for a unifying theme. Lincoln met the challenge of reaching beyond the fissures to the union in a call for compassionate restoration of a common purpose. "With malice toward none, with charity for all, with firmness in the right as God gives us to see the right, let us strive on to finish the work we are in, to bind up the nation's wounds, to care for him who shall have borne the battle and for his widow and his orphan."

A half-century later the nation's pending involvement in a spreading world conflict ordained a statement of mission. Wilson observed: "We are of the blood of all the nations that are at war." He declared and defined America's new vital role in the world. "We are provincial no longer." Events "have made us citizens of the world. There can be no turning back. Our own fortunes as a nation are involved whether we would have it so or not." The speech was less sacramental than an effort at public enlightenment. In fact, Wilson's later experience with the League of Nations raised doubts as to whether the country was prepared to assume a more global status. Still the address deserves its place among featured presidential rhetoric.

Programmatic addresses are less soaring, being directed more to immediate issues. Lincoln's first understandably concentrated on secession. He was inaugurated as the union was collapsing. This first address was four times the length of his second. It reads like a legal brief, citing the lack of a constitutional basis for a separation without the concurrence of all. One could better imagine him arguing his case in a courtroom than on the East Portico of the Capitol.

Theodore Roosevelt's inaugural address in 1905 was the first by a vice president subsequently elected to a full presidential term. He took the oath upon McKinley's death on September 14, 1901, just seven months into his term as vice president. Therefore, Roosevelt had served nearly a full term as president when he was elected in 1905. His speech was a relatively brief, workmanlike message that implored Americans to acknowledge their greater role in the world due in large part to "the extraordinary industrial development of the last half century." In acknowledging this shift, however, Roosevelt clarified both the humanity and strength of America's growing world status. "No weak nation that acts manfully and justly should ever have cause to fear us, and no strong power should ever be able to single us out as a subject for insolent aggression."

Wilson's first inaugural address was among the most in need of a talented speechwriter. This man of the academy, as scholar and president of Princeton University (not to mention former president of the American Political Science Association), produced one of the least erudite speeches delivered on inauguration day. A sample: "Some new things as we look frankly upon them, willing to comprehend their real character, have come to assume the aspect of things long believed in and familiar, stuff of our own convictions." And more: "We see that in many things that life is very great. It is incomparably great in its material aspects. . . . It is great, also very great, in its moral force. . . . We have built up, moreover, a great system of government. . . ."

Why include this address? Because it came at a change point in history. Wilson's election marked the end of Republican dominance, if not the start of Democratic hegemony. Wilson acknowledged this in his opening remarks, among the more partisan of the addresses. Further, he identified specific reforms that Democrats were expected to endorse, many of which were enacted during his first term. Finally, it is worth noting that however "great" our "material aspects," "moral force," and "system of government," the Presbyterian minister's son acknowledged that "the evil has come with the good, and much fine gold has been corroded."

My final choice of an address is a bit of an outlier. James A. Garfield was shot on July 2, 1881, just two days short of his fourth month in office. He died on September 19, 1881. His short tenure offers little basis for evaluating his presidency, though he was ranked twenty-ninth in the C-SPAN survey. The final third of his address is unremarkable, more like a state of the union message offering a legislative agenda. It is the early portion that merits history's recognition for the clarity and purposefulness of a courageous message regarding post–Civil War integration of freed slaves into American society.

Garfield began by acknowledging the historical context of his address: "It is now three days more than a hundred years since the adoption of the first written constitution of the United States—the Articles of Confederation and Perpetual Union." He then offered a four-paragraph review of the American experience prior to the Civil War and its aftermath. He exclaimed: "The supremacy of the nation and its laws should be no longer a subject of debate." He pointed out that "the elevation of the Negro race from slavery to the full rights of citizenship is the most important political change we have known since the adoption of the Constitution in 1787. . . . Those who resisted the change should remember that under our institutions there was no middle ground for the Negro race between slavery and equal citizenship. There can be no permanent disfranchised peasantry in the United States."

Equally powerful was Garfield's response to those claiming that "honest local government is impossible if the mass of uneducated negroes are allowed to vote." Acknowledging the bad effects of ignorance for democratic rule, he doubted that it was a condition exclusive to blacks and recommended "the savory influence of universal education." "Let our people find a new meaning in the divine oracle which declares that 'a little child shall lead them,' for our own little children will soon control the destinies of the Republic."

Although Garfield's address has mostly been lost to history, it is one of the most articulate, passionate, and well-argued statements ever made regarding full citizenship and governing. Without question, Kennedy's inaugural address deserves acclaim in spite of his presidency having been cut short by assassination. Similarly, Garfield's bold statement on full citizenship for blacks deserves to be reclaimed.

Crafting the Address in the Modern Era

Advances in electronic communication guaranteed larger and larger audiences for presidential speeches. What had been a message to colleagues, political friends, petitioners, and supporters was increasingly heard, and later seen, by national, then world, audiences. Specialists were employed to craft the right message for the occasion, the times, and the audiences.

Naturally enough, the speechwriting process changed from one primarily initiated by the president and close friends to one initiated by specialists, ordinarily guided by the president's preferences as interpreted and enforced by his staff. The process evolved into speechwriting by committee, with several drafts pored over sometimes to the last minute.

The dynamics also changed, with Hess's length, style, tone, and theme growing in importance within an interactive network involving the president, staff, and the speechwriting team. Speechwriters themselves specialize in understanding presidents well enough to put the right words in their mouths. As Clark S. Judge, a Reagan speechwriter, put it: "Speechwriters learn to 'hear' the voice of the president, fitting their habits of language and argument within his."[12] Presidents can facilitate this process by clarifying their goals, interests, and preferences to such an extent that they are comfortable with this exercise.

Asked to react to Judge's "hearing the voice of the president," Baer noted: "I think you typically hear those voices even in the middle of the night when you are trying to sleep. . . . It has to become almost second nature to you." Baer stressed the importance of having both political and personal sympathy for "what the president really is trying to do for the nation." "Writing for someone else, in that person's voice, is about as personal an act as you can imagine." Preparing oneself for this task is difficult. "It is something you learn as you read and you listen. . . . But at the end of the day you have to have . . . a natural sympathy for what they're trying to talk about and with who they are in order to do that."

The speechwriters on the panel (Anderson, Baer, and Price) contributed other insights into writing the modern-day inaugural address, notably in regard to audience, delivery, and the role of the president.

Audience

"The audience is the broader audience," explained Price. "You are speaking to the nation and the world. . . ." Baer agreed, noting: "It is arguable that the physical audience matters the least for an inaugural address than for any other kind of speech."

Ken Khachigian, a Reagan speechwriter, explained that he was so conscious of the television picture accompanying the address that he had cameras placed to provide pictures of various monuments as Reagan mentioned them, including Arlington National Cemetery. The effect was to convey symbolic images that the physical audience never saw but that greatly enhanced communication to the larger audience.

Mention was also made of those sitting behind the president—the dignitaries, including those representing the continuity of government as well as the defeated candidate and outgoing administration officials. Each writer cited a grace note. For example, in 1977 Carter's first words were "For myself and for our nation, I want to thank my predecessor [Gerald Ford] for all he has done to heal our land," and in 1993 Clinton said to Bush: "On behalf of our nation, I salute my predecessor, President Bush, for his half-century of service to America." Price revealed that Nixon believed Kennedy offended Eisenhower in what has been heralded as one of the most memorable lines of his address: "the torch has been passed to a new generation of Americans," with Eisenhower representing the old generation.

Delivery

However well crafted a speech may be, its effectiveness can be lessened or enhanced by how the president delivers it. Baer emphasized that delivery was especially critical for the inaugural address. It is delivered in an open-air setting, lacking audible applause because of the president's distance from the audience and the muffled sounds of gloved hands on a January day. "These are politicians after all. They are used to speaking to large crowds of people who give them love back. You don't get that. . . . You don't know what the reaction is." The challenge is to speak to the unseen audience at home rather than the one directly present.

The speechwriters agreed that understanding the difference between the written and the spoken word is the key to effective delivery. Price noted that this difference "is too little understood and needs to be stressed." Baer explained why: "Every convention that we think about in terms of what works well in writing has to be rethought when you're dealing with the spoken word and nowhere more so . . . than in an inaugural address." An inaugural address has to move along quickly, almost as a "string of epigrams."

Role of the President

Who should write the speech? When asked this question, Patrick Anderson responded: "He [the president-elect] should as much as he is able and willing to. The more of him that is in it the better it is, but writers do have a role in it. . . . It's a very personal speech."

The relationship with speechwriters is also quite personal, depending on trust, a comfort level born of experience with the president-elect, and the writer's knowledge of his subject's "voice." Price had a very close attachment to Nixon and "it was just made clear from the outset that I would be the one working with him on it." He stressed, however, "It was not that I was writing for him; I was writing with him or helping him to write."

The process has come to be a "collective enterprise," as Price referred to it. Presidents-elect want and receive a great deal of advice. "Outreach" has become "an established part of the process" with all major speeches. Among other advantages, outreach may help in building support and getting media attention.

Selected Addresses in the Modern Era

Twenty one inaugural addresses were delivered in the period 1925 to 2005—thirteen first-term addresses, six second-term, and one each for third and fourth terms. Relying on the same criteria for selecting addresses as in the earlier period—historians' rankings, choices of outstanding speeches, and change points—I selected seven for special attention: FDR (1 and 2), Truman, Eisenhower, Kennedy, Johnson, and Reagan. All six presidents were ranked in the top third in the C-SPAN survey; all but Kennedy and Johnson were also so ranked in the *WSJ* survey. FDR's first and Kennedy's were designated by Safire as great addresses and all took office at change points of varying significance.

Table 4.3 displays the extent to which the addresses achieved the Sorensen-Price goals. The most striking feature in comparing the modern addresses with those before 1925 is that most were lofty, sacramental, or both.

Whether this difference is attributable to speechwriters or to the growing need for uplifting rhetoric is uncertain. But a scan of the speeches not included in Table 4.3 suggests that all presidents of the period strived for exalted messages.

The two FDR addresses were models of the message satisfying the needs of the times. The first was a crisp review of the problem to be solved—"unemployed citizens face the grim problem of existence"—and his proposals for taking action—"put people to work . . . by direct recruiting by Government itself." Roosevelt projected confidence that "conditions in our country today" would be conquered: "This great Nation will endure as it has endured, will revive and prosper." The second address in 1937 reported on the progress made—"We refused to leave the problems of our common welfare to be solved by the winds of change and the hurricanes of disaster"—and what yet had to be accomplished—"I see one-third of a nation ill-housed, ill-clad, ill-nourished."

Realism and idealism were masterfully bonded in both speeches. In addition to the oft-repeated phrases, there were serious points that deserve time-honored repetition: "The Constitution of 1787 did not make our democracy

Table 4.3. Presidential Inaugural Addresses, 1925–2005
Meeting the Goals in Selected Cases

President (date of inaugural)	Goals Achieved
F. Roosevelt (March 4, 1933)	Lofty, Uplifting, Sacramental, Visionary, Summoning, Realistic, Healing, Basic principles, Appeal to better angels
F. Roosevelt (January 20, 1937)*	See above
Truman (January 20, 1949)	Sacramental (comparison with communism), Realistic, Nonpartisan, Basic principles
Eisenhower (January 20, 1953)	Lofty, Visionary, Nonpartisan, Basic principles
Kennedy (January 20, 1961)	Lofty, Uplifting, Sacramental, Visionary, Summoning, Realistic, Nonpartisan, Appeal to better angels
L. Johnson (January 20, 1965)	Lofty, Visionary, Nonpartisan, Basic principles
Reagan (January 20,1981)	Lofty, Uplifting, Sacramental, Summoning, Realistic, Basic principles, Appeal to better angels

*Date of inauguration changed from March 4 to January 20 by the Twentieth Amendment, ratified January 23, 1933.

Source: Compiled by the author, based on an analysis of inaugural addresses, relying on goals identified by Theodore Sorensen and Raymond Price (http://www.pbs.org/newshour/inauguration/speech4.html).

impotent." "Government is competent when all who compose it work as trustees for the whole people." "To maintain a democracy of effort requires a vast amount of patience. . . ." The speech was said to have been written by Raymond Moley. But Arthur M. Schlesinger, Jr., reports: "Six days before [the inauguration], Roosevelt in his Hyde Park study, writing with pencil on a lined, legal-sized yellow pad, had made a draft of his inaugural address." Schlesinger also notes that the president-elect made a last-minute change in the opening sentence just before delivering the speech. "This is a day of consecration" became "This is a day of national consecration."[13]

Like Theodore Roosevelt, Truman served nearly a full term as a takeover president. Only the third such president to be elected to a full term, Truman had in mind specific proposals, notably the Point Four program for European recovery from World War II and for world peace. The early portion of the address, however, employed sacramentalism by favorably comparing American democracy with communism. As he explained in his memoirs: "I wanted to make it clear that lasting freedom and independence cannot be achieved among free nations unless they possess the means to maintain their free institutions and their national integrity against movements that seek to impose totalitarian regimes upon them."[14] That exercise provided a rationale for his Point Four program, which offered needed balance in postwar world politics. "I state these differences [between communism and democracy], not to draw issues of belief as such, but because the actions resulting from the Communist philosophy are a threat to the efforts of free nations to bring about world recovery and lasting peace."

Interestingly, one finds no hint of the bitter 1948 election in Truman's inaugural address. It was nonpartisan, if not healing. It concentrated almost entirely on international issues, avoiding the more divisive domestic conflicts that dominated the campaign.

The 1952 election ended twenty years of Democratic Party control of the White House. This change point was not the equal of FDR's victory in 1932, but it certainly made a difference in Washington politics.

The new president was a national war hero, not as singular as Washington in 1789 but as close as the United States had come since that time. As with Washington, Eisenhower's popularity ensured an above-politics mood. In fact, his status caused worry among some Republicans that the president would not be faithful to party ideals. The speech itself was not reassuring in that regard. As noted in Table 4.3, it was lofty (almost ethereal), visionary, and wholly nonpartisan. It began with "a little private prayer of my own" followed by frequent references to God. As he recounts in his memoirs, Eisenhower didn't want the address to be a sermon, but from boyhood he had "a deep faith in the beneficence of the Almighty" and was anxious to "make this faith clear."[15] He succeeded.

Beginning with a prayer was a first in inaugural addresses. Eisenhower judged it unusual enough to explain the circumstances in his memoirs. Upon returning from church he got the idea for a prayer and wrote one on a scratch pad. He tested it on family and friends, who believed it to be suitable.

Eisenhower set forth "certain fixed principles" in "pressing our labor for world peace." Most were standard guidelines for the conduct of international relations and commerce and the maintenance of national security. Domestic issues received little attention, except by inference.

The president-elect had himself been a speechwriter for General Douglas MacArthur and thus was likely to be active in crafting his first inaugural address. His principal assistant for this address was Emmet J. Hughes, whom he described as "a writer with a talent for phrase-making."[16] Stephen Ambrose reported that Eisenhower wrote in his diaries, "my assistant [Hughes] was of no help—he is more enamored with words than with ideas."[17] Sherman Adams, however, recounts that the two worked closely with one another through many drafts. Apparently Eisenhower read the draft of the address to a pre-inauguration cabinet meeting, hoping for constructive criticism. He got little.

In his book Kennedy, Theodore Sorensen described the process by which he and the president-elect crafted what Hess refers to as the gold standard for inaugural addresses: "He wanted suggestions from everyone. He wanted it short. He wanted it to focus on foreign policy. He did not want it to sound partisan, pessimistic or critical of his predecessor. He wanted neither the cold war rhetoric about the Communist menace nor any weasel words that Khrushchev might misinterpret. And he wanted it to set a tone for the era about to begin."[18] All of these purposes were met. Dissatisfied that his and Sorensen's efforts to include domestic goals sounded too partisan, Kennedy finally said: "Let's drop out the domestic stuff altogether."[19] As described by Sorensen, the president-elect and his alter ego sifted through themes and ideas suggested by others and reviewed campaign speeches in the drafting process.

The final product was masterful, well deserving of the praise it has received, including that from all the speechwriters attending the Miller Center symposium. The change point was eloquently marked: "the torch has been passed." The new president solicited, even demanded, a world audience: "Let the word go forth . . ." "Let every nation know . . ." "To those old allies . . ." "To those new States. . . ." As with FDR's addresses, current issues were treated in the context of familiar ideals. Common sense had seldom been so movingly stated. As shown in Tables 4.2 and 4.3, most addresses were summoning, often justified by the president's need for support. Kennedy's summons was more that of realizing the demands of world statesmanship ("ask not what America can do for you") and American citizenship ("ask not what your country can do for you"). It was a call for responsibility and energy in governance.

Lyndon Johnson's inaugural address came after a very active year of legislating in 1964. He promised to enact what remained of Kennedy's program as a legacy for the assassinated president. His huge win in 1964 was accompanied by two-thirds majorities for Democrats in both houses of Congress. Thus change was already well under way and conditions were perfect for enacting more legislation to build the "Great Society."

Johnson's theme was an "American covenant." "Conceived in justice, written in liberty, bound in union, it was meant one day to inspire the hopes of all mankind; and it binds us still." There was little in the speech to signal what kind of presidency to expect beyond what one already knew from his service to that point. It was more like Eisenhower's first inaugural than Kennedy's. The "Great Society" that was to mark Johnson's presidency was mentioned but once, and rather peculiarly: "I do not believe that the Great Society is the ordered, changeless, and sterile battalion of ants."

Johnson violated Hess's advice to "sound like yourself." The address was not in his "voice." Lofty and visionary though it was, it did not sound like Johnson: "[America] is the uncrossed desert and the unclimbed ridge. It is the star that is not reached and the harvest sleeping in the unplowed ground."

Oddly, Johnson makes no reference to his inaugural address in his memoirs, nor is there a picture of him taking the oath in a book with more than the usual number of photos for a presidential memoir. Doris Kearns does not mention the address either in her book, *Lyndon Johnson and the American Dream*. She does cite his 1965 state of the union message, which is in Johnson's voice. It was as though the inaugural ceremony was not so important in Johnson's political life. We know, however, what the 1964 election result was. Kearns quotes him as saying: "For the first time in all my life I truly felt loved by the American people."[20]

Whatever else might be said of Ronald Reagan's first inaugural address, one could hardly claim that it didn't sound like the fortieth president. Note in Table 4.3 that his was one of the few addresses clearly partisan in tone. Thus, for example, after praising his predecessor, Jimmy Carter, for his "gracious cooperation in the transition process," Reagan immediately recounted the grim problems left behind by the Carter years. "These United States are confronted with an economic affliction of great proportions." After a candid review of the "crisis," Reagan concluded: "In this present crisis, government is not the solution to the problem; government is the problem."

Surrounding and interspersing the list of woes was classic Reagan optimism. "We have every right to dream heroic dreams. Those who say that we are in a time when there are no heroes just don't know where to look." The speech was sacramental: "This every-4-year ceremony we accept as normal is nothing less than a miracle." It was summoning, with appeals to our better angels: "The crisis we are facing today . . . require[s] . . . our willingness to believe . . . that together, with God's help, we can and will resolve the problems which now confront us. And, after all, why shouldn't we believe that? We are Americans."

Lou Cannon, in his book *President Reagan: The Role of a Lifetime*, provides one of the best descriptions of the writing of this first inaugural address. Ken Khachigian was designated to draft it. He had a great deal to work with because Reagan had formed "The Speech" over several years of corporate-sponsored talks. Cannon refers to "the script" in conveying the consistency of theme, message, and imagery. As he notes: "It was the script that was compelling, and it was Reagan who wrote it." Khachigian's challenge was to frame the elements of the script to suit the ceremonial occasion.

Reagan had his own ideas about the inaugural speech. In reading Khachigian's draft, the president-elect first tried editing the text. "Then he gave it up, took out a yellow legal pad and began to write another speech working both from the Khachigian draft and from ideas of his own." He was particularly anxious to end the speech with "a more personal and dramatic link to the past."[21] And so the address ends with Reagan quoting from a World War I soldier's commitment to serving his country, as revealed in the soldier's diary. It was exactly the dramatic ending Reagan wanted, even if the story itself was not exactly accurate.

Addresses and Transitions

The inaugural address has become part of the ceremony of installing new or continuing presidents. Greatest public attention is paid to new presidents, for obvious reasons. The addresses by presidents continuing in office are primarily notable if events merit special emphasis: the ending of the Civil War for Lincoln, the probability of U.S. participation in a world war for Wilson, and the testing period for new programs designed to cope with the Great Depression for FDR. Other special cases involve takeover presidents elected to continue in office, notably Theodore Roosevelt in 1905, Truman in 1949, and Lyndon Johnson in 1965. For them too, events warranted notice: the greater world role for the United States (Roosevelt), post–World War II recovery (Truman), and advancing the greatest federal expansion of domestic programs since the New Deal (Johnson).

These distinctions suggest different criteria for judging the effectiveness of the addresses. For first inaugurals by new presidents (ten of the sixteen cases), the following tests are appropriate: Was there an effective transition from the campaign to governing? Were policy changes clearly identified? For the second, more events-driven inaugurals, the tests are: Were the issues clearly defined? Was a future course specified?

Table 4.4 offers my judgments regarding each set. As shown, seven of the ten addresses by new presidents evidenced successful shifts from campaigning to governing, either definitely or moderately. Three did not. Lincoln was faced with secession and could hardly ignore the regional and political partisanship that fueled that divisive issue. Wilson and Reagan each had promised bold changes in domestic policy and confirmed that intention in their addresses, with Reagan the more pronounced of the two.

First inaugural addresses also varied in their treatment of the transition from the previous to the new administration. Six addresses were quite explicit about what to expect—those by Jackson, Lincoln, Garfield, Wilson, FDR, and Reagan. The two generals, Washington and Eisenhower, provided few details, opting instead to offer reassurances about their leadership abilities. Jefferson and Kennedy left it to others to interpret what changes they had in mind from their eloquent statements of governing principles.

Events-driven second inaugural addresses had the most transitional features in common. They were uniformly nonpartisan and healing in regard to the shift from campaigning to governing and explicit in specifying the course to be followed in post–Civil War reconciliation (Lincoln), almost

Table 4.4. Effectiveness of Inaugural Addresses

First Addresses President	Transition to Governing?	Transition to New Presidency?
Washington (1789)	Yes (limited campaign so more toward governance)	Limited (few details)
Jefferson (1801)	Yes	Moderate (stated as principles)
Jackson (1829)	Yes	Yes (quite explicit)
Lincoln (1861)	Qualified (difficult to ignore campaign)	Yes (an explicit brief on secession)
Garfield (1881)	Moderate	Yes (explicit)
Wilson (1913)	Limited	Yes (explicit)
F. Roosevelt (1933)	Moderate	Yes (explicit)
Eisenhower (1953)	Yes	Limited (few details)
Kennedy (1961)	Yes	Moderate (limited on domestic)
Reagan (1981)	Limited (campaign carrying over to governance)	Yes (explicit)

Second Addresses President	Issues Defined?	Course Clarified?
Lincoln (1865)	Yes	Yes
Wilson (1917)	Yes	Yes
F. Roosevelt (1937)	Yes	Yes

Takeover (Full-Term) President	Issues Defined?	Course Clarified?
T. Roosevelt (1905)	Yes	Moderate
Truman (1949)	Limited to foreign policy	Limited (foreign policy emphasis—European recovery)
L. Johnson (1965)	No	No (focus on general principles)

Source: Compiled by the author from reading texts of relevant addresses.

certain entry into war (Wilson), and continued attention to the effects of the Great Depression (FDR).

Takeover presidents winning a full term were individual in defining issues and clarifying the course to be followed. Theodore Roosevelt was the most successful in these regards, though more explicit about the questions than the answers. Truman was characteristically forthright but limited himself to an important but singular foreign policy issue. And Lyndon Johnson decided to be more idealistic than realistic in defining the issues and proposing remedies.

Conclusion

I have relied on two sets of measures in evaluating inaugural addresses—goals to be achieved as identified by former speechwriters and practical effects in transitioning from the campaign to governing. Presumably goals and effects are related—achieving the first enables the second. There are risks in identifying great speeches across time and between issues. Historians warn against such exercises, even as they frequently take these risks themselves. I am willing to take the plunge, again under cover of the typology proposed earlier: *thematic* and *programmatic.*

> *Thematic:* Jefferson, Lincoln second, Wilson second, Kennedy
> *Programmatic:* Jackson, Lincoln first, Garfield, Reagan
> *Balanced:* FDR first and second

A notable omission from this list is George Washington. His place in history is as a great president. An extraordinary man gave an ordinary first inaugural address. That he was willing to take the job itself made the moment and laid the foundation for all of his successors.

Did these great speeches contribute to great presidencies? Judged by historians' ratings, apart from Garfield, whose short tenure prevented a reliable ranking, the answer is "yes." The reader may properly ask, weren't those rankings instrumental in selecting the cases? Absolutely. But not all of the top-ranked presidents in the sample gave great speeches (Theodore Roosevelt, Truman, Eisenhower, and Lyndon Johnson, along with Wilson's first address, did not make the list). Further, in scanning all of the inaugural addresses, even those of William Henry Harrison and Franklin Pierce, I can report that it is not common for lesser-ranked presidents to produce outstanding addresses. As it happens, the best in office may not always deliver great orations but the middling and worst in office surely don't.

Notes

1. Note the treatment of "special inaugural addresses" of "ascendant vice presidents" in Karlyn Kohs Campbell and Kathleen Hall Jamieson, *Presidents Creating the Presidency: Deeds Done in Words* (Chicago: University of Chicago Press, 2008), ch. 3.

2. James D. Richardson, *A Compilation of the Messages and Papers of the Presidents, 1789* (Washington, D.C.: Bureau of National Literature and Art, 1905).

3. None of the other twentieth-century takeover presidents—Theodore Roosevelt, Coolidge, Truman, Lyndon Johnson—offered remarks upon being sworn in, primarily because of the urgency and location of the ceremony.

4. The source for quotations from inaugural addresses is The Avalon Project at Yale Law School: http://www.yale.edu/lawweb/avalon/presiden/inaug.html.

5. Both quotations taken from "The Speech: Inauguration, 2001," http://www.pbs .org/newshour/inauguration/speech4.html.

6. Quotations taken from Chapter 5, "White House Speechwriters Symposium," June 20–21, 2008, Panel on Inaugural Address. All other quotations from panel participants (Patrick Anderson, Donald Baer, and Raymond Price) are likewise taken from this source and will not be further noted in this chapter.

7. Stephen Hess, *What Do We Do Now? A Workbook for the President-Elect* (Washington, D.C.: Brookings Institution Press, 2008), 132–134.

8. Ibid., 134.

9. Today, the Judson Welliver Society, started by William Safire, is a bipartisan social group of former presidential speechwriters. Welliver was said to have also aided Harding.

10. Quoted in Lou Cannon, *President Reagan: The Role of a Lifetime* (New York: Simon & Schuster, 1991), 96. Khachigian, a participant in the symposium, reiterates this point in Chapter 5.

11. As presented in C-SPAN Historical Survey of Presidential Leadership, 2004 (http:// www.americanpresidents.org/siurvey/historians/overall.asp) and Federalist Society–*Wall Street Journal* Survey on Presidents, 2000 (http://www.opinionjournal.com/hail/rankings .html).

12. Clark S. Judge, "Bearing the Burden of Writing the Speech," *Wall Street Journal*, August 24, 2005.

13. Arthur M. Schlesinger, Jr., *The Crisis of the Old Order* (Boston: Houghton Mifflin, 1957), 7.

14. Harry S. Truman, *Memoirs*, vol. 2, *Years of Trial and Hope* (New York: Signet Books, 1965), 265.

15. Dwight D. Eisenhower, *Mandate for Change, 1953–1956* (New York: Doubleday, 1963, 100. Sherman Adams, Eisenhower's chief of staff, confirms the importance of religion for the president. It was "a dominant and living force in his life and in his purposes." Sherman Adams, *First-Hand Report: The Story of the Eisenhower Administration* (New York: Harper & Brothers, 1961), 65.

16. Eisenhower, *Mandate for Change*, 100.

17. Stephen E. Ambrose, *Eisenhower: The President* (New York: Simon & Schuster, 1984), 36.

18. Theodore C. Sorensen, *Kennedy* (New York: Harper & Row, 1965), 240. The omission of domestic issues was upsetting to some aides. "You can't do this . . ." said Harris

Wofford upon reading the final draft. He argued for saying something about the equal rights struggle "at home." Kennedy agreed and added "at home" to a sentence regarding human rights abroad. It was but one of thirty-one changes made in the last hours before delivering the speech. Richard Reeves, *President Kennedy: Profile of Power* (New York: Simon & Schuster, 1993), 39.

19. Sorensen, *Kennedy*, 242.

20. Doris Kearns, *Lyndon Johnson and the American Dream* (New York: Signet Books, 1976), 219.

21. All quotes taken from Cannon, *President Reagan*, 88–100. Khachigian confirms the story in Chapter 5.

Chapter 5

Speechwriters on the Inaugural Address

Patrick Anderson, Don Baer, Raymond Price

This session of the symposium featured Patrick Anderson, speechwriter for Jimmy Carter; Don Baer, speechwriter for Bill Clinton; and Ray Price, speechwriter for Richard Nixon. The session was moderated by Charles O. Jones, Professor Emeritus of Political Science at the University of Wisconsin and a nonresident senior fellow at the Miller Center of Public Affairs, University of Virginia.

Jones: The inaugural address is surely the most exclusive of the addresses, occurring once every four years, and certainly the most ceremonial. So it is very special. The preparations for it, especially for a first-time president, have to be made very carefully. In addition you're dealing with a transition from the campaign to governing, and often with a shift from one president to the other. So there's an institutional transition.

The first question is: What is an effective inaugural address? I want to start with Ray Price because he has been quoted on that subject. According to Ray, it should be "uplifting," "sacramental," "summoning," "realistic," "healing," and it should appeal to "the better angels."[1] Do you stick with that?

Price: I do indeed. Better angels are sometimes rather difficult to find, but they're very useful when you do find them.[2] They're very useful in governing too, and useful to a democratic process. I think the word "sacramental" is the key to it. The inaugural is one of the great sacraments of democracy.

In preparation for today, I looked at the first lines of Nixon's first inaugural, which were "Senator [Everett] Dirksen, Mr. Chief Justice, Mr. Vice President, President Johnson, Vice President [Hubert] Humphrey, my fellow Americans, and my fellow citizens of the world community, I ask you to share with me today the majesty of this moment. In the orderly transfer of power, we celebrate the unity that keeps us free."[3] To me that sums up what the sacrament is. Through most of human history, power has not been transferred in such an orderly way, as it was in our case. Ours was different in other ways too. It was a change of parties. And we were beginning the final third of the century. The middle third ran from FDR [Franklin Delano Roosevelt] through LBJ [Lyndon Baines Johnson]. So we were starting a new third, and we were trying to start a new way of looking at the process of governing.

Jones: So the historical context comes to be very important.

Price: Yes.

Jones: Patrick?

Anderson: I agree with Ray. In your acceptance speech, you introduce yourself as a candidate; in your inaugural, you introduce yourself as president. It is solemn. It is historic. I think it is also, under the surface, a very competitive situation, because you are very aware that you are going to be judged against [John F.] Kennedy and [Ronald] Reagan and other great speeches of the past—which tends to inspire both the candidate and his writers to make their best effort.[4] It shouldn't be partisan or political. It should be inspirational and personal, I think. It should be an attempt to unite the nation for a new start, which all new presidents think they're going to accomplish.

I think that Carter had a good inaugural address.[5] The interesting thing to me about Carter's inaugural address—and I worked on the early drafts—was that, if you recall, after he made the speech and after he met with the congressional leaders, he and Rosalynn [Carter] got in the motorcade to go toward the White House, up Pennsylvania Avenue. After a few blocks he stopped the motorcade, and to the horror of the Secret Service, he and Rosalynn got out and walked hand in hand for a number of blocks up Pennsylvania Avenue. There were cheering crowds, a beautiful moment. I think he was trying consciously to contrast what he thought would be the openness of his administration with the lack of openness of some previous administrations. He totally upstaged his speech, but it was a beautiful image, and I think, for all the problems he had ahead, he did start off with a great day.[6]

Jones: It was physical communication.

Anderson: Yes.

Jones: It was almost the introduction.

Anderson: Instead of talking, he was walking.

Jones: Right. Don?

Baer: I agree with what has been said here. I think that inaugural addresses ought to be elevating. I think they need to remind the nation more of what we have in common than of what divides us. So the words that opened President Nixon's first inaugural address are certainly interesting.

President Clinton's second inaugural address, which is the one that I worked on, focused very much on the idea that he wanted to be a repairer of the breech, as he said in that speech.[7] He wanted to help the country realize that we were one America more than we were many Americas in the things that matter most. I think also that most of these speeches, those that work and even those that don't work, quite often are trying to lift the country in two ways: first, to recognize, as you point out, Ray, where we stand in the larger arc of history at any given time, and second, to set a theme for the time and the moment that we're in—not so much programmatically as thematically.[8]

In the case of President Clinton's second inaugural address, you'll remember that his reelection campaign had been run around the theme of building a bridge to the twenty-first century. It was very future oriented. We recognized that ours would be the last inaugural address of the twentieth century. We felt it was important, then, to look back across the great span of that century at what had been accomplished, but also to recognize what still needed to be accomplished as we moved into a very different new century.[9] I think that these speeches have the potential to do all of those things.

As a matter of history, we were writing a second inaugural address, of which there have been even fewer than first inaugural addresses. They can be more difficult, or at least more challenging in some ways. When it comes to unifying or trying to persuade the nation that it is one nation, in the case of the Clinton administration, we had come through four years of pretty severe partisan combat at that point. We were unaware of just how severe the partisan combat would be for the next four years, but it creates a slightly different perspective.[10] I remember that one writer, at the time of President Clinton's first inaugural address, had a lead in a story that said something to the effect that "every baby is new, and every new president gets the benefit of being that new baby." But when you're coming into your second term, you don't have that benefit anymore.[11]

Jones: Ray, what about second vs. first, again in regard to effectiveness?

Price: The first is more dramatic because it is the start of something new. The second is a continuation. Don, I think, hit the key: thematic, not programmatic, for an inaugural address. Programmatic comes later in other ways. The inaugural is a ceremonial occasion. It is not a time for hortatory or that sort of thing. There's a lot less drama to the second inaugural. You're trying to keep something going, knowing that most administrations tend to go downhill in their second term. My guess is it's rare that the second term matches the first.[12] You lose steam. The people who came in are tired. New people are coming in and so forth. Most people have no idea how exhausting the White House can be for people in it, unless they've been there. People wear out quickly.

Jones: Including speechwriters?

Baer: Especially speechwriters.

Price: You're trying to inject a little new vigor and new life, some new ideas in the second term, but knowing that it is a different kind of newness.

Jones: Of course Nixon, in '72, came in having won practically everything.

Price: Except the Congress.

Jones: That's right. Clinton, on the other hand, once more had a narrow victory.

Baer: A pretty wide victory, but he had not gotten 50 percent of the vote, which he had hoped to get. He won 49.3 percent, which was a disappointment. But he won by seven or eight points in the popular vote.[13]

Jones: There's no doubt who won.

Baer: Right. But we were going into the second term without Congress, which was a very different perspective than the first term, when the Democrats controlled both houses of Congress and there was more of a sense that all things were possible. Perhaps too many things were possible. I think 1997 was a very different time and therefore did require more of an outreach. I don't know if you want to get into specific detail, but let's not forget that the presidential campaign itself and the year of 1996 had been relatively calm. I say *relatively* because it was compared to 1995, which was one of the more harshly partisan years in the history of the country, with the Republican revolution and Newt Gingrich and all of that.

Jones: That's interesting. You had Clinton come back with a Republican Congress and Nixon with a Democratic.

Baer: And the truth is, most of '96 was a hiatus from harsh partisanship because the Republicans didn't quite know where to go after having lost in the government-shutdown period. There had been some bridging of the gaps with welfare reform and other legislation that had been passed just before President Clinton was nominated for the second term.[14] So there was unfinished business. The 1997 inaugural was the launch into how the country would deal with that unfinished business going forward, into what everyone hoped would be a productive four years.

Jones: I've always heard that in writing a speech for someone, who the audience is is so important. In this setting you have a tremendous physical audience out in front, but of course, it's the rest of the nation, and indeed the world, in many cases, watching it. Who do you see as the audience for this great ceremonial occasion?

Price: The audience is the broader audience. You are speaking to the nation and to the world, and you're very conscious of doing that, too. The people who are sitting in their seats outdoors at the Capitol are the ones who happen to be present for the event, but they are not the ones to whom you are speaking. You're also conscious of the people who are on the stand behind you, who include some very serious people, but who represent part of the continuity that the inauguration symbolizes.

Jones: There are not many occasions like that. Is that a consideration—that is, this physical audience and then the broader audience on television—in your structuring of the speech?

Price: Well, there's one small item. When we were preparing the first inaugural, which we did over a long period of time, working back and forth on it, Nixon read all of the previous inaugurals. And as he gathered ideas, one comment he made to me was, "It's important not to kick the predecessor," as he thought Kennedy had done to [Dwight] Eisenhower in saying, "A torch has been passed to a new generation." He wanted to be very careful that he did not insult Johnson in any way.

Anderson: The first line in Carter's inaugural is, "For myself and our nation, I want to thank my predecessor for all he has done to heal our land," which was rather gracious, and it got him off to a good start, I think.

Baer: In terms of the stagecraft of these various presidential speeches, it is arguable that the physical audience matters the least for an inaugural address than for any other kind of speech. There's less opportunity, or need, for that matter, to play off of the audience that is there, including the people who are standing behind you.

In the state of the union, you have the vice president and the Speaker of the House behind you, and depending on who those are, there could be things that need to be done. There are facial expressions that one has to be careful about. But in the words of Kennedy's inaugural, "Let the word go forth." This speech is very much about projection and broadcast to a much wider audience. At the same time, with inaugural addresses, depending on what has happened from the standpoint of politics, you can have a very interesting collection of people on whom the cameras will now be focused. So of course Bob Dole was there on the stage in 1997, as was Newt Gingrich. I think that creates some concern or sensitivity about how the words are put together.

Anderson: If you recall Kennedy's inaugural address, when he and [Theodore] Sorensen were working on it, Kennedy said, "This is getting too long. Why don't we just cut all this domestic stuff?" Which they did. "Let the word go forth . . ." is a speech to the world saying we're going to be strong, and we're going to be tough, and we're not afraid of anybody, and so forth. If you had domestic concerns, you had to wait for a later speech.

Baer: I want to come back to this question of the balance between the thematic and the programmatic, because I don't want to leave the wrong impression. I think speechwriters find out very quickly—although inaugural addresses are, perhaps, special challenges in this respect—that writing only about the thematic can leave the listeners pretty empty. The concrete and specific do come into play in very important ways. I hope we're not just referencing back to Sorensen's 1961 work the whole morning here, but if you think about that speech in particular, it's a very specific speech with a great deal of very concrete and focused policy woven into it. I think we've all struggled with that challenge. You want to make sure that everyone understands precisely what you're talking about even as you're trying to frame it in language that is more inspirational for the country.

Jones: I've wondered whether the second address tends to be more programmatic because it's about continuity. There has been an affirmation in the reelection, so there is some attention to the continuity of the administration.

Baer: In the case of the one I worked on, we might have been better off if we had been more specific. We were very mindful that not two weeks later we were going to do the first state of the union address of the second term. There was a bit of a conscious, though not completely conscious, effort to separate some of the theme from the program, knowing that we were trying to set up something broader and more inspirational to the nation in the first speech, and that we would be coming back with a very focused agenda in the second one.

Jones: Who should write the speech?

Anderson: The president should, as much as he is able and willing to. The more of him that is in it, the better it is. But writers do have a role in it.

Jones: Who should assist him then?

Anderson: Us!

Baer: *Only* us! [*laughter*] All the better if it could be only us, but it doesn't always work out that way.

Jones: I remember in Lou Cannon's book that he describes Ken Khachigian's selection as a speechwriter.[15] Clearly there was a process for doing it, and he describes what characteristics the person ought to have. You can say,

"Well, I have these fine personal characteristics," but is there some decision making that goes on in choosing who will assist the president in this first, absolutely crucial, speech?

Baer: I have to confess that I am a bit of a fraud here because I wasn't technically called a speechwriter at the time of the inaugural that I worked on. I was the White House communications director and therefore part of dreaded management, as compared to being one of the lofty speechwriters. But having been the head of speechwriting before and having been a writer and editor in any event, I always remained pretty heavily involved in the speeches, much to the chagrin of the speechwriters sometimes. I believe there is a sorting out that goes on over time, and by the time you get to the inaugural address, the president or president-elect has a pretty good idea of who he or she wants to work with, feels comfortable with, and can throw ideas around with.

Jones: That's what I'm reaching for.

Price: I think so. The inaugural is a special kind of speech, and different writers have different skill sets and so forth. In our case, Nixon asked for recommendations from everybody on the staff, and outside, too. He got a lot of unsolicited ideas pouring in for things that might be in the inaugural. But on the first one, it was made clear from the outset that I would be the one working with him on it. But again, with him it was always a collaborative thing. It was not that I was writing *for* him; I was writing *with* him, or helping him write.

Anderson: With Carter, I had much more of an impact on the acceptance speech, and that was more of a group process. I was involved in the early parts of the inaugural, but at some point he took it over. It's a very personal speech. It had things in it that I might not have suggested, but it was very personal with him.

Price: I might add one little color postscript on the first inaugural. Nixon and I had been working on it for a long time, back and forth. Finally the inauguration was on a Monday. We were going to fly down to Washington on Sunday. On Saturday night we worked in his transition office in New York until about midnight. By midnight he felt that we finally had it right.

There was one bottle of Heineken in his refrigerator. So he got that out and we shared the bottle of Heineken. [*laughter*] Then Rose Mary Woods, his longtime secretary, and I walked him around the corner to his home, and I went home, and I figured we'd done it.[16] But then the next morning my phone rang. He had had a couple more thoughts to help the opening. We worked those back and forth through about three or four phone calls, and it was finally done.

Baer: Again, I didn't work on President Clinton's first inaugural, but I remember an encounter with the people who were working on it, and it involves the very city we're in right now: Charlottesville, Virginia. I was a journalist at *U.S. News & World Report*, and I had spent some time covering the Clinton campaign in '91 and '92. If you remember, in early '93, just before the inauguration, the Clinton entourage began its movement into the capital from here in Charlottesville with an event at Mr. Jefferson's home.[17] I drove from Washington down here, and I hooked up with the Clinton campaign. I remember we drove around to one of the hotels in the downtown area here, which is where everyone was overnighting before the events. Then we drove the bus tour into Washington.

Here I encountered the two people who had the principal responsibility for working with the president on the speech. One was David Kusnet, who was the chief speechwriter through the campaign and was the chief speechwriter for the first year and a half or so in the Clinton White House.[18] The other was Michael Waldman.[19] It was the second time I'd met Michael Waldman, who was not a speechwriter at the time. He was a policy person, a very smart one, and a very good writer. The two of them were working on the speech, and I remember standing in the lobby of this hotel, and the elevator opened up and these two fellows stumbled out. They needed some fresh air because they had been locked away somewhere upstairs in the hotel working on this speech. This was barely forty-eight hours before it was to be delivered.

I will tell you, remembering that Michael Waldman had been involved in that was one of the things that led me to want him to be my successor when I became communications director, because I knew he knew how to deal with the pressures of these kinds of things.

Anderson: Chuck, you asked earlier about personal touches in the speeches. Carter, after thanking [Gerald] Ford for his role, the next thing in his inaugural address was a quotation from his high school teacher, Ms. Julia Coleman. She was a very old lady at that point. She had written him a letter, and he gave it to me and said, "Read through this and see what you see." There was a line in there in which she said, "We must adjust to changing times and still hold to unchanging principles." I thought that was a nice line, and I thought it would be nice to quote his high school teacher, so we put that in there. I thought it was a good touch.[20] A little later he had a line, which I take to be pure Carter—it certainly wasn't me—speaking to the people, "Your strength can compensate for my weakness, and your wisdom can help to minimize my mistakes." I would have argued against that line. I thought it was giving away too much. He went on. There were a lot of personal touches.

Jones: You started to talk about process. Let's talk about it more specifically, the process of constructing the speech, including the relationship with the president-elect and how that interaction goes.

Baer: Ray talked about how President Nixon sought out advice or offered the opportunity for input from outside people. For all of these big speeches, the state of the union and then for the inaugural, we always sought out advice and counsel from a fairly wide circle of people: authors, former speechwriters, typically Democrats.

Jones: Was that on your initiative or—?

Baer: By the time I got there, it was so ingrained. I started in 1994, and it had been done repeatedly already. I don't remember whether he asked for it or whether it was an established part of the process from one White House to another at that point. But we would put together a book, a binder of these various memos that had come in, and we would highlight some of the ideas that we thought might work. Then we'd give that to the president in order to provoke thoughts and whatnot. Of course any number of things would come in over the transom in the Clinton White House. Our president had his own outreach that sometimes we didn't know about. Part of the trick was to bring that into the circle as much as possible so that we could help to control it, at least to understand what the thoughts were and where they were coming from. You typically start as far out in advance with these things as you can.[21]

I think something that already has been alluded to here is very important, which is that it is hard to imagine just how exhausting it is to work in a White House and what the pace is like. Then you add on top of that a reelection campaign, which is pretty enervating in its own right. All of those things taken together make it difficult to create a second inaugural. You don't get the opportunity of a full halt after a reelection any more than you do after an election.

But added to the burdens of transition—because there is a transition from the first to the second term—is the fact that you're still governing every day.[22] It's very difficult to find the moment to pause and step aside to think through what is, in some respects, one of the most important addresses that any one of these people will ever make, to build a process that helps you do that while you're also churning out the daily speeches, and to put some people on the side to think about it some more. And finding some side time to think about it with the president can be even more difficult. But we tried to do that. The process begins to break down the closer and closer you get to the speech. I laugh; it's almost ludicrous to think about the process. There were some long nights of the soul in the four or five days leading up to the speech.

I'll tell one anecdote and then I'll let the others speak. You do get a lot of quasi-advisors who get brought in or who come into the process. President Clinton had a number of friends who were good writers in their own right who wanted to be around this. They recognized that it was history. They wanted to make sure that he put his best foot forward. One of them, quite a renowned writer in his own right, while searching around for themes that we ought to be throwing into this, threw out—not with the president but with others of us down in my office in the West Wing—"How about the 'New Freedom'? Let's make this the 'New Freedom.'" He had, I think, three or four days before the speech, an elaborate way of how the New Freedom would roll out. We all nodded and said okay. Michael Waldman pulled me aside and said, "You have to tell him that that was Woodrow Wilson's theme," which I did.[23] [laughter]

Anderson: I'll tell you a little bit about the process with Carter. It began in December. We talked about the speech, and he said that he had been reading the earlier inaugurals. He thought that Wilson's first and Kennedy's were the best. He thought his speech should be a relatively brief statement, which it was; it's about 1,200 words. He said it should reflect the themes of the campaign, which I certainly agreed with. I wrote him a draft and sent it down to Plains around the first of the year, and then I went down shortly after the first of the year.

He had taken my draft and had used it as the basis for his own draft, and he made quite a few major changes, which was fine. My idea had been that, given the nature of his campaign, "the people" should be the theme. "I went to the people. I listened to the people. The people have spoken," etc. My opening line was, "Once again the people have spoken." He had cut that and added a new opening, which I did not like at all. Let me quote it here: "I have just taken the oath of office on a Bible my mother gave to me many years ago, opened to an admonition and a promise from God to King Solomon, still applicable to our people, our leaders, and our great nation: 'If my people, which are called by my name, shall humble themselves and pray and seek my face and turn from their wicked ways, then I will hear from heaven and will forgive their sin and heal their land.'"[24]

It sounded to me like he was confusing himself with King Solomon and perhaps with God, and I thought it was an utterly inappropriate quotation. So I sent him a memo in which I said, "I liked the opening reference to the Bible, but I question whether that particular biblical quotation is appropriate. It could be interpreted as your suggesting that the American people humble themselves and turn from their wicked ways and their sins. But you've been arguing all along that the government was bad and that the people were good." So I sent him that memo, and I went over to his house that night. He read the memo while I sat there, and finally he looked up and said, "Pat, you don't like my biblical quotation." I said, "No, sir, I don't think it's the right one." He looked at me in some dismay and started talking about Christians and original sin and explained that no reasonable person could possibly misunderstand that quotation. I said, "It's your speech, but I would recommend against it."

Eventually two things happened. One, I was leaving the campaign at that point, and I was not involved in later drafts. Other people, and I think Jody Powell was probably the central one, convinced him not to use that quotation, that it was the wrong quotation. So he didn't. He substituted a totally okay quotation from another part of the Bible.[25] But two or three weeks after he was inaugurated, Carter went to a prayer breakfast with religious leaders, and he got up and used that quotation and said, "My staff wouldn't let me use that. I still think I should have."

Jones: Do you know whether he was aware that Eisenhower wrote a prayer and began his first inaugural with a prayer?[26]

Anderson: We did not discuss it, but he said he'd read all the previous ones, so he must have known that.

Jones: I'm not sure that any other president was inaugurated by forming his own prayer, which is a little surprising.

Anderson: There was much to pray about.

Jones: Eisenhower had had experiences in which prayer was probably pretty important.[27]

Nelson: Patrick mentioned that President Carter was able to keep the speech short. With state of the unions, everybody says they are too long, but they end up being long anyway. With inaugural addresses, they come out short. How is that discipline maintained, keeping it from becoming a forty-minute address with lots of applause lines and the other things that make state of the unions longer than anybody thinks they should be?

Price: I think one of the key differences is that the state of the union is essentially a programmatic speech, whereas the inaugural is essentially a ceremonial speech with a programmatic content. You're suggesting the direction that you want to go, but you're not detailing those directions. Whereas in the state of the union, you're telling Congress what you want to do for the coming year. I'm thinking aloud, but I think that probably lends itself to a longer speech and to the expectation of something longer.

There was one thing I would like to throw in that I didn't mention before when we were talking about the first inaugural. I think it made ours a little different. A lot of people today forget it. I've talked before about our inheriting the legacy of the 1960s, which I consider the second most disastrous decade in American history. But just a couple of things to put that time into a perspective, which most people today are no longer aware of. This is something I sometimes use when I'm talking to a group. I tell them that I'm going to ask a question, I give them a moment to think, and then I ask them for a show of hands on a range of numbers.

The question is, what would be your guess is the combined number of completed bombings, attempted bombings, and bomb threats in the U.S. during our first sixteen months in office? That's January of '69 to April of '70.[28] I throw out numbers like 1 to 10, 10 to 30, 30 to 50. By the time I get up to 200–300, there are very few hands. The answer was 14,000. There were 14,000 actual bombings, attempted bombings, and bomb threats in those sixteen months. That was just part of the culture of the 1960s.[29] In the inaugural parade, Nixon's car was pelted with rocks and bottles from the sides of the street.[30] That was the climate in which we came in and against which he had to speak in his first inaugural.

Baer: Were you thinking about that climate as you wrote?

Price: We were. Basically he was trying to bring peace to a troubled land, and he made that explicit. He was trying to bring peace to a troubled world, but also bring peace to a troubled land. That was one of the principal themes. The country was absolutely tearing itself apart. Also in the 1960s, it became fashionable to set whole sections of cities afire. People tend to forget that. In one day in New York alone, there were 400 bomb threats. That's what we were coming into.

Jones: Clark Judge, in an article—I think it was in the *Wall Street Journal*—suggested that speechwriters learn to hear the voice of the president, fitting their words in along the way.[31] I thought that was an interesting characterization of how you go at writing a speech for someone else. Can you talk about that relationship, and about how you came to know the president well enough to make these words credible from his standpoint and from the standpoint of the whole campaign and of the people listening?

Baer: I think you typically hear those voices even in the middle of the night when you're trying to sleep. But I agree with Clark—it has to become almost second nature to you. I think it's clearly something you learn over time, but it's also a hard thing to learn. It's much better if you start with a level of sympathy. It is a kind of merger, a blending of a political sympathy in terms of what the president is trying to do for the nation and with the nation from a political standpoint. But I think it is also a personal sympathy. Writing for someone else, in that person's voice, is about as personal an act as you can imagine, aside from things that we shouldn't talk about here.

Remember, again, that I was brought into the Clinton White House early in 1994, so the presidency had been ongoing for a little over a year. I had never been a speechwriter before. In fact that's one of my little side stories. I was asked very late in the job interview process, by someone, impertinently, "Have you ever written a speech before?" The only answer I could give was "No." But I had written a lot *about* President Clinton, and I had spent a lot of time with him when then-governor Clinton was a candidate, writing about things and talking with him about things that were very personal.[32] I was the first journalist he ever talked to about the violence in his household when he was growing up, things that became somewhat mythic in the Clinton world. We talked a lot about those things and about his religion and various things like that. That gave me a little bit better sense of his voice when he wasn't in a public setting. I thought it was useful. I was from North Carolina; he was from Arkansas. So there was a sense of a new-southern perspective that we shared.

I remember going in to the White House that I was advised by David Gergen, another former speechwriter and communications director who was then working for Clinton, that I'd better ask for and get some time alone with the president, without any other aides around, in order to talk with him about what he wanted from speechwriting.[33] There had been some concern that maybe he wasn't getting what he wanted through the speechwriting process. So I asked for that. [Thomas] Mack McLarty, who was the chief of staff, graciously allowed me to come in on a Saturday morning, into the Oval Office with the president, and we talked.[34] I asked him, "What do you want from your speechwriters?" The point of the story is he said, "I have no idea. Up until a year and a half ago, I never had a speechwriter." When he had been governor, he never had a speechwriter on staff. He did all this work himself. Those words were personal.

Nowadays in the modern White House, it takes a fairly large team of writers to understand that voice and to be able to capture it and reproduce it.[35] Inaugural addresses are one thing, but presidents are now giving 400–500 speeches a year. To be able to bottle that and to make sure that it is always coming through becomes a much more difficult process.

In any event, I think the president's voice is something you learn as you read and you listen. A lot of times, the off-the-record remarks that these people make are even more important than those they make on the record. You go back and you study it. You try to pull forward sentences and words and different ways that they convey things, and you help others understand that. But at the end of the day you have to have what I would think of as a natural sympathy with what they're trying to talk about and with who they are in order to do that.

Edmonds: Clinton was also a student of the Bible and of religion. One of the reasons that I think I resonated with him was that I also was raised in the church.[36] We worked well together on those types of speeches. He also had a strong affinity and concern for racial issues, for racial harmony, the whole "One America" theme.[37] When I joined the staff, I worked more closely with him on those speeches because I also had an interest in the civil rights movement and that kind of thing. I think each speechwriter brought something different to the process, and they resonated in different ways with the president.

Baer: I think that's correct.

Anderson: When I joined the Carter campaign in May of '76, he had been campaigning for more than a year. He had a basic stump speech, which I had heard as a journalist in '75 and had heard again when I joined him. You may recall that there were some famous lines in there. There was, "I'll never tell a lie," and "We need a government as good as our people," and various other lines.[38] I thought it was wonderful. I thought it was a great speech, and I thought it worked. It touched people's mood at that moment in history. I thought it was very nice. But by the time I was brought aboard, he had lost a couple of primaries, and they were getting worried. My mandate was to come up with something new.

I came up with "I see an America that does this," and "I see an America that does that." If anything, I would say it was Kennedy-esque rhetoric as opposed to the rather different rhetoric that Carter had been using. So I wasn't adapting myself to him; I was giving him something I thought might be useful to him. He delivered it in one speech, and it won a lot of praise in the newspapers. So when we made the acceptance speech, that was central to the ending in the speech.

In general, anytime I could come up with a phrase or something that I knew he'd like to say, some southern expression that would fit in, that was great. I'd use that when I could. But in general, my approach with him and with other people I'd written for was that if you just give them simple English that is intelligent and inspirational, it's like an actor reading his lines:

they will use it and make it theirs. I think a good speaker will take basic English and make something good out of it.

Jones: Ray?

Price: No thoughts in particular, just again that I dealt principally with Nixon, who was a very accomplished speaker for many years before I met him. He did it simply as part of his life. He would adapt things, but as I've so often said, with him it was not so much writing for him as writing with him. He was very much a part of the process. Again, about nineteen out of twenty of his speeches were not written; only about one out of twenty was.

Jones: It occurred to me that there probably is a difference between a great speech and a speech that is suited to the president or the president-elect. Is that right?

Price: I think probably so. There are presidents for whom something that might be good for somebody else would just not fit. With Nixon, I've often said that I had been a professional writer, but he taught me speechwriting as a special form of the craft. There was some long, patient tutoring—sometimes a little impatient. But he could curb his impatience pretty well. It worked out. Basically I was writing in his idiom when I was writing for him.

Jones: I thought of that when I read in manuscript a short book that Steve Hess is doing, a briefing book for the transition period for the president.[39] He evaluates a number of inaugural addresses there. In regard to George [W.] Bush's first inaugural address, he says, "It was a great speech—for some other president." It seems to me that there is a fitting to the person that has to go on.

Anderson: When we were working on the acceptance speech and we were going through various drafts and slowly getting what we wanted, we had some informal advisors who were not our people. The one I'm thinking of was a Kennedy person, but he was giving us advice now and then. He despaired that Jimmy Carter would ever be able to deliver an acceptance speech that would be listenable. At one point he came up with the suggestion that maybe we should not have an acceptance speech, but that he should have an interview, perhaps, with some journalists, a panel or something. Happily we ignored his advice, and it was an extremely successful acceptance speech because he got the speech he wanted through his own process.

Jones: How important is delivery, and does that affect how you write and what you're saying?

Baer: I'm of the mind that it's extremely important, especially with this speech, because it is delivered outdoors in a big open-air setting, as large a one as any human being ever speaks at. The impact of the words is very different. You don't get applause. These are politicians, after all. They are used to speaking to large crowds of people who give them back the love. You don't get that at an inaugural, because you cannot hear any of the applause. You don't know what the reaction is in that rather large "room." So it is difficult. To reveal some of the tricks of the trade, you help coach and train the president to deliver it well to a very different kind of audience. But it is very difficult to give that coaching and training because there is almost nothing else like it.

It is also quite often the case—and this is where there is a bit of a risk, because I'm sure every president or president-elect who is about to give an inaugural address reads every one of the predecessors' remarks—that written words in this context often play very differently than spoken words. I think that makes it much more challenging to pull one of these off well.

Price: That difference you mentioned about the written word and the spoken word is too little understood and needs to be stressed. The written word and the spoken word are very different. Also with a speech, you have to keep the audience awake.

Baer: Right, and this difference was probably the hardest thing for me to get used to because I was a magazine writer, so I very much worked in the context of the read word rather than the spoken word. Not to get too much into it, but the transitions are completely different. Every convention that we think about in terms of what works well in writing has to be rethought when you're dealing with the spoken word—nowhere more so, I think, than in an inaugural address. On Ray's point, even if they're longish, they have to move very quickly to work well. There's not a lot of dwelling on themes or subthemes and dealing with them for very long. They are almost a string of epigrams that are put together and that move along very quickly.

Anderson: I was certainly aware with Carter that Carter was good for Carter. He had his own style, but he was not the orator that Reagan was or that Kennedy was, and that was sometimes frustrating. Sometimes he would make unfortunate slips, like in the acceptance speech, he referred to "our I-talian cousins." It was disturbing to some people, mainly to the "I-talians," that he put it that way.[40]

Nelson: Ray Price mentioned earlier that inaugural addresses have a sacramental quality. It made me think that the inaugural address is a ten- or fifteen-minute part of a great inaugural ceremony, which in some cases begins before the day of the inauguration, as when Clinton and [Albert] Gore [Jr.] made that trek from Charlottesville to Washington. But the address is preceded by a prayer, by the oath taking.[41] After the address comes the parade and the balls. I wonder, as you all were participating in the writing of inaugural addresses, were you thinking of yourselves as contributing to a larger theme for the launch of the presidency?

Price: In my case, I doubt that I was. I recognized that the speech would be a part of it, but that it was a distinct part, a substantive part, that included not only detail but also direction and so on. It was the substantive part of the entire inaugural event—the inaugural event including all the inaugural balls and everything else afterward. It is a grand ceremonial occasion. But this is the centerpiece of that.

Baer: We very much were thinking about the larger audience. Again, as the communications director, a big chunk of my job was to work on the orchestration of these many pieces of the puzzle, not just during the inaugural focus itself, but for about a monthlong period from the holidays in 1996 through the state of the union address. I'd say we were more or less successful. The theme of it was the notion of repairing the breach and bringing the country back together again after the difficulties of 1995. The president was determined to achieve a bipartisan balanced budget in the course of that first year of the Congress. He felt that part of the reason he had been reelected was to deal with Social Security in a bipartisan way, which was not accomplished, and with a number of other things. It was going to require people to work together more rather than to be at odds with one another.

You may remember that one of the things we did in the period between the inaugural address and the state of the union address was to announce the World War II memorial that was to be started on the National Mall, at the White House, with Bob Dole present.[42] Of course Dole was one of the principal representatives of the "Greatest Generation" in Congress at that time, and this announcement was a way to kind of bring them back together after the election. That was meant to be symbolic as well as concrete. There were some other things along those lines that we were trying to do. So while we didn't come up with anything that was particularly symbolic in that respect in that twenty-four-hour period, we certainly were thinking about the inaugural in the context of the whole.

One of the lines in President Clinton's inaugural address was, "Nothing big ever came from being small," which I allowed into the speech. I got a lot of guff from my colleagues for allowing it. It was the president's line. He loved it. I thought it was fine. Many of them thought it was trite, but it was in there. The point being, we needed to rise above some of these petty differences.

Going back to something that Patrick talked about before, I think that Jimmy Carter getting out of the car with Rosalynn on the day of the inaugural was as important as any words he spoke. Now every president has to do it. So there is an accretion of symbolic acts that have taken place over time.

Anderson: I think I was working on two levels. You are aware of history, and you are aware that you will be judged against the great speeches of the past. But at a more immediate level, you're thinking, *My God, how can I take all this material and boil it down to 1,000 or 1,500 words?* It's a very great challenge.

Jones: I have a final question before we open it up to the other folks here: How does the president react after the address? Happy? Sad? Anticlimactic? Or is there no time because there are so many other things going on?

Anderson: Carter had no reason to be anything but very happy after the speech and after the walk down the street and entering the White House. It was the greatest day of his life. I think that was an easy one. The second inaugural might be a more difficult situation, but he should have been very happy.

Baer: Of course you have parties and everything. Presidents have to go to the reviewing stand and stand around in very cold weather for many hours looking like they're enjoying themselves. In the case of President Clinton, I think he loved every bit of it. At the time—and I think it reads much better than it was received at the time—President Clinton's second inaugural address was very badly received by the instant critics whom we have now on cable television all over the place. I can remember, in particular, Chris Matthews, who I think wrote Rose Garden speeches for President Carter, savaged the speech, disliked it intensely.[43] Peggy Noonan disliked it.[44] There's a little cottage industry now of all of our brothers and sisters who get to go out there and trash the next president's speeches once they've gotten through their gauntlet. It was badly received.

I called the president, who was in the residence. He was back there changing before he went out to some of the balls that night. I said, "It's not being well received. I think it is going to play better over time once people read it. I think they will understand it, and we're just going to move on. I'm sorry for you. I wanted this to work for you."[45] He said, "I'm sorry for you. I wanted it to work for you," which was an interesting thing. It's a sign of the bond that we had established, and I think that he had established, as Terry pointed out, with a number of his writers. He knew that we all cared together about these words and about the impact that they should have. So that is just one very personal reaction.

Jones: I particularly want to hear from Ken Khachigian on this.

Khachigian: The critics of the inaugural speeches usually have never written one—or have never written a good one—so I wouldn't ever worry about that. It's a daunting task, obviously. I was nervous when I got the assignment. I probably didn't know any better, especially because it was for Ronald Reagan, who was such a gifted speaker, so the standards were high. I did two things. I read all the inaugural addresses—and after reading [Abraham] Lincoln's second, I should have stopped there and turned the assignment over to someone else. It is so dramatically poetic and excruciatingly well written, you can't come up to that standard.[46] The second thing I did was to reach out to my colleagues, like Ray and Lee and Bill Gavin and Noel Koch and others from the Nixon administration, for help and ideas, many of which got into the speech.[47]

I want to talk about the audience you write for. Something shameless we did for the Reagan inaugural—not that I'm embarrassed about it, but it was still shameless. Nevertheless, it was the first time in history that the inaugural was given from the west front of the Capitol instead of from the east front. Of course the symbolism, the metaphorical nature of it, was that

Reagan was from California and that his looking from east to west was good. But also, as you sat on the presidential platform, and because it was wintertime, the trees weren't in the way, and you could see all the monuments.[48]

The thematic end of the speech was based on the great monuments that we have to great presidents: [George] Washington, Lincoln, and [Thomas] Jefferson. Noel Koch, I must say, provided some wonderful rhetoric about those monuments and those presidents. Beyond those monuments was the Arlington Cemetery, which made room for a wonderful story that the president brought to the speech. I tipped off our TV media people, Mark Goode, at the time.[49] I gave them an advance copy the night before and I said, "You might want to position these cameras while the president is speaking, because he's going to start mentioning these monuments." If they hadn't had this advance notice, the camera positions wouldn't have been there. As I watched the tape of the speech later, I saw that, as Reagan would mention one of the monuments and say, for instance, "President George Washington, upon whose shoulders America stands," the camera would show the Washington Monument and then fade back.[50] Of course there was no way to capture the Arlington Cemetery from the Capitol, so there had to be a camera positioned pretty much out there. It made for an extremely dramatic television address.

In terms of the audience, remember it's cold, so everybody is wearing gloves, so when they clap, it's always muffled. You don't count on that. There was another little twist to the speech. He had a little insert of his own that if the hostages were released on Inauguration Day, he was going to get a signal, and then he was going to announce to the country that the hostages were released. That's the only part I argued with him about. I said it would interrupt the historical quality of the speech, that he could easily do something about that after the speech. It wouldn't fit into the nature of the inaugural address. But had they been released during that speech and had he gotten that signal, he would have read that insert.[51]

There wasn't much collaboration after we went through all this and after I talked to him and after there was a draft. He wasn't crazy about his first draft. He thought it was a little too flowery. He wanted more meat and potatoes and basics. At that point he took it, and when he flew back to Washington, he basically edited, rewrote, redrafted, and made it his own speech. After that, with the exception of that anecdote about Martin Treptow, I didn't have much more to say about the speech. I just had to correct a little fact.

Huebner: Did it get corrected? As I recall, it was a question of where this person was buried and whether the grave was at Arlington.

Khachigian: It was a story given to him by a friend of his, Pres [Preston] Hotchkis,[52] and it was about Martin Treptow, who was a young enlisted man in World War I who kept a diary about how intensely he would go through the struggle and devote himself to it. It was very strong. As the president finished talking about Arlington Cemetery, he said, "And under one such marker lies Martin Treptow." Then he told the story. First of all I had to find out if there was an enlisted man named Martin Treptow in the First World War. We confirmed that. Then we had to find out where he was buried. It turned out he was buried in Wisconsin.[53] [*laughter*]

Baer: Did you move him? [*laughter*]

Khachigian: That alternative was considered. [*laughter*] After all, we had all of the military at our command at that point. So I went back and told Governor Reagan about this. He didn't react. I said, "We're going to have to amend that." He didn't react. Basically he wasn't going to change it, because it would change the drama of his story. Ronald Reagan obviously understood the theater of big speeches. So I struggled with the integrity of the speech, and I came up with the resolution by saying, "Under one *such* marker" lies Martin Treptow. So I had to talk the president into changing that little bit of the line. I told him that they would immediately go look for where Martin Treptow was buried. They would want to know if it was a true story. So it survived, and it helped the beauty of the conclusion of that speech.

Ray, this is a good time to thank you publicly for one of the lines that has endured in that speech, where Ronald Reagan said, "This time government is not the solution, but government is the problem."[54] It is an oft-quoted line from the speech, so due credit at this point.

Shapiro: Hearing about the acoustical challenges of an inaugural address, I realized that after Clinton's first inaugural address, in my journalistic guise, I had a long talk with Taylor Branch, who had spent a lot of time with Bill Clinton on or about the first inaugural.[55] There's nothing like remembering an interview without having looked at it in fifteen years and then citing it, so there may be a few inaccuracies here. But I remember Taylor saying in essence that the president was startled by the lack of feedback from the audience, because Mr. Khachigian had moved the speech to the west front of the Capitol. Also, nothing had prepared Bill Clinton for the fact that most of the audience, because we had moved to the west front of the Capitol, was far beneath him. So it was a very strange thing. Also, as I recall from this interview, he was buffaloed by the echoes he was getting back, which was something, again, that an entire presidential campaign does not prepare you for.

Baer: Four years later—that was what I was alluding to, all of those things. For Bill Clinton at least, that setting was the least suited to his great skills, because he knew how to work a crowd and how to draw from that crowd.

Judge: I'd like to make a couple of observations and ask a question. The first observation is, I did some television commentary at the time of the second Clinton inaugural, and I thought it was a good speech.

Baer: I didn't see you!

Judge: I thought it was a good speech, and I thought the theme, particularly of racial reconciliation, was an outstanding one for a president at that time and for Clinton in particular. There was some question about delivery. I'm sure Peter Robinson and Ken can reflect on this, too. I was a speechwriter for Ronald Reagan and I saw Ronald Reagan deliver speeches where I put in paragraphs that I thought had a clear, specific meaning. And yet when they came out of his mouth, the words were the same, but the meaning had changed. A phrase appeared in the speech, and he teased out a different meaning, and he had infused it through his delivery. That may have been peculiar to Reagan.

Jones: Can you give an example of that?

Judge: No.

Robinson: I can.

Anderson: Are you saying he improved—?

Judge: The meaning was different. It was appropriate. It was, in some ways, better. I guess what I'm saying is that he had the capacity to edit through delivery. It wasn't a requirement that we change the words.

Let me make an observation, and then I think Peter ought to pick up on that observation, which is an historical observation. If you look at inaugural addresses from FDR's first to the most recent one, you find that FDR's first two were domestic and then, with World War II coming, were global and then remained global for every presidential inaugural from then until JFK. They are all international. Then LBJ becomes domestic, and it is domestic through the first inaugural address of the current president [George W. Bush]. Of course the current president's second inaugural was totally international. It says something about the times, the world of the Cold War, the balance of priorities in the country, but also, in the domestic period, it was a more divisive period. With that in mind, I'd like your comments.

Robinson: This is a very small example of the way President Reagan could change the meaning in the course of delivery. Legislation passed on some form of reparations. I can't remember the bill, I can't remember the formal name, but it was reparations of some kind for Japanese Americans who had been interned during the Second World War. I wrote the speech. Two facts about it stand out in my mind. One is that there were a number of Japanese names, and after every name we put in its phonetic spelling. The second was that I found Ronald Reagan, on the record, early in the '40s, as having opposed these internments.

As the president was giving this speech before an audience of Japanese Americans—it was in Room 450, that top room in the Old EOB [Executive Office Building]—he stumbled over every Japanese name. He was conscious that he was stumbling. As he continued, he was beginning to establish such a rapport, you could feel it. They were mostly his generation. They were older people, and you could feel that they'd been through this large experience of the Second World War together. I began to sense that having him quote himself to these people was going to be too self-congratulatory. "I got it right way back when," was certainly what I had in mind when I wrote it, but I could feel that it was going to be wrong as I was listening to him deliver it.

Then he came to the passage and said, "There was one person back in 1945 who disagreed with what had taken place, and gee, I hope I can pronounce this name correctly. Ronald Reagan." Of course it was perfect. He was mocking his mispronunciations. It was relaxed. It got a laugh and applause. Every so often I was given to the temptation that besets all speechwriters, which is to think, *I'm doing a pretty good job putting the words in that fellow's mouth.* Then just often enough there would be an event like that, at which you would say, "Boy, is he good."[56]

Judge: Before this is all done, we each ought to see if we can give, in our man's voice [*imitating Reagan*], a few lines. [*laughter*] I'm sure you can do Clinton.

Baer: I can, but it would be like a bad Leslie Nielsen movie. [*laughter*]

Khachigian: May I make a couple of observations? One is general about the inaugural address, and one is specific about President Reagan. One thing that struck me about reading all the inaugural addresses is that they are a history of America. You can go through, beginning with Washington, and you can learn all about the country just by reading them. If you did nothing else, you'd know almost all about the history of the Civil War, about the Depression, about World War I, about World War II, and about the Vietnam War. It's fascinating. If you sometime want some history students to get a quick lesson, have them read all of the inaugural addresses.

Second, a little story about Reagan and his lack of ego. When we sat down to begin to look at the address, at the very beginning of it, he handed me several index cards from his old speeches, which obviously helped guide the process tremendously. There was a wastebasket in a little cluttered room we had because they were moving. There was a wastebasket full of 3-by-5 cards. There must have been hundreds of them. He said, "One of the good things about moving is that you get rid of stuff you don't need."

I said, "Governor, you're going to be president of the United States. We're going to rescue every one of those because every one of those is history." I went outside and had someone salvage these hundreds and hundreds of index cards, all in his own writing, all from old speeches going back to the '40s. They probably made their way into Marty Anderson's book somehow.[57] But he had no self-image. To him it was just old stuff he had to get rid of.

Nelson: We heard earlier about the difference between writing for the ear and writing for the eye, between spoken prose and written prose. I wonder what you speechwriters get out of reading the inaugural addresses of the pre-radio era, which were pretty much written for the eye. Lincoln's second inaugural was not meant so much for the audience there, who were surely disappointed by it, but for the many people who would read it in the news-paper the next day. What do you get out of reading those old inaugurals that helps you write a twentieth- or twenty-first-century inaugural?

Baer: Lincoln's second is a poem. It's almost written as a poem, with ca-dence and rhythms that are built into it. I think that is one of the reasons that it resonates to this day as a written product. Many of the others were written as reports, in the same way that state of the union addresses were just written reports.

Jones: Kennedy's came close to it.

Baer: It's poetic. That goes back to my point about the epigrammatic quality of some of the better ones: they are almost couplets that are strung together and fashioned together for those that work the best. It's harder to get prac-tical politicians to feel comfortable with that during this most important moment.

Judge: If I could weigh in to second that: if you read Eisenhower's first and then Kennedy's, the themes and points they make are very similar. There are some elements in Eisenhower's that directly track Kennedy's. But one is remembered and one isn't. The distinction is that Kennedy's is such a mag-nificent piece of small literature and theater and the spoken word. Eisen-hower's, much like Eisenhower himself, is more "Well, here it is."

Baer: I'm not going to answer your question directly, but in hearing all this and thinking about it, there are other national communal moments that have come to take on greater meaning, even in the last, say, twenty to twenty-five years. The state of the union address, I think, is one of them, which didn't play much of that role until Ronald Reagan, for the most part. We have had episodic experiences: Lyndon Johnson's speech on civil rights to the Con-gress and George Bush after September 11, and other such opportunities.[58]

The state of the union has become one of those national communal mo-ments. You've talked about that before, and I have made this point before: in a nation and in a world that is moving so quickly and in which people are distracted so much, to have that one communal moment a year when the country comes together is one of the reasons why the length of these speeches doesn't matter anymore. The country actually craves it. We learned that our audience grew the longer the president went on, even though it filled me with shame that I would put him out there and he was going to go on for so long.

I think the inaugural address is the one communal national moment that we have had right along, throughout the entire history of the country. It has been done better or worse at different times. On Clark's point, it would be interesting to explore whether it's easier and more effective to talk about world affairs than domestic affairs for any of these presidents because of the naturally unifying role that that plays. But I would offer that it is a national catechism, tailored to the historical moment that the nation faces at any given point. That is its greatest purpose, as a national catechism.

I remember when we prepared for President Clinton a book, for which we pulled together a bunch of quotes. There was something in the *Wall Street Journal* about what worked and how history judged presidents and what worked in these inaugural addresses. Unfortunately I don't remember which historian said, "The ones that work the best are the ones in which a president is basically trying to inspire or reinspire the nation's faith in itself." At the core of the best of these, that is what it is about.

Huebner: In the long history of the inaugural address, the only president who addressed his speech to his fellow citizens of the world as well as to the American people was Nixon in 1969.[59] These speeches go back and forth, as Clark said, between being focused on the nation and the world. But even the world-oriented speeches are addressed to the American people, probably out of the sense of commitment and spirit that you just described. Nixon's preoccupation was with his role on a global stage, I think, and that was reflected in the opening lines of the address.

Price: He also saw that as the most important thing because the stakes were the greatest. A fair amount of the first inaugural was devoted to the foreign as well.

Khachigian: When a president comes in with a change of party, you can't separate the notion that there has to be a sea change in American politics and government and policy. Of course Reagan's first inaugural dealt with the fact that America's image was down because of the hostage situation in Iran and because of a terrible economy: inflation was at 11–12 percent, interest rates at 18–19 percent, unemployment in very high numbers. So while it is a cathedral event, there are politics, and politics becomes a great source of inspiration for the speech.

You can't be shy about changing the dynamics of the American government. That's why that first inaugural talked about being strong and tough and never surrendering to terrorism on the one hand, and on the other, about making a huge change in the nature of government: less government, lower taxes, and promises of a smaller, balanced budget, which never came about. Still, he had to make clear that there was going to be a change in America, just as Kennedy did in '60 and as Clinton did in his first inaugural.

By the second one, you don't have those elements. You're running against yourself. For President Reagan's second inaugural, it was an icy, frozen, cold day, and they had to move it into the Rotunda, and all the theater was taken away from it.[60]

Price: Incidentally, on Nixon's first inaugural, something that a lot of people may have forgotten is that we were then a nation at war. We had 570,000 troops fighting in Vietnam. There was no visible plan in place either to win it or to end it. Of course that was one of the key things tearing the country apart and also tearing the world apart.

Jones: I want to make a recommendation. If you have not read [James] Garfield's only inaugural address, I highly recommend you read it. The first half, perhaps even 60 percent, deals with integration following the Civil War. It remains one of the finest and clearly, for the time, bold statements regarding the need to integrate African Americans into American society. He acknowledged the point that in many local governments the argument was we should not integrate, because they are not educated enough, and democracy can't survive with uneducated voters. Garfield took that idea and said, "That's true. We need educated people. But that is not only true of African Americans." He used it to make the argument for the need for *universal* education, broadly educating. It makes you even more disturbed that James Garfield was assassinated, because it suggested a bold and effective president.[61]

Nelson: Great thanks to you, Chuck Jones, for guiding this discussion, and to Don Baer, Patrick Anderson, and Ray Price for contributing so much. Thanks also to others of you at the table, speechwriters in other administrations, for your insights.

Notes

1. These words are drawn from an interview Price gave (with Ted Sorensen) to the PBS program *NewsHour* in relation to President George W. Bush's first inauguration in 2001. See "The Speech: Inauguration 2001," available at http://www.pbs.org/newshour/inauguration/speech4.html.

2. The term "better angels" is taken from the conclusion of Abraham Lincoln's first inaugural address. That text can be found at http://millercenter.org/scripps/archive/speeches/detail/3512.

3. The text of Nixon's first inaugural can be seen at http://bartelby.org/124/pres58.html.

4. Texts of these two addresses are available at the Web site of the University of Virginia's Miller Center of Public Affairs, http://millercenter.org/scripps/archive/speeches.

5. Text also available at http://millercenter.org/scripps/archive/speeches.

6. The front page of the *Los Angeles Times* included a story (with photos) the next day (January 21, 1977) headlined, "Carter Takes It in Stride, Walks to the White House." Richard T. Cooper wrote, "Carter's decision to walk the entire parade route was as unexpected as it was dramatic. . . . Daughter Amy skipped along beside Carter and his wife, Rosalynn, most of the way but, apparently mindful of the nursery rhyme warning 'Step on a crack, break your mother's back,' she prudently hopped over all the lines in the Pennsylvania Avenue crosswalks" (1, 17).

7. Text available at http://millercenter.org/scripps/archive/speeches.

8. On the subject of broader themes in presidential rhetoric, but especially the inaugural address, see Colleen J. Shogan, *The Moral Rhetoric of American Presidents* (College Station: Texas A&M University Press, 2006).

9. Clinton's embrace of this rhetorical theme was occasioned by a perceived strategic error on the part of his campaign opponent in the 1996 presidential election. Republican senator Bob Dole, seeking to emphasize his formative experience as a World War II veteran, spoke at the Republican convention that year about the fabled America of his youth—and implored voters, "Let me be the bridge to an America that only the unknowing call myth. Let me be the bridge to a time of tranquility, faith, and confidence in action"—in other words, a bridge to the past. Clinton contrasted himself as the candidate of the future, eager to build a bridge to the twenty-first century. Dole's speech is available at http://www.pbs.org/newshour/convention96/floor_speeches/bob_dole.html, Clinton's at http://www.pbs.org/newshour/convention96/floor_speeches/clinton_8-29.html.

10. Much of the Clinton presidency was characterized by severe partisan conflict, some occasioned by policy differences (over such issues as gays in the military, health-care reform, and gun control); some by Clinton's personal history (avoidance of military service, alleged womanizing, and his marriage to a wife with an independent professional career); and some by the real prospects for changing partisan control of the government

in Washington (including Republican ascendancy in the House of Representatives after the 1994 midterm elections for the first time in forty years). The partisan divisions heightened in Clinton's second term, culminating in his impeachment in 1998.

11. Columnist Mark Shields has said that "the second inaugural speech is a speech writer's nightmare because you can't use the 'new' the same way. It isn't a new celebration of a different direction for the country. You have to take continuity and sort of make it into a form of renewal." See *"NewsHour* Special: Reaction to President Clinton's Inaugural Address," transcript of Jim Lehrer's *NewsHour* broadcast of January 20, 1997, available at http://www.pbs.org/newshour/inaugural97/reaction_1-20.html.

12. See, for example, Lou Cannon, "Can Bush Break the Second-Term Jinx?" *New York Times*, November 9, 2004, A23.

13. The Clinton team believed that it was well on the way to getting beyond the 50 percent threshold, when a summertime controversy erupted over fundraising practices, especially in relation to China and the Chinese American community. In one instance, Vice President Al Gore was caught in the embarrassing position of collecting large sums of money from a Buddhist temple in California.

14. After twice vetoing legislation from the Republican-controlled Congress reforming the American welfare system, Clinton signed a welfare reform bill into law in August 1996. President Clinton reflected on that experience ten years later, in "How We Ended Welfare, Together," *New York Times*, August 22, 2006, A19, available at http://www.nytimes.com/2006/08/22/opinion/22clinton.html.

15. See Lou Cannon, *President Reagan: The Role of a Lifetime* (New York: PublicAffairs, 2000), 73-74.

16. Rose Mary Woods would later become a minor political celebrity, because she claimed to have been responsible for accidentally creating an eighteen-and-a-half-minute gap on a crucial Oval Office recording that Nixon's critics said, from the context, must have included conversations incriminating the president in covering up the Watergate break-in.

17. See R. W. Apple, "Inaugural Week Begins with Pomp and Populism: By Bus, Clinton Makes a Festive Entrance into His Capital," *New York Times*, January 18, 1993, A1.

18. David Kusnet was Clinton's chief speechwriter from 1992 to 1994. He also wrote speeches for Democratic presidential nominees Walter Mondale and Michael Dukakis and consulted for a number of executive agencies later in the Clinton years. Some of Kusnet's thoughts on the inaugural address can be found in Kusnet, "Bush's Inaugural Speech Must Walk the Middle Road," *Los Angeles Times*, January 14, 2001, M3. Available at http://articles.latimes.com/2001/jan/14/op-12115.

19. Waldman, whose background was in consumer-interest lobbying, was special assistant to the president for policy development from 1993 to 1995 and, thereafter, until 1999, served as director of White House speechwriting. He is author of *POTUS Speaks: Finding the Words That Defined the Clinton Presidency* (New York: Simon & Schuster, 2000).

20. Anderson's assessment of the Coleman quote is not shared by scholars Karlyn Kohrs Campbell and Kathleen Hall Jamieson, who condemn its use as an "inappropriate" and trite personalization of the inaugural address. Mrs. Coleman, they claim, did not have the stature necessary for that genre of speech. They do not acknowledge, however, that in the specific context of Carter's inaugural—the aftermath of Watergate and the age of the imperial presidency—the homespun reference to Coleman may have sounded a powerful note "reconstitut[ing] the audience as the people," which they claim to be the first duty of the president at the inauguration. A survey of press accounts from January 1977 reveals virtually no contemporaneous criticism of its use. Apparently the critics of the day agreed with Anderson. See Campbell and Jamieson, *Deeds Done in Words: Presidential Rhetoric and the Genres of Governance* (Chicago: University of Chicago Press), 23–24.

21. This process of outside consultation is discussed in Waldman, *POTUS Speaks*, and is a central theme of Benjamin R. Barber, *The Truth of Power: Intellectual Affairs in the Clinton White House* (New York: W. W. Norton, 2001).

22. Charles O. Jones examines the forces Baer touches on in "From Campaigning to Governing: Perspectives on the Second Clinton Transition," Research and Commentary Report from the Brookings Institution, Winter 1997, available at http://www.brookings.edu/articles/1997/winter_politics_jones.aspx.

23. Michael Waldman identifies the author as Pulitzer Prize–winning biographer Taylor Branch. *POTUS Speaks*, 153. "The New Freedom" was the broad heading used to describe Wilson's governing program—and not coincidentally the title of a book of his speeches from the 1912 presidential campaign. See Wilson, *The New Freedom: A Call for the Emancipation of the Generous Energies of a People* (New York: Doubleday, Page, 1913).

24. 2 Chronicles 7:14.

25. Carter spoke the following words: "Here before me is the Bible used in the inauguration of our first President, in 1789, and I have just taken the oath of office on the Bible my mother gave me a few years ago, opened to a timeless admonition from the ancient prophet Micah: 'He hath showed thee, O man, what is good; and what doth the Lord require of thee, but to do justly, and to love mercy, and to walk humbly with thy God.'" (Micah 6:8)

26. Eisenhower's prayer reads: "Almighty God, as we stand here at this moment my future associates in the Executive branch of Government join me in beseeching that Thou will make full and complete our dedication to the service of the people in this throng, and their fellow citizens everywhere. Give us, we pray, the power to discern clearly right from wrong, and allow all our words and actions to be governed thereby, and by the laws of this land. Especially we pray that our concern shall be for all the people regardless of station, race or calling. May cooperation be permitted and be the mutual aim of those who, under the concepts of our Constitution, hold to differing political faiths; so that all may work for the good of our beloved country and Thy glory. Amen." This inaugural address is available at http://millercenter.org/scripps/archive/speeches/detail/3356.

27. Among other things, Eisenhower had directed the World War II invasion forces into France on D-day.

28. These dates are corrected from the original.

29. For an extensive bibliography documenting the violence of the 1960s, see "Years of Violence: Urban Civil Unrest in the 1960s—Resources Available from the Thurgood Marshall Law Library," available on the Web site of the University of Maryland, at www .law.umaryland.edu/marshall/specialcollections/riotbib.doc.

30. Further details are provided by David Greenberg, *Nixon's Shadow: The History of an Image* (New York: W. W. Norton, 2003), ch. 3.

31. "Speechwriters learn to 'hear' the voice of the president, fitting their habits of language and argument within his." Judge, "Bearing the Burden of Writing the Speech," *Wall Street Journal*, August 24, 2005, D10, available at http://www.whwg.com/thefirm/sample.php/72/Clark_S._Judge.

32. One of Baer's interviews with Clinton was published in the May 30, 1992, issue of *U.S. News & World Report*.

33. David R. Gergen had been a Republican political operative before voting for Bill Clinton in 1992. He subsequently served in the Clinton White House, beginning in 1993, as counselor to the president on domestic and foreign policy. He later became a special advisor to Secretary of State Warren Christopher. He has written about his diverse experience serving several American presidents in *Eyewitness to Power: The Essence of Leadership, Nixon to Clinton* (New York: Simon & Schuster, 2001).

34. Thomas F. "Mack" McLarty III served as White House chief of staff from 1993 to 1994. He was a kindergarten classmate of Bill Clinton's in Hope, Arkansas, and became a prominent businessman. Later in Clinton's term, McLarty was a special envoy for Latin America.

35. The *2000 Federal Staff Directory*, which lists J. Terry Edmonds as the director of speechwriting for President Clinton, includes fourteen people in the speechwriting shop, nine of whom are directly identified as presidential speechwriters.

36. The importance of religion to Clinton is addressed in several places by David Maraniss in *First in His Class: The Biography of Bill Clinton* (New York: Simon & Schuster, 1995), 35, 57–58, 432–435.

37. One of President Clinton's signature projects during his second term was an initiative on race relations in the United States called One America. Although the president's advisory board on race held numerous meetings across the country—and received considerable press attention, pro and con—little concrete came of the effort. The board's final report was issued in 1998 and is available at http://clinton2.nara.gov/Initiatives/OneAmerica/PIR.pdf. See also Stanley Renshon, ed., *One America? Political Leadership, National Identity, and the Dilemmas of Diversity* (Washington, D.C.: Georgetown University Press, 2001).

38. See Robert W. Turner, ed., *I'll Never Lie to You: Jimmy Carter in His Own Words* (New York: Ballantine Books, 1976).

39. Stephen Hess, *What Do We Do Now? A Workbook for the President-Elect* (Washington, D.C.: Brookings Institution Press, January 2009).

40. Carter's actual line was, "Ours is the party that welcomed generations of immigrants—the Jews, the Irish, the Italians, the Poles, and all the others, enlisted them in its ranks and fought the political battles that helped bring them into the American mainstream." Audio of Carter's speech (including this reference) can be found at http://www.americanrhetoric.com/speeches/jimmycarter1976dnc.htm.

41. Article II, Section 1, provides this language: "I do solemnly swear (or affirm) that I will faithfully execute the office of President of the United States, and will to the best of my ability, preserve, protect and defend the Constitution of the United States." President Barack Obama's oath taking in January 2009 was marred by a slight and unintentional rewording by Chief Justice John Roberts—and because the Constitution is explicit about the language to be used, a proper oath was readministered in private quickly after the public inaugural event.

42. President Clinton held a White House ceremony on January 17, 1997, to announce the winning design for the memorial. Dole was soon thereafter named national chairman of the campaign for the memorial. See Douglas Reid Weimer, "Legislative History of the World War II Memorial and World War II Commemorative Legislation," *CRS Report for Congress*, Library of Congress, Washington, D.C., April 16, 2002, CRS-15.

43. Christopher Matthews hosts a television talk show focused on American politics. He has also been a print journalist, a congressional aide to several Democrats—including Speaker of the House Thomas P. "Tip" O'Neill—and a onetime Democratic candidate for a seat in the U.S. House of Representatives from his native state of Pennsylvania.

44. Margaret E. "Peggy" Noonan was a speechwriter for Presidents Ronald Reagan and George H. W. Bush. She subsequently became a commentator and political analyst, most notably with the *Wall Street Journal*. Her personal account of the Reagan presidency and her role in it is published as *What I Saw at the Revolution: A Political Life in the Reagan Era* (New York: Random House, 2003).

45. For example, Todd Purdum authored the following analysis in the *New York Times* the day after the speech: "Snap judgments in such matters are notoriously unreliable, but after Mr. Clinton finished his 22 minutes in the chill midday sun today, a sampling of reaction from his audience on the Mall and professional, though largely partisan, wordsmiths elsewhere indicated that he had fallen somewhere short of the outfield wall." A mid-page graphic accompanying the piece reported that "Clinton gets an A+ for effort, but a C- for oratory." January 21, 1997, A14.

46. The text of Lincoln's second inaugural, along with the Gettysburg Address, is engraved on the walls of the Lincoln Memorial in Washington. The speech concludes with these familiar words: "With malice toward none; with charity for all; with firmness in the right, as God gives us to see the right, let us strive on to finish the work we are in; to bind up the nation's wounds; to care for him who shall have borne the battle, and for his widow, and his orphan—to do all which we may achieve and cherish a just and lasting peace, among ourselves, and with all nations."

47. Noel Koch was special assistant to President Richard Nixon from 1971 to 1974,

serving primarily as a speechwriter. He was assistant secretary of defense and director for special planning at the Defense Department from 1981 to 1986.

48. When Russell L. Riley included Khachigian's assertion about the Reagan team moving the location of the ceremony in an op-ed piece he wrote for the *Washington Post* on the occasion of Barack Obama's inauguration ("Still Editing? A Few Words of Advice," January 18, 2009, B03), he received a vigorous objection from one reader that Reagan had nothing to do with this decision. This objection is authoritatively sustained by Senate historian Donald Ritchie, in "Who Moved the Inauguration? Dispelling an Urban Legend," *OUPblog*, Oxford University Press USA, at http://blog.oup.com/2009/01/moving_inauguration/. It seems that the Joint Committee on the Inauguration had decided to make the change a month before Reagan was even nominated, based primarily on economic grounds.

49. Mark Goode (1932–1998) was the first full-time television advisor to work in the White House. He moved from the entertainment industry to politics and back, providing media guidance to Presidents Nixon, Ford, and Reagan, while also producing the situation comedy *Three's Company* and *The Johnny Cash Show*. Maureen Dowd provides an account of his operating style in "Bush Seeks the Glow of Leadership," *New York Times*, August 11, 1988, D19.

50. Reagan's actual words were: "Directly in front of me, the monument to a monumental man, George Washington, father of our country. A man of humility who came to greatness reluctantly. He led America out of revolutionary victory into infant nationhood."

51. Khachigian's reference here is to the American diplomats taken hostage in Tehran as part of the Iranian revolution in 1979. The hostages were held for 444 days and were released shortly after Reagan took the oath of office on the day Jimmy Carter departed (but evidently not early enough for Reagan to have received this signal). Arguably Carter's inability to resolve the crisis opened the way for Reagan's presidency.

52. Preston Hotchkis was a Reagan supporter and chief executive officer of the Bixby Ranch in California.

53. Additional details on the Treptow story appear in Lou Cannon, *The Role of a Lifetime*, 98–100.

54. Reagan's direct quote is "In the present crisis, government is not the solution to our problem; government is the problem."

55. Author Taylor Branch was a longtime friend of Bill Clinton's going back to their days working together for presidential candidate George McGovern in Texas during the 1972 campaign. Branch was frequently consulted by Clinton during his White House years, and, it was learned after Clinton had left office, Branch conducted scores of secret oral history interviews with Clinton in the White House residence, to be consulted by Clinton for writing future histories of his presidency. See Taylor Branch, *The Clinton Tapes: Wrestling History with the President* (New York: Simon & Schuster, 2009).

56. On August 10, 1988, Reagan signed into law the restitution act for wartime

internment of Japanese American civilians. The president noted that several show-business personalities had, in 1945, celebrated contributions of Japanese Americans, and then quoted one in particular, saying, "The name of that young actor—I hope I pronounce this right—was Ronald Reagan." The text of Reagan's remarks is available at http://www.ncrr-la.org/NCRR_archives/88dayofcelebration/press/President's%20remarks%20on%208-10-88.pdf.

57. The book Khachigian mentions is probably George P. Shultz, Kiron Skinner, Annelise Anderson, and Martin Anderson, eds., *Reagan in His Own Hand: The Writings of Ronald Reagan That Reveal His Revolutionary Vision for America* (New York: Simon & Schuster, 2001).

58. Lyndon Johnson's March 15, 1965, civil rights address, pressing for congressional action on the voting rights act (wherein he assures the nation that "we shall overcome") can be both read and heard at http://www.americanrhetoric.com/speeches/lbjweshallovercome.htm. George W. Bush's post–September 11 speech to a joint session of Congress was delivered on September 20, 2001, and can be read and heard at http://www.americanrhetoric.com/speeches/gwbush911jointsessionspeech.htm. Note that chapters 8 and 9 deal with such special-event speeches, often occasioned by crisis.

59. In Nixon's opening in 1969, he first addressed the constitutional dignitaries seated behind him and then "my fellow Americans—and my fellow citizens of the world community."

60. Contemporaneous press accounts report that Reagan's second inauguration was the coldest on record, at 7 degrees. Details of that day ("Traffic lights, their timers frozen, stared vainly up the empty length of Connecticut Avenue") are provided in Edmund Morris, *Dutch: A Memoir of Ronald Reagan* (New York: Random House, 1999), 508–513.

61. The Garfield inaugural can be read at http://millercenter.org/scripps/archive/speeches/detail/3559.

Chapter 6

The State of the Union Address:
Process, Politics, and Promotion

Kathryn Dunn Tenpas[1]

Article II, Section 3, of the U.S. Constitution states, "He shall from time to time give to the Congress information of the state of the union, and recommend to their consideration such measures as he shall judge necessary and expedient." This provision makes the state of the union address the president's only constitutionally mandated speech. During the first 125 years of the republic, most presidents delivered a written state of the union message to Capitol Hill. However, this humble address has since evolved into a media event characterized by the president's prime-time delivery before a joint session of Congress. What was once a task designed to appeal to Congress has been transformed into an annual event in which the president seeks to appeal not only to legislators, but also to the vast audience watching the speech on television.[2] As such, the speech is written with the dual goal of garnering congressional and public support. Not surprisingly, members of the White House staff and the president take great care when drafting this annual address, attempting to project a ceremonial air of grandeur while speaking of the nation's proud history, present condition, and vision for the future—no small task for even the best of writers. According to Nixon speechwriter Lee Huebner, "Presidents have felt the demand to make it an uplifting, ceremonial, rhetorical success."

This chapter examines presidential state of the union addresses from the Dwight D. Eisenhower through the George W. Bush administrations—a fifty-five-year period of American history spanning ten presidents in which television emerged as the primary mode of presidential mass communication. The state of the union addresses of these ten presidents constitute a sample that includes only those speeches delivered in the television era. Although Harry Truman was the first president to deliver a televised state of the union message, he did not do so until partway through his term. Eisenhower was the first president to deliver all of his state of the union addresses to television audiences.

Although the speech itself is of paramount importance, it is also worthwhile to consider its aftermath by examining the effects of this address on public approval of the president. Since Eisenhower, the president and his staff have become increasingly aware and interested in public approval ratings for a variety of reasons: the systematic and frequent polling that occurs and is reported, the media's proclivity to write about the president's approval ratings, the technological advances that enable presidents to monitor these ratings, and the simple fact that the ratings themselves have emerged as the most visible barometer of presidential performance. In a sense, this chapter offers bookends to the actual delivery of the address. It examines the period before the address is written to describe how the modern White House produces such a speech, and it explores the post-address period to determine its political effects.

This study has been heavily informed by the work of many scholars of rhetoric who have examined the annual address from a variety of perspectives, and in the process have explained the ways in which the speech defines the presidency itself—how its content has changed over time, its ability to shape the national agenda, and its consequences for the polity.[3] In addition, speechwriters, historians, and political scientists have addressed this topic in presidential memoirs and studies of White House communications.[4]

In an effort to build upon these contributions and advance our understanding of the mechanics of presidential speechwriting, the first part of this chapter explains the speechwriting process within the White House and identifies key stages in the development of the state of the union address. Although this study examines ten presidents over a fifty-five-year period, it is possible to identify a set of common tasks that explain how the modern presidency approaches this important annual address. Part two moves from the speech itself to an analysis of its perceived political consequences. Specifically, what defines a successful speech? This section addresses the broad range of definitions of success in an attempt to understand the myriad political expectations and potential effects of the state of the union address. Part three selects one measure of political effect, presidential approval, and analyzes whether state of the union addresses from 1953 to 2008 positively influenced these approval ratings. The fourth section places these findings in their proper context by identifying alternative political effects that point more broadly to the power of presidential rhetoric. As the transcribed speechwriters' discussions in this book illustrate, presidential speechwriters firmly believe in the power of words and their ability to influence the American people. According to one former Reagan speechwriter, "A speech is part theater and part political declaration; it is a personal communication between a leader and his people: it is art, and all art is a paradox, being at once a thing of great power and great delicacy."[5] What has become eminently clear in recent years is that what once was a relatively humble address, usually submitted to Congress in writing, has become a media spectacle often deemed not only to be the most important speech of the year, but also a political opportunity to expand presidential support.

Mechanics: Writing the State of the Union Address, 1953–2008

Although Presidents George Washington and John Adams went to Congress to deliver the state of the union address, their nineteenth- and early twentieth-century successors were content to send a lengthy written message to Capitol Hill. Not until 1913 did Woodrow Wilson reinstate the original tradition by personally delivering his state of the union address to a joint session of Congress. Since Eisenhower became president in 1953, there have been fifty-seven state of the union addresses, of which only four were submitted in writing.[6] (These four were excluded from this analysis.) The written state of the union addresses were much longer than those presented to a televised audience. Televised state of the union addresses have ranged from roughly 3,500 to 9,200 words, while the four written addresses in this period ranged from 6,210 to 33,667 words.[7] The average length of Jimmy Carter's televised state of the union addresses was 3,750 words. His one written address was 33,667 words. The contrast clearly reflects the constraints on the president imposed by television and its viewers.

During this period, the speechwriting process for the state of the union address remained remarkably constant, despite the expected variation in presidential style and level of engagement in the speechwriting process.[8] To be sure, "Each White House does things differently," says Reagan speechwriter Clark Judge. "President Reagan was more disciplined and had more of a process in place. . . . President [George W.] Bush does a lot of editing himself but is also more in the Reagan mold, in terms of discipline, versus the Clinton mold, in terms of a lot of last-minute work by the president himself."[9] But all administrations experience what often is referred to as the "death march,"[10] during which presidents and their staff members spend substantial time and resources developing the roughly 5,000-word address. Generally speaking, the speechwriting process can be broken down into three stages that occur over a period of roughly five months. Under Clinton, a new, fourth stage of the process emerged.

Stage One: "Casting a Wide Net"

Stage one typically begins in the early fall preceding the January or February address and involves soliciting advice from a broad range of sources—cabinet members, pollsters, members of Congress, business leaders, economists, historians, authors, and others. In terms of formal advice, cabinet secretaries and other political appointees press the White House to showcase initiatives and achievements emanating from their department. Well-known scholars and best-selling authors have also been invited to submit their thoughts and ideas. According to Clinton speechwriter Michael Waldman, "Before Christmas, we had sent Clinton a book of memos from two dozen writers and academics—from Arthur Schlesinger Jr. to Garrison Keillor."[11] Casting a wide net ensured a variety of perspectives and enabled the White House to move "beyond the beltway."

This early period of trolling for ideas and advice is helpful to the speechwriting team. However, the challenge comes when presidential speechwriters must choose among the many ideas and solicitations, often offending those whose ideas or departmental achievements go unmentioned in the address. According to one news report, "The push also comes from Congress, private groups and anyone with a policy idea that would benefit from having the president discuss it on TV."[12] In short, stage one is characterized by intense lobbying for "mentions" in the state of the union address. As Waldman wrote, "Policymakers wage fierce competition to have their proposals included in an address. . . . The role of the speechwriter is to help the president sift through the dozens of competing visions for the speech."[13] Before Clinton's last state of the union address, speechwriter Terry Edmonds said, "We are being lobbied, assaulted, bombarded, beseeched from all quarters— from within the White House, from the agencies, even from outside. . . . Some little old lady called up from somewhere and said, 'How can I get something in the State of the Union?'"[14] Speechwriters wading through these many requests while trying to write a thematic, coherent speech are put to a severe test. As former Reagan speechwriter Peggy Noonan wrote, "Here's an image: Think of a bunch of wonderful, clean, shining, perfectly shaped and delicious vegetables. Then think of one of those old-fashioned metal meat grinders. Imagine the beautiful vegetables being forced through the grinder and being rendered into a smooth, dull, textureless puree."[15] This "excruciatingly collaborative"[16] stage, although painful for speechwriters, is unavoidable and most likely explains why many disparagingly refer to this speech as a "laundry list" of programs and policies designed to please every viewer.

Stage Two: Consolidation

Over a period of weeks, even months, speechwriters' discussions with the president and senior staff narrow the range of possible themes and policy initiatives. As such, the second stage of the state of the union drafting process involves the speechwriters' efforts to identify themes through a series of conversations with the president, eventually resulting in a rough outline. During this period, there are frequent discussions about the overall tone of the speech, the appropriate mix of foreign and domestic policy elements, and which policies and achievements to highlight.

By December, speechwriters have heard enough from the president, cabinet, and senior staff to write a first draft. With roughly four to six weeks remaining before the address is delivered, speechwriters begin the editing exercise, circulating the draft, receiving suggestions, and modifying the text accordingly. This "staffing cycle"—the term used to describe the process of sending the speech out for review to all relevant parties, receiving feedback, and determining which changes to make—not only can seem interminable but also may strike at the heart of speechwriters who have labored over every word and phrase. Generally, a senior staff member makes the toughest decisions. In the case of the Reagan administration, Richard Darman had final say about which suggestions to the writers must be included. According to Noonan, "I didn't always agree with Dick's decisions, but he was open to appeal. He also didn't mind offending people if it meant preserving a script. . . . He didn't care who got mad."[17]

Apart from the pivotal role of the president's staff, presidential pollsters have become prominent behind-the-scenes advisers on the state of the union address.[18] Although they are not formally members of the White House staff because they do not draw a government salary and are not listed on official staff rosters, their advice on speeches can be influential: incorporating data from polling, testing themes and phrases with focus groups, and measuring reactions to the speech in real time by using pulse-meters. Such data are often used to inform both the delivery and content of the address. Pollsters claim to provide a "scientific" approach to identifying what will resonate, what will fall flat, and what parts of the speech still need work.

Once a close-to-final draft has been approved, efforts to promote the speech begin. During the Clinton administration, the communications team seized the opportunity of the winter news vacuum created when Congress goes on recess to preview important proposals from the forthcoming speech. "They left a couple of items to be announced in the speech itself, but for the other policy proposals, there were stories focusing on the particulars of what the president would offer in the address."[19] Although these efforts laid the groundwork for early, pre-address news stories, reconciling remaining disagreements among staff members and advisers remained a difficult task subject to significant wrangling. At some point, however, speech-writers must submit a complete draft to the president. The chief executive then makes changes to reflect his voice and preferred tone, resulting in yet another draft.

The specifics of this stage appear to vary across administrations. In 2006, for example, the Bush administration adopted a process in which proposals were vetted by four policy councils: domestic, economic, homeland security, and national security. In addition to the policy councils, the administration required the Office of the Staff Secretary to provide a comprehensive review of the speech, essentially footnoting every sentence to verify accuracy and consistency.[20] After this exhaustive review, the speech was reviewed by the president's senior advisers—the chief of staff, deputy chief of staff, and counselor to the president.[21] This approach formalized the substantive division of labor that occurs in the process of writing the state of the union address, as well as the emergence of new policy issues such as homeland security and the administration's incorporation of them.[22]

Stage Three: Practice, Practice, Practice

In stage three, perhaps the least labor-intensive part of the process, the president rehearses the address, modifying the text along the way. As in stage two, significant variation occurs across administrations. At one end of the spectrum was Clinton, who tinkered with the speech until minutes before delivery. At the other end, Reagan preferred not to edit the speech in the days before delivery, even though he would rehearse it. As in the previous

Table 6.1. First-Term Domestic Presidential Travel

President	Year 1	Year 2	Year 3	Year 4	Overall Trips Term 1	Average Trips by Year
Eisenhower	19	30	21	24	94	24
Nixon	22	50	48	38	158	40
Carter	28	62	52	125	267	67
Reagan	25	58	50	111	244	61
G. Bush	69	102	77	254	502	126
Clinton	93	111	98	212	514	129
G. W. Bush	110	160	118	284	672	168

Source: Successive volumes of the *Public Papers of the President*; see also Emily J. Charnock, James A. McCann, and Kathryn Dunn Tenpas, "First-Term Presidential Travel from Eisenhower to George W. Bush: The Emergence of an 'Electoral College' Strategy," *Political Science Quarterly* 124, no. 2 (Summer 2009): 323–339.

stages, presidential pollsters and political consultants continue to evaluate the speech, in this case focusing on the president's delivery.

Stage Four: The Post–State of the Union Road Show

Beginning with Clinton, a new stage of the state of the union address has been added to the process—the promotional road show. In hopes of continuing the publicity created by the address itself, Clinton and his successors traveled the country afterward, promoting key administration initiatives. The road show represents the president's attempt to promote important aspects of the speech in strategically selected cities across the country. The practice emerged when Clinton visited fourteen cities after the address.[23] Bush engaged in this strategy even more vigorously than his predecessor, making twenty-eight post–state of the union trips across the country. According to Bush press secretary Scott McClellan, the reason for such travel was that "it will be an opportunity for the president to lay out in greater detail his 2006 agenda."[24] A Clinton speechwriter indicated that the trips were designed to continue public discussion of the president's major initiatives and keep attention focused on him. "You needed a systematic strategy to build on the message so you create many events to amplify a single message."[25] If presidents continue to employ the road-show strategy, it will become clear that the state of the union address is no longer a single event, but the first of a series of presidential engagements designed to bolster administration support.

Increased travel means more presidential interaction with the electorate and ultimately more work for White House speechwriters. According to the political scientist Martha Joynt Kumar, Clinton and Bush each delivered roughly 500 speeches per year.[26] Such efforts require a vigorous speechwriting team capable of mastering the president's views and drafting his words on multiple issues, a task for which the modern White House has prepared by expanding the size of the speechwriting office. The penchant for domestic travel is reflected in Table 6.1, which summarizes first-term domestic travel from Eisenhower to Bush and demonstrates the significant and steady increase in presidential trip taking.

One consequence of increasing presidential travel as it relates to the state of the union address has been the opportunity for presidents to engage in a post-address "rollout." Eisenhower, Kennedy, Johnson, Nixon, and Ford did not travel in the immediate aftermath of the state of the union address. Carter took one trip after his 1978 address to meet with campaign volunteers, suggesting that he was not seeking to broaden the appeal of his message as much as to rally his base. Reagan took one trip each after his 1983 and 1984 addresses for a total of two post-address visits in eight years. George H. W. Bush took one trip after the 1990 state of the union address and another after the 1992 address. In short, prior to Clinton, presidential travel after the state of the union address was infrequent. Recent presidents, however, have concluded that such appearances may bring favorable attention to their programs and initiatives.

This review of the four stages in the development of the president's state of the union address demonstrates the sheer length of the process as well as the challenges that speechwriters encounter when drafting this pivotal address. Most recently, it has become clear that the speech is not simply a speech, but the opening salvo in the president's annual battle to sell his agenda to Congress and the public.

Defining a Successful Speech

All who are involved in preparing the state of the union address consider it to be the "Super Bowl"[27] of presidential speeches, capable of influencing the future course of an administration. Even members of Congress consider this speech to be pivotal. According to Republican senator Lamar Alexander of Tennessee, the president "is the nation's agenda setter . . . and the state of the union is the best opportunity for him to set that agenda."[28] Reagan speechwriter Clark Judge similarly observed, "Our objective was to lay down the agenda for the year ahead, to put the president in the best possible position vis-à-vis Congress."

The state of the union address has multiple objectives and audiences, resulting in multiple definitions of success. For the sake of clarity, it is useful to divide these audiences into two categories: the White House and the larger Washington community. Although at first glance it may seem odd that the White House seldom has a unified definition of success, a closer look at its specialized offices reveals why. Consider the White House Office of Congressional Affairs, the Press Office, and the speechwriting team, noting that each has a specific constituency to whom it devotes its time and attention. Congressional Affairs will focus on what it hears from members of Congress about whether the president sufficiently reached out to them. The Press Office will be concerned with the media's impressions as reflected in the tone and content of news stories about the address. The speechwriters have yet another understanding. One Clinton speechwriter quipped that "applause lines" were the true measure of success and recalled that writers would compete to see who could write the most. Reagan speechwriter Clark Judge indicated that "we would have lots of places where I structured in applause . . . I would pace a speech by applause lines and laugh lines."

Of course, the White House is not the sole judge of the president's performance. External groups within the Washington community include the executive departments, interest groups, and the media. After the address has been delivered, cabinet secretaries and their staff will be satisfied if their issues were allotted significant airtime. Lobbyists and interest groups will watch a speech to see if it discusses and promotes their cause. The media want a speech that makes news either because it unveils dramatic new initiatives or because the president's delivery is somehow unusual or particularly inspirational.[29] Beyond the beltway lies public opinion: did the American people react favorably to the speech? Was the speech too long? Did it address the needs of the majority of viewers?

Although different audiences for a state of the union address employ different measures of success, most of these perspectives are inherently difficult to measure. For example, how does one determine whether the speech positively influenced Congress? Surely a victorious vote in the House and Senate on a presidential initiative constitutes a victory, but it is impossible to attribute legislative passage to a single speech when so many factors influence each member's vote. Perhaps the very complexity of defining success leads to mixed results—some internal assessments may be positive, others negative. External groups may be similarly divided, enabling a president to avoid the extremes of utter failure or euphoria and ultimately derive some semblance of satisfaction after delivering the speech.

One Measure of Success

One measure of success is easily identifiable and reveals the impressions of perhaps the most influential audience for a state of the union address, the public. According to Clinton speechwriter Terry Edmonds, "You're looking at the polls to see whether the speech was viewed favorably by the public the next day." This sentiment is bipartisan. Reagan speechwriter Clark Judge indicates that "if you get a bounce in the polls after a State of the Union address, you've signaled to all those on the other side, as well as to your own camp, that you have struck a public chord and that they'd better be careful about how they oppose your legislative agenda. . . . [I]f he does well, [the president] will get that bump in the polls." Without a doubt, the president's political advisers carefully monitor the president's political standing in hopes that the state of the union address will provide an upward bump in the president's ratings.

In an effort to assess the effect of the state of the union address on public opinion, George C. Edwards's *On Deaf Ears* provides a useful approach.[30] Edwards examined Gallup presidential approval ratings in the period 1981–2001 both before and after major speeches and found little movement in the polls, suggesting that presidential speeches generally did not have much effect on their approval scores.[31] "It is one thing to go public," notes Edwards, "it is something quite different to succeed in moving public opinion."[32] In examining approval change after nationally televised addresses, he found that, "typically, the president's ratings hardly move at all."[33] In short, Edwards refuted the widely accepted notion that major televised addresses lead to heightened political support for the president.[34]

In the case of the state of the union address, the White House leaves nothing to chance—drafting and redrafting, checking and rechecking for accuracy and consistency, using focus groups to test key phrases, previewing important initiatives for the media, and intensively rehearsing—essentially precluding any risk of outright failure. How then could this "Super Bowl" of speeches not boost the president's approval rating? Extending Edwards's study to include all state of the union addresses from 1953 to 2008, one

Table 6.2. Significant Changes in Presidential Approval Scores after the State of the Union Address, 1953–2008

President	Date	Percentage Bump
Eisenhower	January 10, 1957	–6
Eisenhower	January 7, 1960	–13
Kennedy	January 14, 1963	–6
Johnson	January 7, 1968	–8
Nixon	January 22, 1971	–7
Reagan	January 27, 1987	–6
G. Bush	February 9, 1989	+6
G. Bush	January 31, 1990	–7
Clinton	February 17, 1993	+8
Clinton	January 23, 1996	+7
G.W. Bush	January 20, 2004	–10

Note: These figures were calculated by comparing presidential approval scores before and after the state of the union address. Figures obtained at the Roper Center Public Opinion Archives, http://137.99.31.42/CFIDE/roper/presidential/webroot/presidential_rating.cfm.

can determine whether this particular speech successfully moves public opinion.

The Gallup Poll has been asking respondents whether they approve or disapprove of the president's overall performance throughout the period of this study (1953–2008) and thus provides a consistent tool of measurement. Of the fifty-three state of the union addresses delivered in this period, approval data are available for fifty-one. Of these fifty-one addresses, only eleven produced changes in presidential approval of six or more percentage points, and eight of these eleven were in the negative direction (see Table 6.2). Of the three addresses that resulted in a significant positive bump, only one was technically a state of the union address—Clinton's 1996 address.[35] This positive bump could plausibly be explained more by the political context in which the speech was delivered than by the speech itself. It was given in the aftermath of two government shutdowns and the first full year of Republican majorities in the House and Senate. Nonetheless, political consultant Dick Morris called the 1996 state of the union address the "speech that changed everything."[36] Before the speech, Clinton's approval rating was 46 percent. Afterward, it never went below 52 percent and rose as high as 73 percent in December 1998.[37] The political consultant's exuberance aside, the post–state of the union bump Clinton experienced in 1996 appears to

Table 6.3. Box-Tiao Estimates of the Effect of State of the Union Addresses

	Coefficient	Standard Errors	Significance
$\theta1$ (AR1)	.94	.014	P=.000
ω	.016	.67	P=.98
δ	−.043	.039	P=.27
Number of cases	627		
Wald test	χ^2=4608 (p=.00)		
Portmanteau test for white noise	Q statistic=37.53 (p=.58)		

be the exception rather than the rule, suggesting that White House political advisers might be better off focusing on an alternate measure of success.

Edwards's approach, taken by itself, however, has shortcomings. Gallup approval ratings do not isolate the singular effects of a speech and therefore cannot be the sole determinant of whether the speech moved public opinion in a favorable direction. As one critic notes, "Political scientists . . . tend to examine major policy addresses with an eye toward short-term changes in public opinion."[38] An alternative approach that addresses this critique is the Box-Tiao Intervention Model, which establishes a prior level of approval for the president and then determines whether the state of the union address was so important that it disrupted the preexisting level of approval. Technically, the model estimates two parameters of the effect of an intervention (in this case, the state of the union address): an initial shift parameter (i.e., the "immediate effect" of the event) and a "decay" parameter that shows how the "immediate effect" changes over time.[39] This model focuses not only on short-term changes, but also on the effect of an address over a long time period to determine whether the ability to boost approval ratings exists at any point.[40] (For an explanation of the full model, see the Appendix.)

Table 6.3 reports both parameters to see whether the effect of the state of the union address is statistically significant and how that effect changes over time.

The results in Table 6.3 indicate that the data contain a significant autoregressive process (.94), meaning that the president's approval rating is closely correlated with itself over time. It also indicates a sustained decline of presidential popularity over time. Neither the initial shift parameter (ω) nor the decay parameter (δ) is statistically significant, indicating that the state of the union address does not have a significant effect on presidential approval ratings in any form.[41] In short, even a sophisticated time-series model reveals no noteworthy effects of the state of the union address.

What is most striking about both the Edwards approach and the Box-Tiao Intervention Model is that neither the expansion of the White House's public relations and political outreach staff nor the increasing use of pollsters has enhanced presidents' ability to move public opinion in a favorable direction. The White House staff grew steadily in size and specialization during the half-century from Eisenhower to Bush and in ways that considerably enhanced its ability to interact with the public. In fact, the public components of the staff, including the speechwriting office, flourished far more than its managerial, policy, and other components. The period witnessed the creation of the White House Offices of Communications, Public Liaison, Congressional Relations, Political Affairs, and Intergovernmental Affairs. Along with their increased ability to reach out to the public through the staff, presidents since Nixon have hired personal pollsters to gauge and test public opinion throughout their tenure in office. These efforts have become more technologically sophisticated, enabling presidents to fine-tune their speeches to selective audiences and to alter subsequent efforts based on polling results. It seems, however, that these innovations have not provided enough assistance to boost a president's image in any meaningful or consistent way.

Not the Last Word

Nothing in this chapter wholly undercuts the importance of the state of the union address. Rhetoric scholar Roderick Hart struck the right chord when he wrote that "rhetoric's effects are broader and deeper than can be captured by paper and pencil measures."[42] Hart notes a number of the potential contributions made by a presidential address: it can change the national conversation, crystallize vague concepts and put new issues on the agenda, alter the national imagination, change the way we define current political events, change people's presuppositions, and even change the arc of time and space.[43] Carol Winkler demonstrates, for example, that the George W. Bush administration used a Cold War narrative to explain the nation's war on terrorism, concluding that "America's leadership not only understands the psychological import of the narrative but has, at times, manipulated public depictions of terrorism threats to fit within the Cold War's rhetorical expectations," ultimately leading to an expansion of executive power.[44] Many other examples of the influence of presidential rhetoric may be offered, reflecting the concerted efforts of a collection of gifted scholars who have researched and documented the varied effects of presidential rhetoric.[45] As such, it is important to place this study's findings in their proper perspective, noting that public approval ratings are merely one measure of a speech's influence. Although a state of the union address will likely fall short if its goal is to raise the president's approval ratings, it may make other meaningful and tangible contributions.

Conclusion

"My fellow Americans, the state of our Union is strong":[46] a powerful sentence to be sure, but President Clinton's optimistic assessment in 1997 was destined to have limited consequences in terms of boosting his public approval rating. Nevertheless, the White House may have rightly celebrated after the address when television pundits and newspaper columnists gave him high marks for the speech. White House staff members may have received positive feedback from key interest groups or members of Congress. Cabinet officials may have been delighted that the president showcased one or more of their programs. The "inside the beltway" feedback may have been sufficient for speechwriters to declare it a success and move on to the next speech. If, however, Clinton's top political advisers were hoping for a bump in the polls, they were disappointed. Instead, they needed to take solace in other assessments of presidential support, understanding that this address serves a much broader purpose in American democracy.

Future presidents and their speechwriters would do well to understand what the state of the union address cannot reasonably be expected to do so that they can better appreciate its potential to achieve alternative goals, such as highlighting legislative priorities, securing congressional support, and bringing new issues into the nation's political dialogue. Try as they might, the public activities of presidents cannot overcome the many obstacles to leadership that inhere in our political system—the constitutional separation of powers, the declining audience for presidential addresses, the volatility of public opinion, the active participation of interest groups, the polarization within the electorate, and the mean-spirited political debate that often circulates in cyberspace and on cable television. These are just a small sample of the forces confronting presidents, their speechwriters, political advisers, and supporters, thereby making the quest to boost presidential approval ratings a frustrating one at best.

Appendix: Pre-estimation Analyses before Box-Tiao Intervention Model

1. Dickey-Fuller test for stationarity

	Test statistic	5% critical value
Z(t)	–4.63	–2.86

MacKinnon approximate p-value for Z(t) = 0.0001

2. ACF and PACF of the series

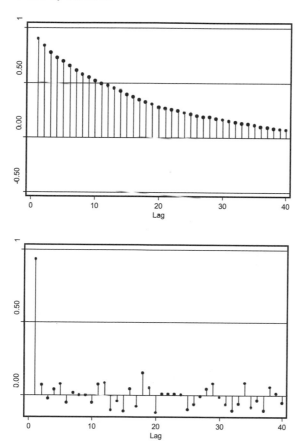

3. The full model Box-Tiao intervention model is expressed as

$$Y_t = c + \varepsilon_t + \sum_{i=1}^{p} \varphi_i Y_{t-i} + \sum_{i=1}^{q} \theta_i \varepsilon_{t-i.} + \frac{\omega}{1 - B\delta} X$$

Y is the dependent variable series (approval rating). X is the intervention (state of the union address). c is a constant. ε_t is white noise. p is the order of autoregressive process (AR). q is the order of moving average process (MA). φ and θ are parameters for AR and MA respectively. B is the back shift operator, for example, $BX_t = X_{t-1}$. ω estimates the strength of the impact of the intervention (addresses) on the series. δ indicates how quickly that impact builds and then decays over time.

Notes

1. The author would like to thank Min Tang and Professor James McCann of Purdue University for their valuable contributions, Dana Rehnquist of the University of Pennsylvania for her diligent research efforts, and the former White House speechwriters who generously gave of their time to teach me about the state of the union address.

2. Note, however, that the audience size (as a percentage of the total population) for presidential speeches has been steadily declining since the Carter administration. During the Clinton years, the largest audience for a state of the union address was approximately 53 million viewers in 1998. During the George W. Bush administration, the 2003 address garnered the largest audience, estimated at 62 million viewers. President Obama's first speech to a joint session of Congress on February 24, 2009, captured an estimated 52 million viewers. See Nielsenwire at http://blog.nielsen.com/nielsenwire/media-entertainment/audience-estimates-for-president-obamas-address-to-joint-session-of-congress/. See also Samuel Kernell and Matthew Baum, "Has Cable Ended the Golden Age of Presidential Television?" *American Political Science Review* 93 (March 1999): 99–114. For an examination of the declining political effects of the state of the union address, see Garry Young and William B. Perkins, "Presidential Rhetoric, the Public Agenda and the End of Presidential Television's Golden Era," *Journal of Politics* 67, no. 4 (October 2005): 1190–1205.

3. For a discussion of the status of rhetorical research pertaining to the state of the union address, see "The Report of the National Task Force on Presidential Communication to Congress," ch. 12 in *The Prospect of Presidential Rhetoric*, eds. James Arnt Aune and Martin J. Medhurst (College Station: Texas A&M Press, 2008), 279–281. See also Kurt Ritter and Martin J. Medhurst, eds., *Presidential Speechwriting: From the New Deal to the Reagan Revolution and Beyond* (College Station: Texas A&M Press, 2003), especially ch. 3, "Dwight D. Eisenhower: The 1954 State of the Union Address as a Case Study in Presidential Speechwriting," by Charles J. G. Griffin, 67–91; Ryan L. Teten, "Evolution of the Modern Rhetorical Presidency: Presidential Presentation and Development of the State of the Union Address," *Presidential Studies Quarterly* 33, no. 2 (June 2003): 333–346.

4. A partial listing of helpful sources includes Robert Schlesinger, *White House Ghosts: Presidents and Their Speechwriters* (New York: Simon & Schuster, 2008); Reed L. Welch, "Presidential Success in Communicating with the Public through Televised Addresses,"

Presidential Studies Quarterly 33, no. 2 (June 2003): 347–365; Michael Waldman, *POTUS Speaks: Finding Words That Defined the Clinton Presidency* (New York: Simon & Schuster, 2000); Karen M. Hult and Charles E. Walcott, "Policymakers and Wordsmiths: Writing for the President under Johnson and Nixon," *Polity* 30, no. 3 (Spring 1998): 465–487; Carol Gelderman, *All the President's Words* (New York: Walker, 1997); James C. Humes, *Confessions of a White House Ghostwriter* (Washington, D.C.: Regnery, 1997); Todd M. Schaefer, "Persuading the Persuaders: Presidential Speeches and Editorial Opinion," *Political Communication* 14 (1997): 97–111; Peggy Noonan, *What I Saw at the Revolution: A Political Life in the Reagan Era* (New York: Random House, 1990).

5. Noonan, *What I Saw*, 68.

6. The premier Web site for archived presidential documents is The American Presidency Project, http://www.presidency.ucsb.edu/sou.php, sponsored by political scientists John Woolley and Gerhard Peters. Three of the speeches classified in this chapter as state of the union addresses were characterized differently by the administrations in which they were given. In 1989, soon after taking office, George H. W. Bush delivered a speech called "Administration Goals" on February 9. Clinton followed suit after his first inauguration by delivering an "Administration Goals" speech on February 17, 1993. In 2001, George W. Bush delivered a speech called "Administration Goals" that focused on budget issues on February 27. Woolley and Peters chose to include these speeches in the state of the union count because the "impact of such a speech on public, media and congressional perceptions of presidential leadership and power should be the same as if the address was an official State of the Union." (See http://www.presidency.ucsb.edu/sou.php.) As such, I have included them in my analysis. For a printed compendium of the state of the union addresses examined in this chapter, see Deborah Kalb, Gerhard Peters, and John T. Woolley, eds., *State of the Union: Presidential Rhetoric from Woodrow Wilson to George W. Bush* (Washington, D.C.: CQ Press, 2007).

7. The average number of words in the fifty-three state of the union addresses delivered to joint sessions of Congress from 1953 to 2008 is 5,063 (author calculations from word counts at The American Presidency Project).

8. For an informative example of Eisenhower's unique process and involvement in the 1954 state of the union address, see Griffin, "Dwight D. Eisenhower," in Ritter and Medhurst, 68–87. Griffin demonstrates how Eisenhower's approach to speechwriting reflected his overall leadership style.

9. Clark Judge, "Former Speechwriters Describe State of the Union Drafting Process," *Online NewsHour*, January 23, 2007, http://www.pbs.org/newshour/bb/white_house/jan-june07/message_01-23.html.

10. Former George W. Bush speechwriter Matthew Scully indicated that this phrase was coined by his colleague, John McConnell. See Matthew Scully, "Present at the Creation," TheAtlantic.com, September 2007, www.theatlantic.com/doc/print/200709/michael-gerson.

11. Waldman, *POTUS Speaks*, 95.

12. David Jackson, "State of the Union Address: A Meshing of Many Ideas," *USA Today*, January 29, 2006, www.usatoday.com/news/washington/2006-01-29-sotu-speech_x .htm.

13. Waldman, *POTUS Speaks*, 93.

14. Marc Lacey, "Guarding the President's Words and, Maybe, His Legacy," *New York Times*, January 24, 2000, obtained online from Lexus-Nexus.

15. Noonan, *What I Saw*, 72.

16. Terry Edmonds.

17. Noonan, *What I Saw*, 76.

18. Presidential pollsters emerged during the Nixon administration and include David Derge (Nixon), Robert Teeter (Nixon, Ford, George H. W. Bush), Patrick Caddell (Carter), Richard Wirthlin (Reagan), Fred Steeper (both presidents Bush), Stanley Greenberg (Clinton), Mark Penn (Clinton), Douglas Schoen (Clinton), and Jan van Lohuizen (George W. Bush). In addition, political consultants Stuart Spencer (Ford and Reagan), James Carville (Clinton), Paul Begala (Clinton), Mandy Grunwald (Clinton), and Dick Morris (Clinton) played key roles in providing political advice during the speechwriting process. See Lawrence Jacobs and Robert Shapiro, "The Rise of Presidential Polling: The Nixon White House in Historical Perspective," *Public Opinion Quarterly* 50 (1995): 519–538; Kathryn Dunn Tenpas, "The American Presidency: Surviving and Thriving amidst the Permanent Campaign," in *The Permanent Campaign and Its Future*, eds. Thomas Mann and Norman Ornstein (Washington, D.C.: Brookings/AEI Press, 2000); Diane J. Heith, *Polling to Govern: Public Opinion and Presidential Leadership* (Palo Alto, CA: Stanford University Press, 2003); Robert M. Eisenger, *The Evolution of Presidential Polling* (New York: Cambridge University Press, 2003); Kathryn Dunn Tenpas, "Words vs. Deeds: President George W. Bush and Polling," *Brookings Review* (Summer 2003): 32–35.

19. Martha Joynt Kumar, "The Office of Communications," in *The White House World: Transitions, Organization and Office Operations*, eds. Martha Joynt Kumar and Terry Sullivan (College Station: Texas A&M University Press, 2003), 258.

20. See Karen M. Hult and Kathryn Dunn Tenpas, "The Office of the Staff Secretary," written for the White House Transition Project, Report 2009-23, http://www .whitehousetransitionproject.org/resources/briefing/WHTP-2009-23%20Staff% 20Secretary.pdf.

21. Jackson, "State of the Union Address."

22. The Clinton administration had two speechwriting teams: foreign and domestic. For the state of the union address, these teams would be merged and overseen by chief speechwriter Terry Edmonds.

23. Trips are considered post–state of the union events only when the president's remarks promote or emphasize content from the state of the union address.

24. Greg Kelly and the Associated Press, "White House Prepares for State of the Union," FoxNews.com, January 31, 2006.

25. Interview with Clinton speechwriter, September 7, 2008.

26. Martha Joynt Kumar, "Presidential Public Appearances and Interchanges with Reporters," in *The White House Transition Project, 2009-04*, 1, www.WhiteHouseTransition Project.org.

27. Terry Edmonds. Among the many speeches that a White House staff member drafts, this one is the most visible and therefore is deemed the most significant.

28. Jackson, "State of the Union Address."

29. Schaefer, "Persuading the Persuaders," argues that the state of the union address is less likely to influence editorial endorsements in major newspapers than the political context, especially presidential popularity and degree of elite support, 106–109.

30. George C. Edwards III, *On Deaf Ears: The Limits of the Bully Pulpit* (New Haven, Conn.: Yale University Press, 2003).

31. Since FDR, the Gallup Poll has regularly asked the question, "Do you approve or disapprove of the president's performance?" Note, however, that this approach to measuring a speech effect is somewhat crude because many other events can contribute to the movement of public approval ratings. It is impossible to isolate the effect of a single speech using Gallup presidential approval ratings. Nevertheless, this approach reveals the absence of a "bump" in approval ratings after most televised presidential addresses.

32. Edwards, ix.

33. Ibid., 29.

34. Numerous scholars have also sought to understand the effects of presidential addresses from a variety of perspectives. For an interesting analysis of the effects of presidential rhetoric on the public's economic perceptions, see Jeffrey E. Cohen and John A. Hamman, "The Polls: Can Presidential Rhetoric Affect the Public's Economic Perceptions?" *Presidential Studies Quarterly* 33, no. 2 (June 2003): 408–422. See also Lyn Ragsdale, "Presidential Speechmaking and the Public Audience: Individual Presidents and Group Attitudes," *Journal of Politics* 49, no. 3 (August 1987): 704–736.

35. The other two speeches were Bush's 1989 speech "Administration Goals" and Clinton's 1993 "Administration Goals" speech.

36. Dick Morris, *Behind the Oval Office* (Los Angeles: Renaissance Books, 1999), 218.

37. Beginning with President Clinton, Gallup cosponsored their polls with CNN and USA Today. I analyzed only those ratings (Gallup/CNN/USA) for the Clinton and Bush administrations.

38. Aune and Medhurst, *Prospect of Presidential Rhetoric*, 281.

39. For an interesting application of Box-Tiao in the context of presidential approval ratings, see Robert Yaffee, "Presidential Scandals and Job Approval: Impact Analysis with SAS," www.nyu.edu/its/statistics/Docs/scandals.html.

40. The Box-Tiao Intervention Model is a sum of the autoregressive moving average of a stationary series (ARMA) and an intervention term. ARMA is composed of two components: autoregressive (AR) and moving average (MA). AR means that the present value of a time series is a weighted sum of its previous values and a white noise error. MA means that the present value is a linear sum of the error terms of the previous time points plus a

white noise. Taken together, ARMA means that the present value of a time series can be expressed as a linear combination of the sum of its previous values and a sum of the error terms of the previous time points. A stationary series is a time series that has a constant mean and remains constant over time. Stationarity is required for ARMA because the estimation will be biased if the mean and variance are dependent on time. (See Appendix for pre-estimation analyses, including Dickey-Fuller test for stationarity as well as tests for Autocorrelation [AC] and Partial Autocorrelation [PAC].)

41. Since the parameters of intervention are insignificant and the parameter of AR (1) is significant, the significance of the whole model as indicated by the Wald test mainly comes from the significance of AR (1). The Portmanteau Q test was used to examine the residuals. Its null hypothesis is that none of the autocorrelation coefficients were statistically significant from zero. That is, the values of the residual series were not correlated over time. When the Q statistic is larger than its critical value (55.76), we can reject the null; otherwise, we cannot reject the null. Since it was smaller than the critical value in this sample, it was not possible to reject the null hypothesis. Thus I conclude that the residual series is white noise (that is, the residuals have a constant mean and variance over time and have no correlation over time).

42. Roderick P. Hart, "Thinking Harder about Presidential Discourse," in *Prospect of Presidential Rhetoric*, eds. Aune and Medhurst, 244.

43. Ibid., 244–246.

44. Carol Winkler, "Revising the Cold War Narrative to Encompass Terrorist Threats," in *Prospect of Presidential Rhetoric*, eds. Aune and Medhurst, 202.

45. For an extended review of these contributions, see Part 1 of Aune and Medhurst, *Prospect of Presidential Rhetoric*, especially the chapters by James Aune, John M. Murphy, Marouf Hasian, Jr., Trevor Parry-Giles, Carol Winkler, and Marilyn Young. See also Jeffrey E. Cohen, "Presidential Rhetoric and the Public Agenda," *American Journal of Political Science* 39 (February): 87–107.

46. See Clinton's 1997 state of the union address at http://www.presidency. ucsb .edu/ws/index.php?pid=53358.

Chapter 7

Speechwriters on the State of the Union Address

J. Terry Edmonds, Lee Huebner, Clark Judge

This session of the symposium featured J. Terry Edmonds, speechwriter for William J. Clinton; Lee Huebner, speechwriter for Richard Nixon; and Clark Judge, speechwriter for Ronald Reagan and George H. W. Bush. The panel was moderated by Professor Kathryn Dunn Tenpas of the University of Pennsylvania.

Dunn Tenpas: The topic of this panel is state of the union addresses. What is perhaps most interesting and what distinguishes the state of the union from other speeches is that it is the only constitutionally mandated speech.[1] It has been referred to by former speechwriters as "the mother of all speeches" and as "the biggest policy speech of the year." Some people call the process of creating it the "death march." Since all of you have worked for different administrations, from Nixon through Clinton, I wonder if you could talk about that process. At what point do you start to prepare for the state of the union, and could you describe the various stages of this preparation?

Huebner: I happen to have one piece of research. I found the language in the Constitution that says the president "shall from time to time give to the Congress Information of the State of the Union, and recommend to their Consideration such Measures as he shall judge necessary and expedient," which is a pretty loose and open definition.[2] I'm told that the "State of the Union" term wasn't used to define the address until the New Deal era.[3] Franklin Roosevelt saw the magic of calling it that.

I think it is a schizophrenic speech. On the one hand it is an administrative tool. It is a way of managing the government. The process begins very early, often in the fall before the speech is given. It is a way of defining priorities, of getting the input of, I think, every bureau and agency and department in the government. Then it gets mashed together into an overlong, often very dull speech.

On the other hand, it is a state occasion. It has become a great ceremony. I think this happened mainly when Lyndon Johnson decided to move it from noon to evening, I believe in 1965.[4] Suddenly, instead of it being a speech for well-informed people who follow government closely, it became a speech for the general public. Presidents have felt the demand to make it an uplifting, ceremonial, rhetorical success. These two objectives, I think, clash.

I'll say very quickly that my experience—and the reason I think I'm part of this discussion—is that I was very much involved in Richard Nixon's attempt to reconcile those two opposites by effectively creating two state of the union communications. He went back to doing what was done all through the nineteenth century. [Thomas] Jefferson decided not to give a state of the union speech because he thought it was too monarchical, like a speech from the throne of the king or the queen. So he suspended it. He started sending written messages.[5] Woodrow Wilson then picked the speech-giving tradition up again, consistent with his own view of presidential leadership.[6]

When I was working for him, Nixon asked the speechwriting staff to turn out a written state of the union message, which was very long, very technical, very administratively oriented, giving every department and agency its due. He also gave a much shorter, much more generally themed, warmer, and more publicly appropriate state of the union speech. He began the speech by handing copies of his written message to the president of the Senate and to the Speaker of the House, making the comment that he had delivered that more extensive message to the Congress that morning and now he would address the public about it.[7] Ray Price, who is here, often worked on those state of the union speeches. It seemed to me like a good way to try to have it both ways.

Dunn Tenpas: After the period in which you solicited feedback from the various departments and agencies and anybody else who wanted to give feedback, was the next stage then to sit down with Presidents Ford and Nixon and talk to them about what they were hoping to get across in this address? What would follow after that sequence?

Huebner: It was mainly a matter of attending meetings where priorities were sorted out. I don't think I ever dealt directly with President Nixon, who is the only president I worked for, although I helped Ford a little bit when he was vice president. I don't think I ever dealt directly with President Nixon on that particular assignment—on other assignments, sometimes, yes. But it was such a huge, complex mass of material that it would get sorted out by committee. I could understand speechwriters who tried to create a single address out of that process facing a very difficult time.

I think one of the reasons why the state of the union speeches are not so memorable in this current era is that they're awfully long. They've become applause-line contests. They try to put everything but the kitchen sink into them. I think Nixon had a good idea that I wish other presidents would have emulated.

Judge: I think in the Reagan administration we thought of the state of the union address a little differently, not so much as an administrative tool, although there were those elements in the process, but as part of the ongoing game with the Congress. The president came out of a union background. That's often forgotten about President Reagan. He had been a union leader while he was a movie star.[8] He thought a great deal of what he did in the presidency in terms of a negotiation. The state of the union address was part of setting up our agenda on domestic policy with the Congress for that year, and rallying congressional support for the budgets that we were going to need in support of our foreign policy. So there was a fair amount of stating basic themes in President Reagan's state of the union address.

There was also a great deal of setting a tone that we are doing this *together*. In later addresses—I know you'll discuss this, Terry—in Clinton addresses, you have examples of President Clinton setting up applause lines and then coming back with a zinger at the other party afterward. This particularly happened after the government shutdown, where he set up a hero and then everybody applauded, and then the hero turned out to be somebody who had been without a paycheck for a time because the government was shut down.[9] We didn't do that. Our rhetorical frame was "Party is set aside," which in essence put the opposition in a position of saying, "No, we're partisan."

So there are different ways of approaching this. Our objective was to lay down the agenda for the year ahead, to put the president in the best possible position vis-à-vis Congress, marshaling public opinion to the extent that you can at a state of the union address. It is not your only hit, but it is a very important hit because you have so many people watching and because it will be so intensively reported by the media. The media itself is an important constituency, even if they are skeptical and even adversarial, as they were with us. They are a constituency you're always playing.

So far as process goes, a well-run process will run much as Lee described: you'll be in meetings; you'll hear from people; you'll start to put it together.

It may be a handful of people on the staff—that is to say, two or three people on the staff who do most of the work. In other cases it was the entire staff. In one case, after Iran-Contra, for us, there were tremendous fights in the White House on domestic policy—much more at that time than on foreign policy—to the point that there were warring camps. Ken Khachigian was brought in to deal with that because it got to a point where the speechwriting staff was too identified with one camp. So with us the process changed according to circumstance, but the objective was always the same.

Dunn Tenpas: And was the time line similar in the sense that you would start in early fall to corral suggestions?

Judge: That's too early. You start a little before Christmas.

Dunn Tenpas: Then it's a death march from Christmas until January?

Judge: I wouldn't call it a death march. In this one instance I referred to, the '87 address, we had huge fights that went on throughout the White House for weeks. But we had a coalition government.[10] We had conservative Republicans, liberal Republicans, Scoop [Henry] Jackson Democrats, and some other elements.[11] So there was always a lot of mediation and negotiation for the speechwriting staff.

In his recent book, *White House Ghosts*, Robert Schlesinger remarks on this being a particular attribute of the Reagan White House, that we did quite a lot of fighting among ourselves.[12] It was a bit like, I think it was in the Korean War, after American generals had fought out their differences in the press, one British general said, "Why can't you Americans wash your dirty laundry in private?" We were a little bit that way.

The results were very good, in large part because President Reagan had set down such clear objectives and clear principles early on. It was easy to write to that. But still, in getting the detailed policy and in determining how we would be positioned, vis-à-vis Congress and other elements in the large game that you're playing when you're in the White House, there was quite a bit of tension. Our role, which almost always was successful, was to mediate, to negotiate, and to get the speech to where the president would want it while taking account of all of the elements in the government and of the political coalitions, which also weighed in.

Dunn Tenpas: Can you approximate how many drafts you went through to get to that endpoint where you had resolved—

Judge: I think some White Houses must put a number at the top that says how many drafts there are. Perhaps out of embarrassment we never did that. We put the date and time. So all you knew was that this draft you were looking at was a relatively recent draft, and nobody ever quite knew how many dozens, or tens of dozens, of drafts we'd gone through. It is like thinking back on great pain: you don't want to remember it. I probably shouldn't say that. It was great fun, but we never counted how many drafts we had. Some scholar—we're here among scholars—will be able to do an important paper on the large number of drafts that were written for some Reagan speech. Believe me, you'll spend a long time counting.

Dunn Tenpas: Terry, what about you? Can you comment on the Clinton process?

Edmonds: I would call the state of the union the Super Bowl of speeches for a White House speechwriter. It is the most labor-intensive project of the year for speechwriting. It is interesting to talk and meet with other administration speechwriters because everybody is different. In the Clinton White House, writing for him was excruciatingly collaborative, with him being the number-one collaborator, of course. But there were so many other people involved, from the chief of staff to his college roommate, especially around the state of the union time.[13]

President Clinton also loved ideas and collecting ideas from all sorts of sources.[14] So our process began before Thanksgiving. One of the first things he would do was canvas the great thinkers in the country and ask, "If there were one thing you would want to see in the state of the union, what would it be? Give me a one-page synopsis of what you would like to see in the state of the union." We would collect those. Not many of them made it in, but it was a great process to get the president's mind thinking.

He was also, unlike the way Lee described Nixon, very involved with staff in the process. We would meet with him multiple times. In fact, we would go into his office with a tape recorder and listen to him and let him tell us his thoughts. A lot of times that language would make it right back into the speech. He also did a lot of the writing himself. We would give him passages, and we would find them crossed out, and he did a lot of his own writing. He is a very good writer. I would say that he was more involved in that speech than any other, of course.

The speech I am most associated with is his last state of the union, in 2000, which also served a dual purpose, like that convention speech I spoke about earlier. It was meant both to look at the coming year and at what we wanted to accomplish legislatively and programmatically, but it was also a chance to remind the country "You had it pretty good for eight years, so let's keep it going." So there was a fair amount of that, too.[15] There's a lot of stagecraft in the modern state of the union speech, too, as Clark alluded to. It is almost standard now that you point to somebody in the gallery as an example of success. In that speech, I think we had about four or five people stand up, including Hank Aaron, one of my heroes.[16] It is very labor-intensive and, as I said, it was the most excruciatingly collaborative experience of my life.

Dunn Tenpas: Did you count your drafts?

Edmonds: Yes, I think we did thirteen drafts of that state of the union.

Judge: I've heard a story that on one of his major speeches, a camera from one of the television networks caught the limousine on the way to the Capitol, and there was a computer screen glowing as they were doing the last entries. Tom Brokaw or someone said, "Now, kids at home, don't do your papers like this."

Edmonds: Yes, I think it is no secret that President Clinton worked on his speeches almost to the last minute, and yes, there were a couple of instances when we were in the limo on the way to the Capitol or to an event and he was still tinkering. I'm sure that there were some instances where, as he was standing at the podium, he was still tinkering.

Huebner: Following up on that, my memory is of a story where the wrong text or something other than the last text was written into the teleprompter.[17]

Edmonds: I wasn't there at the time, but I believe it was a speech on health care before a joint session of Congress.[18] Yes, but President Clinton is the most intelligent, brilliant man I have ever met. I think everybody would attest to his intelligence. He was able to wing it flawlessly so that people didn't know that the wrong text was in the teleprompter.

Dunn Tenpas: Lee, to stick on process for one more round of questions, I've read a great deal about how certain presidents, after they have a draft that is somewhat agreeable, spend some time rehearsing in the family theater.[19] Did you sit in on any of those rehearsal sessions when the presidents would practice the speeches and say, "This isn't my voice. Let's change it"? Did you experience any of that?

Huebner: I never had that experience. Ray can correct me. He's shaking his head. I think Nixon would go over the speech very carefully. If you look at the delivery text, the text in the archives that he delivered the speech from, you see his underlining of words, line by line, as he went through it and practiced it, I think, very rigorously to himself. He was a very private person in many ways, and I think, in that respect, probably rehearsed in private.

Dunn Tenpas: What about President Reagan?

Judge: He rehearsed everything out loud, including thirty-second public-service announcements. I used to go watch those tapings, in part to get a feeling of how he handled a script in front of a camera, usually a script I hadn't written. He'd tape ten or fifteen or so at a time, whatever was on the schedule. One time they were clearing things off and getting ready for the next one, and he said, "This ran a little long last night, a little more than a minute, so I'm going to speed it up." In other words, he had gone through it with a stopwatch the night before.

For state of the union addresses, he'd do it in the theater in the White House, and there would be aides present. But my guess is, he also did it at night, polishing. He had an extremely good memory, so once he had been over something a couple of times—at least he was reputed to be able to do this—he basically knew it. Struggling with getting through the words was not his problem. He was extremely disciplined. Everything was rehearsed, and that was true of state of the union addresses as well.[20]

Edmonds: Do you think that was because of his Hollywood background?

Judge: People ask me that, and I think it was. In Hollywood you learn that kind of discipline. But there's another aspect of that. It goes the other way, too. I think, as I look at his career, the qualities that made him successful in Hollywood made him successful in the other aspects of his career. So they precede Hollywood. There was tremendous personal discipline.

I didn't appreciate this until the administration was over and I had watched some tapes of him and of others doing similar kinds of ceremonial events where I knew that there was tape marking his spot on the floor. I knew that his remarks were set to an audience, and it all looked very natural. Then I'd look at other people doing things, and there was no such discipline in it. There is nothing harder, that requires more discipline, than to appear spontaneous in front of a mass audience. It requires a lot of thinking and lining up, of audiences with remarks with moment. Those qualities and his demand for them he communicated through his staff—he wanted that kind of discipline, that kind of thinking-through. Those are the same qualities that made him successful in Hollywood, made him a successful union leader, allowed him to jump from radio to movies to television to politics, and you find this in the ways he approached things. Some of it is the Hollywood training, but the Hollywood training fed on something that was innate to him.

Edmonds: I think President Clinton, on the other hand, was more like a jazz musician.[21] He did a lot of riffing onstage. But for the state of the union, yes, he did rehearse in the theater with the speechwriters. In fact, we would have the twelfth copy of it, the twelfth rendition of it, in the computer, and as he was reading it, we would make those final edits right there, and hopefully that would be the last time we would see it. Unfortunately it probably wasn't. But he would rehearse the state of the union. That's one of the few speeches that he put on a teleprompter. He was aware that it was being timed, that there was limited time because of the networks. One of the worst things is to have it cut off, or for the headline the next day to be, "He went on for too long." He had gotten those headlines before.

Judge: If I could say, I think this is probably why he liked your speechwriting. I think of presidential speeches as music. I think of the Clinton speeches as improvisational jazz, brilliant riffs. They didn't always line up one with another, but they were brilliant riffs, each one. You had that sense of spontaneity even when they weren't spontaneous. I'll add that I think of the first

President Bush as rock-and-roll—simple, driving beats—and the current President [Bush] as country music—strong structure, invocation of values, note the beat of evangelical lyricism. I think of President Reagan as symphonic. He could handle every range, the entire range of emotion and meaning, and give depth to it. But President Clinton was clearly improvisational jazz, and that's probably why he liked your work so much.

Dunn Tenpas: Lee, I'm also interested in the speechwriting office and its relation to other offices within the White House and to the specific senior staff members who seemed to be the most intimately involved in major speeches, such as the state of the union address. When President Ford was getting ready for the state of the union address, who was involved? Was it Dick Cheney?[22] Which senior staff members were needed to oversee or to read the drafts? What other offices? Was it domestic policy? Was it political affairs?[23]

Huebner: I wasn't there in the Ford years, so it would be the Nixon experience that I would try to remember distantly. It was a very disciplined staff much of the time, and on policy questions most of the time. There were other elements of the White House at that time that were much less disciplined, as we know, but the policy process evolved under the direction of the Domestic Policy Council. It was earlier called the Urban Affairs Council. Pat [Daniel Patrick] Moynihan headed that at the beginning—John Ehrlichman later on—with substantive experts in each area. The speechwriters, the writers in general, would work very closely with those people and with people from other departments and agencies of the government who would be brought into the process. Similarly in foreign policy, of course, Henry Kissinger was watching things.[24]

One of the elements of discipline that I remember appreciating was that, for all of the criticism he has taken through the years, Bob [Harry Robbins] Haldeman, who ran that staff in a rather military way sometimes, ensured that the speechwriters got the last crack at the rhetoric, that somebody wasn't going to fool around with what they thought was a great phrase—except the president himself—unless the speechwriters were part of that.[25] Of course the president himself was, we all said—and, I think, genuinely still believe—the best speechwriter of all. He personalized these texts and the state of the union speech, as distinguished from the written message. He got very much involved.

I think Nixon's was the first staff historically that was called the "writing staff." Up until that time, people doubled as speechwriters, or they were speechwriters but had other titles. With Nixon it was a writing staff, but the writing role was honored, and Nixon took his rhetoric very seriously. He wanted to be sure that this was the case. I would say that among other things, the writing staff, out of a collection of often scattered policy suggestions that came up from the government, felt a responsibility to put these into coherent wholes, into thematically unified expressions. That was a challenge that the president was particularly concerned about. He was never quite satisfied that we had done it well enough. He was always looking for a great theme that would sum up his presidency in some special way. We always kept trying to help in that search. We were protected in that role by the disciplines of the White House and by the readiness, as a result, of some very able people on that staff to work with us.

Judge: I think we in the Reagan administration were very influenced by those elements of the Nixon White House. We had a similar but I think somewhat evolved policy process. What you did not have in the Nixon White House was the cabinet council system that was the product of Nixon veterans thinking about how to evolve the process into a way in which the departments had more say rather than everything being subsumed within the White House staff.[26] So when we came in, there were a lot of elements of our White House that were modeled after yours, with the benefit of having done some thinking about what the strengths and weaknesses were. I think that example had a lot to do with the success of the Reagan administration.

Huebner: I'm sure that's right. My criticism of the Nixon White House is that too many things got collected in the White House in the end.

Judge: I agree. People, including yourself, who were in the Nixon White House felt that way, and basically, to a large extent, we fixed it with our White House.

Edmonds: I don't know what the division of duties was in other White Houses, but in the Clinton White House, there was a domestic policy speechwriting team and a separate foreign policy speechwriting team, which was overseen by Sandy [Samuel] Berger when I was there.[27] When the state of the union came, we had to merge the two staffs. As the chief speechwriter, it was my job to be the final maestro of the process. On the domestic policy side, I relied heavily on the Domestic Policy Council folks to give us the policy, the meat and potatoes. That was Bruce Reed at the time.[28] For the economic policy, we relied heavily on Gene Sperling and his staff for the guts of the speech.[29] Sometimes they would actually provide us "language," which we would have to translate into—

Judge: English.

Edmonds: You got it. I hope Gene's not listening! I think both of my colleagues would agree that there was also input from outside the White House proper. Most of the agencies of the administration weighed in. In fact we would meet with certain cabinet secretaries to find out what they wanted in the speech. It became a game of what do you put in and what do you leave out. A lot of times the hardest part was telling someone, "No, it's not going to be in the speech. I'm sorry. It's too long already. While that program is worthwhile and wonderful, the president will do a speech on it later."

Dunn Tenpas: What other senior staff members were involved? We know that at the end of the Clinton administration the pollster was Mark Penn.[30] Was the chief of staff involved?

Edmonds: The chief of staff was always involved on every speech. He would be the final eye before it went to the president. The pollster, Mark Penn, was involved quite a bit in helping us with policy points that we wanted to make. Again, as I said, it was excruciatingly collaborative. The president was the final word. Many times when you gave him something to review, at the end it didn't look anything like what you had given him originally.

Nelson: The way you're talking, it sounds like the president comes onstage very late in the process.

Edmonds: Not in the state of the union, not in my case.

Nelson: Okay, talk about the president at the front end.

Judge: There are differences between administrations.

Edmonds: In my case, as I said before, the president was involved early and often and consistently in the state of the union. He wrote whole sections of it.

Nelson: You said the process began around Thanksgiving. Was he involved around Thanksgiving?

Edmonds: Yes. We would put together that notebook of ideas, and he would read that over the Thanksgiving holiday and then come back. And then we would start drafting, meeting with him in his office and that kind of thing.

Nelson: And Reagan and Nixon?

Huebner: In terms of the great themes, in an effort to strategize about the speech, the president would start thinking about it very early. There were two speeches—I think maybe his first and second—which would have been in the year of the congressional reelection. That would have been 1970 and then '71. I wasn't deeply involved in those, but I remember that the strategy in '70 was that the speech would challenge the Democrats and set the stage for the fall campaign, which went very badly for the Republicans.[31] In '71 it was all reconciliation and national unity and partnership and working together.[32] I think we would have been aware of those general thematic elements very early, and that would obviously reflect the president's judgment about what this opportunity would be.

Judge: I think we had, in many respects, an administration that was almost unique in American history—maybe [Abraham] Lincoln's was comparable—in the sense that we came in with a clear agenda, an agenda that was much more detailed than most administrations', and that was President Reagan's own agenda. It wasn't the result of a last-minute cobbling in the campaign or pollster work. The movement that brought President Reagan to office had been about sixteen or twenty years in development.[33] So by the time he got to office, he had a clear agenda of what he was going to do in domestic policy and what he was going to do in foreign policy.[34] Then, if you look at where we were on the final day he saluted to the new President Bush and got in the plane, which at that point was not designated *Air Force One*, and flew back to California, we had gone through everything.

What that meant with the state of the union address was that in many respects, the president was involved in the entire year leading up to it because he was involved in setting the parameters and the priorities. But President Reagan was also a master of pushing responsibility down. This is one of the reasons why there was so much conflict within our administration, because the responsibility was pushed down in order to determine lots of elements of what we were pursuing, how we were pursuing it, and the like. So the president, in one sense, was involved *very* early. Quietly he would make it clear what his priorities were, if he felt that he had to send policy in a new direction. That happened much more in foreign policy than in domestic.

If things had gone well, by the time it got to him, he was resolving the last few issues. He didn't need to have the intense early involvement because he'd already resolved many of the issues that you resolve early on in the course of the prior year and as the premise for how he entered office. So the process for us was much more evolved, without him directly putting his hand in until fairly late.

Dunn Tenpas: What about within the White House—with whom did you work, or with what other offices did you work, and who else played a role?

Judge: Let's expand this beyond the state of the union because what we're talking about here is not particularly unique to the state of the union address. Whenever he had a major policy address, I would ask, "What offices have direct policy input here? Who has an interest in this issue?" I'd go talk to them. I might talk to them formally—or it might be informally—to see what they wanted to do with the state of the union address or with the policy address or whatever. In the lead-up to the Moscow summit, I wrote a major policy address. Some of the elements of it came from a discussion over the lunch table at the White House mess with the senior strategist at NSC [National Security Council]. I took back his thinking, and I played around with it, added my own thoughts, added what I knew other elements wanted, added what I knew the president would want to have on his desk, and it evolved from there.

After the speech is in draft, it is going to go back to those same people for clearance. It is best if you know where they are beforehand rather than make it up and then have them say, "Yes, but we've been working for a year and a half on something else." You get some tension when there are offices that have overlapping responsibilities and they're not on board with one another. Then we had to resolve the differences. Sometimes it was just, "Find a way to make them both happy"; sometimes it was, "Well, one office is off the reservation that the president has defined." Then we took the bullet, basically, for bringing them back. It varied according to the speech. In the state of the union address, because every state of the union address has an economic, a social, and a foreign policy element to it, it varied according to what section of the address you were dealing with.

Huebner: Nixon finally decided that another way to handle the mammoth length of all of this was not to talk so much about foreign policy, but to draft what he called the "State of the World message."[35] This was another long, written state paper that Henry Kissinger would labor over and then give to the speechwriting staff with instructions to put the verbs back in the right place, because he always joked about his Germanic background and syntax.[36]

Judge: And that went on for two paragraphs?

Huebner: Sometimes, I guess. But that was another effort to adapt to the fact that the president has to talk about too many things on these state occasions.

Dunn Tenpas: I want to switch gears a little bit and focus on the political impact of these speeches and ask: What is your goal when you write these speeches? Are you hoping that there will be a bounce in the public approval polls? Are you hoping that the speech will generate support within Congress? Are you hoping that the speech will inoculate the public because you're going to introduce something that is a little bit controversial, or maybe it is bad news and you're hoping that by introducing it in this major speech, the public will get accustomed to it? Maybe we can start with you, Terry.

Edmonds: You've basically answered the question by asking it. I think it has all of those objectives.

Dunn Tenpas: But weren't there some years when there was more—like, for instance, in 2000, you knew it was Clinton's last annual message? Maybe your definition of success then was the degree to which analysts talked about his legacy or the degree to which they talked about a successful Clinton administration. It could change from year to year.

Edmonds: Yes, but I think the overall objective is to nudge Congress to do what you want them to do, sometimes to embarrass them to do it, to put them on notice that this is something you're going to fight for. Also, you're right, to roll out something to the public and to see the reaction. Yes, everything has a political element to it. You're looking at the polls to see whether the speech was viewed favorably by the public the next day. But it is one of those assignments that has to be done. I don't think anybody, including the president, wants to give a speech that long and that detailed and that full of different proposals. But you do the best you can, and you hope that it is viewed favorably.

One of the interesting things I'm sure everybody notices about the state of the union is that one side of the aisle sits on their hands while the other side applauds at certain points. It can be a partisan moment, too, because you're challenging the Congress to do things the way you want them done. So it has a lot of different purposes.[37]

Dunn Tenpas: Were your state of the union addresses deemed successful, the ones that you participated in?

Edmonds: Yes.

Judge: All of the Clinton ones, I think, were, even when they went long.

Edmonds: Yes, that's the only sort of criticism that we got: that they went on rather long. But it was unavoidable. President Clinton was a policy wonk in addition to being a visionary. So he wanted to get into the details of policy in those speeches. As much as we tried to push back on it, he usually won.

Huebner: I think they're increasingly partisan events, too, and I think part of that is this new tradition of a Democratic or a Republican response to the president, the speech that comes later. I asked somebody about that. Their memory of the history of that was that it came right after Johnson started doing these speeches in the evening, thereby making them into public political events.[38]

Judge: That's right.

Huebner: I'm not sure that's entirely good. I think it's a little silly now with the Congress leaping up and down every few seconds to applaud or to show their disapproval by refusing to applaud. It's like *Saturday Night Live*.

Edmonds: The great moment is when everybody stands up.

Huebner: You remember that *Saturday Night Live* did this business where poor Vice President [J. Danforth] Quayle didn't know whether to stand up or sit down because it got so confusing. I could sympathize with him.[39] I think it is too bad that we don't have many great, ceremonial, national occasions. That occasion on that evening in January always starts out that way as the Justices of the Supreme Court and the ambassadors and the military leaders all walk in. The speech often doesn't rise to that occasion. I think it is because of some of these conflicting purposes.

Judge: In the state of the union addresses of recent years, the foreign policy section comes toward the end. That's because even if there are divisions between the parties, as there clearly are right now, you can invoke the military and you can invoke other elements of the national purpose that are consensus elements within our society, within our country.

The other thing is that politicians are like market speculators: they're betting on the value of any one stock—which is to say, issue or whatever—six months off. You're giving Congress a sense of how powerful your arguments are versus the opposition's arguments. If you get a bounce in the polls after a state of the union address, you've signaled to all those on the other side, as well as to your own camp, that you have struck a public chord and that they'd better be careful about how they oppose your legislative agenda. That is what the opposition response speeches are trying for as well. Now most of these responses are forgotten even as they're being given.

Edmonds: As is the state of the union.

Judge: Less so, though. The only one I know that was successful was Bob Dole's response on health care to Clinton. That was partly because he used a graphic chart rather than his language.[40] But in each case, the two sides are playing a game of who is striking the responsive chord with the public. The president, if he does it well, will. He will get that bump in the poll, and that will be read by all these market speculators, who are politicians, that this is a stock that has some oomph in it.

Dunn Tenpas: Can I draw you back into the question about how you define whether you had written, or helped draft, a successful state of the union? How did you define success? What were you hoping for?

Huebner: That's the question that I think good, responsible speechwriters defer to whoever they're writing for—that is, what is the objective? I suppose anybody who is in a position of leadership, but the president especially, has so many cross-pressures and so many different objectives all at the same time. That, to me, is what sorts good leaders from less good leaders: making the judgment about what the objective is at that moment. I think a speechwriter has to keep asking himself, "What does the president want to accomplish with this speech?" What is his prime goal, and how do you measure success?

Dunn Tenpas: Are there tangible goals? Do they have tangible goals?

Edmonds: Two tangible goals: (1) that the president likes the speech and is happy and comfortable with it, and (2) that it resonates with the public. Those are the two goals that define whether the speech is successful, from my point of view.[41]

Judge: I would add a third goal. Those are correct, but I'd also add whether it sets up the president for a successful year, vis-à-vis Congress and the other elements of his objectives.

Dunn Tenpas: Do you think a single speech can do that?

Judge: Sure, that's why you do it.

Huebner: Sometimes you don't know.[42] This doesn't apply to the state of the union so much, but President Nixon had a rule that anybody who wrote a speech for him, or who even provided most of the material, would have to be present when the speech was given, whether it was given on the other side of the world or on the other side of Washington. He wanted them to feel the audience reaction and to be part of the moment, because it is sometimes so hard to tell how a speech works.

Edmonds: Also, a lot of times there are things that you put in the state of the union that you know are not going to happen, that you're not going to accomplish in that year. But you put them out there as a statement of your purpose and your vision. I don't think that any president expects that every proposal he puts in his state of the union is going to be enacted by Congress.

Judge: Yes, but there are a lot of proposals—for example, we had the line item veto and the balanced budget amendment.[43] There was no chance we'd get them. But mentioning them is part of keeping the pressure on in the area of controlling spending. So we had things in the speech that wouldn't necessarily get enacted, but they helped set up the president for what he was trying to achieve that year.

Huebner: They set the agenda for the longer-range future.

Judge: Exactly.

Nelson: Every president gives live, prime-time speeches. Some of them involve speaking to a live audience—the state of the union being the most regular—and others involve just talking to the camera. Which did your presidents prefer: speaking to the American people live in prime time or speaking to just a camera? Which did they do better? How did it affect the way you wrote the speeches?

Edmonds: There were big differences between those two styles of delivery. Usually if the president is speaking from the Oval Office directly into the camera, it is to announce a crisis or to declare war or to say that something bad or good is going to happen. Those speeches are generally short—five, six minutes' worth of talking directly to the American people.[44]

The state of the union, of course, is a sprawling speech that can go on for an hour. In President Clinton's case, he loved people, so he loved being in front of a live audience. He was just as good speaking from the Oval Office, but I think he enjoyed interacting with live people.

Huebner: I'm thinking of reasons why Nixon was comfortable in both cases. It was often said that he was more comfortable with an audience of 5,000 than with an audience of five in his office. He could be personally shy and reserved and even awkward in personal conversation. When he got before a large audience, he was transformed. On the other hand, he had great success with the one-on-one experience, getting into people's living rooms through the eye of the camera, often keeping other people out of the room while he gave the speech so as not to be distracted.

He had a great appreciation, growing up as a young adult, for Franklin Roosevelt's fireside chats,[45] on which I think he modeled perhaps his most important speech early in his career, the so-called Checkers speech, the fund speech of 1952, when he turned national public opinion around in twenty-something minutes.[46] He modeled it on the fireside chat, even with the set that he was on at the time. He was so successful on that occasion that I think he later overestimated his ability to turn around public opinion with that kind of speech, although he did it again in the case of his very first big Vietnam speech.[47] So I think there is evidence that he liked both settings and probably had successes in both, although there probably were less successful speeches in both media.

Nelson: Reagan, of course, made a career out of connecting with the American people through the lens of a camera. Did that carry over to his speechmaking in the White House, where he was most comfortable?

Judge: I think he was comfortable in both. He was highly practiced as a podium speaker. He was highly practiced as a speaker to a camera. He had tremendous skills in each. With the podium style, I think I've heard people talk about rhetorical flourishes—not here, but in other instances—and devices and whatever. In our case, rhetoric was, in a sense, a hidden art. Even as we were pulling out the applause lines or whatever in front of a live audience, he was always, to one extent or another, speaking to the camera, and in essence having an intimate talk with people in their living rooms. That was very much part of our style.

Before audiences we would have lots of places where I structured in applause—structured in jokes and the like—which you can't tell in an Oval Office speech, because you don't have anybody laughing, except for the camera crew, and you sure don't want that. I would pace a speech by applause lines and laugh lines. The fact is, if I missed one, it wasn't unusual for the president to ad-lib something in. If there was an obvious hole in a speech, he'd ad-lib a story or something else that would get a reaction from the audience. That was, at least for me and I think for all of my colleagues, part of how we thought of live speeches. Our televised speeches didn't have those structural elements, didn't have those zings and whatever. We were still going for the sound bite; we were still going for other elements. The president was equally at home with either one. Again, returning to music, he was a tremendous symphony to have at your disposal.

Dunn Tenpas: I understand that Richard Wirthlin was the pollster for President Reagan, and he would conduct something called "pulse-meters," where people would be watching speeches and they would register on a dial meter whether it was positive or negative.[48] He would produce these reports, which are all available at the Reagan Library, and you can actually see the responses to a particular speech and the various lines. Did you analyze those?

Judge: The only time Dick came in with a pulse meter in my tenure was after the '88 state of the union address. He showed the ups and the downs. I was very pleased with one particular way up. I won't say why I was pleased with it, but I was very pleased. We did not get very much, if any, direction from Dick: "The public wants to hear this," or "You have to use this word," which is common now. "Use 'exuberant'" or something like that because it tested well. We didn't get much of that. I'm going to turn here to my two colleagues, Peter Robinson and Ken Khachigian. Did you ever hear of this?

Robinson: Zero. I can recall only two Dick Wirthlin briefings.

Judge: That was one of them.

Robinson: That's one, and the other was before the campaign for what became the 1986 tax reform, when Dick came over and with a very long face said, "The polls are all against us on this one."[49] He had just come from the Oval Office. He said, "I tried to talk the president out of this one. I want you to know that this is going to be an uphill battle." So the only polling advice we got was, don't do it.

Khachigian: I was struck in the president's diaries by how often Wirthlin came to report on polls to the president and how much attention the president seemed to pay to them in terms of his mood. I've just seen the edited version, and I'm eager for the full three-bound volumes to come out.[50]

But as I said, with all due respect to Dick, the one time I listened to him was in that '82 campaign stump speech, when the phrase "Stay the course" was in there. It was, as I look back, the worst thing to say when the economy was not going well and people didn't feel like they were doing well. With all due respect, it is the only criticism I have.

At one point the younger President Bush was using "Stay the course" in Iraq, which was when body bags were coming home. It was the wrong wording.[51] It means status quo when people don't want status quo. You sometimes have to go with your instincts instead of with polls. The one time I didn't and I was told what I was supposed to do, it was the wrong thing, in my judgment.

Judge: I would second that, by the way. I'm not going to say the issue or what happened, but the only regret I have from the White House was that one speech I wrote for the president was in support of a candidate, and the line was dictated by a political consultant for the candidate, and it was not successful. I deferred, figuring that he knew what he was doing.

I think the way President Reagan thought of polling was that it told him what the sensitive points were with the public, but he knew where he wanted to go. He wanted to be informed about those sensitive points, but he wasn't going to change his course because of something a pollster told him.

Edmonds: I would agree with that. That's the way President Clinton used pollsters.[52] Sometimes they did grate on speechwriters because they would suggest things that we thought didn't make sense or weren't rhetorical. But in the end, the president made the decision based on what he thought was the best thing to do. I think, if I might say, that during this current campaign [2008], we may be seeing a shift away from too much reliance on pollsters. Mark Penn was involved with the Clintons, and I think he may have done his last campaign for the Clintons.[53] I don't know. I'm just saying that if you rely too heavily on them, sometimes it can backfire.

Judge: We have two candidates now [Obama and McCain] who the pollsters said couldn't get nominated, right? Good point.

Dunn Tenpas: Dick Morris talks a lot—this was before Terry was there—about how they held focus groups with people to figure out which words to use and how best to present initiatives.[54] It was Clinton's idea, but they talked about what vocabulary would resonate most with the listeners and things like that.

Edmonds: I was there for a brief period when Dick was there.

Dunn Tenpas: Was it different pre and post his involvement?

Edmonds: After he left, Mark Penn filled that role. But yes, there was some resistance, we should say, by the speechwriters to his input. [*laughter*]

Judge: This is what you learn in the White House, how to phrase things exactly right.

Dunn Tenpas: I'd like to open the discussion to the broader audience and ask if anybody else wants to add anything.

Khachigian: I'll make an observation: I hate state of the union speeches. [*laughter*] I think it has become so tawdry, the way it happens now. It is becoming a spectacle of partisanship, where they jump up and do standing ovations on one side and sit on their hands or stand up on the other side. Then we have, who is going to be in the gallery? It has taken away from the majesty of the presidency. The presidency used to be such a majestic office, and it still is, but there's no dignity in the state of the union speech whatsoever. There's nothing memorable anymore that comes out of it. The agenda doesn't stick.

In this last go-around—I can't remember; it was probably the previous January—I was frustrated with the way it was going. I sent a note to Bush's speechwriters, and I said, "Why don't you send up your written state of the union with your big agenda on it and go before the Congress in the state of the union speech and say, 'I know that in the past we've had speeches where people who agree with what I say tend to cheer, and people who disagree tend to not cheer, but tonight I want to talk very seriously about the war in Iraq in a way that gets our message across for all Americans and without responding in a partisan fashion. You may disagree with me or you may agree with me, but let's do it outside this hall. Tonight I want to address what I feel is important about what our men and women are doing 8,000 miles away.'" You can imagine what happened.

Judge: But, Ken, what did happen was they decided to drop the gallery stuff this year, and they decided to drop it pretty early, in part because they felt it was trite. That may have been because of your input.

Khachigian: I'm sure it wasn't, but that's a minor part of the show now. I don't even watch it because I feel saddened by the spectacle of this clown show that goes on.

Price: It's Hollywood on the Potomac.

Khachigian: Yes, it's sad.

Huebner: Even forty years ago, Nixon was uncomfortable with that speech, and it was reflected in this fact. I think Ray recommended me to edit a collection of Nixon speeches, which still hasn't quite happened. Nixon picked thirty speeches from his entire career, going back to the Alger Hiss case and going right up through the last one, his comments at his wife's funeral.[55] Of those thirty speeches, none was a state of the union address, which we tend to think of as the glory moment. I don't think Nixon was embarrassed by them, but he found it a difficult forum even with his two-tier approach.

Edmonds: I think everybody knows that the best speeches are short—like Abraham Lincoln's Gettysburg Address.[56] It is very hard to be rhetorical or to be memorable when you're talking for more than an hour. You have so many different subjects. We even did away with transitions; forget the transitions. It was, "And another thing. . . ." Just go to it.

Riley: Since everybody within the speechwriting shop seems to recognize problems with this speech, was there ever serious discussion about breaking the mold?

Edmonds: I think there is always discussion about it, but we always fall back to the norm because it is expected that the speech is going to be so wide-ranging.

Riley: But where does the pressure come from? Is it from elsewhere within the executive branch of the government? Is it from the media?

Huebner: I think the speech plays a very useful role, that is, the laundry list. We haven't used that term yet, but that's the term used for it. It plays a useful role in disciplining the government. It's very good for people to begin thinking in October or November or December about what they want to prioritize with the president. In the aftermath of that speech, it is combed over for signals, hidden or not, as to what the president's agenda is in terms of their own responsibilities. I think it is a very useful management document. I just think it probably could be accomplished in a written document.

Price: The president used to hand a written state of the union message, which was *the* state of the union message, to the Speaker and the president of the Senate, and then he did a shorter talk. But then it metastasized, and now it is back to its old self again.

Judge: Yes, but remember, in his final state of the union address, President [Dwight] Eisenhower noted that the U.S. had had divided government for, at that point I believe, the longest period in its history.[57] We've had a divided government for most of the last forty years. From '68 on, we've usually had divided government.[58]

Price: A lot of people don't think about what the source of our problems was, that Nixon was the first president since Zachary Taylor, 120 years before, to take office with both houses of Congress controlled initially by the opposition.[59] Of course they remained in opposition control throughout until they finally got rid of him, which they did.

Judge: It creates a dynamic. A successful presidency keeps control of the agenda in Washington, and that requires setting terms early and then keeping the pressure on. President Reagan, for example, did his economic policy address in '81, a kind of mini–state of the union.[60] He set the agenda early. He used each state of the union address to reassert his agenda, to freshen it, and to keep the pressure on. With a divided government, that is an essential function if you're going to have a successful presidency. Pretty much the definition of a presidency that has lost its way is one that doesn't control the agenda in Washington.

Milkis: Terry, your administration experienced both of those situations, situations where your party controlled the Congress and then when the Republicans took control of Congress in '94. Was there a difference in the preparation of the state of the union message in those different environments?

Edmonds: No, the purpose is still the same: to lay out the agenda for the year. Even though you don't have unanimity, even within your own party sometimes, I think it is still important to lay out the agenda.

Price: Also, with the spoken state of the union, your audience is not the Congress; it's the public.

Rudalevige: If I can build on that point and on Clark's: If it is the case that the annual message is for the public, how does that relate to the question of bureaucratic control? Is it the case that this could be a written message if in fact it needs to be public?

Judge: The president's authority derives from the public, from the American people. If the American people are seen to be behind the president and if he is seen to be in charge, his authority rises. If he is seen to be losing the backing of the public and not to have an aggressive agenda that is doable, one that can control the doings in Washington, his authority declines. It isn't just with the public; it's with all the political players—bureaucratic, legislative, and the like—in Washington, and with those who feed into them. So there isn't a conflict. Those two things go together.

Rudalevige: Would a written message work?

Edmonds: Not in this modern media age where there is a proliferation of cable-news networks and YouTube. I think people expect to see the president deliver this once-a-year address. It doesn't have to be as long or as unwieldy as it has become, but I think it is a moment that just cries out for public presentation.

Huebner: The Nixon answer wasn't a written address. It was both. It was a combination of the two.

Rudalevige: As long as the bureaucratic signal is received, right? It struck me that you're saying that you could do that in writing.

Huebner: I think most White Houses, though, spend a lot of time on written messages to Congress in which the legislative program is written out.

Judge: One of the current president's [George W. Bush's] early agenda items in his first year was to get the written material on the budget out on time in order to show that he was in charge in Washington. There are multiple constituencies in Washington. I've talked about how the public feeds in, but there is also a sense that you have to convey that the administration has its act together. The kind of written document that Lee and Ray are talking about conveys to the entire apparatus of the government, "Here are the details, and here's where we're going, on the level of detail that matters to you down in the agencies and bureaus."

Khachigian: I wonder if anybody can remember what came out of President Bush's January [2008] state of the union speech that guided his administration between January and today, June 20.

Judge: Support for the Iraq war.

Khachigian: That's obvious.

Judge: That was the big theme of the agenda.

Khachigian: The state of the union hasn't done what everybody thought it would, which is to set the agenda. The later you get into your administration, the more difficult it is, which is why, for the 1987 speech, I was brought in to mediate between all you warring factions.

Robinson: Ken was the paratrooper. When we got hung up in the hedgerows, we looked to the sky.

Khachigian: We made a great effort and didn't change the debate. It was so poisonous.

Judge: I think you're being too tough on yourself, Ken.

Khachigian: It was a poisonous atmosphere. Iran-Contra was dominating the debate, and the president had just had an operation in December, over Christmas.[61] They were wondering about his health, whether he was up to the rigors of the presidency. I scrounged around for people to give me an agenda for that year. It wasn't my responsibility to set the president's agenda. I came in as a volunteer to help write the speech, but there wasn't any agenda. The "Mice," as they've been described, were coming in saying one thing, and you all were discouraged because you were fighting rearguard actions on another front.[62] At the end, we barely made it through.

Judge: Yes, but Ken, remember several things about this. First of all, in '87 the president was going through the toughest part of his presidency. Iran-Contra had just happened, he lost [Robert] Bork a little bit later, but by the next year he was coming back.[63] He was in charge of his foreign policy agenda. He did the "Tear down this wall" speech that Peter Robinson wrote.[64] Toward the end of '87, he recaptured the agenda in foreign policy matters, which he had never quite lost. Then he had a very successful last year in foreign policy, and he left with his own vice president [George H. W. Bush] succeeding him.[65]

Part of what you achieved in that state of the union address, Ken, was to set the predicate for what came later, even though we had to pass through the valley of the shadow of death. The rule in politics is, you pass through the valley of the shadow of death, and you keep on marching. You don't stop and look around. You helped us do that.

Robinson: Everyone else, listen in as we reassure Ken that he wrote a wonderful speech! [*laughter*] That '87 state of the union speech may not ring in history, and it may not even have done much to set the agenda for the rest of that year or for 1988, but Reagan did it, and you're exactly right. There were questions about Reagan at that point. But he walked into the chamber, people looked around, the television camera was on him, and by the time he walked out of the chamber, everybody was saying, "He's still got it. We're okay." So that was an accomplishment at the most human, basic level. That was important.

I agree. I'm with you. I hate the damn thing, and I consider the state of the union one of the central mysteries of modern American life. The president doesn't want to give it, Congress doesn't want to listen to it, the networks don't want to cover it, and every year the damn thing happens all the same. [*laughter*]

Nelson: It's in the Constitution.

Robinson: The founders backed their way into it, and we're stuck with it in the Constitution. Then Woodrow Wilson grasps it, Lyndon Johnson gives it a flip, and now we have it. I would argue with Clark that in a certain sense it is now a permanent ritual. The question is, how well does any administration stand up to the discipline of doing this peculiar act that everybody has to do and which, if done correctly, is useful? At the animal level, the public gets to see whether the president of the United States has it.

And at the staffing and bureaucratic level. . . . Listen, in a Republican administration, it is the only time of year that you say to yourself, "There is a Department of Housing and Urban Development. What the heck are we going to do with that thing?" That's an essential discipline. And frankly, as I said, the networks don't want to cover it. There is something to be said, then, for the moment when those folks up in New York, making their networking decisions, go "Ugh, think of all the advertising revenues we're going to lose." But they have to do it because it's the president of the United States in a joint session of Congress.

Judge: We've been awfully Reagan-oriented here. Terry, you had some tough moments. How did you guys feel you handled it?

Edmonds: I wasn't there in '98, but I think I know what you're talking about.[66]

Judge: That was a very tough moment. Set aside the usual elements of it. It was a very tough moment, and you guys had to do the same thing Peter is talking about. President Clinton had to go in and show that he could get through it.

Edmonds: And he did. Yes, President Clinton was very good at compartmentalizing, focusing on the people's business, and he got through that speech at a very difficult time.

Judge: And the speech, the way he delivered it, gave a sense that he was still in control.[67]

Dunn Tenpas: I would add one more paradox to your list of paradoxes about the state of the union address. A lot of you said, "That speech gave us a big bump." I looked at state of the union addresses from Eisenhower through [George W.] Bush in 2008. Of all those speeches, there was only one bump in a positive direction, and that came after President Clinton's speech in 1996. That was a difficult time, after the government shutdown, after Newt Gingrich's Contract with America. You want to ascribe a lot of blame or credit to these speeches, but in most cases they don't give you a bump.

Judge: In Washington it is perceived, one way or the other, as successful, as driving things, or not. There will be expectations, and if the president meets the expectations, then he has had success.

Huebner: One question mark, though, is whether this tendency to count the number of standing ovations as the way of measuring the success of the speech doesn't blur that a little bit. It is a little bit of a sporting contest rather than—

Judge: That's something the media does, and you want to get that affirmation. But look, we've had divided government for a long time. Even when the two parties come together—and they come together on a lot more stuff than you would believe from their rhetoric[68]—you are not going to see people in the two houses joining hands and singing "Kumbaya" and toasting marshmallows. At least not in this environment, until we pass through this period of perpetually divided government.

Jones: I have a partial solution to the problem of the state of the union address. That is, require the members of Congress to wear seat belts. [*laughter*] You can still count the applause.

Nelson: I think there is something quite wonderful about there being millions of people who choose to watch this speech. When I was a kid, you had no choice because there were just three channels, and they were all carrying the state of the union. Now almost everybody has choices, yet they still tune in.

What they see, I think, Ken, is a wonderful ritual of raucous but civil partisanship. When the president walks into that room and people are waiting to shake his hands on both sides of the aisle, there is something quite wonderful about that, affirming the unifying value of the presidency. Then during the speech, some people cheer and some people show their displeasure, but they're all there in that same room, and they leave on good terms. I think there's something there that tells us that we can have raucous partisanship within the framework of a political system in which people deeply believe and are interested.

Edmonds: Has anyone done a study or survey of the ratings of these speeches? Are they going up or down?

Nelson: They're going down, but they're not going down to where you'd think they would go based on the comments in this room about how awful they are.[69]

Judge: Televised presidential speeches—I think I'm right on this—peaked during the Nixon years, and they have slipped steadily since then.[70] I think they've plateaued in recent years.

I agree with you. I think the way the public sees the standing and cheering on one side and not on the other is a little bit like the Army-Navy game, or two football rivals, and part of it is the fun and sport of it. There is an element of sport about American politics, as well as an element of camaraderie at the end.

Nelson: On that cheerful note, it's time to bring this wonderful session to a close. We can make an exception if Ken Khachigian wants the last word.

Khachigian: To have written a speech and to go home and feel that you didn't achieve what you wanted to achieve for the president is such a discouraging feeling. We went through those in the Nixon years, too. We had some tough times. The president got up there for one state of the union and said, "One year of Watergate is enough."[71] It turned out that one year of Watergate was not even close to enough.

Nelson: Great thanks to Lee Huebner and Terry Edmonds and Clark Judge, and Katie Tenpas for leading this discussion, and to all of you for your contributions.

Notes

1. See Article II, Section 3, of the U.S. Constitution.

2. This passage was corrected from the original.

3. Huebner's assertion about FDR's role in popularizing the term "state of the union" is corroborated by the National Archives. See http://www.archives.gov/press/press-releases/2005/nr05-35.html.

4. See Alex Hawkes, "Briefing, the State of the Union address," [London] *TimesOnline*, January 28, 2003, http://www.timesonline.co.uk/tol/tools_and_services/specials/article857197.ece.

5. Andrew Burstein writes of Jefferson, "After the inaugural, he took to sending his messages to Congress, where they were read by the clerk of the House. While a reflection on his own limitations, this departure from the first two presidents also expressed Jefferson's preference for republican simplicity over ceremonial government." Jeffrey K. Tulis asserts that "Jefferson's main objection was to the . . . peculiar way that the president's physical presence might affect the deliberative process." See Burstein, "Thomas Jefferson, 1801-1809," in *The American Presidents*, ed. Melvin I. Urofsky (New York: Garland Publishing, 2000), 36; Tulis, *The Rhetorical Presidency* (Princeton, N.J.: Princeton University Press, 1987), 56.

6. The standard work associating a different theory of presidential leadership with Wilson's position on rhetoric is Tulis, *The Rhetorical Presidency*. See 56, 117-144.

7. For example, in his third annual message, delivered in January 1972, Nixon noted, "There is ample precedent, in this election year, for me to present you with a huge list of new proposals, knowing full well that there would not be any possibility of your passing them if you worked night and day. I shall not do that. I have presented to the leaders of the Congress today a message of 15,000 words discussing in some detail where the Nation

stands and setting forth specific legislative items on which I have asked the Congress to act. . . . I am presenting only vital programs which are within the capacity of this Congress to enact, within the capacity of the budget to finance, and which I believe should be above partisanship—programs which deal with urgent priorities for the Nation, which should and must be the subject of bipartisan action by this Congress in the interests of the country in 1972." Nixon also handed a 22,000-word written message to the Speaker of the House and the president of the Senate in 1974. Both speeches are available at The American Presidency Project Web site, http://www.presidency.ucsb.edu/sou.php.

8. Biographer Lou Cannon writes that "Reagan's first significant political training ground was the Screen Actors Guild." See Cannon, *Governor Reagan: His Rise to Power* (New York: PublicAffairs, 2005), 85.

9. Clinton's 1996 state of the union address included the following passage:

"I want to say a special word now to those who work for our Federal Government. . . . Our Federal Government today is the smallest it has been in 30 years, and it's getting smaller every day. Most of our fellow Americans probably don't know that. And there's a good reason. . . . The remaining Federal work force is composed of hard-working Americans who are now working harder and working smarter than ever before to make sure the quality of our services does not decline.

"I'd like to give you one example. His name is Richard Dean. He's a 49-year-old Vietnam veteran who's worked for the Social Security Administration for 22 years now. Last year he was hard at work in the Federal Building in Oklahoma City when the blast killed 169 people and brought the rubble down all around him. He reentered that building four times. He saved the lives of three women. He's here with us this evening, and I want to recognize Richard and applaud both his public service and his extraordinary personal heroism. But Richard Dean's story doesn't end there. This last November, he was forced out of his office when the Government shut down. And the second time the Government shut down he continued helping Social Security recipients, but he was working without pay.

"On behalf of Richard Dean and his family, and all the other people who are out there working every day doing a good job for the American people, I challenge all of you in this Chamber: Let's never, ever shut the Federal Government down again."

Clinton's challenge sparked thunderous applause among Democrats—and stony silence among Republicans.

10. In the 1986 midterm elections the Democrats reclaimed the U.S. Senate, giving them control of both houses of Congress for the first time in Reagan's presidency.

11. Henry M. "Scoop" Jackson (1912–1983) was a U.S. representative and senator from the state of Washington. He was most known for holding strongly conservative views on U.S. foreign and defense policy. Accordingly, "Jackson Democrats" are typically seen as being hawkish on national security issues.

12. Robert Schlesinger, *White House Ghosts: Presidents and Their Speechwriters* (New York: Simon & Schuster, 2008).

13. The inclusiveness of Clinton's speechwriting process is touched on throughout speechwriter Michael Waldman's memoir of the Clinton years, *POTUS Speaks: Finding the Words That Defined the Clinton Presidency* (New York: Simon & Schuster, 2000).

14. Clinton's interest in tapping intellectual sources outside the White House is a central theme of Benjamin R. Barber's *The Truth of Power: Intellectual Affairs in the Clinton White House* (New York: W. W. Norton, 2001). Barber's Chapter 4 is entitled "The Art of Speechwriting."

15. Early in the 2000 speech, Clinton credited the following developments to the genius of the American people—and by implication, his own leadership:

"We restored the vital center, replacing outmoded ideologies with a new vision anchored in basic, enduring values: opportunity for all, responsibility from all, a community of all Americans. We reinvented government, transforming it into a catalyst for new ideas that stress both opportunity and responsibility, and give our people the tools they need to solve their own problems.

"With the smallest federal work force in 40 years, we turned record deficits into record surpluses, and doubled our investment in education. We cut crime, with 100,000 community police and the Brady law, which has kept guns out of the hands of half a million criminals.

"We ended welfare as we knew it, requiring work while protecting health care and nutrition for children, and investing more in child care, transportation, and housing to help their parents go to work. We've helped parents to succeed at home and at work, with family leave, which 20 million Americans have now used to care for a newborn child or a sick loved one. We've engaged 150,000 young Americans in citizen service through AmeriCorps, while helping them earn money for college."

16. Henry L. "Hank" Aaron played outfield for the Milwaukee/Atlanta Braves and was a designated hitter for the Milwaukee Brewers; in 1974 he broke Babe Ruth's all-time home run record by hitting number 715. Aaron's public stature was enhanced because of his grace under extreme pressure—as he was constantly subjected to race-based threats while pursuing the home run record. See Tom Stanton, *Hank Aaron and the Home Run That Changed America* (New York: Harper, 2005).

17. The teleprompter is an electronic device that allows the text of a speech to be projected onto almost transparent screens at eye level of the speaker, on either side of his field of vision, so as to permit a speech to be delivered without the speaker having to look down constantly to papers on a lectern. The machine's operator scrolls the text of the speech to keep pace with the speaker.

18. Oral history interviews confirm that Clinton often did work on speeches up to the very moment of their delivery—and indeed would often extemporize while speaking. The story of the teleprompter and the health-care speech is recounted in George Stephanopoulos, *All Too Human: A Political Education* (Boston: Little, Brown and Company, 1999), 199–203. The wrong speech was initially loaded into the machine, an accident brought on by the fact that the text was being worked on so late that no time was left

to check the process. For several minutes, Clinton was forced to speak before a national television audience while an alphabet soup of verbiage spooled past his eyes on the teleprompter screens.

19. More on the family theater, including photographs, can be found at http://www .whitehousemuseum.org/east-wing/theater.htm.

20. Reagan's longtime political advisor, Stuart Spencer, has affirmed Judge's point. Spencer reports that Reagan had "great self-discipline. He would make sure—there are only two or three examples in his whole career that I can think of where he didn't—he was prepared for every event. He took pride in that. He was professional in getting prepared for them. He had the discipline that it takes to do that." See Stuart Spencer Interview, Miller Center, University of Virginia, Ronald Reagan Presidential Oral History Project, November 15–16, 2001, 23.

21. George Stephanopoulos uses the jazz metaphor, too, in *All Too Human*, 202–203.

22. Cheney was Ford's White House chief of staff.

23. The relationship of the speechwriting staff to the White House's policymaking offices is discussed in Bradley H. Patterson, *The White House Staff: Inside the West Wing and Beyond* (Washington, D.C.: Brookings Institution Press, 2000), 165–169.

24. Kissinger served as both national security advisor and secretary of state for Nixon, for a time holding both posts simultaneously.

25. Haldeman (1926–1993) was Richard Nixon's White House chief of staff. He was known for his no-nonsense style and devotion to the president and was convicted of several felony offenses in relation to the Watergate scandal. His published diary contains a wealth of information about the interior life of the Nixon presidency. See *The Haldeman Diaries: Inside the Nixon White House* (New York: G. P. Putnam's Sons, 1994).

26. The emergence of these cabinet councils is described by Reagan aide Martin Anderson in *Revolution: The Reagan Legacy* (Stanford, Calif.: Hoover Press, 1990). "A cabinet council was really a smaller, tailor-made version of the cabinet. Each cabinet council was designed to deal with certain specific issues of national policy. . . . The members of the cabinet councils were selected primarily on the basis that the departments they headed were deeply involved in the specific issues that would be discussed at the cabinet council meetings. . . . Initially there were five cabinet councils. One on economic affairs, one on natural resources and the environment, one on commerce and trade, one on human resources, and one on food and agriculture." Anderson, *Revolution*, 224, 226.

27. See Patterson, *White House Staff*, 163–164.

28. Bruce Reed was Bill Clinton's second chief domestic policy advisor, following Carol Rasco. Reed had previously written speeches for Tennessee senator Al Gore, and had been an influential advisor during the 1992 Clinton campaign. He was among a small group of aides who served all eight years in the Clinton White House.

29. Gene B. Sperling was one of the Clinton White House's chief economic policy advisors. He was a deputy to Robert Rubin at the newly created National Economic Council beginning in 1993 and later rose to head that office in the period 1996 through 2000.

30. Mark J. Penn was Bill Clinton's chief pollster for the 1996 reelection effort and into the second term. He filled the role earlier performed by Stanley Greenberg.

31. Nixon made pointed references several times in the 1970 address to the failure of Congress to act on important legislation he had previously submitted. For example, "Last year this administration sent to the Congress thirteen separate pieces of legislation dealing with organized crime, pornography, street crime, narcotics, crime in the District of Columbia. None of these bills has reached my desk for signature."

32. The tone of the 1971 address was markedly different, emphasizing the upside to what could be accomplished together, rather than pointing a censuring finger at failure:

"I ask this Congress to be responsive. If it is, then the 92d Congress, your Congress, our Congress, at the end of its term, will be able to look back on a record more splendid than any in our history. This can be the Congress that helped us end the longest war in the Nation's history, and end it in a way that will give us at last a genuine chance to enjoy what we have not had in this century: a full generation of peace. This can be the Congress that helped achieve an expanding economy, with full employment and without inflation—and without the deadly stimulus of war. This can be the Congress that reformed a welfare system that has robbed recipients of their dignity and robbed States and cities of their resources. . . . But above all, what this Congress can be remembered for is opening the way to a new American revolution—a peaceful revolution in which power was turned back to the people—in which government at all levels was refreshed and renewed and made truly responsive. This can be a revolution as profound, as far-reaching, as exciting as that first revolution almost 200 years ago—and it can mean that just 5 years from now America will enter its third century as a young nation new in spirit, with all the vigor and the freshness with which it began its first century. . . . So let us pledge together to go forward together—by achieving these goals to give America the foundation today for a new greatness tomorrow and in all the years to come, and in so doing to make this the greatest Congress in the history of this great and good country."

33. Lou Cannon affirms Judge's claim, reporting that most of the ideas that Reagan brought to Washington had been shaped in the 1950s. See *President Reagan: The Role of a Lifetime* (New York: PublicAffairs, 2000), 88–97.

34. Supporting Reagan's policymaking efforts was a think-tank community that also had spent years working on issues in preparation for the arrival of a committed conservative president. First among these was the Heritage Foundation, which had produced a vast and detailed set of policy blueprints headed *Mandate for Leadership 1980*. Heritage's founder, Ed Feulner, later recalled that "seven days after the election, we met with Martin Anderson, Dick Allen, Ed Meese and others in the basement of the Hay-Adams and we delivered them the first draft copies of 'Mandate for Leadership,'" which became known as the "Bible of the Reagan transition." See Tevi Troy, *Intellectuals and the American Presidency: Philosophers, Technicians, or Jesters?* (Lanham, MD: Rowman & Littlefield, 2003), 147–149.

35. For example, in 1970 Nixon commented on the broad outlines of his foreign policy within the annual message but alerted Congress to the fact that he would deal more

extensively with his thoughts in a forthcoming paper. On February 18 of that year, Nixon transmitted what was styled as the "First Annual Report to Congress on United States Foreign Policy for the 1970s." The print version ran to 160 pages. An electronic version can be found at http://www.presidency.ucsb.edu/ws/index.php?pid=2835&st=&st1=.

36. German language syntax is highly structured, with verbs always occupying the second position in a simple declarative sentence, and compound verbs divided between the second and the final position.

37. John Dickerson asserts that excessive applause has ruined the state of the union message. "After Kennedy's first State of the Union, the *New York Times* devoted a separate story to the topic: 'Capitol statisticians reported that President Kennedy's State of the Union was interrupted thirty-seven times by applause from one or both sides of the center aisle. . . . In seven State of the Union appearances before Congress President Eisenhower scored as high as fifty-seven interruptions for applause. . . . His average was thirty-three.' If the press was going to take the clapping seriously, what were politicians left to do but get into an arms race? Now there is clapping interrupted by speaking." See "The Silliest Speech in the Union: What's Wrong with the President's Annual Address," *Slate*, January 30, 2006, http://www.slate.com/id/2135101/.

38. Although opposition-party responses began in 1966, with replies to President Johnson by Senator Everett Dirksen (IL) and Representative Gerald Ford (MI), there was a much earlier practice of issuing *institutional* responses to the president's annual message. "Following British practice," notes Jeffrey K. Tulis, "the president received formal replies to his address from both houses of Congress," a practice that lasted only during the terms of Washington and John Adams, before being discarded by Jefferson as too monarchical (Tulis, *Rhetorical Presidency*, 55–56). A complete list of opposition party replies appears at http://www.senate.gov/artandhistory/history/resources/pdf/RespondStateUnion2.pdf.

39. Vice President Quayle served with President George H. W. Bush and developed a media reputation as not up to the challenges of high public office, based partly on a much-lampooned incident in which he encouraged a young spelling bee participant to add an "e" to the end of the word "potato."

40. Dole replied to Clinton's 1994 annual message using a devastatingly complex flowchart—stoking popular fears about government red tape in executing the Clinton healthcare plan. See Nigel Hamilton, *Bill Clinton: Mastering the Presidency* (New York: PublicAffairs, 2007), 262–263.

41. On the topic of resonating with the public, see Lyn Ragsdale, "Presidential Speechmaking and the Public Audience: Individual Presidents and Group Attitudes," *Journal of Politics* 49, no. 3 (August 1987): 704–736.

42. A leading skeptic of the president's ability to move Congress through the force of rhetoric is George C. Edwards III. See *On Deaf Ears: The Limits of the Bully Pulpit* (New Haven, Conn.: Yale University Press, 2003). See also Richard J. Powell, "Going Public Revisited: Presidential Speechmaking and the Bargaining Setting in Congress," *Congress and the Presidency* 26 (1999).

43. In his 1986 annual message, for example, Reagan included these lines: "And tonight, I ask you to give me what 43 Governors have—give me a line-item veto this year. Give me the authority to veto waste, and I'll take the responsibility, I'll make the cuts, I'll take the heat."

44. An example was President Clinton's June 11, 1999, address from the Oval Office, announcing a cessation of air strikes in Yugoslavia and the beginning of a new phase of that conflict. Clinton's remarks lasted twelve minutes. The text of the speech is available at http://clinton4.nara.gov/WH/New/html/19990611.html.

45. Franklin Roosevelt perfected the art of communicating to the American people on the radio, through what came to be called "fireside chats," because of FDR's captivating informality. He made some thirty of these addresses, from 1933 to 1944. Audio and texts are available on the Web site of the Miller Center of Public Affairs, at http://millercenter.org/scripps/archive/speeches. For analysis of FDR's communications skills, see Halford R. Ryan, *Franklin D. Roosevelt's Rhetorical Presidency* (Westport, Conn.: Greenwood Press, 1988).

46. Richard Nixon, as a vice presidential candidate on the ticket with General Dwight Eisenhower in 1952, found himself under attack for maintaining a fund raised by supporters to defray personal expenses associated with campaigning. Sensing his vulnerability, Nixon left the campaign trail and flew to Los Angeles, where on September 23 he delivered on national television what came to be called the "Checkers" speech—defending himself against ethics charges. He asserted that he and his wife, Pat, were of modest means, and deflected allegations that they were enriching themselves through political friends by noting that "Pat doesn't have a mink coat. But she does have a respectable Republican cloth coat." He also said that he had no intention of dignifying the opposition charges by returning money to donors, noting, too, that a supporter had given the Nixon family a cocker spaniel puppy, which daughter Tricia had named Checkers. "And you know, the kids, like all kids, love the dog and I just want to say this right now, that regardless of what they say about it, we're gonna keep it." The speech was a terrific success—Tom Wicker later called it "an American masterpiece"—notwithstanding Nixon's own immediate sense that he had failed. See Wicker, *One of Us: Richard Nixon and the American Dream* (New York: Random House, 1991), 85–108. Nixon's own account of the experience constitutes one chapter in his 1962 book, *Six Crises* (New York: Touchstone, 1990). Text and audio of the speech are available at the Web site of the Miller Center of Public Affairs, http://millercenter.org/scripps/archive/speeches/detail/4638.

47. This reference is probably to Nixon's November 3, 1969, speech to the nation about Vietnam. That text is available at http://www.vietnamwar.net/Nixon-2.htm.

48. Richard B. Wirthlin polled for Ronald Reagan both before Reagan's presidency and during his White House years. His survey-research studies are now archived at the Hoover Institution in Stanford, California. Pulse-meters, more commonly referred to as "dial meters," are now a standard tool for political strategists, especially those who are testing audience reactions to particular phrasings or who are trying to gauge intensity

of reactions. See Dennis W. Johnson, *No Place for Amateurs: How Political Consultants Are Reshaping Democracy* (New York: Routledge, 2001), 108–111.

49. In 1986, President Reagan joined with Democrats in Congress to pass a landmark law simplifying the tax code. The issue was politically problematic because polling indicated that many in the American public saw the bill as an effort to smuggle into law a tax increase. The story of the passage of this law is thoroughly documented in Alan Murray and Jeffrey Birnbaum, *Showdown at Gucci Gulch: Lawmakers, Lobbyists, and the Unlikely Triumph of Tax Reform* (New York: Random House, 1987).

50. Ronald Reagan, *The Reagan Diaries* (New York: HarperCollins, 2007).

51. The phrase "stay the course" had an uneven history in the George W. Bush White House. The president did use the term to describe his Iraq policy at various times in his presidency, ranging at least from 2003 to 2006, but on other occasions—evidently motivated by the kinds of concerns voiced by Khachigian here—he sought directly to distance himself from the term. This resulted in press accounts in October 2006 that the White House was dropping the phrase. See, for example, Peter Baker, "Bush's New Tack Steers Clear of 'Stay the Course,'" *Washington Post*, October 24, 2006, A1.

52. Edmonds's assertion about President Clinton's use of polling is contrary to the conventional wisdom on this point. Popular perceptions during the Clinton presidency were that his White House was particularly responsive to what the pollsters were saying—based on press accounts that had the president polling to determine such things as the site of a family holiday in 1996. Even Clinton pollster Dick Morris has reflected, "Sometimes I carried polling too far," in a chapter devoted to "The Presidential Vacation" (Morris, *Behind the Oval Office: Winning the Presidency in the Nineties* [New York: Random House, 1997], 235). A wholly accurate picture will await the opening of the Clinton archives, but the scholarship on this point is summarized in Caroline Heldman's assertion that "President Clinton polled like no other president to date, staking out policy positions and crafting agendas based on public opinion." See John G. Greer, ed., *Public Opinion and Polling around the World: A Historical Encyclopedia* (Santa Barbara, Calif.: ABC-CLIO, 2004), p. 429. A dissenting interpretation is available in Joe Klein, *The Natural: The Misunderstood Presidency of Bill Clinton* (New York: Broadway, 2003).

53. Penn was responsible for designing and directing the strategy for Hillary Clinton's failed bid for the presidency in 2008.

54. Richard S. Morris served as a political consultant for Bill Clinton both when Clinton was running for public office in Arkansas and later when he was president. Morris was a controversial figure in part because he was willing to work for candidates from both political parties. When he ran for president in 1992, Clinton did not use Morris, but he invited him back into the fold after the devastating loss of the House of Representatives to the Republicans in the 1994 midterm elections. Clinton initially insisted that Morris's return be hidden from all but a few of his very closest advisors, but eventually the relationship became known publicly. Morris left the Clinton team in disgrace in the middle of the 1996 presidential campaign, because of press reports of Morris's

assignations with a prostitute. His own account of those years is found in *Behind the Oval Office.*

55. Alger Hiss was an official in the U.S. Department of State in the 1940s who was accused by journalist Whittaker Chambers—who had admitted to being a Communist earlier in his life—of being a Soviet spy. The resulting legal and political conflict between the two set off an enduring culture war between those who sided with the urbane Hiss and others who believed Chambers's charges to be correct. Richard Nixon developed a national reputation in relation to this case, as he sided with the conservative Chambers as a member of the House Un-American Activities Committee. Nixon's investigations helped turn up incriminating evidence against Hiss in the form of microfilm documents hidden in a pumpkin on Chambers's Maryland farm. For more on the Hiss case, see G. Edward White, *Alger Hiss's Looking Glass Wars: The Covert Life of a Soviet Spy* (Oxford: Oxford University Press), 2005.

56. The Gettysburg Address comes in at 272 words.

57. In his 1960 annual message, President Eisenhower observed, "I am not unique as a President in having worked with a Congress controlled by the opposition party—except that no other President ever did it for quite so long! Yet in both personal and official relationships we have weathered the storms of the past five years. For this I am grateful." Eisenhower lost both houses of Congress to the Democrats in the 1954 midterms, so he served for six years with divided government. David R. Mayhew reminds us, however, that "divided control is not a new phenomenon. During a twenty-two year stretch between 1874 and 1896 . . . the two parties shared control of the government for sixteen years." *Divided We Govern: Party Control, Lawmaking, and Investigations, 1946–1990* (New Haven, Conn.: Yale University Press, 1991), 1.

58. Judge's comments here were corrected from the original.

59. Zachary Taylor (1784–1850) served as president from March 1849 to July 1850, when he died in office from gastrointestinal distress (allegedly brought on by an overconsumption of cherries and cold milk on the Fourth of July). He was a Whig and came into office with both the House and Senate controlled by the Democrats.

60. Reagan spoke to a joint session of Congress on economic recovery on February 18, 1981. The text of that speech is available at http://www.reagan.utexas.edu/archives/speeches/1981/21881a.htm.

61. President Reagan underwent prostate surgery on January 5, 1987.

62. "Mice" was a derisive nickname for the several junior aides an unpopular Donald Regan brought with him to the chief of staff's office to help run the White House in the second term. See Cannon, *Role of a Lifetime,* 500–503.

63. Robert H. Bork was a conservative jurist whom Reagan unsuccessfully tried to place on the U.S. Supreme Court in 1987.

64. Reagan spoke at the Brandenburg Gate in Berlin on June 12, 1987, and urged Soviet leader Mikhail Gorbachev to tear down the wall. Robinson speaks at length about the construction of this speech in Chapter 9.

65. The magnitude of this success is placed in proper perspective by noting that George H. W. Bush was the first sitting vice president since Martin Van Buren, in 1836, to be elected directly to the presidency.

66. Bill Clinton's 1998 state of the union message was delivered mere days after news broke that the president had been sexually involved with a young White House staffer.

67. For contemporaneous commentary confirming the immediate reaction to Clinton's 1998 state of the union message, see "Addressing History," transcript of *NewsHour* with Jim Lehrer, January 28, 1998, available at http://www.pbs.org/newshour/bb/white_house/jan-june98/historians_1-28.html.

68. The productivity of divided government is the core thesis of Mayhew's *Divided We Govern*.

69. Extensive evidence documenting the decline in viewership of presidential speeches can be found in Edwards, *On Deaf Ears*, ch. 8. See also Matthew A. Baum and Samuel Kernell, "Has Cable Ended the Golden Age of Presidential Television?" *American Political Science Review* 93, no. 1 (March 1999): 99–114.

70. By one of Edwards's measures, Judge appears to be correct: "[The] percentage of households owning televisions that watched the president for an average minute decreased steadily from the Nixon administration through the Clinton years." But the overall evidence seems more ambiguous. For example, in a chart Edwards provides based on a 1999 study, the lowest percentage-of-homes viewership for a state of the union message occured in 1974 (Nixon), and the highest in 1981 (Reagan). *On Deaf Ears*, 190–191.

71. This quote is taken from Nixon's 1974 state of the union address.

Chapter 8

The Crisis Speech and Other Landmark Addresses: Managing Speechwriting and Decision Making[1]

Andrew Rudalevige

Theodore Roosevelt's "bully pulpit" is more bully than ever, these days, propelled physically across the world and aurally across all manner of airwaves. Its expansion has engendered an immense amount of scholarship. Students of the "rhetorical presidency" have assessed nearly every aspect of presidential discourse: its literary merit, its influence on its various audiences, its implications for presidential personality, even its role in authoring a "second Constitution" governing the meaning and role of the office itself.[2] Scholars studying the "institutional presidency" have tracked instead the growth of the staff and coordinating resources needed to support presidents' propensity to "go public" with increasing frequency and geographic dispersion.[3]

This chapter takes a rather different approach to the topic by bridging these literatures to examine presidents' discretionary addresses.[4] Grounded in notions of presidential staff management, what follows is more "institutional" than "rhetorical." But the distinction is largely artificial in the first place. Any bargaining with the public, through speechmaking, over the problems and solutions facing the nation must first reflect the president's bargaining within the executive branch over those same matters. If the most important resources a president controls are his time and his words,[5] managing the speechwriting process intertwines those assets. The issue is less one of speechwriting and decision making, perhaps, than of speechwriting as decision making.

Indeed, as Richard Neustadt put it soon after his tenure as a White House aide, a president's communication to the outside world cannot be separated from decision making within his inner circle. "Messages, speeches, . . . and the like," Neustadt said,

are not merely vehicles for expressing policy, they are devices for getting policy decided. They have deadlines attached. And there is nothing like a deadline on the
statement of a policy for getting a decision on what that policy shall be. . . . [Speech-
writing includes] not only the power that goes with choosing the words but also the
power that goes with presenting the issues for decision. The preparation of these
great "action" documents was rarely an editorial matter. Ordinarily it was a matter of
helping the President decide what to say, as well as how to say it.[6]

In today's White House, speechwriters do not give that help on their
own—at least not always—and some argue they should not. Their advice
comes as part and parcel of a wider set of presidential choices about decision
making, shaping how information flows within and through the executive
office. Although it is common to impute conclusions about presidents' personality from their speeches, it might be more useful to derive them from
their decision-making process instead. How well does the "power to choose
the words" mesh with the "power to present the issues for decision"? How
does that power reflect, and itself affect, presidential power more broadly?
Speeches and rhetoric are often regarded as the independent variable caus-
ing change in other aspects of the polity.[7] Here they will be treated as the
dependent variable, the outcome created by other processes.

This chapter centers on "landmark" presidential addresses, often made
in reaction to ongoing national problems. Examples include Richard
Nixon's "Silent Majority" speech on the Vietnam War in November 1969
and Jimmy Carter's speech on America's "crisis of confidence" (a.k.a. the
"malaise" speech) ten years later. Such speeches respond to events, circumstances, or even proximate emergencies, as did George W. Bush's addresses
to the nation after the September 11, 2001, terrorist attacks. These are by
their nature exceptional speeches and represent, of course, a small subset of
presidential rhetoric. "Presidents are now giving 400–500 speeches a year,"
estimates Clinton speechwriter Don Baer, devoting much time and verbiage
to what LBJ staffer Bill Moyers called "Rose Garden Rubbish."[8]

To be sure, even putatively banal events may serve as a platform for policymaking or for sending signals to key constituencies. Still, landmark addresses are those speeches most likely to "stick," the ones returned to by
historians and used as benchmarks for assessing presidential influence on
specific policies. Studying them allows us to focus on presidential proactive-
ness: that is, on the elevation of specific issues to presidential attention and
the process by which informational inputs are transformed into presidentially

uttered outputs.[9] And such a focus highlights the impressive variance in that process, from Truman's organized speech conferences to Nixon's self-isolation with his legal pads, from Carter's frenzied consultations to Clinton's speeches born (his staff thought) by "immaculate conception." Indeed, the cases here show little in the way of pure patterning, for landmark speeches tend to be at one remove even from the normal institutional flow of a given White House.

That variance, in turn, itself tells us something important, not just about presidential prolixity but about presidential power. Defense Secretary Donald Rumsfeld memorably observed that "stuff happens, and to that stuff, presidents may or must react."[10] But presidents also make things happen. The force of their leadership—both within their administrations and across the nation and world—is expressed in each case by their timely words.

Presidential Staffing as Agenda-Setting

In framing the discussion that follows it is useful first to think about agenda-setting. Using the term with regard to the president's rhetoric and its effect on external audiences is perhaps unproblematic; certainly much scholarship and punditry study the influence of presidential speech on legislators, bureaucrats, and the wider public. Along these lines, George W. Bush's few stated regrets about his presidency centered on issues of communication. As he noted with some chagrin, "As President of the United States, you better be careful what you say."[11]

Using the term with regard to staffing is perhaps less intuitive. As before, the key is the transmission of information. But while with external communication there is at least the implication of information scarcity—one listens to the president to find out something one doesn't know, perhaps the explanation of an action or policy position—the internal face is different. Here, the starting point is that presidents have too much, rather than too little, information potentially available to them. As Nobel laureate Herbert Simon has argued (with regard to the top of any large organization), "the scarce resource is not information," it is attention, and the simple "processing capacity to attend to information."[12]

Recent work on presidential hierarchy builds on this insight. It posits staff institutions as a limiting structure imposed upon a chaotic informational environment.[13] Shorn of the jargon of the public choice literature, this just means that staff serve as a filter or screen—or, just as accurately, as an agenda, similar to those used by legislatures to order and restrict their potentially limitless alternatives. Advising hierarchies guides the consideration of policy alternatives, creating outputs from the sequential consideration of different options; they reduce the ocean of information at the bottom of the organizational pyramid to a manageable puddle at the top. They are, in short, agendas, only in the form of an organization chart.

Students of game theory know that legislative agendas are not neutral: even assuming the same preferences and the same basic options, the sequence and combinations in which alternatives are considered can lead to different results. This is why the Rules Committee in the House of Representatives, which governs that ordering, is so powerful. Like other agendas, hierarchies are always biased in some way. Some information vanishes and some makes it to the top: which does what depends on how presidents organize their advising, either formally or through the routines and cultures that they develop or encourage. As a result, presidents' ongoing choices in this area will affect their future options for subsequent decisions.

Structure is not the whole story, certainly. No one would argue that presidential personality, or the relative skills of administration staffers, have no effect on policy choices—and we will see that in spades below. Still, advisory institutions are an important starting point for examining decision-making outcomes: those traits and abilities are wielded on a field of play at least bounded by organizational design and reporting relationships.

So how can presidents structure their staffs to obtain the best information? Most of the relatively limited research on this question points to the need to integrate different lines of advice, as a means of (in Richard Rose's nice phrase) "institutionalizing distrust."[14] It argues that presidents should ensure that generalist expertise is brought to bear on technical policy, thereby suggesting that institutions should be built around functional tasks—such as communications—rather than hiving those tasks off from foreign and domestic policy advising.[15] After all, the kind of information any executive needs will span different issue-arenas, and different problems interact across those arenas that affect both the intended and unintended consequences of policy choice.

This research also argues that presidents must empower diverse preferences and viewpoints as a vital cross-check on basic assumptions and conclusions, correcting for existing lines of bias—including their own. This can be done systematically (as in Franklin Roosevelt's "competitive" staff system) or by less intentional structural means (as in Ronald Reagan's staff "troika").

Either way, presidents overlap staff jurisdictions in an attempt to glean the best advice through a sort of marketplace of ideas.[16] Or it can be done on an ad hoc basis by seeking information far down the hierarchical pyramid, allowing the president to monitor that ongoing informational winnowing in making accurate decisions about which data are extraneous to his needs. John F. Kennedy, for example, was known to call on bureaucrats at all levels of the organizational chart in search of additional information.

These strategies generate a wealth of information for the president and ensure that he will maintain final control over decisions. They do not guarantee that he will make good decisions, but instead give him the chance to do so. Even so, they involve trade-offs, in time and in staffs' and presidents' personal, sometimes duplicated, efforts. Nor do staff members typically enjoy competitive processes.

Staff members' enjoyment shouldn't matter much: the process is meant to protect presidential choice, not staff perquisites. But in recent decades, with the development of a large and substantively specialized White House operation, presidents have veered away from the managerial efforts involved in the methods recommended here. They have tended toward more formal hierarchies and staff systems. Some observers suggest that this protects their time at the expense of their knowledge.[17] As we will see, the same may be true for their speechwriting.

Integrating Communication with Decision Making

What are the implications of these findings for the management of speechwriting and rhetoric? The growth of the White House staff and its increasing specialization pervade the communications arena.[18] For instance, under the Clinton administration, as Terry Edmonds recalls, "there was a domestic policy speechwriting team and a separate foreign policy speechwriting team." The National Security Council achieved formal control over foreign policy speeches in what NSC speechwriter Jeremy Rosner concedes was "the biggest turf grab in White House history." Clinton national security adviser Anthony Lake, however, characterized his staff's incursion as "simply efficiency."[19]

Enhanced efficiency was the justification for another important change as well. Nixon speechwriting head Jim Keogh, fending off the "heavy hand" of Lake's predecessor (and former boss) Henry Kissinger, told Chief of Staff H. R. Haldeman that "if this office is to have responsibility for these speeches then we should have control of them."[20] Instead speechwriters gradually were removed from policy deliberation. Raymond Moley could describe his writing job for Franklin Roosevelt as one that would "sift proposals for him, discuss facts and ideas with him, and help him crystallize his own policy."[21] Into the late 1960s, those who constructed speeches were employed not as writers first but rather as government generalists, and most saw, in Kennedy-Johnson aide Richard Goodwin's words, "the two roles—writer and policy-maker—[as] symbiotic."[22] But although "the Johnson White House was not the first to employ specialized speechcrafters . . . it was the last not to."[23] Richard Nixon systematized a late-term Johnson innovation that has been maintained by every president since: organizing writing specialists in a separate White House unit. This was deferential to the notion of writing as a craft, but it valued that craft rather low in the White House hierarchy.

The import of Nixon's move was initially disguised by his real effort to include speechwriters in meetings as active members of his policy development team, aided by what Lee Huebner calls Chief of Staff H. R. Haldeman's "rather military" adherence to Nixon's wishes in such matters.[24] But the pressures of Watergate, combined with staff turnover, eroded this process. In time, speechwriters were downgraded in the hierarchy. They found it hard to gain White House mess privileges or even security passes that would allow them unchaperoned access to the West Wing. Such slights put a symbolic stamp on their declining prestige while complicating their attempts to mingle with, and gain insight from, policy staff. It became hard for someone like the Reagan administration's Clark Judge to conduct the sort of invaluable informal policy coordination that he describes as occurring "over the lunch table at the White House mess with the senior strategist at NSC."[25]

Such narrowing of the speechwriters' role and diminution of their status also encouraged the expansion of a "staffing out" gauntlet that allowed as many as a dozen offices to review and edit speech drafts. Under Gerald Ford, even the president's remarks to a Christmas party for the White House press corps required approval from eight different staff units.[26] Reagan speechwriter Peggy Noonan compared the process to "sending a beautiful newborn fawn out into the jagged wilderness where the grosser animals would pierce its tender flesh."[27] Speeches developed in such a manner could lose not just their rhetorical flair but also their policy coherence.

Certainly there are costs to arming Bambi as he ranges into the policy world. Populating the Great Society through presidential oratory sometimes meant that major policy initiatives emerged mainly as a means for curing writers' block. LBJ budget director Charles Schultze complained that the "damned speechwriters spend more money than all the rest of the Executive Branch put together."[28]

But the wider discussion of staffing makes clear that "simply efficiency" is not always the prevailing value when it comes to the informational economics of the presidency. Less literal costs also attend the specialized separation of speechwriters from policy staff; indeed, Martin Medhurst dismisses as "myth" the notion that speechwriting is best when divorced from the policy process.[29] Huebner notes the potential constructive role of the communications staff in coordinating the myriad "often scattered policy suggestions that come up from the government." Likewise, Reagan speechwriter Peter Robinson echoes the earlier Neustadt quote in suggesting that the various staff councils "chugging decisions towards the President" did not achieve policy closure until "there was a speech on the schedule and a deadline and you had to do it." The competitive White House structure Ken Khachigian and Robinson describe elsewhere in this volume allowed Reagan's communications staff an occasional voice in that process and a more common role as "referee" coordinating "all th[e] internal disputes." This system produced creative jockeying even as it also produced "blood on the floor."

In sum, policymaking and speechwriting are most successful when closely integrated—that is, when brought together as part of a diverse institution built around the need to produce relevant presidential rhetoric—rather than segregated by walling off policymaking from "wordsmithing." Such integration can take place in the same person, as in the Truman White House, or it can be organizationally separate. Coordination can be centered in the president, or in an aide, and it can be collaborative or competitive. But either way, making speeches and making decisions are not separate tasks. Presidents, then, face a managerial task along with their communicative burden.

The Staffing of the Speech

How are these themes made manifest in the landmark discretionary addresses that are the focus of this chapter? In some ways it would be nice to approach this question quantitatively, coding staff inputs and impact, and tracing within the universe of speeches the variance in outputs produced by different staffing structures. In the present case, though, there are two reasons to take a different tack.

One is purely pragmatic. In a recent article, two scholars using archival records from the George H. W. Bush presidential library sought to track and measure the influence on presidential rhetoric exercised by various White House aides on Bush's policy and writing staffs. Their approach is interesting, their efforts immense—and for all that, they achieved the quantitative study of a single speech by a single president.[30] Yet presidents give hundreds of speeches annually, some of which become landmark addresses.[31] There is not space enough, or time, to work through a representative sample of these speeches.

There are also theoretical reasons not to do so. For one thing, landmark speeches are outliers, not those that fit on a regression line. They are the exceptions that prove the rule—or rather, as we will see in the cases themselves, the rule is that they are exceptions. The speechwriters' discussions throughout this volume make clear that, as Robinson puts it, "the large speeches . . . were different."[32] Note that major addresses, almost by definition, receive sustained presidential attention; they flow from the standard speechwriting template but they are also set apart from it. In such cases assessing the particular process involved in creating a speech, and assessing it through the prism of staff management may well be more instructive than a larger study could be. The latter might identify trends (the what) but not processes (the why).

In this spirit five examples follow. The first lays out the Truman model, as the classic "functional" template of organizing the communications process that had developed by the time of the Korean War. The others—from the Nixon, Clinton, George W. Bush, and Carter administrations—all came after the shift to a separate writing office and thus serve as contrasts, chosen to show variations on the theme of staff specialization. The Carter speeches are particularly useful in suggesting the limits as well as the benefits of a functional approach, and are presented out of chronological order for that purpose.

Truman, 1950: Clearing the Air

During the Truman years, the roles of policy aide and speechwriter were combined in the same persons. As Truman's administrative assistant George Elsey later recalled, "We did not have neat little compartments, little boxes, one person being assigned or one group of people being assigned to one area of work and another group to another. . . . [The White House counsel] and I, and the people that we would borrow from time to time from the Bureau of the Budget or other Government agencies, did what had to be done.

There wasn't a matter of one group being domestic and another group being foreign and another group being political [and] another group concerned with Capitol Hill relations."[33]

Nor was a single writer usually assigned to a speech. Instead, drafting was a collaborative process among three or four staffers under the direction of the president's special counsel—first Clark Clifford, then Charles Murphy—who received initial guidance from Truman himself. Aides from the White House staff and the Bureau of the Budget (BoB), which at that time were nearly interchangeable, would work with staff from one or more executive departments (on foreign affairs, this included State and Defense, as well as the Mutual Security staff under Averill Harriman). Then relevant cabinet members would be asked to read the draft and try to improve it, usually after the president had already seen it. These were productive but occasionally scathing sessions. Future BoB director David Bell, at the time a White House staffer, remembered "a classic occasion, during the Korean war. We had worked hard and prepared a draft, and. . . . Dean Acheson said with that magnificent English manner of his: 'You can't ask the President of the United States to utter this crap.' And he was probably right." Acheson's saving grace, Bell added, was that he was one of those who when he "did something like that, would get up and take off their coats and say, 'Where's the nearest typewriter?'"[34]

None of the core group working on Truman's speeches were primarily writers. They were, instead, as BoB aide Richard Neustadt recalled, "lawyers and economists and public administration types who had picked up along the way a skill as generalists in government." They did not necessarily possess much literary polish, but since Truman's idea of a good speech was "a direct statement of the facts without trimmings and without oratory," the process seemed to work. It also forged a tight connection between policy and rhetoric. Another BoB staffer, James Sundquist, wrote of Murphy that he "controlled the flow of words from the presidential office. . . . By being in charge of the words that explained the president's program, Murphy became perforce the coordinator of program development as well."[35]

The integration of policy with rhetoric is clear in the lead-up to the major wartime speech that Truman delivered in December 1950—his "Report to the American People on the National Emergency."[36] As the title makes clear, the stakes were high. The speech followed on the heels of a roller-coaster half-year, with early disaster in Korea averted by the Inchon counteroffensive, then threatened anew when General Douglas MacArthur dismissed

both the Chinese threat and the president's authority. A long military struggle seemed in the offing; there were hints of Soviet involvement, if only to
take advantage of America's distraction, and already the limited "police action" was unpopular. Truman was about to issue a proclamation declaring
a national emergency stemming from Korea and the threat of "world con-
quest by communist imperialism," thereby activating additional presidential
powers over economic and military mobilization. He wanted, in the opening words of the speech, to explain to Americans "what our country is up
against, and what we are going to do about it."

To answer those questions for the public, Truman had to answer them
for himself. To do that, he scheduled an address to the nation. "It's funny,"
the president observed, "how a pending speech will clear the air on policies."[37] Two weeks of consultation followed, involving the White House
staff, including counsel and "boss of the drafters" Murphy;[38] the cabinet; the
members of the NSC, including Vice President Alben Barkley; British prime
minister Clement Attlee; and two large bipartisan groups of congressional
leaders.[39]

The speech itself, after ten drafts, was finalized in an evening conference with Murphy sitting at the president's right hand and Secretary of State
Acheson at his left. At least five other White House and BoB aides who had
worked on the speech were present, as well as Council of Economic Advisers
chairman Leon Keyserling, economics aide Robert Turner, and an aide to
foreign policy adviser Harriman. Secretary of Defense George Marshall and
General Omar Bradley had weighed in on the draft earlier that day. "I've put
a lot into this thing," Truman noted as they wrapped up after nearly three
hours of going through the text line by line.[40]

Such a process allowed the president both to learn and to synthesize competing views. Advice was openly solicited; Mutual Security counsel Theodore
Tannenwald recalls that Truman's last question was always "'Does anybody
have anything to say?' And the rule of the house was that you could be the
lowest man on the totem pole, and if you thought there was something that
ought to be said, you could do it."[41]

As Truman later wrote, "Until the decision was reached, I wanted [my
staff] to argue. . . . And we had to do a good deal of arguing that December."
Such dissensus did not help external perceptions of the administration,
which was derided as divided and weak. But Truman thought it worthwhile,
given the magnitude of the venture at hand. He was asking for authority to
reinstate centralized direction of the national economy to boost production,

only a few years after World War II's controls had expired; he was going to accelerate the draft to remobilize millions of soldiers and sailors; and he wanted to raise taxes to pay for all this and for more aid to America's allies. Even in so doing, the best result he could predict was that "we hope we can prevent another world war."[42]

Truman was pleased with the speech—"one of the best we ever did," he told his assembled drafters. This claim is hard to assess. It was not a rhetorical masterpiece; nor did it do him much immediate political good, as far as Gallup Poll ratings can measure.[43] That said, the speech allowed him to say what he wanted to say and, more important, it showed that he controlled the direction of his administration. As a mechanism for internal agenda-setting, then, and for asserting presidential authority over the other branches of government, the speech was clearly a success.

Nixon, 1969: A Majority of One

At the other end of the spectrum in terms of open argument, but evoking a similar sense of presidential control, is the example of Richard Nixon in the autumn of 1969. The president's November 3 "Address to the Nation on the War in Vietnam" is notable for who wrote it: the president. "He did [it] entirely by himself," says longtime Nixon writer Ray Price. Nixon, Richard Reeves has observed, "believed writing—clarifying and transferring ideas into enlightening and persuasive rhetoric—was the most important part of the presidency."[44]

On Vietnam, there was much persuading to do. Having inherited half a million troops in country, with over thirty thousand Americans dead, Nixon faced pressure both to withdraw American forces and avoid making "Johnson's war" his own and to escalate the fight to win the war. Nixon's intention to give the speech was announced on October 13, setting off three weeks of fevered speculation about its contents.

Nixon provided no advance notice, or even hints, about the direction he proposed to take.[45] He immersed himself in writing the speech, retreating to Camp David in late October and putting in twelve-hour-plus days. He produced at least twelve longhand drafts on legal pads before announcing to Chief of Staff H. R. Haldeman after an all-night session that "the baby's just been born!"[46]

Meanwhile, Nixon sent out for food, and for information. On October 27, for instance, he sent a brief memo to National Security Adviser Henry

Kissinger: "Is it possible we were wrong from the start in Vietnam?"[47] He received advice and draft language from staff, cabinet officials, congressional leaders (including Democrats such as Senator Hubert Humphrey and Senate Majority Leader Mike Mansfield), and outside contacts like British military adviser Robert Thompson. "Mostly, though," Reeves notes, "he asked himself. The others, including Kissinger, did not know what he was thinking or exactly why he was asking."[48] This made the speech-drafting process one that implicitly encouraged competition to offer the best idea, the approach that would most appeal to the president.[49] As a result he received wildly varying advice, some of it internally contradictory: Thompson, for instance, told him both that the United States could not escalate and that "the future of Western civilization is at stake" in Vietnam.[50]

Pundits expected a new and dramatic peace overture.[51] Yet Nixon concluded in the speech that "precipitate withdrawal would . . . be a disaster of immense magnitude" for U.S. interests. Instead he renewed his commitment to strengthen South Vietnam's capacity for self-defense. "In the previous administration, we Americanized the war in Vietnam. In this administration, we are Vietnamizing the search for peace." This process would take time, and in what became the speech's signature moment, Nixon assured vocal antiwar protesters that he shared their goals, but not their tactics. Instead, he sought to outflank their movement by calling on "the great silent majority of my fellow Americans" for patience and support. He also warned the North Vietnamese that any escalation of the fighting on their part would be met in kind.[52]

Although Nixon asked a lot of questions during the drafting process, it is hard to believe that he did not have answers already in mind. Still, the process clarified for him the stakes involved on each side and the choices he needed—and wanted—to make. If he arrived at a middle option, it was one he had synthesized effectively and affirmatively selected.

Nixon was happy with the results, to the point of grandiosity. He later wrote that "very few speeches actually influence the course of history. The November 3 speech was one of them."[53] Of course, by that standard, other speeches crafted by mortal hands—even those of writers as talented as William Safire, Ray Price, and Pat Buchanan—were bound to disappoint. As noted earlier, Nixon was adept at matching writers to topics, depending on what stylistic and ideological spin he wanted a speech to have. He also linked writers to the policy decision process and was good at giving clear guidance, through "initial instructions and aggressive editing," about theme, topic, and tone.[54]

But such two-way communication took effort and extended the preparation time for speeches. The president complained constantly about this process, as well as about the writers' inability to draft the down-to-earth material he claimed to want, with fewer "facts" and more "heart."[55] In the end, of course, Nixon's heart was in his splendid isolation, and that caused its own problems. But his example suggests that there is no single model of a functional advising structure. Good information can flow via either meeting or memo, if the president is willing to invest a substantial amount of attention in the process.

Clinton, 1994–1995: Immaculate Conception

A very different example of a president guarding his power of choice through a sort of isolation—directly relevant to notions of "competitive ad-hocracy"— is provided by Bill Clinton.

In the wake of the 1994 midterm elections that returned both chambers of Congress to Republican control for the first time since the early 1950s, Clinton was unsure how to proceed. "The president is relevant here! . . . I have shown good faith!" he assured the nation (or perhaps himself), but how to prove it? Distressed and seeking a new approach, Clinton renewed his relationship with his longtime consultant, Dick Morris, thereby forming an alliance against his own staff, whom Clinton termed "the children who got me elected."[56]

Morris was soon in constant but secret contact with Clinton, establishing a "beachhead" of influence through speechwriting: "that's where he invaded Normandy," Clinton aide Jonathan Prince later noted. One early result was a December 1994 speech proposing a Middle Class Bill of Rights. "Nobody knew how it got on the schedule; no one knew what it was supposed to be," recalls speechwriter Don Baer, who was told to work on the speech with domestic aide Bruce Reed: "it was only supposed to be the two of us." The mysterious genesis of the initiative was dubbed the "immaculate conception."[57]

Clinton's speech was not well reviewed by liberal Washingtonians, but the president was nonetheless pleased that he had competing advice from Morris and his allies with which to work. The relegation of most of the president's staff to a "Potemkin Village White House" counterpoised to "another whole White House which was really driving things," as Baer put it, suggested that Clinton had regained the ability to set the agenda he wanted.

Perhaps not coincidentally, late 1994 also marked Clinton's turn to serious reading of presidential history.[58]

As early as the "immaculate conception" speech, Clinton went so far as to type or, in his own hand, to copy Morris's suggested drafts to disguise their source. But as his influence grew, Morris found centrist allies in the White House. Chief of Staff Leon Panetta was no fan of Morris, but he knew that Clinton wanted to use the consultant and accepted the president's preroga-tive to seek advice from a wide circle. Indeed, Morris expanded policy par-ticipation quite importantly by combing the broader bureaucracy for ideas that fit his model of "triangulation" between and above liberal Democrats and the new Republican majority, making Clinton's speeches relentlessly substantive, if also relentlessly poll-tested.[59]

By the spring of 1995, Clinton was ready to wrest the initiative back from Congress and the Republicans' "Contract with America." In this pe-riod Clinton gave an important speech that was truly discretionary in both timing and content: the so-called Pile of Vetoes address. Morris—still hidden from most of the White House staff—was pushing the president to draw a line in the sand, to specify where he could find common ground with the GOP, and where he could not. But the faction-ridden White House staff split, able to agree only that the president should argue against cuts in fed-eral education funding.

Clinton chose to move ahead with a broader agenda. In April 1995, without informing key domestic staffers such as George Stephanopoulos, he shelved the education speech two days after signing off on it. In its place he gave the members of the American Association of Newspaper Editors a long, detailed address on where compromise with the Republican agenda might be possible—remarks drafted by Morris, polished by Baer, and then largely ad-libbed by the president. "I do not want a pile of vetoes," Clinton said; "I want a pile of bills that will move this country into the future. . . . I want us to surprise everybody in America by rolling up our sleeves and joining hands and working together." He listed a number of areas where bargaining with Congress might take place: "We both want tax cuts, less intrusive Gov-ernment regulations, the line-item veto, the toughest possible fight against crime." At the same time, the president promised to block a slew of "ex-treme" GOP proposals and promoted his own dormant legislative program, including the items in the Middle Class Bill of Rights.[60]

The management process for this speech involved the president holding the cards and playing the White House staff against an invisible opponent.

(Morris was often described as a black hole: unseen, but exerting a powerful gravitational pull.) Most of the staff, unsurprisingly, hated this. But what prompts staff approbation is not always good for the president. The process, Baer later commented, "absolutely served the President well."[61]

Clinton continued to triangulate, adopting in June the Contract with America's pledge of a balanced budget, though at a different pace and with different cuts than those proposed by the Republicans in Congress.[62] Soon thereafter, Clinton eased away from Morris. But competition continued: Morris became one voice among many as Clinton adopted a "pattern of navigating through crosscurrents of conflicting advice, fashioning a course that was distinctively his own."[63]

In fact, as the administration progressed, crossover between policy staff and speechwriters increased to a point not seen since the Johnson administration. According to Robert Schlesinger, Clinton "preferred to work on speeches with aides who could answer substantive questions about policy," seeking what Baer called a "one-stop shop." By 1997, "gone were the days when policy and speeches were developed on separate tracks." In that sense the Clinton process was a "throwback" to the Johnson years[64]—though the Truman experience offers just as apt a comparison, with Dick Morris temporarily in the role of Charles Murphy.

Bush, 2001: The Guy They Quote

Another wartime speech by another president with expansive views of executive authority provides a different, and probably more replicable, model of speechwriter–policy staff integration. George W. Bush would later tell Bob Woodward that, as commander in chief, "I don't need to explain"—but a week after the September 11, 2001, terrorist attacks in New York, Washington, and rural Pennsylvania, he clearly did.[65] On the evening of the attacks, Bush had given a less-than-reassuring brief talk from the White House, followed by several days of meandering bellicosity. He had set neither a firm tone nor a course of action, at least publicly, to which Americans could respond.

That started to change on September 20, when Bush addressed a nationally televised joint session of Congress in the House chamber. "Tonight," he declared, "we are a country awakened to danger and called to defend freedom. Our grief has turned to anger and anger to resolution. Whether we bring our enemies to justice or bring justice to our enemies, justice will be done." Not only must the Taliban regime in Afghanistan hand over Osama bin Laden to the United States, but every nation in the world was warned, "either you are with us, or you are with the terrorists." A long struggle was promised: "our war on terror . . . will not end until every terrorist group of global reach has been found, stopped, and defeated. . . . We will not tire; we will not falter; and we will not fail."[66]

Like most speeches of Bush's first term, the September 20 address was largely crafted by a trio of speechwriters composed of Michael Gerson (who tended to get most of the credit),[67] John McConnell, and Matthew Scully. Presidential counselor Karen Hughes also was closely involved and made many of the final rhetorical calls.[68]

Unlike many speechwriters in previous administrations who found themselves cut off from presidential contact, Gerson, McConnell, and Scully had been with Bush before and during the tough 2000 campaign—he knew and trusted them. Bush was a president who (unlike his father) realized not only that public appearances are important but also (unlike Jimmy Carter or, at the outset, Bill Clinton) that he could productively use speechwriters to help make those appearances successful.[69] And unlike many White Houses, in the Bush administration, the communications chief was arguably the president's top aide.[70] Hughes knew Bush's voice and he trusted her to re-create it. Indeed, she had what Chief of Staff Andrew Card called a "mystical bond" with the president; handed a text, a reporter noted, "she reads with the president's eyes."[71] As a result, despite the extraordinary circumstances that prompted the September 20 address, the process of drafting it was closer to the regular staffing routine of the administration than any of the others discussed here except Truman's.

Even so, the first draft of the September 20 speech was a generic, if eloquent, call to patriotic arms. It was crafted without any specific calls to action or policy declarations—in truth, the writers did not know what the policy was to be. Even NSC speechwriter John Gibson, their normal contact for foreign policy issues, had been cut off from his usual meetings with top national security staffers.

The fact was, there was no real policy yet, and the president was not sure he wanted to give a speech at all until there was. After meeting with his "war cabinet" at Camp David on September 14 and 15, however, important questions were resolved and the speechwriters were quickly plugged back into the process. Scully later wrote, "some of the most moving lines in the joint-session address were just slightly polished versions of what Bush himself . . . told us" in a series of subsequent meetings. These gatherings included counsel from a wide range of advisers. One Oval Office meeting among Bush, Hughes, and the writers was joined by National Security Adviser Condoleezza Rice, who provided the list of demands to the Taliban that Bush had approved at Camp David, as drafted by the State Department; the writers were to translate them from State-ese to English. Other policymakers and political advisers, ranging from NSC experts on terrorism (sent by Rice to work with the writers) to political adviser Karl Rove to Vice President Dick Cheney, also weighed in. The integrated process even led the writers to include the administration's domestic policy agenda until that was cut by the president while rehearsing the speech. Bush also resisted the inclusion of historical citations: "I don't want to quote anyone," he declared; "I want to be the guy they quote!"[72]

That much was achieved. The first-term Bush staffing process, partly as a function of the president's will and partly because of Hughes's influence with Bush, ensured that speechwriters were integrated into the development of the message. It didn't hurt that "message" was such an important part of Bush's war on terror, or that the September 20 speech was more a matter of tone than specific policy prescriptions. Truman in 1950 expanded the draft, raised taxes, and imposed price controls; Bush urged Americans to "hug your children."

But specifics would follow. And tone truly mattered. The speech convinced the public (who gave Bush 90 percent approval ratings that week) that the president had a consistent, and reasoned, agenda for action. It allowed him to define the terms of the debate: among other things it cemented the idea that this was a "war" on terror, not a large-scale criminal proceeding, with all the presidential powers that implied.[73]

Just as important for the president's immediate freedom of action, the speech also won him leeway with legislators. The address was a "home run, a ten," said perhaps the most liberal member of Congress, Representative Maxine Waters, who earlier in the year had refused even to meet with Bush. She added, "Right now the president . . . has support for almost anything he wants to do."[74]

Carter, 1978–1979: Post-Speech Malaise

For Harry Truman, wrote John Hersey, "policy was really and carefully shaped through its articulation."[75] But as James Fallows, Jimmy Carter's chief speechwriter, would tell an oral historian, in Carter's White House it was abnormal for a speech to be "a vehicle for focusing policy. In other administrations, especially in Kennedy's and in Johnson's and in Nixon's, the speech was the main way of bringing policy arguments to a head. That's not the case for Carter."[76]

Indeed, despite a number of promised procedural revamps, Carter's speech management process almost systematically isolated writers from policymakers. There was no formal process for speechwriters to meet with, much less serve as, policy aides: as one put it, "throughout our four years the administrative pattern of speechwriting was the separation of function and responsibility from authority." Another speechwriter, Walter Shapiro, observed that Carter "really did not have time for his speechwriters, because after all they were merely a technical little appendix-like necessity in being president."[77]

To be sure, Truman's speechwriting conferences had been far less methodical at the start of his administration.[78] But Fallows puzzled at Carter's "blissful *tabula rasa*. . . . Why should a man as well-meaning and intelligent as Carter blithely forgo the lessons of experience and insist on rediscovering fire, the lever, the wheel?"[79]

These critiques would seem to condemn Carter's staff structure to the abyss. But, at least with regard to major speeches to which the president gave his full attention, structure may not have been the problem.

Consider the president's foreign policy address at the U.S. Naval Academy's commencement exercises in June 1978.[80] In advance of the speech, the president had altered the staffing process by directing his writers to consult various experts and pass along their advice to him. But after much consultation along these lines (including the solicitation of advice from Alex Haley, the author of *Roots*), Carter changed his mind. Prompted by a plea from Secretary of State Cyrus Vance, the president decided instead to use the occasion to "spell out more clearly" his approach to the Soviet Union, which observers argued had been rendered incoherent by profound policy disagreements between Vance and National Security Adviser Zbigniew Brzezinski.[81] Although the writers were thus shut out once again, Carter did seek widely ranging advice, soliciting competing memos from Vance, Brzezinski, United Nations ambassador Andrew Young, and CIA director Stansfield Turner. Their responses ranged from the broadly hawkish to the nonconfrontational. Carter then spent the weekend composing the speech himself.

This process could have worked—as it had for Nixon. The resolution of thesis and antithesis might have resulted in sharp synthesis, a new and clear presidential policy. But Carter, unlike Nixon a decade before, did not square the circle with any decisiveness. His effort to unify his advisers' two conflicting worldviews resulted instead, as the *Washington Post* headlined the next day, in "Two Different Speeches." At the start of the speech, Carter told the midshipmen that "we seek a world of peace," of "accommodation, . . . improved trade and technological and cultural exchange." But his tone then darkened dramatically, condemning the "totalitarian and repressive" Soviet government for its "abuse of basic human rights," "excessive" military buildup, and actions and "proxy forces" that caused a "threat to regional peace." Fallows later argued that Carter "assembled the speech essentially by stapling Vance's memo to Brzezinski's, without examining the tensions between them. . . . It had an obvious break in the middle, like the splice in a film." After the speech was delivered, those in the White House, Pentagon, and State Department who had provided the basic text all distanced themselves and even U.S. policy from it, noting that because Carter had written the speech himself it contained mistakes and ambiguities that "should not be subjected to rigorous diplomatic analysis."[82]

The speech, then, suffered from imprecision both in policy and in rhetoric, the worst of both worlds. It established neither an external agenda nor an internal one and even undercut presidential authority over his departments. Still, the president had given himself the chance to make decisions based on wide-ranging advice. It is not clear that his failure to clearly make those decisions—or to make them clear—was a failure of advice.

Consider along those lines Carter's famous "crisis of confidence" speech in July 1979. By June of that year, crises of energy and inflation had converged in the headlines and on the streets, as truckers barricaded highways and gas lines stretched into breakdown lanes. Carter, attending an economic summit in Japan, hurried back to Washington, skipping a planned vacation in Hawaii. A speech on energy was planned for early July—against the advice of speechwriters, who feared the president did not have the sort of "bold, new, and ambitious policy to announce" that would attract an audience— and then abruptly cancelled thirty hours before airtime, highlighting the lack of such a policy.[83]

Carter decided instead to widen the scope of his deliberations and give a different speech, inspired perhaps by pollster Pat Caddell, who had taken to drafting voluminous musings on the American spirit (and its relation to the 1980 election). The president went to Camp David for eleven days, hosting a wide range of business, labor, academic, religious, and government leaders and taking occasional secret helicopter flights to call on "average middle class families."[84] Although this hiatus horrified domestic aide Stu Eizenstat and made the politically astute vice president, Walter Mondale, "distraught," the president enjoyed the extended conversation. He later wrote that he found those days to be "some of the most thought-provoking and satisfying of my presidency."[85]

Speechwriters Gordon Stewart and Rick Hertzberg were at Camp David, too, but "off in some cabin in a [writing] sweatshop," as Hertzberg recalls. "Every once in a while you would look out the window and see some *Time* magazine cover subject wandering around."[86] In the end, the president did hold a freewheeling, contentious session with a wide array of advisers, including the speechwriters. Some wanted him to discuss the substance of the energy crisis and incorporate very specific solutions into the new speech; others wanted to emphasize Caddell's larger message of spiritual stagnation. Some wanted the president to be optimistic, others more measured and self-critical.

Faced with this range of advice, Carter again decided that the final speech should incorporate all of these things. But this time the melange approach (with the help of Hertzberg and Stewart) worked better than it had in Annapolis. The broad theme of a "crisis of confidence. . . . that strikes at the very heart and soul and spirit of our national will" set the tone. "All the legislation in the world can't fix what's wrong with America," the president proclaimed. Then the speech pivoted to a discussion of "energy [as] the immediate test of our ability to unite this nation," leading to a battery of policy proposals fleshed out by Eizenstat. All in all, Carter gave a speech whose text and delivery were generally well received. "The speech itself . . . was, overnight, quite effective," Shapiro recalls. "The response of the TV talking heads was good."[87]

Why, then, is the speech remembered instead as a symbol of the administration's failings? Although it did not use the word "malaise," a state of malaise nevertheless resulted. The problem was not a lack of diversified advice to the president, though the process that provided that advice was not particularly thoughtful or intentional. Instead, the failings resulted from the linkage of the speech to other real-life happenings and a wider set of policies. True, energy was a near-impossible proving ground: establishing a test of national unity on such fissured ground was a dangerous undertaking. But worse was the president's dismissal of his own call: two days after the speech Carter blithely ignored the unifying internal agenda it set. He showed his own crisis of confidence by asking all his cabinet members to resign, but only firing those who were at odds with his inner circle of "Georgians."

The reaction was fateful. As Shapiro recalls, "the markets were totally roiled. Europe reacted like the government was going to fall. . . . The word 'malaise' got into the universe." Soon, Ronald Reagan would contrast his sunny optimism against Carter's malaise, and win the 1980 election. Overall, Carter's address failed to adhere to his actions, and he paid the political price.[88]

This is not to pick on Jimmy Carter; similar examples could be found in other administrations. But it is notable that two of Carter's best-known speeches proved dramatic exceptions to his generally maligned staffing process—and yet both failed to impose a coherent presidential agenda upon his own administration or the public sphere. Why?

One answer highlights the limits of using advisory structures as a frame of reference. What we have found in these cases is that important "one-off" addresses can generate ad hoc management structures that diverge from the usual staff operation. This suggests that presidents would be better served by routinizing the integration they seek through extra-organizational means when these important occasions arise. This seems to be a lesson of which Bill Clinton took hold and Richard Nixon eventually lost track. But the cases also suggest another key conclusion—that no matter how solid the advice, presidential leadership, in the end, depends on the president making good choices.

New Approaches to an Old Agenda

A tension pervades the relationship between the president as individual and the presidency as institution. But presidents can help themselves by attending to the institution. They can frame issues in their favor by setting the agenda within their administration, gathering information, and translating it into policy decisions.

The integration of speechwriting with policy formulation is a critical variable in formulating good policy: the staffing of a speech matters for its making. George H. W. Bush's communications director said that the president "felt that he would be judged—and should be judged—on action and on decisions and on policies" rather than on his communication of those actions. But the articulation of policy is a major factor in thinking through its virtues. As Ted Sorensen noted of the Cuban Missile Crisis, "the answer . . . was not resolved until it was effectively worded."[89]

One can overstate the benefits of connecting policy decisions and writing. David Gergen points out that Ronald Reagan's famous Normandy speech on the fortieth anniversary of D-day "was drafted by a young Peggy Noonan who had come to the White House four months earlier *and had never talked to the President about that or any other speech!*" Yet Gergen concedes that such isolation of speechwriter from president is "a lousy way to run a White House"; only Reagan's long-standing consistency of theme and tone allowed Noonan to capture his voice so accurately.[90]

Another caveat is that the sort of integration urged in this chapter is largely an artifact of an earlier era in presidential history. The Truman system of staff work, one could argue, has been rendered irrelevant by the leap in demands on the twenty-first-century chief executive, not least in the area of media relations. The distinction Neustadt drew a half-century ago between presidential leverage derived from professional reputation (among Washington insiders) and prestige (among the general public) seems far less sharp than it did then. Reputation these days seems driven by prestige. As importantly, if the rise of technocracy and the huge growth in the size of government necessitate the rise of White House specialization to manage complex substance, it might be dangerous when speechwriting ends up "dictating policy rather than describing it." Certainly the 1960s development of a hierarchical, substantively specialized "standard model" of White House staffing, as Karen Hult and Charles Walcott conclude, may be added "to the list of formidable obstacles in the path of a president who wishes to succeed in a 'rhetorical' presidency."[91]

Still, words matter—not always, but often. As Reagan speechwriter Tony Dolan noted, "a semantic infiltration" can change the way people view an issue—it can tell them not just what to think about, but also how to think about it.[92] This is most likely to occur when the president takes an issue that is percolating and seeks to set his mark on it through a landmark address.

The addresses discussed above provide contemporary examples of how presidents can successfully manage their production. Whether by employing a formal staff process or evading it, contemporary presidents still can use their time and their words to protect their power to choose. But as those examples also clarify, doing so does not relieve them of the burden of making good choices.

Notes

1. Thanks to all who participated in the Miller Center of Public Affairs' speechwriters symposium, especially Michael Nelson, for their helpful comments and feedback.

2. Jeffrey Tulis, *The Rhetorical Presidency* (Princeton, N.J.: Princeton University Press, 1987). A very small sampling of the relevant literature includes Karlyn Kohrs Campbell and Kathleen Hall Jamieson, *Presidents Creating the Presidency: Deeds Done in Words* (Chicago: University of Chicago Press, 2008); Brandice Canes-Wrone, *Who Leads Whom? Presidents, Policy, and the Public* (Chicago: University of Chicago Press, 2006); George Edwards III, *On Deaf Ears: The Limits of the Bully Pulpit* (New Haven, Conn.: Yale University Press, 2003); Lori Cox Han and Diane Heith, eds., *In the Public Domain: Presidents and the Challenge of Public Leadership* (Albany: SUNY Press, 2005); Roderick P. Hart, *The Sound of Leadership* (Chicago: University of Chicago Press, 1989); Martin Medhurst, ed., *Beyond the Rhetorical Presidency* (College Station: Texas A&M University Press, 1996); Martin Medhurst and James Arnt Aune, eds., *The Prospect of Presidential Rhetoric* (College Station: Texas A&M University Press, 2008); Lee Sigelman, "Two Reagans? Genre Imperatives, Ghostwriters, and Presidential Personality Profiling," *Political Psychology* 23 (December 2002): 839–851; David Zarefsky, "Presidential Rhetoric and the Power of Definition," *Presidential Studies Quarterly* 34 (September 2004): 607–619.

3. Samuel Kernell, *Going Public: New Strategies of Presidential Leadership*, 4th ed. (Washington, D.C.: CQ Press, 2006); and see John P. Burke, *The Institutional Presidency*, 2nd ed. (Baltimore: Johns Hopkins University Press, 2000); Matthew J. Dickinson, *Bitter Harvest: FDR and the Growth of the Presidential Branch* (New York: Cambridge University Press, 1997); Charles E. Walcott and Karen M. Hult, *Governing the White House* (Lawrence: University Press of Kansas, 1995); Martha Joynt Kumar, *Managing the President's Message: The White House Communications Operation* (Baltimore: Johns Hopkins University Press, 2007); Martha Joynt Kumar and Terry Sullivan, eds., *The White House World* (College Station: Texas A&M Press, 2003); Bradley Patterson, *The White House Staff*, rev. ed. (Washington, D.C.: Brookings Institution Press, 2002).

4. Even if one is tempted to ask, as Truman speechwriter George Elsey once wondered aloud to an inquisitive graduate student, whether all of this is "just a little bit more academic than any of us [in the White House] ever had the time for." See George Elsey's July 10, 1969, oral history, held at the Harry S. Truman Presidential Library (hereafter HSTL), http://www.trumanlibrary.org/oralhist/elsey4.htm, 178.

5. This is what Richard Neustadt used to tell his students. As Neustadt also noted, in *Presidential Power* (New York: Free Press, 1990), 3, "the male gender is justified historically but not prospectively when referring to a President." In that spirit—especially in light of Campaign 2008—"he" should be read throughout as "he, someday she."

6. Francis Heller, ed., *The Truman White House: The Administration of the Presidency, 1945–1953* (Lawrence: Regents Press of Kansas, 1980), 99.

7. For sophisticated treatments with very different assumptions and conclusions, see Edwards, *On Deaf Ears*, and Zarefsky, "Presidential Rhetoric."

8. Moyers quoted in Robert Schlesinger, *White House Ghosts: Presidents and Their Speechwriters from FDR to George W. Bush* (New York: Simon & Schuster, 2008), 165. His denigration of sports team visits to the White House is well taken but clearly must exclude those by the 2004 and 2007 World Series champions.

9. Of course, responding to an emergency presumes that events have forced presidential action: Bush could not have chosen *not* to address the nation after September 11. Still, even when such occasions are thrust upon the White House, presidents must still choose how to respond. And presidents often have more choice than Bush did over timing and subject matter. Thus, with caveats, they are rightly termed "discretionary addresses."

10. Rumsfeld, press briefing of April 11, 2003, available at http://www.defenselink .mil/transcripts/transcript.aspx?transcriptid=2367.

11. CNN interview, November 11, 2008, transcript at http://edition.cnn.com/2008/ POLITICS/11/11/bush.transcript/index.

12. Herbert A. Simon, "Applying Information Technology to Organization Design," *Public Administration Review* 33 (May/June 1973): 270. See also the very useful work of Bryan D. Jones, e.g., *Politics and the Architecture of Choice: Bounded Rationality and Governance* (Chicago: University of Chicago Press, 2001).

13. Thomas Hammond, "Toward a General Theory of Hierarchy," *Journal of Public Administration Research and Theory* 3 (January 1993): 120–145.

14. Richard Rose, "Organizing Issues In and Organizing Problems Out," in James P. Pfiffner, ed., *The Managerial Presidency* (Pacific Grove, Calif.: Brooks/Cole, 1991), 108. More generally, see Andrew Rudalevige, "The Structure of Leadership: Presidents, Hierarchies, and Information Flow," *Presidential Studies Quarterly* 35 (June 2005): 333–360.

15. Much of this literature is from organization theory or strategic management; see Hammond, "General Theory"; Herbert Simon, *Administrative Behavior*, 3rd ed. (New York: Free Press, 1976). But see also Alexander George, *Presidential Decisionmaking in Foreign Policy: The Effective Use of Information and Advice* (Boulder, Colo.: Westview, 1980) and, for a bibliography, Rudalevige, "Structure of Leadership."

16. For a comparison of such models, see Richard Tanner Johnson, *Managing the White House* (New York: Harper & Row, 1974); Roger Porter, *Presidential Decision Making* (New York: Cambridge University Press, 1982); Rudalevige, "Structure of Leadership."

17. See, e.g., Dickinson, *Bitter Harvest*; Burke, *Institutional Presidency*. Richard Neustadt lamented as early as 1978 the "five-way spread of titles," which "wreaked havoc" on the idea that having the phrase "to the president" in one's title signified "a close, continuing relationship with *him*, and serious engagement on *his* work from day to day." Neustadt, "Staffing the Presidency: Premature Notes on the New Administration," *Political Science Quarterly* 93 (Spring 1978): 7.

18. For a review, see Karen M. Hult and Charles E. Walcott, *Empowering the White House: Governance under Nixon, Ford, and Carter* (Lawrence: University Press of Kansas,

2004), ch. 8. Further, as the publicity contemporary speechwriters often receive indicates, they—like other White House staffers—seem to have abandoned the "passion for anonymity" expected by the original architects of the Executive Office of the President (EOP). (The phrase is from the Brownlow Report of 1937.)

19. Schlesinger, *Ghosts*, 409–410; and see Dick Morris, *Behind the Oval Office* (New York: Random House, 1997), 245.

20. Schlesinger, *Ghosts*, 206. Keogh was resisting Kissinger's effort to make writer Ray Price his "stenographer." For another "writer v. Kissinger" story, see Safire, *Before the Fall* (Garden City, N.Y.: Doubleday, 1975), 136–142.

21. Raymond Moley, *After Seven Years* (New York: Harper & Row, 1939), 55. Carol Gelderman holds up the example of Harry Hopkins instead, whose integration with the president's thought process (and household!) made him the "ideal" speechwriter. See *All the President's Words: The Bully Pulpit and the Creation of the Virtual Presidency* (New York: Walker & Co., 1997), 15.

22. Richard Goodwin, *Remembering America* (New York: Harper & Row, 1989), 268.

23. Schlesinger, *Ghosts*, 165.

24. Hult and Walcott, *Empowering the White House*, 155–156; Karen M. Hult and Charles E. Walcott, "Policymakers and Wordsmiths: Writing for the President under Johnson and Nixon," *Polity* 30 (Spring 1998): 465–487.

25. Schlesinger, *Ghosts*, 367; Hult and Walcott, "Policymakers and Wordsmiths."

26. Hult and Walcott, *Empowering the White House*, 160; Schlesinger, *Ghosts*, 243–246.

27. Peggy Noonan, *What I Saw at the Revolution* (New York: Random House, 1990), 76.

28. Quoted in Schlesinger, *Ghosts*, 173.

29. Martin J. Medhurst, "Presidential Speechwriting: Ten Myths That Plague Modern Scholarship," in *Presidential Speechwriting: From the New Deal to the Reagan Revolution and Beyond*, eds. Kurt Ritter and Martin J. Medhurst (College Station: Texas A&M Press, 2003), 12–13.

30. Justin S. Vaughn and José D. Villalobos, "Conceptualizing and Measuring White House Staff Influence on Presidential Rhetoric," *Presidential Studies Quarterly* 36 (December 2006): 681–688.

31. In practice, of course, such opportunities are carefully husbanded. Their elevation is itself important to the tenor and perception of presidential communication, and frequency is not a virtue: note that FDR gave no more than four of his famous fireside chats in any given year, and only twenty-eight in twelve years; see Gelderman, *All the President's Words*.

32. He adds that in the Reagan White House, even the "little speeches could be nonroutine surprisingly often."

33. Elsey, HSTL oral history of March 9, 1965, 83. See also Matthew J. Dickinson and Andrew Rudalevige, "Presidents, Responsiveness, and Competence: Revisiting the 'Golden Age' at the Bureau of the Budget," *Political Science Quarterly* 119 (Winter 2004–2005): 633–654.

34. David Bell, 1968 oral history, HSTL, 81–82; see also Theodore Tannewald, Jr., 1969 oral history, HSTL, 40–41.

35. Neustadt in Heller, *Truman White House*; Seymour Fersh, *The View from the White House: The Study of the Presidential State of the Union Messages* (Washington, D.C.: Public Affairs Press, 1961), 123; James Sundquist, "The Last Truly Anonymous White House Aide," *Washington Post*, September 1, 1983, A23.

36. "Radio and Television Report to the American People on the National Emergency," December 15, 1950, available at http://www.presidency.ucsb.edu/ws/index.php?pid=13683. This and the other speeches cited here are drawn from the excellent database of the public papers of the presidents compiled for The American Presidency Project by John Woolley and Gerhard Peters at the University of California, Santa Barbara. This section otherwise relies heavily on John Hersey, "A Weighing of Words," *The New Yorker*, May 5, 1951, 36–53, which Truman staffer Bell, who helped draft the speech, has called "*very* accurate." Bell, 1968 HSTL oral history, 79, emphasis in original. See also the Elsey and Tannenwald oral histories cited above; Robert J. Donovan, *Tumultuous Years: The Presidency of Harry S. Truman, 1949–1953* (New York: W. W. Norton, 1982), 319–320; Harry S. Truman, *Years of Trial and Hope, 1946–1953* (Garden City, N.Y.: Doubleday, 1956), 439–457.

37. Hersey, "Weighing," 40.

38. Ibid., 36.

39. It is notable how much space in his memoirs Truman devotes to seeking congressional advice, despite his refusal to seek legislative sanction for the war itself. And indeed, the consultation was important, as a number of members were doubtful about the need for a new declaration of emergency.

40. Hersey, "Weighing," 37; though Truman would soon add, "but I want to take it home now and hash it over some and see if I can make it better" (52).

41. Tannenwald, HSTL oral history, 47.

42. Truman, *Years*, 442; speech of December 15, 1950.

43. Hersey, "Weighing," 52. Truman's Gallup rating did rise slightly, from 33 to 36 percent approval—but the latter poll was not taken for nearly a month after the speech, in early 1951.

44. Richard Reeves, *President Nixon: Alone in the White House* (New York: Simon & Schuster, 2001), 140. See also Nixon's later comment that "thinking a speech through helps a leader think his policy through." Richard Nixon, *In the Arena: A Memoir of Victory, Defeat, and Renewal* (New York: Pocket Books, 1990), 150.

45. Advance copies of the text were never provided outside a small White House circle, though National Security Adviser Henry Kissinger did brief legislative leaders several hours before Nixon spoke.

46. Richard Nixon, *RN: The Memoirs of Richard Nixon* (New York: Grosset and Dunlap, 1978), 409; see also Raymond Price, *With Nixon* (New York: Viking, 1977), 160.

47. Reeves, *President Nixon*, 142.

48. Ibid., 140. Kissinger, in his own memoirs, cannot resist insisting that "the core [of the speech] was provided by my staff and me." Henry Kissinger, *White House Years* (London: Weidenfeld & Nicolson, 1979), 306.

49. A similar situation arose in 1970, when Nixon asked Ray Price, Pat Buchanan, and Kissinger for competing speech drafts concerning a televised "progress report" on Vietnam. Hult and Walcott, *Empowering the White House*, 157.

50. Nixon, *RN*, 405.

51. Nixon, *RN*, 404; Rick Perlstein, *Nixonland: The Rise of a President and the Fracturing of America* (New York: Scribner, 2008), 436.

52. "Address to the Nation on the War in Vietnam," November 3, 1969, available at http://www.presidency.ucsb.edu/ws/index.php?pid=2303.

53. Nixon, *RN*, 409. More pragmatically, the silent majority did, apparently, approve—Gallup Polls after the speech showed a sixteen-percentage-point jump in Nixon's job approval ratings (to 68 percent); Republican governors were elected the next day in New Jersey and Virginia. "Euphoria continues," Haldeman would write in his diary. Yet soon afterwards the Senate rejected Nixon's first nominee to the Supreme Court, Clement Haynsworth.

54. Hult and Walcott, "Policymakers and Wordsmiths," 479–480.

55. Schlesinger, *Ghosts*, 205–207; Hult and Walcott, "Policymakers and Wordsmiths," 483; Hult and Walcott, *Empowering the White House*, 156–158.

56. "The President's News Conference," April 18, 1995, available at http://www.presidency.ucsb.edu/ws/index.php?pid=51237; Morris, *Behind the Oval Office*, 98.

57. Prince quoted in Schlesinger, *Ghosts*, 424.

58. John Harris, *The Survivor: Bill Clinton in the White House* (New York: Random House, 2005), 156 and 163.

59. Schlesinger, *Ghosts*, 426–427; Harris, *Survivor*, 171; see also David Gergen, *Eyewitness to Power* (Simon & Schuster, 2001), 314.

60. "Remarks and a Question-and-Answer Session with the American Society of Newspaper Editors," April 7, 1995, available at http://www.presidency.ucsb.edu/ws/index.php?pid=51198; Michael Waldman, *POTUS Speaks: Finding the Words That Defined the Clinton Presidency* (New York: Simon & Schuster, 2000), 80; Schlesinger, *Ghosts*, 431–433; Harris, *Survivor*, 174–175.

61. FDR's style of staff management, which also featured competition among advisers, was fiercely disliked by his subordinates; see Dickinson, *Bitter Harvest*.

62. "President's Radio Address," June 17, 1995, available at http://www.presidency.ucsb.edu/ws/index.php?pid=51508.

63. Harris, *Survivor*, 186.

64. Schlesinger, *Ghosts*, 437 and 444.

65. Quoted in Woodward, *Bush at War* (New York: Simon & Schuster, 2002), 144.

66. "Address on the United States Response to the Terrorist Attacks of September 11," September 20, 2001, available at http://www.presidency.ucsb.edu/ws/index.php?pid=64731.

67. Many reports—to the dismay of Matthew Scully, op cit.—claim that Gerson (in Bob Woodward's version) wrote "all of Bush's memorable post-9/11 speeches." Woodward, *State of Denial* (New York: Simon & Schuster, 2006), 342. Scully later wrote a long magazine piece in rebuttal, noting that "great works carried out collaboratively make for an undeniably less interesting story than the solitary genius scribbling away." Matthew Scully, "Present at the Creation," *The Atlantic*, September 2007, 77–89.

68. D. T. Max, "The Making of the Speech," *New York Times Magazine*, October 7, 2001, 32–37; Scully, "Present at the Creation."

69. See Peter Robinson (on G. H. W. Bush) and Walter Shapiro (on Carter) in Chapter 9 of this volume.

70. Note that in Reagan's "troika," Communications Director Michael Deaver held like prominence.

71. Card quoted in Ron Suskind, "Mrs. Hughes Takes Her Leave," *Esquire*, July 2002, 103; Max, "Making of the Speech."

72. Quoted in Schlesinger, *Ghosts*, 468.

73. For a broader discussion of the notion that Bush's rhetoric allowed him "to dominate public interpretation of the events" of September 2001, see John M. Murphy, "'Our Mission and Our Moment': George W. Bush and September 11th," *Rhetoric and Public Affairs* 6 (Winter 2003): 607–632.

74. It is worth noting that not all of Bush's speeches on the war on terror would integrate rhetoric and specific policy detail so smoothly—this was especially true with the various intelligence estimate–based speeches that justified the war in Iraq. Waters is quoted in Carolyn Lochhead and Carla Marinucci, "'Freedom and Fear Are at War': Message to Americans, Warning to Taliban," *San Francisco Chronicle*, September 21, 2001; for her boycott of Bush's January 2001 meeting with the Congressional Black Caucus, see Robert Draper, *Dead Certain* (New York: Free Press, 2007), 112.

75. John Hersey, *Aspects of the Presidency: Truman and Ford in Office* (New York: Ticknor and Fields, 1980), 164. This insight stems from Hersey's (much) later access to the Ford White House, whose own process of articulation Hersey found quite inferior by comparison; he was "profoundly disturbed" by its "aimlessness" and the lack of policy thought incorporated into the drafting process. This was perhaps not wholly fair, given the different portions of the two processes he observed, though others also criticize the Ford process.

76. James Fallows, 1978 exit interview, Jimmy Carter Library (JCL), 8.

77. Hendrik Hertzberg, quoted in John H. Patton, "Jimmy Carter: The Language of Politics and the Practice of Integrity," in *Presidential Speechwriting: From the New Deal to the Reagan Revolution and Beyond*, eds. Kurt Ritter and Martin J. Medhurst (College Station: Texas A&M Press, 2003), 173. Fallows would likewise observe that his policy suggestions vanished into thin air since they were not part of his "strictly limited tasks." Schlesinger, *Ghosts*, 291.

78. See Schlesinger's discussion on the process as of April 1945 in *Ghosts*, 31–37, and George Elsey's more detailed description of the shifting processes in his oral history of July 10, 1969, 150–153.

79. James Fallows, "The Passionless Presidency," *The Atlantic Monthly*, May 1979, available at http://www.theatlantic.com/unbound/flashbks/pres/fallpass.htm.

80. "United States Naval Academy Address at the Commencement Exercises," June 7, 1978, available at http://www.presidency.ucsb.edu/ws/index.php?pid=30915.

81. Jimmy Carter, *Keeping Faith: Memoirs of a President* (London: Collins, 1982), 229. The process behind the speech is not discussed in his memoir.

82. Murray Marder, "Carter Challenges Soviet Leaders: Two Different Speeches," *Washington Post*, June 8, 1978, A1, which went on to ask, "which of two speeches did the Kremlin hear?" One administration "specialist" even complained of its "very, very bad English": see Robert Kaiser and Walter Pincus, "Carter as Speechwriter," *Washington Post*, June 8, 1978, A18; Schlesinger, *Ghosts*, 287-290; Fallows, "Passionless Presidency."

83. Schlesinger, *Ghosts*, 299-301.

84. Burton I. Kaufman, *The Presidency of James Earl Carter* (Lawrence: University Press of Kansas, 1993), 139, 143-146; the quote is from 144.

85. But his Camp David meetings with economists were exempted from the parts he enjoyed—they were "a waste of time." Jimmy Carter, *Keeping Faith*, 115, and, on economists, 118. For Stu Eizenstat ("less than happy with it, to say the least") see Eizenstat's JCL exit interview of January 10, 1981, 9-10.

86. Schlesinger, *Ghosts*, 301.

87. "Address to the Nation on Energy and National Goals," July 15, 1979, available at http://www.presidency.ucsb.edu/ws/index.php?pid=32596; Schlesinger, *Ghosts*, 302-305; Patton, "Jimmy Carter."

88. For a good discussion of this point, see Patton, "Jimmy Carter," 181.

89. David Demarest quoted in Schlesinger, *Ghosts*, 364; Sorensen quoted in Gelderman, *All the President's Words*.

90. David Gergen, *Eyewitness to Power* (New York: Simon & Schuster, 2001), 241; emphasis in original. As Peter Robinson noted, "there were fourteen of us who moved through that office, five or six writers on staff at any given time, and yet Ronald Reagan always sounded like Ronald Reagan."

91. Neustadt, *Presidential Power*, chs. 3-4, 10; Martha Joynt Kumar, "The White House Office of Communications," in *White House World*, eds. Kumar and Sullivan, 269; Hult and Walcott, "Policymakers and Wordsmiths."

92. Quoted in Gergen, *Eyewitness*, 242; more systematically, see Zarefsky, "Presidential Rhetoric."

Chapter 9

Speechwriters on the Crisis Speech and Other Landmark Addresses

Kenneth Khachigian, Peter Robinson, Walter Shapiro

The featured participants in this session—about major presidential speeches that do not recur on a regularized schedule—were Kenneth Khachigian, speechwriter for Ronald Reagan; Peter Robinson, speechwriter for Ronald Reagan; and Walter Shapiro, speechwriter for Jimmy Carter. This session was moderated by Professor Andrew Rudalevige of Dickinson College.

Rudalevige: I want to begin by mentioning that we're talking in all these sessions about a very small fraction of presidential rhetoric. One way to dramatize that is to have a look at the volumes of *Public Papers of the Presidents*. These [*dropping two thick volumes on the table*] are Jimmy Carter's, from 1977.[1] Replicate this over the seventy-plus years that these have been collated in this form and you have pages and pages, feet and feet, of rhetoric. Obviously much of that vanishes, if not into thin air, then at least into these pages—and out of public memory.

The notion of landmark addresses, though, assumes that some of these words are remembered, that some are kept, that lots of people listen to at least some of what presidents say. Our topic is to look at the subset of these vast shelves of documents, the parts that people really pay attention to. Our focus is on addresses that are prompted by a crisis or by a particular issue that the president wants to elevate to a major part of his national agenda or into the national spotlight.

I'd also like to get into the differences between the routine utterances that the president gives every day and those that reach landmark status. It seems to me that these have fascinating implications for agenda-setting of all sorts, both for the national agenda and for agenda-setting within the administration, as well as for trying to enforce the president's preferences on the

235

rest of the bureaucracy in a coherent way. So I'd like to explore that connection of rhetoric and policymaking.

I wonder if we might move from the specific to the general and perhaps ask each of the panelists to talk about an address that he found memorable that he worked on. What made that address memorable? What made it important? How did it succeed in setting out what the president wanted to do in that area? Why don't we go chronologically? We'll start with Walter.

Shapiro: First of all, this panel is listed as "The Crisis Speech and Other Major Addresses." I worked for Jimmy Carter in the White House in 1979, and given what was happening to him politically, I think every single speech was a crisis speech. [*laughter*] I was not actively part of Jimmy Carter's major crisis speech of 1979, which is now remembered as the "malaise speech," though he never used the word "malaise."[2] But I was involved in some of the before-and-after of it.

I can think of no speech in American history that has been more mal-remembered. First of all, it was described using the word "malaise." The speech itself, as I recall, was quite effective overnight. The response of the TV talking heads was good. I remember trying to write a follow-up speech. I was given buckets of mail that came into the White House—in those days, when people actually wrote letters. People were pouring their hearts out. Jimmy Carter resonated with something.[3]

As I remember, it was a two-step process: (1) give the speech, (2) purge the disloyal elements out of the Carter Cabinet. Approximately four members of the Cabinet were fired about two days later, including the head of the Federal Reserve, G. William Miller, who went from the Federal Reserve to the Treasury Department.[4] The markets were totally roiled. Europe reacted like the government was going to fall because that's what happened in traditional European settings. The word "malaise" got into the universe. Jimmy Carter ended up having to appoint Paul Volcker, the man who eliminated inflation, as the head of the Federal Reserve, a major accomplishment.[5] Jimmy Carter was the only president who went into his reelection in the middle of a recession that his appointee deliberately brought on.

I think the shorthand version of this is that so much was going on in that week in the summer of 1979 that the malaise speech, as rhetoric, *was* effective. As part of a broader set of policies, it was disastrous.

Khachigian: What's interesting about being in the White House during a very controversial period is that you tend to lose perspective. In the Nixon White House, I was a full-time employee, so during all the difficulties of the Vietnam War—and then of course, later, of Watergate—there was constant pressure. You're in a pressure cooker. You get a little bit of a bunker mentality. That leads me to how I helped President Reagan through what I considered to be the first major, personal crisis of his presidency.

It was, in a nutshell, that he was going to visit Germany, and in an act of reconciliation was going to put a wreath on the tomb of some German soldiers.[6] When the advance folks went over to Germany, it was wintertime, so the gravestones were covered, and no one noticed that the soldiers were SS Nazis. Once this was determined, there was a great uproar that he would be commemorating Nazi Germany and the worst storm troopers of the Nazi regime. Several people asked that he not make the trip. An enormous controversy erupted within Washington and the nation. Chancellor [Helmut] Kohl, however, wanted President Reagan to go on this trip.[7] It was important for him. Leading up to this, there was a Holocaust commemoration in the East Wing, and Elie Wiesel, who was a victim of the concentration camps, lectured the president from the podium of the East Room, so there was an enormous personal controversy going on.[8]

I wasn't inside the White House at the time. I was in California. Those of you who were in the White House probably know the internal perspective, but I sensed that there was some panic about what the president should do. I was called in from California to help address this. The remediation for this great controversy was for the president—in addition to finding a way to lay a wreath at a tomb that would commemorate the end of World War II—to go to a concentration camp and speak. Bergen-Belsen was chosen, perhaps symbolically, because it was the gravesite of Anne Frank.[9]

When I got to the White House, there was great unhappiness, and everyone was upset. My first meeting with the president was with only the president and Michael Deaver.[10] I think it was the first time I had met with the president when he was personally distraught. It showed in his face. It showed in his eyes and in his voice. Usually when I worked on a speech with the president, I made a point of coming in with a lot of ideas because I thought he expected that of me. But as I started to talk, he interrupted and began talking. I started writing as fast as I could.

He started his conversation by saying, "None of us can fully understand the enormity of the feelings carried by the victims of these camps." I wrote that down as quickly as I could, and that was the opening of his remarks at

Bergen-Belsen.[11] It flowed from there. He continued talking about his passionate feelings. He was wounded that anyone would think that he was a bigot or that he would honor the Nazis. Emotion poured out of him. That emotion found its way into my notes and into his remarks.

There was also a personal side to this. At the end of April, almost at the same time that the Holocaust remembrances were taking place in America, the remembrances to the Armenian genocide took place. There was a commemoration at Arlington Cemetery on April 24.[12] I happened to be in Washington, and I went to that. Since my father was a genocide survivor, these feelings infused into me a sense of how I could convey how those victims felt in those camps, because of the stories I had heard from my dad. So it all came together.

I think part of the benefit of getting me involved was that I was able to come in without the pressure cooker. The staff was fighting and arguing with each other—"Whose fault was this, and who did what?" The president determined how he would fix this situation with Germany. He did fix it. He called me about four days after he returned from Germany, and he was elated. He chuckled and said, "I think I could have been elected president of Germany."

Robinson: In the spring of 1987, the assignment came to me for the Berlin Wall speech. We—the scheduling office and the advance office—knew that the president would stand in front of the Berlin Wall, with the Brandenburg Gate behind him.[13] The audience would be 10,000 to 40,000 people. I'm giving you my guidance in total: "He should speak for perhaps twenty to thirty minutes, and he should discuss foreign policy." That was the total guidance, which wasn't unusual. In our White House, you'd get very general guidance, and it was up to the speechwriters to take a first draft at what the president ought to say. By the way, there was no sense that this would be an historic speech or anything that would be remembered.

I took my kids—who have, as children tend to, a very low opinion of me—to the Reagan Library. This was a couple of years ago. Lo and behold, in that new *Air Force One* pavilion, there is a section of marble with phrases from the president's speeches.[14] My kids wandered off. Later I saw them standing there slack-jawed, and it was because of a phrase from this speech. The idea that anything their father had drafted would be carved into stone brought me about ninety seconds of credit with those kids.

At the time, I knew and the speechwriting shop knew that this was going to be one of the larger speeches of the year. We would usually have half a dozen that broke the mold of the usual Rose Garden, or political convention, or political fundraiser speech. This was going to be one of those half-dozen or so. I'll tell the story very briefly.[15]

I flew to Berlin with the pre-advance team, and I spent about a day and a half in Berlin. The first stop was at the office of the American consul general. I believe he was the ranking diplomat. He was full of ideas about what Ronald Reagan should *not* say. He wanted to make sure that the president understood that Berlin was the most left-leaning of the West German cities, home to a couple of universities, a large academic population. Because these people were surrounded by East Germany, they were acutely sensitive to nuance. He said, "Don't have Ronald Reagan come here and be a cowboy, don't have him be a commie-basher, and don't go on and on about the Wall. They've all gotten used to it by now." So I walked out of there, in a certain sense, worse off than I had been before I went in. Not only did I not have material, but I had a long list of things I wasn't allowed to write about.

The next stop was at the site where the president would speak. There was the Wall, and there was the Reichstag with the shell markings, still scarred from bullet fire.[16] You could climb up the observation platform, as they had us do, and peer over and look down Unter den Linden, the historic street in East Berlin, almost empty, guards walking back and forth. The next stop was at the Tempelhof Air Force Base, where I climbed onto a U.S. Army helicopter and was given a flight over the wall.[17] As bad as it looked from inside West Berlin, from the air you could see the other side—dog runs, guard towers, barbed wire, very carefully raked gravel. I asked through the headset what the gravel was for. The reply was, "So that the young East German guards know that if they want to let a girlfriend or a member of their family escape to the West, they'll have to explain the footprints the next morning to their commanding officer." I had the feeling that they had thought of everything.

Finally for me that day, I broke away from the Americans, got in a cab, and went out to a suburb in West Berlin for a dinner party that some West Berliners were putting on for me. I'd never met these people, but the man of the family, Dieter Elz, had spent twenty years at the World Bank. He had just retired back to Berlin with his wife, Ingeborg [Elz].[18] We had friends in common. This friend had said, "Let Robinson meet some Berliners." So we chatted. I told them what I'd been told: that they'd all gotten used to the Wall, and it would seem naïve or crude if the president mentioned it. I said, "I flew over the thing. Is it true? Have you gotten used to it?" There was a dead silence. I thought, *Oh no, I've been the kind of crude American that the diplomat doesn't want the president to seem.*

Then one man raised his arm and pointed and said, "My sister lives just a few kilometers in that direction. I haven't seen her in more than twenty years. How do you think we feel about the Wall?" We went around the room. Everybody told a story about the Wall. It was clear, perhaps, that they had stopped *talking* about it, but they still hated it. Then Ingeborg Elz, who was a lovely woman then probably in her late 50s, became quite angry. She took a fist and slammed it into the palm of her hand and said, "If this man [Mikhail] Gorbachev is serious with his talk of *glasnost* and *perestroika*, he can prove it by coming here and getting rid of that Wall."[19] I was taking notes, and I put an arrow next to that note. This doesn't ascend to the level of analysis that I feel I ought to be offering to a Harvard doctorate, but a little lightbulb went off. I knew immediately that if Ronald Reagan had been there in my place, he would have responded to the decency and power of that remark, and to the central truth that it contained.

So back to the White House I went. I drafted a speech, and I built it around that comment. I have to confess that I'd love to say that I sat down and simply composed the speech as the gods gave it to me, but I was very conscious that the audience in front of him would be German, and that the television audience would be American. So I put the key line in German, "Herr Gorbachev, machen Sie dieses Tor auf!" Tony Dolan, then the chief speechwriter, said, "Peter, when the president of the United States is your client, give him his best lines in English. Try, 'Mr. Gorbachev, tear down this wall.'"[20] So in it went.

Again, to compress this a little bit. There was a meeting with the president. He got the draft on a Friday, he looked at it at Camp David, and we met with him on a Monday. We went around the table talking about various speeches. We got to my speech. We always wanted more of him. So Tom Griscom, then the communications director, said, "Mr. President, Peter's Berlin draft.[21] What do you think?" [*imitating Reagan*] "That was a fine draft. I think that's about what I'd like to say." I don't know if you did this, Ken, but Clark, Josh Gilder, and others of us—if you had a chance to ask him a question, you'd think through what question would get him talking.[22] You'd want to elicit more of him.

I explained that I had been told in Berlin that they would be able to hear the speech by radio on the other side of the Wall, and if weather conditions were just right, they could hear it clear to Moscow, across much, if not all, of

Eastern Europe.[23] "Mr. President, is there anything you want to say to people on the other side of the Wall?" I remember that he thought for a moment and said, "Well, there's that part about tearing down the Wall. That's what I want to say to them: that Wall has to come down." Fool that I am, I thought, *I didn't get anything fresh from him.*

Next the speech went out to circulation. And it was the Reagan White House, so of course a fight broke out. The fighting took place at a number of levels. It turned out—I didn't piece this together until the middle of the fight—that his consul general in Berlin had been working with the State Department and the National Security Council. He had produced his own draft. Their effort was to strangle the speechwriter's draft and to let his prevail.

I won't go on and on, but we've been talking about individual speech-writers, and in the Reagan White House, so much of what we did was the effort of the shop. In this case for example, Tony Dolan, my boss, knew about this other draft, and he kept me ignorant of it so that I would produce a fresh piece of work. Then the fighting broke out. Tony fought far harder than I was aware of at the time while I was rewriting. We felt that we had to compromise and include about a page and a half of the State Department draft. You can tell when you get to it because if you're listening to the speech, that's a bit where it suddenly turns boring for about three minutes. It went back and forth and back and forth.

Not long before the party left for Europe, the secretary of state ended up in the White House chief of staff's office and said, "This line about tearing down the Wall has to go. It's going to put Gorbachev in too much of a tight spot." Tommy Griscom argued and argued, and [George] Shultz backed off for the time being.[24] I later found out that when they were in Europe, the president was going to Italy first for the Venice Economic Summit.[25] George Shultz insisted to Ken Duberstein that this line come out.[26] So Duberstein— Duberstein gives me this account; I wasn't there—sat the president down in the garden of whatever Italian palazzo they were resting in. Duberstein gave him all the State Department arguments, which were essentially that it was too crude, that it would put Gorbachev in a tough position, and so forth.

They talked about it for a moment, then Ken said that there was one of those Ronald Reagan moments. The eyes twinkled, and the president said [*imitating Reagan*], "Now, Ken, I'm the president, aren't I?" "Yes, sir, we're clear about that much." "So I get to decide if that line stays in?" "It's your decision, Sir." "Well then, it stays in."

I stayed in the White House, but Tony traveled with him, so he is my source on this. The day the party left Venice to fly to Berlin, where the president was only going to be for a few hours—that is to say, the morning of the day he was to deliver the speech—the State Department faxed over the seventh or eighth alternative draft. They tried even at that last moment to get the president to swap it out, but he refused. He delivered the speech, and that was that.

What I would like to stress is (a) the speech was the effort of the speech-writing shop in all kinds of ways, and (b) those are the bare outlines of the story, and everything I've said is true. But my story can be misleading, because it sounds as though I wrote the thing and all Ronald Reagan did was deliver it. I promise you that by that point in my career in the White House, I had Ronald Reagan living in my head. When I was in Berlin, I very explicitly was looking for items that *he* would find arresting, looking for comments that *he* would want to adapt and deliver. I'd worked for George H. W. Bush, the vice president. There's not a chance I would have written such a speech for him, and if I had, the first thing he would have said—the first thing he always said when you gave him a foreign draft, as Clark will attest—was, "What does State say about this?" So it is true that I did the drafting. The president adjusted it and so forth. But I want to convey that in the deepest sense, from beginning to end, it is Ronald Reagan's work.

Khachigian: Here's the key element. Reagan knew good theater when he saw it. It wasn't just the policy. Half of that decision was his anti-Communist head thinking. The other thinking was, *What great theater this is going to be.* He knew a great theatrical moment. Hollywood and showbiz dominated so much of what was in his communicating mind, whether it was picking out people in audiences to eyeball when he was giving a speech, or even that use of the word "well." He explained that that was a stage pause that would allow him a split second to think of his next line. I can't be in his head, but I'm convinced that he could picture the theater of the Wall behind him, and history rolling up. He would never let the line change.

Robinson: Once he got that draft and saw it himself, right.

Shapiro: Since we've all dealt with the State Department drafts, through this story I have been sitting here trying to imagine what the timid State Department version would have been, and the closest I've come is, "Mr. Gorbachev, could you perhaps consider bilateral negotiations?" [*laughter*]

Rudalevige: That gets us to an interesting point about this staffing-out process, the integration of speechwriting with policymaking. Back in the days of the [Harry] Truman administration, there was no distinction between the two, in the sense that these were the same people, right? Clark Clifford was counsel to the president, but he was writing speeches with his assistants and he was also very much a policy advisor.[27] By the time you get to later presidencies, these are separate organizations. You talked a little bit about getting very vague guidance, for example. So the chance to write the first draft of policy, was that typical? How did the speechwriting shop integrate with these White House and bureaucratic inputs?

Robinson: I am sure that every White House is different in this regard. In my experience in the Reagan speechwriting shop, one reason why the speeches tended to be fought over so often, and frankly so viciously—you could hardly walk down those marble floors of the Old EOB [Executive Office Building] for all the blood on the floor, a slippery place—was that the speeches were an occasion of making policy.[28]

I'll give you an example. As Dave Barry would say, this is true.[29] In 1984, Dick Wirthlin began to pick up that education was an issue rising in importance, and the president was going into a reelection campaign. He scheduled a speech to a convention of high school principals.[30] Suddenly, we have to talk about education. Somebody had better figure out what our education policy is. I got the job of writing the speech. I called the then-secretary of education, the one before Bill Bennett.[31] Anybody remember?

Rudalevige: Dr. [Terrel] Bell.[32]

Robinson: Exactly. And his office said that he was at the beach. I said, "Well, this is the White House calling about a presidential address," blah, blah, blah. I didn't often have to pull rank like that, but you try. "Well, I'm sorry. He's at the beach." Finally they faxed over a draft that he had composed at the beach. I must tell you that for a guy who was running American education, there were grammatical errors, one non sequitur after another, and furthermore, it was clear that we had no policy. We had *this* program and *that* program but no overarching education policy.

So I, panic-stricken, called Dick Darman, who was temporarily the director of communications, and I asked for time to see him.[33] Darman, whose time was so much more valuable than anyone else's, wouldn't give me time on his schedule. He called and said, "What's the problem?" "Well, education speech. Talked to the secretary of education. Have a draft." Darman said, "What you're telling me is we don't have an education policy." "Yes, Dick, that's what I'm telling you." "Then make one up." He hung up on me. [*laughter*] I promise this is true. So I knew a fellow in the Old EOB named Bob Sweet, who was our liaison with education.[34] I went to talk to him. Bob introduced me to a fellow, then unknown to me, named Bill Bennett. Those two guys knew a lot. Over a period of a couple of weeks, I drafted a speech, a ten-point plan that was our education policy for the second term.

In the Reagan White House, there were domestic policy councils and foreign policy councils. All of that was taking place. All of that was producing good paper. All of that was chugging decisions toward the president. But quite often, in my experience, the final decision or the final framing did not take place until there was a speech on the schedule, and a deadline, and you *had* to do it. Don Baer's nodding, so I think there are two White Houses in which that must have been the case.

Shapiro: First of all, as a very secular person who did not channel Jimmy Carter's religiosity, I do remember, speaking of vague instructions, a particular moment of stomach-churning horror, even in recollection: the moment when Jerry Rafshoon, then the communications director, called me in and said, "The president needs a speech to the Baptists for next Sunday. Please fill it with moral uplift." End of instructions.[35]

But the serious thing is that writing for Jimmy Carter was, I think, a sui generis sort of situation against the modern backdrop of speechwriting, because in so many different ways Jimmy Carter looked at words as the awkward building blocks of his engineering mind.[36] "Rhetoric should never be used because we are into unadorned policy." As a result, in the wake of the energy crisis, I wrote a series of speeches, as did everyone, about alternative energy. The phrase that lingers in my mind is "low-head hydroelectric power." I have often wondered what would happen if one could get Peggy Noonan, Ted Sorensen, and the Abraham Lincoln of the second inaugural around a table and say, "You have one challenge. Take all the time you need. Write something of soaring eloquence that uses the phrase 'low-head hydroelectric power.'" [*laughter*]

The only writing guidance I got, which is framed in my office, is a handwritten memo from Jimmy Carter, written sometime, I think, in the summer of 1979. It says, "To Jerry Rafshoon and the speechwriters." We all got our

Xeroxed copy. It is in classic Jimmy Carter style. It is a list of nine things, including instructions on correct grammar. Point number three: "It is 'with Jerry and me,' not 'with Jerry and I.'" Point number five: "Do not start sentences with 'and' or 'but.'" Number seven: "Do not use contractions. Let me put them in." Then, as every speechwriter will understand, there were also separate items on "Speech drafts are too long" and "Please get the speech drafts in on time."

When Robert Schlesinger wrote his wonderful book on presidential speechwriting—it came out this year—I tried to push him to write about this document.[37] It is such a window into the technical sense that Jimmy Carter brought to speechwriting. I think, God knows, that Ronald Reagan was the antithesis of Jimmy Carter, but I think that most presidents have been the antithesis of this.

Rudalevige: It is said of Carter, by former staffers, that he saw making a speech as distinct from making a decision, which I understand is different from perhaps both the Nixon and Reagan administrations.[38] How do those processes compare between those two White Houses?

Khachigian: That's interesting. I can give you the 180-degree different version of Peter on policymaking, which is on economic policy in the first Reagan term. In the first few weeks of 1981, right after the inaugural, we were all about changing the economic paradigm in America. We had plenty of input from everyone about economic policy. Reagan made clear in the campaign that cutting taxes, balancing the budget, and supply-side economics were going to dominate. But in that case, I didn't become the maker of policy; I became the referee for the policy guys who were arguing back and forth. David Stockman, who was then the budget director, had the imprimatur to put together the budget slicing, the budget issues. Then Don Regan, over at Treasury, had the imprimatur to put together the tax policy.[39]

We had a lot of meetings and a lot of debates. At the very end we had to referee a little bit because Larry Kudlow, who is now a television personality, had disputes with Don Regan.[40] Regan was over at Treasury, and Kudlow was in the White House, so he had proximity to power, which is, as you all know, very important. But that was the antithesis of what Peter was going through. I had no skin in the game. I didn't have a position on this. For me it was getting what would be right for the president. Then at the end, after refereeing these internal disputes and presenting a draft to the president, nobody else had a say in the final product. *He* was going to determine which way we went.

So you had the first economic address in early February of '81 and then a speech to a joint session of Congress later in February. Both of them had the input of his entire administration, and not any one person was happier than the other, but in the end it reflected Ronald Reagan, because he knew how to put the words to the policy. But I thought that worked out rather well, very frankly.

Rudalevige: You were a policy coordinator then, in a sense. You were obviously working on the presentation of that policy.

Khachigian: And not trying to impose myself on it, which I think is a problem with a lot of aspiring speechwriters—whether it is for the president or for an executive or for cabinet officers, imposing their views on the principal. Sometimes you have to—in this case, I suppose. Of course the great debates in the Reagan White House were between the folks who wanted to let Reagan be Reagan and those who wanted Reagan to be Nelson Rockefeller.[41] [*laughter*]

Robinson: Dick Darman would never have said something like, "Make up the education policy," if the issue had been tax policy. I thought that was atypical. Clark and I both worked for George H. W. Bush. In fact we worked for him so long ago that he only had two initials. He was called GB. Now he is GHWB. But the contrast was very vivid between working for him and then working for Reagan. With Vice President Bush, who is a wonderful man in a hundred different ways, speeches were something that he had to do in addition to the real work of being vice president. It was clear, if you saw the way he scheduled himself, that he was at his best and was most animated when he was making phone calls, lobbying members of Congress, and presiding over policy meetings. "Oh, and now I have to give a speech."[42]

We were pretty good at giving him speech drafts on time, but very often he wouldn't mark them up. It was absolutely typical. You'd be on *Air Force Two*, and when you'd feel the plane begin to descend, Joe Hagen, the personal aide, would come back and say, "By the way, Peter, he's ready for you now."[43] Then I would give him the half sheets.[44] He'd hold the cards like this and say, "Pretty good speech, but it feels too heavy. Cut it in half." Again, perfectly typical.

The timing was a little tighter in this example than it was at other times, but I remember him speaking someplace in Ohio. He was speaking at a high school. I was making the changes, making the changes. Photocopier was a little bit slow. Finally I got a fresh draft for him, and I was directed by the Secret Service through the basement of this high school. "Turn here. Turn there. Up those stairs." Suddenly I was on a stage. The curtains were closed. The vice president was standing there looking around for me, and on the other side I could hear someone saying, "Ladies and Gentlemen, the vice president of the United States." I handed the thing to him, and then I ran off as the curtain was opened. It was not all that atypical that the first time he would see a speech was in the act of delivering it.

With Reagan, in so many ways, it was the reverse. Giving speeches and talking to the public was his first instinct. That was, in some ways, his central impulse, his central tool of governance. You'd send the drafts over—of course we got them in on time—and the following morning they would always come back with the "RR" in the corner. Sometimes his changes would be quite extensive, and sometimes they would be minor. I can remember one morning—I can't remember what the speech was—but for some reason I remember it was six pages. No changes on the first page, none on the second. I said, "For once he watched television instead of doing the markups." The last page, next-to-last line, he had changed one word. In some ways that had more of an effect on me. I thought, *That old guy is reading every single word I write. I'd better stay on my toes!*

He took the text seriously and his view was—I don't know whether he formed it this way in his mind—if he could move the country, Congress would fall into place. That '86 tax reform was typical. The polls were all against it. I can remember one senator, [Robert] Kasten [Jr.], of Wisconsin, a Republican, who declared against it.[45] This is in my mind because I wrote one of the speeches. The president spent a day in Wisconsin. He gave a speech in Oshkosh and Milwaukee, which I recall because I wrote it.[46] About a week later, after his office was inundated with letters and phone calls, Senator Kasten came around and announced that he had found a way to support the president's proposal after all. So for Reagan, bringing people along was instinctive. It was what he did.[47]

Nelson: When Nixon, Reagan, or Carter was going to make a major speech, who decided whether that speech would be to a live audience or whether it would be a prime-time Oval Office address? Once that decision was made, how did that affect what you wrote?

Shapiro: I can answer succinctly in the case of Carter. This was all done at a higher level than speechwriters, because we were mere technicians. Toward the end, Rick [Hendrik] Hertzberg, who was his most successful chief speechwriter, may have had some input.[48] But for the most part, one was told when the speech was and where the speech was, and then you would draft it. There wasn't a "How can we get this message out?" kind of decision.

Nelson: And would you write it differently if it were going to be before a live audience or to a camera?

Shapiro: To a large extent, very few things were to cameras only in those days. Rather, everything was to camera and nothing was to camera, in the sense that very few things broke into television at that point, but it was also at a point when everything a president did was recorded. So I can't recall actually making the distinction. It was a speech, but it wasn't as if this was from the Oval Office with no audience.

Khachigian: I can't imagine ever wasting a chit on determining where the president would speak. There was so much more I had to do as a collaborator than that. Just about everything I ever did was decided by someone else, where it would be. Once that decision was made, I could work on the process.

But sure, the speeches would be different. His early February address on the economy was a televised address from the Oval Office, and it was a lecture, an economics lesson by him to the American people. Two weeks later, before a joint session of Congress, it was totally different. He had a live audience, so there were cheer lines in the speech. Whenever you had a live audience, obviously you wanted some cheer lines, especially if you were in the state of the union, where you had a captive audience of senators and congressmen. So it makes a difference, but it never occurred to me. I had no view one way or the other. I suppose if I had strong feelings, I'd have made them known, but that was a ministerial decision that I didn't waste time on.

Shapiro: The other type of speech for which you are keenly conscious of the audience is when the president makes political speeches. In the case of

Jimmy Carter, he made a series of [Thomas] Jefferson–[Andrew] Jackson Day speeches in the spring of 1979, so I was very much inserting the applause lines there.[49] Again, it amazes me, in hindsight, how little guidance I had. This was eighteen months before the election, before he was nominated for reelection, nine months before Ted Kennedy got into the race against him. It was, again, like you on education policy [*speaking to Peter Robinson*], "Make up the accomplishments of the administration."

Coming after Vietnam, I had a line about how he was the first president, I think, since [Calvin] Coolidge, or something like that, to have no American soldiers die in combat while he was president. That, of course, only lasted until the failed hostage raid.[50] But I can still see myself sitting in my office in the Old Executive Office Building, saying, "We're two and a half years into the administration. What are we proud of?" Again, I think one of the speeches was to the Virginia Democratic JJ [Jefferson-Jackson] Dinner. It was a very odd experience to be given that much latitude.

Khachigian: Andy, I'll circle back to something that Peter talked about in terms of the Berlin Wall speech, which is the importance of knowing the site, knowing the environment of the speech. One of the disadvantages I had, because I was never full-time, except for two periods in the White House, was that I was a volunteer. So when I did the speech for Bergen-Belsen, I was not able to fly to Germany to see where he was speaking or what the camp looked like or anything else. And all of it was integral to the speech.

So I got the advance men on the phone. That's one thing about the White House: you can call anywhere in the world. So I gave Jim Hooley, who was the advance fellow in Germany, and Bill Henkel a set of instructions.[51] I wanted to know what it looked like, where he would be walking. Then I said, "When you guys are flying over between Hanover and Bergen-Belsen, what does it look like? What is the president going to see outside the window?" They asked, "What does Ken want all this stuff for?" But they gave me all this extraordinary detail.

Part of the theme of that speech was the emerging springtime in the German countryside, where the victims of these camps would never again see a leaf turning green or have that springtime of their lives. So through other people's eyes, I was able to write, "Flying here low over the German countryside, I could see the greening of the springtime here."[52] Then he was able to launch into a very sympathetic look at these young people who had died never knowing anything but the desolation of those camps. Had I been a full-time staff member, I would have been flown over and would have looked at the site myself.

That imagery grew out of my training in the Nixon years, where color reporting and knowing the background were essential for President Nixon, before he went into any event. If we have time before this is over, I think Ray and Lee ought to talk about the process we went through in the Nixon years: why he didn't speak from text but spoke extemporaneously on almost every occasion. How he did it was interesting.

Rudalevige: Is it possible to generalize about these major addresses in a staff-process sense? Presumably there is a pretty set routine for what Bill Moyers uncharitably called "Rose Garden rubbish," stuff that is being presented day by day, some of it more important than others, but nonetheless pretty low-level.[53] Is there a routine for that? For these speeches, it seems that in reading about their creation, it is very much ad hoc. There is a particular process that is applied to a particular speech, whether it is because of the location or the people involved or the external events that are shaping the decision to give the speech in the first place. Is it possible to talk in general terms about this?

Shapiro: It is hard, again, generalizing from Carter. Carter had three different chief speechwriters—four, if you count Pat, going back to the campaign —in a four-year period, each one of whom had a different routine and a different relationship with the president. So in addition to the chaos of Jimmy Carter's deteriorating political situation, there was so much turmoil internally that it is very hard to generalize about how anything was done except on an ad hoc basis. This was a president who, for the most part, did not have time for his speechwriters, because after all, they were merely a technical, little, appendix-like necessity in being president. After all, he wrote poetry, and he had written a book, *Why Not the Best?*[54] So if he was the best, then the people working for him clearly were not as good.

Rudalevige: He did write a couple of speeches himself. There was an energy speech early on; there was a foreign policy speech at Annapolis; obviously some of the "malaise" speech.[55] That didn't work very well, in fact, when he did it. I ask rather than state.

Shapiro: I would say that Jimmy Carter was far better as an inspirational leader in certain areas. I don't want to be too critical of Carter, who is responsible for me being here today, but there is another element of presidential speechmaking I should mention, which is how presidents talk about their accomplishments. The big accomplishment for Jimmy Carter in 1979 was that he brokered the Egyptian-Israeli peace agreement.[56] I think Jimmy Carter went about taking credit for it, which he deserved, in the wrong way. In every speech, we had the same eight words, "two courageous leaders, Anwar Sadat and Menachem Begin." Jimmy Carter referred to the agreement repeatedly using the exact same language. In early computers, you could almost put it on the Save/Get key. To some extent, in a bizarre way, by constant repetition, it diminished his accomplishment because he didn't have a fresh way of talking about it.[57]

Robinson: As I said, there would be three, four, half a dozen big speeches each year, and they were different procedurally. But even the little speeches could be nonroutine surprisingly often in the Reagan White House. I remember Josh Gilder. This was the same White House meeting in which we discussed the Berlin Wall speech. The president was going to visit the Pope at the Vatican. Josh hit the jackpot. He mentioned it, and the president started talking about the importance of religious liberty and what he hoped to see in Eastern Europe and maybe someday in Russia. Josh sat there and wrote as fast as he could and came out with two or three paragraphs of fresh, beautiful material. He dropped it into the speech, and the State Department objected.

Josh, on the phone, asked, "Could I ask why you're objecting?" They said, "It's too religious." "This is a meeting with the Pope!" [*laughter*] "Yes, but he's meeting the Pope in the Pope's capacity as head of state of the Vatican City, not as the head of the Roman Catholic Church." Josh said, "Well, would it make any difference if I told you that the author of the paragraphs that you want to delete is the president of the United States?" "Well, I suppose you can have them then, but we'd like the record to show that we object." "Okay." That kind of thing went on a lot.[58]

That little story also demonstrates a constant in our White House: there were fourteen of us who moved through that office, five or six writers on staff at any given time, working on big speeches and small speeches. Yet Ronald Reagan always sounded like Ronald Reagan. He was the constant. Before he came to office, he was a fully formed political figure. His principles were clear. His speaking style was perfectly clear. That was, in many ways, our great ally. As Ken said, there were people around the president such as Mike Deaver during the first term—and in my case, Tommy Griscom for the Berlin Wall speech—people not particularly political in some way who would look at something and say, "That's boring. That's not Reagan." So there was an insistence on the vivid. What you wanted was the ring of a trumpet, and that was Reagan. Everybody had a sense of what was appropriate for him and what wasn't. That was the constant for the speechwriters: the president himself.

Judge: Let me say a couple of things about what Ken and Peter said about the Reagan White House. One detail of what Peter said should be highlighted: it was unusual for the president to be the first one in the staffing process to see a speech. He did with the Berlin Wall speech. In my experience he also did another speech dealing with the Soviets, where he was personally shaping policy. He saw it first.

The thing about his seeing a draft first was that generally we were the only ones, together with the communications director and presumably the chief of staff, who would know that the president had seen the speech. So when the fight would break out, there was a core of people who knew that the president had already declared a section of the speech off-limits. I think it is fair to say that whether on instruction or instinct, we didn't invoke the president in most cases. But he had already gamed the negotiation over the speech. It was a very subtle way of exercising power. Ken talked about the speechwriting reflecting the president, and he talked about refereeing. When this refereeing was going on, particularly in an area where the stakes were way too big for the speechwriting office actually to prevail, the president had already weighed in in a way that signaled to senior staff that we were to prevail in this one area, even if we had to do something to make others as happy as they could be.

The final thing I'd say about Ken coming in from California is that Ronald Reagan always had a team in reserve. You saw this in New Hampshire when he was running for president in 1980. He was disillusioned with John Sears and the people around him, and he took over the campaign. On election night in New Hampshire, he brought in a new team.[59] When Iran-Contra hit, all of a sudden there was a new team around to look things over and more or less to run things outside of the staffing system until he figured out how to resolve it. The same is true with what Ken said about the Bergen-Belsen speech.

Rudalevige: I wanted to ask Don Baer and Terry Edmonds about the Clinton experience. The example that comes to mind, of course, is from late 1994 into '95, when there was another presence—at least this is the way that the accounts of the time tell it—there was an influence on presidential rhetoric, but you're not quite sure where it was coming from. I don't know if this is your phrase, but the "immaculate conception."

Baer: That's one of my phrases, and I've been quoted as talking about gravitational pull. You didn't know that there was another planet out there, but it was pulling things in a certain direction. You're referring to the time after the '94 congressional elections, which the Democrats lost, a low point for President Clinton and for the administration.[60] He had begun just before that to reach out to Dick Morris, who had been a political consultant to him for more than a dozen years when Clinton had been the governor of Arkansas. Other pollsters were Mark Penn and Doug Schoen.[61] Bob Squier, who was a Democratic consultant close to Vice President [Albert] Gore [Jr.], was brought into it.[62] At first none of us knew about it for several months.

There were some speeches that found their way onto the schedule during the early stages of this, one in December of 1994, which was one of the early efforts of President Clinton to reassert himself after [Newt] Gingrich and the Republican revolution in Congress. It was called the Middle Class Bill of Rights speech. Nobody knew how it got on the schedule; no one knew what it was supposed to be.[63] I was assigned to work on that speech with only Bruce Reed, who was at that point the deputy domestic policy advisor, but who had been a speechwriter for President Clinton during the campaign in '92. It was supposed to be only the two of us. Bruce and I both represented, in the mind of the president, this New Democrat perspective, the more moderate, centrist perspective.

Bruce had come from the Democrat Leadership Council, so I think the president trusted that he was going to get from us something different from the pure, more liberal, congressional Democratic perspective that he typically got from others on his staff.[64] So we worked on that speech. There's a long story about that. The drafts changed dramatically and somewhat immaculately without us knowing what was going on. The same thing happened with the state of the union address in 1995, a month or so later. That one became, unfortunately, more of a layer cake, because the president was receiving advice and counsel from different sources.

At that time, of course, I was working in the main White House. I was a staffer reporting to the communications director, since I was running the speechwriting operation. So I needed, to some extent, to take my lead from what I was being told by what I thought of as the daytime White House. Then there was a nighttime White House going on as well. I eventually came to regard the official White House staff as the Potemkin Village White House, because there was another White House that was really driving things. That led to the eighty-one-minute state of the union address in 1995, because there was this layer-cake effect. It was the longest state of the union address in history up to that point. I was proud that a few years later—I think, Terry, when you were the chief speechwriter—the president went to eighty-nine minutes, so I can take that record off my résumé.[65] [*laughter*]

Then several months went by. This was in the early stages of the Republican Congress. Newt Gingrich was viewed, for all intents and purposes, as the prime minister of the United States.[66] President Clinton, in a press conference, said, "The presidency is relevant," and all of that.[67] There is an elaborate story that is told in a number of books about when I was first brought into the picture. I was the first person brought into any of the communications apparatus outside of the chief of staff, one or two of the deputy chiefs of staff, Vice President Gore's chief of staff, and then the president, the vice president, and the first lady.

I was the first one brought to the table on this because they recognized that they needed an ally in the speechwriting shop, which says something, I think, about the importance of speechwriting. They did not bring anyone from communications into it, per se, but they did recognize that they wanted to work much more closely with speechwriting. They either thought that I would be pliable or they were trying to move the administration toward more of a centrist perspective, and they knew that was where I was coming from anyway. It was one of the reasons why I wanted to go into the Clinton presidency in 1994.

I was put into a difficult situation because there were things I was not at liberty to talk about even with my staff, or with the rest of the speechwriting operation, but even more important, with the people to whom I directly reported and worked for. That was at the request of the president. It meant that over time, there were a lot of things going on that I knew about and was even helping with, that I was asked not to dwell on with the very people I was supposed to be working with on a day-to-day basis, including people in the foreign policy apparatus. So that became even more uncomfortable. I used to joke that I had a full head of hair when I started at the White House, though my wife claims that that was never true.

Rudalevige: Was that a process that served the president well? We have a lot of stories of staff competition, in a sense.

Baer: It absolutely served the president well. I never heard him say this directly, but I heard that President Clinton and Vice President Gore both said to themselves, to one another, and to a small group of people around them, that they wanted to take back their presidency—so that it would serve the purposes that they felt they had come there to serve. Who, if anyone, was to blame for them not controlling the presidency before that period, I think, is open to question, because they shared blame in that as well. But I think they felt very strongly that they wanted to do this.

I would argue that the period of time we're talking about—for all of the atmospherics around that and for all of the reporting on both personal habits and infighting and things like that—it was the most productive period of the Clinton presidency, in terms of both domestic and foreign policy advances. I think it did work, and it enabled the president to right himself and to right his presidency for the purposes of getting reelected. But more importantly, I think it enabled the president to make major gains in terms of policy.[68]

This situation made a lot of people angry inside the White House. There were people who quit—not immediately, but in time—who were very alienated. It made a lot of people in the more left-wing Democratic Party establishment very unhappy—some would argue, to this day. I think there are interesting echoes of those fights, which are now more than a dozen years old, even in the [2008] Democratic primary season we've just come through.

Jones: Don, could you say something about the '98 state of the union, which could be called a crisis speech? Arguably the lead-up to the speech was extremely effective. The Republicans were out of town, and the president had essentially taken over during that time to systematically review each of the policy areas that were clearly going to be in the speech. All of the commentary in that period in early January was that this was the second or third presidency of the president and so forth. Was the speech changed very much as a consequence of the [Monica] Lewinsky scandal?

Baer: A major proviso: I was not at the White House. I had left in late 1997, so I was no longer there. Terry was there. But I was around Washington. I can give you some of what I saw but not as firsthand. Michael Waldman was the head of speechwriting at the time. Ann Lewis was the head of communications.[69]

A few things: They had done a very effective job, starting as far back as September of 1997, of planning for the state of the union in 1998. If you remember the unfinished business of the first Clinton term—although I talked in terms of there having been three Clinton terms, but I won't bore you with that thesis at this point. They recognized that, having balanced the budget and having gotten through the major budget fight of 1995 and 1996 with a great bipartisan resolution, they then had the chance to go on to what people thought would be the last productive phase of the Clinton presidency: the last three years. So they had begun to do extensive work on policy development and on what the second-term agenda would be. They had done an effective job of the rollout, which we always worked on, certainly from '96 forward. We had worked on a pretty elaborate rollout, both before the state of the union and then afterward. There was always an important set of road shows and activities going on. I used to write memos that would project out for six months on how we would work off of the state of the union. This happened when I was communications director, so it was an extension of that kind of work.

Rahm Emanuel, who was then the senior advisor for policy and strategy, played a big role in that.[70] Paul Begala was back in the White House at that point.[71] I think Paul played a big role in it, as did Michael Waldman, who was the chief speechwriter. So they had begun, about three weeks after the first of the year, to put out public announcements about what was coming in the state of the union speech and all of that. They did a very good job of building it up and of placing the president back in the center of that relevancy, as it were.

Of course we know that some five days or so before the speech, the Lewinsky scandal broke.[72] I was involved in it at that point because every year after I left the White House, I came back in for part of the state of the union preparation—as more of a favor to me, I think, than anything else. But it was interesting to be around it and to help where possible. There was a lot of talk about what to do with that speech and about how to deal with it given the controversy that was swirling. You may remember that George Stephanopoulos, who by then was an ABC News person, stood on the front lawn of the White House and said, "If this is true, the president is going to be impeached," within a matter of two hours after this stuff broke. This sent shock waves throughout Washington and the White House.[73]

There was a big fight, and it operated on a few levels. There were some people who advocated very much that the president needed to address the nation from the well of the Congress on the issue of the scandal, and that he had to speak to the country about it at this moment when he had everyone's attention focused on him as president. There were other people, fortunately, who prevailed, who understood that the job of the president was to be the president. The country was looking to see, as bad as this thing seemed to be, if he was still in a position to perform the job of the presidency on their behalf, because that is what the country wanted. If you remember, there's not a mention of that scandal in the speech.

I remember being in a meeting. The thing broke on Thursday.[74] This meeting may have been even on Monday. As anyone who has worked on a state of the union address knows, that's still pretty early in the process. There's still a lot going on for a Tuesday night speech. We had a meeting in Richard Nixon's old West Wing hideaway office, which was a conference room that we used over there, to talk about whether, at the top of the speech, the president should say anything very quickly, even parenthetically, that would hint at "I know something is going on, but let's get on with the business of the country."

There was a back-and-forth, and I remember having a pad of paper and asking, "Is there a way to say this in a way that wouldn't overstate anything?" and all that. There was a group of a dozen or so people, outside advisors and whatnot. The decision was ultimately made by the president. "We're not going to say anything about this. My job is to stand up there and tell the country what I'm going to do as president and to show them that I'm going to perform the job every day that they hired me to do."

Indeed he delivered that speech.[75] It was a brilliant speech. It was a well-thought-through, well-wrought, policy-oriented speech with a serious agenda to it. For whatever it's worth, his poll numbers shot up as a result of that speech, because again, the country was focused very much on his ability to perform the job. There are plenty of people—I've not talked to the president about it, but I'd be surprised if he disagreed with this—who believe deeply that he survived in office, given everything that transpired over the course of the next year, because day in and day out after that, he was shown to be and in fact was performing the job of being president. He was not dwelling on being dragged down into the commentary on this other thing.[76] So that's the background of at least that part of that fight.

To reveal some things: On the Sunday after the scandal broke, there was a lot of activity and back-and-forth conversation about "Did he have to call a press conference? Did he have to do something before the state of the union in order to wipe the slate clean so that he could stand there and do the thing?" I had a conversation with the president about this. I know for a fact, based on things he told me and that other people did, that there was a division of opinion, as you can imagine, with some advisors saying, "There's no way you can get through Tuesday night without doing something." Other people said, "Keep your head down." Of course that led not to a press conference or to taking questions, but to the famous statement that he made in the Roosevelt Room later that day.[77] That was because of the cross-pressures and tensions about whether he should say anything.

Rudalevige: It strikes me that a lot of the discussion here is about reacting creatively. Can you set out to write a landmark address? Do we remember these addresses—in fact, your best efforts obviously made part of that possible—because the events surrounding them cause them to be memorable? Where is the balance there? Can you set out to create a memorable speech?

Robinson: In my judgment, the answer is no. You can't set out to write a landmark address. Frankly my overarching goal is always to hit my deadline without embarrassing myself, just to do my job. In the case of the Berlin speech, "Mr. Gorbachev, tear down this wall," the fact is, the speech was recognized as a pretty darn good speech at the time. He delivered it beautifully and so forth. But it wasn't until fourteen, fifteen months later, when the Berlin Wall actually came down, that the speech, in a strange way, retroactively acquired resonance.[78]

Baer: They would play it over and over again.

Robinson: Exactly. So my feeling was that I had done a good job. The president had delivered it beautifully. That would be, perhaps, one of the half-dozen best speeches that he got in that year, but that particular phrase would acquire such resonance. When he gave that speech in 1987, if you had asked me the day before he delivered that speech, or even a year afterward, "What will be remembered as the signature line for the Reagan administration?"

I would have said, "evil empire," which was 1983.[79] Or I would have said, "Marxism-Leninism will end up on the ash heap of history," which was 1982.[80] It seemed to sum up something that happened. It wasn't the speech itself, I don't believe. You just do your best work. That speech acquired such resonance, in my judgment, because Ronald Reagan was right so much of the time about how to pursue the Cold War and about what the ultimate outcome would be. But you couldn't tell that he was right until afterward.

Shapiro: And if it weren't for Gorbachev setting up the situation, you couldn't say, "Mr. Gorbachev, tear down this wall." That would be the kind of rhetoric that the State Department was worried about.

The one time I tried to participate, shall we say, in a "grasp for greatness" was before Carter's 1979 state of the union. There was an effort to come up with a slogan for the administration. A group of men, all men, sitting around a room, came up with the "New Foundation." There are two things on my government résumé which I'm very proud of: one is, no hostages were taken on Shapiro's watch, and the other was, when it was suggested that our slogan be the New Foundation—as has been recorded in the Robert Schlesinger book—my contribution was, "Can't we do better?"[81] [laughter] What stays with me is that this group of seven or eight men came up with a slogan that, when Jimmy Carter said it in his state of the union message, a few people pointed out was exceedingly similar to bra and girdle ads of the 1950s and '60s. [laughter]

Khachigian: That's called BOGSAT, a bunch of guys sitting around a table. I think you can plan a landmark speech. Not everything is reactive. You can make a landmark speech with a form that is already there. I'm thinking of President Reagan's remarks at the United Nations General Assembly, I think in '85, when he set a new tone for the relationship with the Soviet Union. I had been brought in to work on the speech, and I wrote somewhat of a more hard-line speech, thinking that was where Reagan was in relationship with the Soviet Union.[82]

We had our first meeting about the speech. There were several people in the room, and he was very candid. He said, "If we're going to have a new relationship with the Soviet Union, we have to change our rhetoric a little bit." I thought that was very interesting. I thought I was being sabotaged by some squish at the State Department, but it was really the president himself deciding that the tone of his remarks would offer something new. I think that speech was a semi-landmark in terms of opening a new door, in terms of how they dealt with Gorbachev and then of course later on with Reykjavik.[83]

Robinson: I'm so happy to hear that that happened to you, too. There was a meeting with us and Don Regan, when Don Regan was chief of staff. I always liked Don Regan, but he was probably in the wrong job. In the middle of the speech meeting he said, "By the way, fellas, the president would like you to go a little easier on Gorbachev." We gave him hell. We said, in effect, "*You* may want us to go easier," because we'd been through this—the staff, Deaver, and [James] Baker, "Ease up, ease up." We were the true believers. We understood what the president wanted.

Regan said, "All right, if you won't take it from me. . . ." A couple of days later he found time on the president's schedule, and we trooped into the Oval Office, and Ronald Reagan said, "Well, this fellow Gorbachev is a different kind of leader, and I think he's serious about getting out of Afghanistan." It took about a week for us to be able to eat our breakfast in the morning again. It was as if the world had turned upside down. But it was true. It came from the president himself. He was the first person I heard suggest this, not a pundit. Nobody had said at that point that the Soviets would get out of Afghanistan.[84] Reagan sensed it immediately about Gorbachev.

Khachigian: I think it was a sea change in his view of the Soviet Union.

Baer: I think that planning for the landmark speech is quite often dangerous because you have writers who want to write for the granite or the marble. But those kinds of lines almost never make it to the granite or the marble. You have to be careful.

Second, I think that foreign speeches on foreign soil about foreign policy subjects tend to lend themselves more to that opportunity. There's typically a more dramatic setting. That was true with [John F.] Kennedy in Berlin.[85] Ronald Reagan turned this into an art form, which we tried to take advantage of, but we were quite often coming in his aftermath. So we did our fiftieth anniversary of the Normandy invasion. I think we did pretty well, but it was always compared to prior presidents and things like that.[86] But there were always those opportunities.

Finally, on domestic fronts, I think the speeches tend to be reactive because they tend to follow dramatic moments in which presidents find themselves healing the country more than anything else. I think of Oklahoma City or of this President [George W.] Bush after September 11.[87] Those are the times when the country tends to turn to them and listen to them about something that is here on the home front.

Price: I guess it depends a little bit on what you mean by "landmark." You might say we had a landmark in the last speech I did with him [Nixon], which happens to be the one in which he announced that he would resign the next day. That isn't done very often, so that might make it a landmark. Perhaps the key landmark speech, in the normal course of that word, that he gave as president might be the one he did on Vietnam early in his presidency, which nobody saw but him.

Rudalevige: It was November 1969.[88]

Price: Yes, which he did entirely by himself.

Rudalevige: But he understood that it was going to be an important statement.

Price: Oh sure, he intended it to be a definitive speech on that subject. But he did it without help.

Judge: The "silent majority" phrase came out of that speech. He used something close to it about ten times.

Price: Yes.

Judge: The forgotten Americans, the quiet majority.

Price: I forget what that earlier thing was, but the "silent majority" was picked up.

Rudalevige: Ray, do you have any recollections that you can share with us about that resignation speech?[89]

Price: I have a few recollections of it, yes. He'd been up and down on the question of resigning for a period of a week to ten days. We finally got started on that on Thursday. He made the speech on Thursday, August 8, that he would resign on Friday, August 9.

We knew we would have to do a big Watergate defense about that time, so a big meeting was set up in Al Haig's office for Thursday the eighth. Al Haig was then the chief of staff.[90] He organized a big meeting of department heads and me and some others who were involved. They had charts and so forth assigning people for the battle, all the battle stations, and so forth.

Then that was over, and I was chatting with a couple of people outside of his office, and his secretary urged me to come back in. She said, "That was all sham. He wants a resignation speech. Start on that." So I started on that. We were going to go up to Camp David, and then the president decided against it. He was going to make a speech, but instead he was going to pledge to fight on and to answer questions in the well of the Senate under oath, which I thought was a bad idea. Somewhere along the way, as we were getting the vote count, it looked to me as though it was impossible. Better to end it cleanly. It was a fairly momentous decision for a president to make. He wrestled with it up and down. Finally we were up at Camp David that weekend, supposedly wrestling with how we were going to fight the battle. Then I got the word, "We're back on the resignation track," which was, of course, very secret. So it went back and forth, working on that in privacy.

One odd little problem I had was that I had turned over the writing staff at the end of our first term and had moved around the corner to an office by myself, with one assistant and one secretary, still on the first floor of the Executive Office Building (EOB). Then the one assistant finally left. He had postponed his departure twice, but he had to get back to starting law school. So I brought in Ben Stein, Herb Stein's son, who was much thinner then than he is now on television.[91] But he was on our writing staff. He was in Tex's [Harold J. Lezar's] office, which was right across from mine.[92] His office was here, my secretary was in the middle, and then I was over here. So all the time I was working on this, I could have shared with Tex, because he knew how to keep a secret. I didn't know yet whether Ben knew how to keep a secret, and under all the intense pressures, everybody tried to figure out what you were doing. So I had to keep Ben in the dark. This meant that anytime he came into my office, I had to make sure that everything was covered up. This was too bad. It complicated things a little bit.

We went back and forth. We went back through several drafts of the speech from Tuesday to Thursday, back and forth. Finally the president worked it out in his mind to say the things that he wanted to say in the way that he wanted to say them. Finally, on Wednesday night I thought we had pretty well wrapped it up. We went back and forth by telephone several times. I think I logged eight telephone calls between 4:35 A.M. and 5:07 A.M. from him. I'd gone at about midnight to settle down. I went back home and tried to sleep a little bit, but then my phone began ringing again as we worked out some of the final wording of it until it was done. Then I watched him give it on Thursday night, hoping that he would maintain his composure. He did. That was it.

Nelson: Well, I hate to bring this to a close on such a somber note, but it was fascinating in addition to everything else. Let's give our thanks to Ken Khachigian, Peter Robinson, and Walter Shapiro, and to Andrew Rudalevige for guiding this discussion.

Notes

1. For Jimmy Carter alone, the *Public Papers of the Presidents* series (Washington, D.C.: General Services Administration) comprises nine volumes and some 11,000 pages—and weighs nearly fifty pounds.

2. A comprehensive study of that "crisis of confidence" speech in historical context is found in Kevin Mattson, *"What the Heck Are You Up to, Mr. President?": Jimmy Carter, America's "Malaise," and the Speech That Should Have Changed the Country* (New York: Bloomsbury, 2009). Video and text of the speech can be found on the Web site of the University of Virginia's Miller Center of Public Affairs, at http://millercenter.org/scripps/archive/speeches/detail/3402. Carter's own brief account of this episode appears in *Keeping Faith: Memoirs of a Presidency* (New York: Bantam Books, 1982), 115–121.

3. Confirmation that the immediate reaction was positive can be found in J. William Holland, "The Great Gamble: Jimmy Carter and the 1979 Energy Crisis," *Prologue: Quarterly of the National Archives* 22, no. 1 (Spring 1990): 63–79. Holland reports that Carter's approval ratings jumped over ten points. See also Michael J. Towle, *Out of Touch: The Presidency and Public Opinion* (College Station: Texas A&M University Press, 2004), 35–36.

4. Carter asked for resignation letters from most of his senior appointees; under duress, thirty-three White House and cabinet officials offered to resign. In the end, five cabinet secretaries were essentially fired, as well as fifty subcabinet figures. The overall effect was to suggest that his "government" had collapsed; the stock market and Carter's approval ratings went with it. "Carter had . . . exacerbated the very crisis of confidence that his actions were designed to alleviate." Richard M. Pious, *Why Presidents Fail: White House Decision Making from Eisenhower to Bush II* (Lanham, Md.: Rowman and Littlefield, 2008), 105–107.

5. Paul A. Volcker is an American economist who served as chairman of the U.S. Federal Reserve from 1979 to 1987. The Fed, under Volcker's leadership, sought to arrest the high rate of inflation the country was suffering near the end of the Carter presidency by dramatically raising interest rates, which many credit with bringing on recession. See Bernard Shull, *The Fourth Branch: The Federal Reserve's Unlikely Rise to Power and Influence* (Westport, Conn.: Praeger/Greenwood, 2005).

6. On this episode, see Richard J. Jensen, *Reagan at Bergen-Belsen and Bitburg* (College Station: Texas A&M University Press, 2007).

7. Helmut Kohl was chancellor of West Germany from 1982 to 1990, and then of the unified German state from 1990 to 1998. Kohl was a reliable ally during a period of protracted East-West tension during the Cold War.

8. Wiesel's objections were very public, registered in an address before a White House audience. The text of his speech is included in a chapter entitled "Holocaust Witness Elie Wiesel Asks President Reagan to Reconsider a Visit to a German Cemetery," in *Lend Me Your Ears: Great Speeches in History*, ed. William Safire (New York: W. W. Norton, 2004), 735–738.

9. Anne Frank (1929–1945) was a German-born Jew who spent most of her life in the Netherlands. She kept a diary, published after World War II, documenting her life in hiding. She died at the age of 15 in the Bergen-Belsen concentration camp. See Frank's *Diary of a Young Girl* (New York: Bantam, 1993).

10. Michael K. Deaver (1938–2007) was a longtime Reagan aide, whose main responsibilities included media affairs and image building. Deaver was also very close to Nancy Reagan, and accordingly served as her eyes and ears within the official White House. One account of his time with Reagan is Deaver (with Mickey Herskowitz), *Behind the Scenes* (New York: William Morrow, 1988).

11. The actual text of Reagan's opening was: "Chancellor Kohl and honored guests, this painful walk into the past has done much more than remind us of the war that consumed the European Continent. What we have seen makes unforgettably clear that no one of the rest of us can fully understand the enormity of the feelings carried by the victims of these camps." Video and full text of the speech are available at http://www.americanrhetoric.com/speeches/ronaldreaganbergen-belsen.htm.

12. On April 24, 1915, the government of Turkey arrested some 200 Armenian leaders, setting into motion what would become a massive, violent loss of life among the Armenian people. April 24 is thus the day set aside each year to remember the Armenian victims. The Turks vigorously object, however, to use of the term "genocide" to describe these events, claiming that the Armenians were not the victims of methodical elimination, but rather suffered, as did many Turks, from the senseless, tragic violence of World War I. For evidence supporting the Armenian case, see the Web site of the Armenian National Institute in Washington, at http://www.armenian-genocide.org/genocidefaq.html. A Web site professing to offer a balanced treatment of the issue, entitled "Armenian Genocide Debate," can be found at http://www.armeniangenocidedebate.com/.

13. The Berlin Wall was rapidly erected by the Communist police and East German army units in August 1961 to separate the free sector of Berlin, in the West, from the rest of Soviet-dominated East Germany. The Brandenburg Gate is a massive, monumental set of Doric columns that served as a passageway through a different set of city walls dating back to the late eighteenth century. The erection of the Communists' wall effectively made the gate inaccessible to both sides, from 1961 to 1989.

14. The Ronald Reagan Presidential Library is located in Simi Valley, California. In October 2005, the library's museum opened a pavilion containing the airplane that was Reagan's *Air Force One*.

15. A similar version of this account by Peter M. Robinson appears in *The Weekly Standard*, June 23, 1997.

16. The Reichstag is the ornate building that was constructed in 1894 to house the German parliament. It was severely damaged by fire in 1933, and suffered further at the time of the Soviet invasion at the end of World War II. During most of the Cold War it was in ruins and unused, but was reconstructed to a condition near its former glory after German reunification.

17. Tempelhof was, in an earlier time, the main Berlin airport, and was a critical connecting point for the U.S. military during the course of the Berlin airlift. It was permanently closed to air traffic in 2008.

18. Dieter Elz is a widely published author on agricultural economics.

19. Mikhail Gorbachev presided, as final head of the Soviet Union, over the union's breakup, drawing the Cold War to an end. Two policy commitments closely associated with Gorbachev's rule were *glasnost*, which is the Russian word for "openness," and *perestroika*, the word for "restructuring." It was unclear at the time that Robinson made his visit to Berlin how far Gorbachev would go in pursuing these two commitments. See Mikhail S. Gorbachev, *Perestroika: New Thinking for Our Country and the World* (New York: HarperCollins, 1987).

20. Tony Dolan was a Pulitzer Prize–winning journalist before joining the 1980 Reagan-Bush campaign as a speechwriter. He was appointed Reagan's head speechwriter in November 1981, a position he held until the conclusion of Reagan's presidency.

21. Tom Griscom came to the White House in 1987 when Tennessee senator Howard Baker agreed to become White House chief of staff, to help steady the Reagan presidency in the wake of the Iran-Contra scandal. Griscom was serving at the time as Baker's press secretary. In the White House, Griscom served as a key aide to Baker and as director of White House communications.

22. Josh Gilder was a senior speechwriter for President Reagan from 1985 to 1988. He also held a senior post in the State Department under President George H. W. Bush and subsequently became a journalist and novelist.

23. Reagan's speech presumably would have been broadcast on Radio Free Europe.

24. George P. Shultz was Ronald Reagan's secretary of state from 1982 to 1989. Shultz had a distinguished academic and business career before joining the Reagan cabinet, and

had served as secretary of labor, secretary of the treasury, and director of the Office of Management and Budget under President Richard Nixon.

25. The Venice meeting was the annual gathering of the so-called G-7, held to discuss the state of the global economy.

26. During this interval, Kenneth Duberstein was serving as President Reagan's deputy chief of staff. He earlier had worked in and headed the office of congressional affairs, and, after Howard Baker's departure, he became Reagan's final White House chief of staff.

27. Clark Clifford (1906–1998) was a longtime advisor to Democratic presidents from Harry Truman to Jimmy Carter, serving as secretary of defense under President Johnson in 1968 and 1969. He was special counsel to President Truman from 1946 to 1950, but otherwise served in less formal capacities. His autobiography (written with Richard Holbrooke) is *Counsel to the President: A Memoir* (New York: Random House, 1991). On speechwriting, see 73–75, 194–196, 519–526.

28. Richard Reeves has written of the first four years of the Reagan presidency (citing Richard Darman as his source) that "the strategic, political, and philosophical tensions of the administration were worked out in the preparation of the President's speeches. The words were both policy and marching orders." *President Reagan: The Triumph of Imagination* (New York: Simon & Schuster, 2005), 327.

29. Dave Barry is an American humorist, who often introduces outrageous, but true, stories with the claim that "I am not making this up."

30. Although it is not completely clear from Robinson's remarks which speech he is describing, the most likely candidate is Reagan's February 7, 1984, ten-point address to the annual convention of the National Association of Secondary School Principals in Las Vegas, Nevada (available at http://www.presidency.ucsb.edu/ws/index.php?pid= 39400&st=education&st1=principal). However, Reagan also made Oval Office remarks to this same group on July 23, 1983. And on December 8, 1983, he spoke to the National Forum on Excellence in Education, in Indianapolis, Indiana. So the speechwriters had indeed crafted at least passable remarks on education within a year before this address. Moreover, it is worth noting here that in April 1983, the President's Commission on Excellence in Education produced its controversial report entitled "A Nation at Risk," documenting the deficiencies in the U.S. school system. Robinson strongly implies in these comments, then, that the White House had not decided in the aftermath of that report, even going into the reelection season, how to respond to the recommendations made by the president's commission. A copy of the report can be seen at http://www .ed.gov/pubs/NatAtRisk/index.html.

31. William Bennett served as secretary of education under President Reagan from 1985 to 1988. He also directed national drug control policy under President George H. W. Bush from 1989 to 1991, before leaving government service to become a prolific author and conservative commentator.

32. Terrel H. Bell was President Reagan's first secretary of education, serving from 1981 to 1985. Prior to this time, he was a senior official in the U.S. Department of

Health, Education and Welfare (appointed by President Nixon), and then chief executive officer of the Utah higher education system. He authored *The Thirteenth Man: A Reagan Cabinet Memoir* (New York: Free Press, 1988).

33. Richard Darman (1943–2008) served in several high-ranking executive branch positions in five administrations, beginning with Richard Nixon's. Most notably, he was a very powerful, and controversial, director of the Office of Management and Budget for President George H. W. Bush—and is usually credited with helping to devise the 1990 budget agreement with the Democratic Congress, which conservatives repudiated as a violation of Bush's "no new taxes" pledge. He also was deputy secretary of the treasury for President Reagan in the second term. During the period Robinson addresses here, he was the chief aide to White House chief of staff James A. Baker, in which capacity he evidently was the final arbiter of presidential speeches. (See Peggy Noonan's observations to this effect, quoted in Reeves, *President Reagan*, 327.) Darman was serving functionally as communications director, even without the title. Darman's memoir is *Who's in Control? Polar Politics and the Sensible Center* (New York: Simon & Schuster, 1996).

34. Robert Sweet, Jr., is a Republican education policy expert, who has served as a staff member to the Domestic Policy Council for President Reagan (including the time Robinson addresses), as acting director of the National Institute for Education, and as a staff person at the Department of Education. President George H. W. Bush appointed him to head the Office of Juvenile Justice and Delinquency Prevention within the Department of Justice.

35. On Carter's use of religious rhetoric in the 1976 campaign, see Keith V. Erickson, "Jimmy Carter: The Rhetoric of Private and Civic Piety," *Western Journal of Speech Communication* 44, no. 3 (Summer 1980): 221–235.

36. For a discussion of Jimmy Carter's presidential rhetoric, see John H. Patton, "Jimmy Carter: The Language of Politics and the Practice of Integrity," in *Presidential Speechwriting: From the New Deal to the Reagan Revolution and Beyond*, eds. Kurt Ritter and Martin J. Medhurst (College Station: Texas A&M University Press, 2004), ch. 7. Included there (189–193) are extensive footnotes containing valuable bibliographic information on Carter and rhetoric.

37. Schlesinger, *White House Ghosts: Presidents and Their Speechwriters* (New York: Simon & Schuster, 2008).

38. Erwin C. Hargrove, in his award-winning study of Carter, makes a slightly different point. He claims that Carter believed that his powers of persuasion were at their strongest by making highly informed decisions after an immersion in the details of a particular policy. Legitimate political persuasion was thus, for Carter, more the result of finding the best product than of crafting the most elegant or convincing language to sell something inherently inferior. See Hargrove, *Jimmy Carter as President: Leadership and the Politics of the Public Good* (Baton Rouge: Louisiana State University Press, 1988), 24–25.

39. For an especially intimate view of the internal politics of that first year's budget battles, see William Greider, *The Education of David Stockman and Other Americans* (New

York: E. P. Dutton, 1981). It was Stockman's candid cooperation with Greider for an article in *The Atlantic Monthly* that got him "taken to the woodshed" for a scolding by President Reagan later that year.

40. Lawrence Kudlow is a conservative economist and journalist, with government experience in the Federal Reserve Bank of New York and the Reagan administration. He was from 1981 to 1985 (the period Khachigian addresses here) associate director for economics and planning in the Office of Management and Budget. For more on the internal political combat over Reagan's initial economic policies, see Jude Wanniski, "Introduction to the Revised and Updated Edition," *The Way the World Works*, 4th ed. (Washington, D.C.: Regnery, 1998), 345–363.

41. Lou Cannon writes that "the phrase 'Let Reagan be Reagan' became a mantra for conservatives outside the administration who feared the president was being turned from his natural ideological course by pragmatic White House aides." *President Reagan: The Role of a Lifetime* (New York: Simon & Schuster, 1991), 149.

42. For extensive analysis of Bush and speechmaking, see Martin J. Medhurst, ed., *The Rhetorical Presidency of George H. W. Bush* (College Station: Texas A&M University Press, 2006).

43. *Air Force Two* is the nomenclature for the plane flying the vice president. Joe Hagen was deputy White House chief of staff for President George W. Bush, but he evidently was serving here as the first President Bush's personal aide—responsible for handling the president's creature comforts and making sure that his paperwork was in order.

44. Many political figures prefer to have their speeches printed on "half sheets," which are either note cards or paper pages sized to half the length of a regular 8.5 × 11 page. See the description in Cannon, *Role of a Lifetime*, 34.

45. Robert W. Kasten, Jr., a Wisconsin Republican, served in the U.S. House of Representatives from 1975 to 1979, and in the U.S. Senate from 1981 to 1993—including the duration of the Reagan presidency.

46. The Oshkosh, Wisconsin, speech, devoted to selling tax reform, was delivered on May 30, 1985. It can be read at http://www.presidency.ucsb.edu/ws/index.php?pid= 38707&st=Oshkosh&st1=Milwaukee.

47. For more on Reagan's ability to move members of Congress by speaking directly to their constituents, see Samuel Kernell, *Going Public: New Strategies of Presidential Leadership*, 4th ed. (Washington, D.C.: CQ Press, 2006), ch. 6.

48. Hendrik Hertzberg was a speechwriter for Jimmy Carter for all four years of his presidency—serving as chief speechwriter beginning in 1979. He subsequently returned to a career in journalism, including terms leading *The New Republic* and writing for *The New Yorker*.

49. Jefferson-Jackson Day Dinners are held by the various state Democratic parties, usually in February to April of each year, to celebrate the history of the party—and to provide an occasion for seeing some of its most promising orators in action.

50. The failed mission, known as Desert One, occurred on the night of April 24–25,

1980. Eight American soldiers were killed. Carter provides a description of his own engagement with the mission in *Keeping Faith*, 506–519.

51. James Hooley began doing advance work for Ronald Reagan in 1978 and ultimately was designated, in late 1988, assistant to the president and director of presidential advance. He also played a key role in planning Reagan's funeral ceremonies. William Henkel directed the White House advance office from 1982 to 1988. For details about his service, see Joseph Petro (with Jeffrey Robinson), *Standing Next to History: An Agent's Life inside the Secret Service* (New York: St. Martin's Griffin, 2006), 29–33.

52. Reagan's actual words were: "As we flew here from Hanover, low over the greening farms and the emerging springtime of the lovely German countryside, I reflected, and there must have been a time when the prisoners at Bergen-Belsen and those of every other camp must have felt the springtime was gone forever from their lives. Surely we can understand that when we see what is around us—all these children of God under bleak and lifeless mounds, the plainness of which does not even hint at the unspeakable acts that created them. Here they lie, never to hope, never to pray, never to love, never to heal, never to laugh, never to cry."

53. Bill Moyers was Lyndon Johnson's White House press secretary from 1965 to 1967, but he held several different positions in the Kennedy and Johnson administrations, and was for a time Johnson's de facto White House chief of staff. He later developed a prominent career in television journalism, mostly through the Public Broadcasting System.

54. This book was Jimmy Carter's campaign biography, *Why Not the Best?* (New York: Bantam Books, 1976).

55. Carter delivered an important statement about his thinking on American foreign policy with the commencement address to the U.S. Naval Academy in Annapolis on June 7, 1978. That text can be read at http://www.presidency.ucsb.edu/ws/index.php?pid=30915&st=&st1. An extensive study of this speech can be found in Robert A. Strong, *Working in the World: Jimmy Carter and the Making of American Foreign Policy* (Baton Rouge: Louisiana State University Press, 2000), 98–122. See also Hargrove, *Jimmy Carter as President*, 151–155.

56. One full section of Carter's memoir, *Keeping Faith*, is devoted to describing the Middle East peace agreement. See "No More War," 267–429.

57. A text search through Carter's speeches suggests that Shapiro is oversimplifying—but the core point is sustained: Carter constantly emphasized the bravery and courage of the two leaders with whom he worked. For example, in his address to Congress reporting on the Camp David meetings, on September 18, 1978, he began with "The first thing I would like to do is to give tribute to the two men who made this impossible dream now become a real possibility, the two great leaders with whom I have met for the last 2 weeks at Camp David: first, President Anwar Sadat of Egypt, and the other, of course, is Prime Minister Menahem Begin of the nation of Israel. I know that all of you would agree that these are two men of great personal courage, representing nations of peoples who are deeply grateful to them for the achievement which they have

realized." Text of the full address is available at http://www.presidency.ucsb.edu/ws/index.php?pid=29799&st=&st1=.

58. The text of Reagan's address at the Vatican can be seen at http://www.reagan.utexas.edu/archives/speeches/1987/060687a.htm. Earlier in his administration, Reagan established full diplomatic recognition of the Vatican.

59. Reagan and many of his longtime supporters, including Nancy, became disenchanted with the way that campaign manager John Sears had waged the race for the 1980 Republican presidential nomination—especially in the wake of a loss in the Iowa caucuses. Accordingly, Reagan dropped Sears on the night of his victory in New Hampshire, bringing back longtime advisor Stuart Spencer, who had been out of good graces with the Reagans because he had worked for Gerald Ford in 1976. See Cannon, *Role of a Lifetime*, 65–70. Spencer's account of this episode is included in the Stuart Spencer Interview, Miller Center, University of Virginia, Ronald Reagan Presidential Oral History Project, November 15–16, 2001, 38–39.

60. In the 1994 midterm elections, the Democrats lost control of the House of Representatives for the first time since 1954.

61. Doug Schoen is a Democratic political consultant who was brought into the White House with Dick Morris in the aftermath of the 1994 midterm losses to help steady the Clinton White House. He directed polling for Clinton's successful 1996 reelection campaign.

62. Bob Squier (1934–2000) was a longtime Democratic Party political consultant, who had worked for Hubert Humphrey and Jimmy Carter, as well as for the Clinton-Gore campaigns in 1992 and 1996. His background was in documentary filmmaking, and his most important work in these campaigns was in television advertising.

63. On the Middle Class Bill of Rights speech, see Bob Woodward, *The Choice: How Bill Clinton Won* (New York: Simon & Schuster, 2005), 45–47. The speech is reprinted in "The Clinton Tax Plan: Text of Clinton Speech Proposing Series of Tax Breaks for the Middle Class," *New York Times*, December 16, 1994, A36.

64. The Democratic Leadership Council is an organization of conservative and moderate Democrats founded in 1985 by members of the party who were concerned about its leftward movement in the wake of Walter Mondale's massive loss to Ronald Reagan a year before. Both Bill Clinton and Al Gore were associated with the DLC's development, which was, at least in the early years, heavily driven by southern members. The story of the DLC's emergence is chronicled in Kenneth S. Baer, *Reinventing Democrats: The Politics of Liberalism from Reagan to Clinton* (Lawrence: University Press of Kansas, 2000).

65. The 1995 state of the union ran to eighty-one minutes. Clinton's eighty-nine-minute state of the union message occurred in 2000.

66. Gingrich, for example, was designated *Time* magazine's Man of the Year in its December 25, 1995, issue.

67. Clinton was moved to declare that the president was still relevant to the policy process in an April 18, 1995, press conference, as reporters there continually asserted that

the Gingrich-led Congress had seized the initiative on a host of current issues. The following day a domestic terrorist bombed the federal courthouse in Oklahoma City, which had the effect of turning the nation's attention again to the White House for explanation and consolation. On the press conference see Todd Purdum, "Clinton Seeks New Welfare Bill, Saying G.O.P. Plan Is Too Harsh," *New York Times*, April 19, 1995, A1.

68. Charles O. Jones affirms the extraordinary productivity of the 1995-1996 period in *Separate but Equal Branches: Congress and the Presidency*, 2nd ed. (New York: Chatham House–Seven Bridges, 1999), 262-267.

69. Ann Lewis is a longtime Democratic Party activist who served in the Clinton White House from 1997 to 2000, first as director of communications and then as counselor to the president. Before the Clinton presidency, her résumé included leading positions at Planned Parenthood and Americans for Democratic Action. She is the sister of Massachusetts congressman Barney Frank.

70. Rahm Emanuel served in several staff capacities in the Clinton White House, including assistant to the president for political affairs and senior advisor to the president for policy and strategy. He was later elected, initially in 2002, to the U.S. House of Representatives from the state of Illinois, a position he vacated in 2009 to become White House chief of staff for President Barack Obama.

71. Paul Begala was a Democratic political consultant before becoming an author and television commentator. He teamed up with James Carville to help elect Harris Wofford to the U.S. Senate from Pennsylvania in a special election in 1991, over the heavily favored Republican Richard Thornburgh. That surprise victory commended Carville and Begala to Clinton, who hired them to run his successful 1992 presidential campaign.

72. Monica Lewinsky was a former White House intern, later a paid employee, with whom President Bill Clinton developed a sexual relationship. Public knowledge of this relationship, brought to light through the long-running investigation of Clinton's personal affairs by independent counsel Kenneth Starr, eventually resulted in Clinton's impeachment in 1998. There is a vast literature on these scandals and investigations.

73. Stephanopoulos had been among Clinton's most senior and trusted advisors in the 1992 campaign and later held several key positions in the White House, including press secretary and counsel. His relationship with Clinton was strained, however, over the course of the years, and suffered serious damage both because of his assertion of Clinton's likelihood of being impeached and because of the publication of Stephanopoulos's candid 1999 memoir, *All Too Human: A Political Education* (New York: Little, Brown, 1999).

74. The Lewinsky story actually broke in the mainstream media on the morning of Wednesday, January 21, 1998.

75. The text of the 1998 state of the union address is available at http://millercenter.org/scripps/archive/speeches/detail/3444.

76. Speechwriter Michael Waldman makes the same case in *POTUS Speaks*, 219-220.

77. At a news conference on the topic of education, held on January 26, 1998, Clinton made the following statement in response to a question about the developing scandal: "I

want to say one thing to the American people. I want you to listen to me. I'm going to say this again. I did not have sexual relations with that woman, Miss Lewinsky. I never told anybody to lie, not a single time—never. These allegations are false." Given subsequent developments, these words came back to haunt the president. Michael Waldman has commented that Clinton's line about *that woman* "will live as long as anything I ever wrote for him." *POTUS Speaks*, 211.

78. The Berlin Wall opened on November 9, 1989.

79. The oft-cited passages from Reagan's March 8, 1983, address to the annual convention of the National Association of Evangelicals in Orlando, Florida, were: "Yes, let us pray for the salvation of all of those who live in that totalitarian darkness—pray they will discover the joy of knowing God. But until they do, let us be aware that while they preach the supremacy of the state, declare its omnipotence over individual man, and predict its eventual domination of all peoples on the Earth, *they are the focus of evil in the modern world. . . .* So, in your discussions of the nuclear freeze proposals, I urge you to beware the temptation of pride—the temptation of blithely declaring yourselves above it all and label both sides equally at fault, to ignore the facts of history and the aggressive impulses of an evil empire, to simply call the arms race a giant misunderstanding and thereby remove yourself from the struggle between right and wrong and good and evil" (emphasis added). Available at http://www.reagan.utexas.edu/archives/speeches/1983/30883b.htm.

80. See Reagan's speech of June 8, 1982, at Westminster to the members of the British Parliament: "What I am describing now is a plan and a hope for the long term—the march of freedom and democracy which will leave Marxism-Leninism on the ash heap of history as it has left other tyrannies which stifle the freedom and muzzle the self-expression of the people." Full text available at http://www.reagan.utexas.edu/archives/speeches/1982/60882a.htm.

81. See Schlesinger, *White House Ghosts*, 293–296.

82. This speech, delivered October 24, 1984, on the fortieth anniversary of the United Nations, was intended to suggest a "fresh start" to U.S. relations with the Soviet Union. The text is available at http://www.reagan.utexas.edu/archives/speeches/1985/102485a.htm.

83. Ronald Reagan and Mikhail Gorbachev held a summit meeting (or, more properly, a working meeting) in October 1986 in Reykjavik, Iceland. There they discussed nuclear weapons reductions extensively, including the prospect of eliminating nuclear weapons entirely. These negotiations ultimately did not succeed, but they did lay the foundation for an Intermediate-Range Nuclear Forces Treaty (INF) a year later. Moreover, they evidently strengthened Reagan's rapport with Gorbachev, which had an important role in giving the Soviet leader room to maneuver as he pressed reforms leading to the dissolution of the Soviet empire.

84. The last Soviet soldier left Afghanistan in February 1989, "9 years and 50 days after Soviet troops intervened." See Bill Keller, "Last Soviet Soldiers Leave Afghanistan," *New York Times*, February 16, 1989, A1.

85. President Kennedy spoke to a massive audience in Berlin on June 25, 1963—where he famously claimed, "*Ich bin ein Berliner.*" See Arthur M. Schlesinger Jr., *A Thousand Days: John F. Kennedy in the White House* (Boston: Houghton Mifflin, 1965), 884–885.

86. Video and text of Bill Clinton's address at Normandy on the occasion of the fiftieth anniversary of D-day are available at http://millercenter.org/scripps/archive/speeches/detail/3438. Clinton's address suffered by comparison with the speech Reagan had delivered on the fortieth anniversary. Reagan's remarks about the "boys of Pointe du Hoc" are widely considered to be a classic of presidential rhetoric. That speech can be seen and read at http://millercenter.org/scripps/archive/speeches/detail/3410. One interpretive take on this speech is Douglas Brinkley, *The Boys of Pointe du Hoc: Ronald Reagan, D-Day, and the U.S. Army 2nd Ranger Battalion* (New York: William Morrow, 2005).

87. Clinton's speech encouraging a "time for healing" was delivered in the aftermath of the April 19, 1995, domestic terrorist attack on the Alfred P. Murrah Federal Building in Oklahoma City, Oklahoma, which killed 168 and wounded nearly 700 others. The speech can be seen and read at http://millercenter.org/scripps/archive/speeches/detail/3441.

88. Nixon's Vietnam speech was delivered on November 3, 1969. It can be seen and read at http://millercenter.org/scripps/archive/speeches/detail/3873. The term "silent majority" became a catchphrase for Nixon and his supporters, as a note of contradiction to what they saw as the noisy minority disenchanted with the country's leadership. On this speech, see Safire, *Lend Me Your Ears*, 985–997.

89. Nixon's resignation speech can be seen and read at http://millercenter.org/scripps/archive/speeches/detail/3871.

90. Alexander M. Haig, Jr. (1924–2010), was Nixon's White House chief of staff in 1973 and 1974, succeeding H. R. Haldeman, who was forced to resign over Watergate-related improprieties. Haig also had a distinguished military career, and from 1970 to 1973 served as deputy national security advisor to Henry Kissinger. Later, Haig was Ronald Reagan's first secretary of state.

91. Ben Stein worked as a speechwriter for Presidents Nixon and Ford, but later achieved broader fame as a film actor (in *Ferris Bueller's Day Off*) and television personality. His father was economist Herbert Stein.

92. Harold J. "Tex" Lazar (1948–2004) was a speechwriter for President Nixon from 1971 to 1974. He previously had worked for William F. Buckley at the *National Review* and later spent time as a political appointee in the Justice Department in the Reagan administration.

Chapter 10

Crafting the Rhetorical Presidency

Sidney M. Milkis

This volume accomplishes a rare feat. Based on an oral history conference at the University of Virginia's Miller Center of Public Affairs, it brings together speechwriters and scholars to consider a critical development of American politics: the development of the rhetorical presidency. Since Jeffrey Tulis's seminal study recast the foundations of presidential studies in 1987, political scientists and historians have debated the constitutional and political consequences of presidents' obsession with speaking to the people.[1] Although general agreement prevails that presidential leadership of public opinion is an important feature of American democracy, there has been considerable scholarly dispute about the sources and consequences of presidents "going public."[2] Is the rhetorical presidency allied to constitutional government and an enduring feature of the political order? Did it instead emerge in the Progressive era with the precedent-shattering presidencies of Theodore Roosevelt and Woodrow Wilson, and thus transform the nature of representative democracy? Has it become ubiquitous with the growing exposure of the White House, abetted by advances in technology that now make it possible for presidents to communicate with the nation without interruption?

The testimony of speechwriters and the analysis of their work by leading scholars of the presidency shed much light on these fundamental questions. Interestingly, speechwriters themselves express many of the same concerns and engage in many of the same debates that political scientists and historians have waged. Moreover, the attention paid to speechwriters and their craft in this volume reveals another side of the rhetorical presidency that is all too often treated separately from presidential oratory: namely, that speechwriting is part of the development of the White House Office—the West Wing—and, therefore, is central to the administrative presidency. Indeed, presidential communication lies at the busy intersection of ideas and policy. As many speechwriters note, important addresses like the inaugural address

274

and, especially, the state of the union address play a critical role in focusing the administration and setting the agenda for the national government.

Traversing this volume offers a tour not only of the origins and development of the executive office, but also of critical changes in American democracy. As Reagan speechwriter Ken Khachigian says of inaugural addresses, "You could do sort of an historical time line of the United States by reading them. . . . [Each speech] sort of told you what was on America's mind every four years." We also learn how presidents and their aides attempt to take the American people to school, to embrace values and policies that the White House is committed to advancing. What emerges from this dialogue among scholars and speechwriters does not accord with the concerns of many pundits that presidents, supported by a battalion of pollsters and strategists, seek to manipulate public opinion to their own ends. Nor does it seem that the White House merely seeks to find out what is on the American people's mind in order to pander to prevailing opinions. To a surprising degree, presidents and speechwriters are engaged in the complex task of reconciling the core principles of American constitutional government with the imposing challenge of keeping these values relevant in the face of ethnic and racial conflicts, the vagaries of a dynamic economy, and the necessities of world politics. To be sure, in this daunting task, presidents and speechwriters may seek to accumulate more influence in the White House than a healthy constitutional government can bear. But, for better and worse, presidential rhetoric has become an essential ingredient in the never-ending attempt to fulfill the Founders' vision of realizing self-government on a grand scale.

Presidential Rhetoric and American Constitutional Government

Skeptics have long dismissed presidential oratory and the work of speechwriters as "mere rhetoric." This refrain was heard frequently during Barack Obama's 2008 presidential campaign and the early days of his presidency. Widely admired for his oratorical gifts and soaring rhetoric, so too has Obama been criticized for substituting words for action. As the most important building block of his promise to build a "New Foundation," for example, Obama pledged "an historic commitment to reform that will finally make quality health care affordable for every American."[3] Yet criticizing the administration's full court effort to enact health-care reform, fraught with elusive discussions over how to pay for universal coverage, the columnist Charles Krauthammer asked, "What happened to Obama-care? Rhetoric met reality. As both candidate and president, the master rhetorician could conjure a world in which he bestows upon you health care nirvana: more coverage, less cost. . . . But you can't fake it in legislation. Once you commit your fantasies to words and numbers, the Congressional Budget Office declares that the emperor has no clothes."[4]

Whether the Obama administration will fully realize its promise to establish health care as a right of citizenship remains to be seen. But this volume reveals that even a group of savvy speechwriters and distinguished scholars can put too much emphasis on words. Charles O. Jones rightfully praises President James A. Garfield's exalted 1881 inaugural address as "one of the most articulate, passionate, and well-argued statements regarding citizenship and governing." Jones singles out Garfield's powerful defense of African American rights, his proclamation, amid the reactionary tide of Jim Crow, that "under our institutions there was no middle ground for the Negro race between slavery and equal citizenship. There can be no permanent disenfranchised peasantry in the United States."[5] It is important to add, however, that Garfield spoke these words four years after participating in the unsavory "Compromise of 1877." This bargain resolved the controversial 1876 election between Republican Rutherford B. Hayes and Democrat Samuel Tilden by bestowing the White House on Republicans in return for their commitment to end the federal government's efforts to enforce the Fourteenth and Fifteenth Amendments. In the aftermath of this compromise, Garfield's brief presidency was focused not on fulfilling the rights of black citizens, but rather on intramural partisan squabbles over patronage. In truth, his inaugural address merely dramatized Republican hypocrisy during the Gilded Age. Republican rhetoric and party platforms continued to pledge full citizenship for black Americans, even as a virulent system of Jim Crow, sanctified as "separate but equal" by the Supreme Court in 1896, exposed this promise as a sham.[6]

Presidential speeches have not always been "mere rhetoric," however. Indeed, on important occasions, they have been central to approaching Thomas Jefferson's exalted, elusive idea of a "living Constitution"—that is, to making the Declaration of Independence and the Constitution enduringly relevant as generations and political circumstances change. This has been especially so of the inaugural address. As Jones notes, Nixon speechwriter Ray Price was eloquent in placing the address in its cultural and constitutional context. "An inaugural address is uniquely sacramental," Price observed. Not only does it sanctify the peaceful transfer of power that graces American democracy, it also has the potential, as Abraham Lincoln accomplished in his first address, to "speak to the better angels of our nature," while "summoning us to those exertions required to make the future we seek achievable." Although Lincoln is the lodestar of sacramental rhetoric, Jones finds a surprising number of presidents attempting to define the meaning of the social contract for their own time. Even presidents like Dwight D. Eisenhower and Lyndon B. Johnson, seldom celebrated for their rhetorical gifts, spoke to the nation's civic religion. Eisenhower went so far as to begin his first inaugural with a prayer, which he wrote for the occasion. He beseeched the almighty for wisdom "to clearly discern right from wrong," a preamble to his declaration of principles that called on the nation to continue the protracted struggle of the Cold War: "We must be ready to dare all for our country. For history does not long entrust the care of freedom to the weak or the timid. We must acquire proficiency in defense and display stamina in purpose. We must be willing, individually and as a Nation, to accept whatever sacrifices may be required of us. A people that values its privileges above its principles soon loses both."[7]

The most revered inaugural addresses, Jones tells us, not only invoke American creedal values but also mark a new direction for the country. He singles out Franklin Roosevelt's first and second inaugurals for combining the thematic and programmatic. Roosevelt's first address, delivered in the most dire emergency the country had faced since the Civil War, spelled out in clear and uncompromising language both his disdain for age-old practices he thought should be abandoned and his intention to act boldly to deal with the crisis at hand. Laying the blame for the depression squarely on the laissez-faire economic doctrines and halting leadership of his conservative Republican predecessors, Roosevelt summoned the nation to a higher purpose: "The money changers have fled from their high seats in the temple of our civilization. We may now restore that temple to ancient truths. The measure of that restoration lies in the extent to which we apply social values more noble than mere monetary profit."[8]

Just as boldly, Roosevelt made clear that the national government would have to put people back to work and reform the economy, tasks that required the same effort as the "emergency of a war." The Great Depression, Roosevelt anticipated, would thrust the president into the center of politics and governance:

It is to be hoped that the normal balance of Executive and legislative authority may be wholly adequate to meet the unprecedented task before us. . . . But in the event that Congress shall fail to take [action] . . . and in the event that the national emergency is still critical, I shall not evade the clear course of duty that will then confront me. I shall ask Congress for one remaining instrument to meet the crisis—broad executive power to wage a war against the emergency, as great as in the power that would be given to me if we were in fact invaded by a foreign foe.[9]

As the *New York Times* reported, Roosevelt's inaugural address confirmed the hopes of the jubilant crowd that "the day had come when [a] new philosophy was to replace the rejected theories of the old."[10]

Of course, a great deal of presidential rhetoric is far from foundational. Martin J. Medhurst observes that nomination acceptance addresses "are purely political." In part, these addresses reflect the link between presidents and political parties that was forged during the early part of the nineteenth century, a change that diminished somewhat the nonpartisan—even sacramental—luster that the Founders hoped to instill in the executive office. As Price notes, the nomination speech fulfills a critical objective of the presidential campaign: defining the choice between the candidates and parties and urging the voters "to make the right choice." One of the more effective acceptance speeches in recent history, Medhurst observes, was Ronald Reagan's 1984 address, in which, building on Jeane Kirkpatrick's characterization of the opposition party as "San Francisco Democrats," he placed former vice president Walter Mondale to the left of the American mainstream. More fundamentally, Reagan claimed that Democratic liberalism had become so wedded to "tax and spend" policies that it had departed dangerously from the Founders' celebration of individualism and natural rights: "Isn't our choice really not one of left or right, but of up or down? Down through the welfare state to statism, to more and more government largesse accompanied always by more government authority, less individual liberty and, ultimately, totalitarianism, always advanced as for our own good. The alternative is the dream conceived by our Founding Fathers, up to the ultimate in individual freedom consistent with an orderly society."[11]

Reagan's rhetorical joining of the contest between him and Mondale to a fundamental struggle for the constitutional soul of the American people suggests that acceptance speeches are not just about politics as usual. In fact, the acceptance speech was part of a long-standing effort to restore some of the executive office's nonpartisan stature. Presidential candidates only began to accept the nomination of their parties at the convention in 1932. Until FDR broke the hallowed tradition, individual contenders stayed away from the convention hall in deference to their parties' collective identity.

The acceptance speech was not just a change in rhetorical practice; it also represented a self-conscious and sweeping challenge to the traditional, decentralized party organizations. In coming to the 1932 convention, FDR insisted on a direct, unmediated relationship between the candidate and the party's rank and file. The acceptance speech thus marks a critical development in the emergence of the "modern" presidency: the president, not the party, is at the center of campaigning as well as governing.[12] As Medhurst notes, "the acceptance address is a rhetorical representation of the candidate as much as, and in more recent years considerably more than, a representation to the political party to which he belongs." One of the most spectacular failures of this genre, in fact, erred in expressing partisanship too rancorously: Barry Goldwater's nomination speech at the 1964 Republican Convention. Instead of using his address to unify the fractured GOP and display his stature to undertake the responsibilities of the modern chief executive, Goldwater chose to highlight his impeccable conservative credentials and excoriate the Democratic Party. "By condemning the entire Democratic Party and failing to make any appeal to moderate or independent voters, even those who usually voted Republican," Medhurst writes, "Goldwater assured that his address would be a failure even before he got to the part about 'extremism in defense of liberty is no vice.'"

In contrast, Reagan's 1984 acceptance speech allied his conservatism to founding principles and the rebirth of America. Just as the documentary film that preceded Reagan's address rejoiced that it was "morning again in America," so did the president's speechwriters highlight this theme in crafting the dramatic peroration of his address. Invoking the Statue of Liberty, Reagan concluded:

> The poet called Miss Liberty's torch the "lamp beside the golden door." Well, that was the entrance to America, and it still is. And now you really know why we're here tonight. The glistening hope of that lamp is still ours. Every promise, every opportunity is still golden in this land. And through that golden door our children can walk into tomorrow with the knowledge that no one can be denied the promise that is America.
>
> Her heart is full; her door is still golden, her future bright. She has arms big enough to comfort and strong enough to support, for the strength in her arms is the strength of her people. She will carry on in the eighties unafraid, unashamed, and unsurpassed. In this springtime of hope, some lights seem eternal; America's is.[13]

The attempt to link the sacramental with the political represents, Medhurst suggests, the tendency in many acceptance speeches to use a rhetorical form based on the Puritan jeremiad. With the help of their speechwriters, presidential candidates celebrate the "promise" of America, attribute any decline to the ideas and policies of their political opponents, and "join in the 'renewal' of promise—portrayed as a compact between the president and people rather than a covenant between the people and God." By invoking images of Americans striving to build a "city on a hill," modern presidential candidates attempt to secure their status as leaders, not just of a party but of the whole nation—to prove that they are well cast as, to use Theodore's Roosevelt's beguiling phrase, the "steward of the public welfare."

And yet, the modern nomination speech has not necessarily been good for the Democratic and Republican parties. Although the 1984 campaign is praised as a great success by Reagan speechwriter Khachigian, the administration's ostentatiously nonpartisan strategy seemed devoid of serious political content, put forward as if, in some obscure diurnal logic, the Democrats could be made to endorse the night. Not surprisingly, Reagan's triumphant reelection was a "lonely landslide": Reagan won an overwhelming popular and electoral college victory but the Republicans failed to take control of the House of Representatives and actually lost two seats in the Senate, presaging the Democratic takeover of that chamber in 1986.

More broadly, the direct connection between the modern presidency and public opinion risks subordinating rhetoric to "spectacles." As Bruce Miroff has written, "A president's approach to, and impact on, public perceptions are not limited to overt appeals in speeches and appearances. Much of what the modern presidency does, in fact, involves the projection of images whose purpose is to shape public understanding and gain popular support."[14] Kathryn Dunn Tenpas's chapter and the testimony of speechwriters in Chapter 7 reveal that the state of the union address, deemed by presidential aides to be the most important of the year, has become a media spectacle—in the words of Bill Clinton writer Terry Edmonds, "the Super Bowl of speeches for a White House speechwriter."

Citing Article II, Section 3, Dunn Tenpas notes that the state of the union address "is the only constitutionally mandated speech by the American president." And yet this address has been dramatically changed by presidents determined to adapt it to the task of influencing mass opinion. Most important, Woodrow Wilson, breaking a tradition that began with Jefferson, delivered his speeches in person to Congress rather than submitting them in writing. FDR and Johnson further adapted the address to the modern executive: it was Roosevelt who termed it the state of the union, seeing, as Nixon speechwriter Lee Huebner suggests, "the magic of calling it that." Johnson amplified the moment by moving it from noon to evening, so that the address would be delivered on prime-time television. Thus transformed, the speech's principal rhetorical objective of setting the annual agenda for executive departments and agencies as well as for Congress has sometimes been overshadowed by political theater. As Huebner notes, "Suddenly, instead of it being a speech for well-informed people who follow government closely it became a speech for the general public. Presidents have felt the demand to make it an uplifting, ceremonial, rhetorical success," which undermines the objective of "managing the government."

On the face of it, elevating the importance of a speech should elevate the importance of its writers, but the testimony in this volume shows that not all of them are enamored of the state of the union spectacle. Some lament the recrudescence of partisanship in recent years that overwhelmed their efforts to craft statesmanlike words transcending Democratic and Republican differences. Others bemoan the practice, initiated by the Reagan administration, of recognizing "heroes" in the gallery, a ritual that deflects attention from the expressed themes and policy prescriptions of the address. Citing both of these tendencies, Khachigian admits that he "hate[s] state of the union speeches":

> I think it has become so tawdry, the way it happens now. It is becoming a spectacle of partisanship, where they jump up and do standing ovations on one side and sit on their hands . . . on the other side. Then, we have, who is going to be in the gallery? It has taken away from the majesty of the presidency. The presidency used to be such a majestic office, and it still is, but there's no dignity in the state of the union speech whatsoever. There's nothing memorable anymore that comes out of it. The agenda doesn't stick.

Huebner agrees: although the speech itself is still potentially important as a "laundry list" that, if properly framed, "disciplined the government," he thinks that task could be better "accomplished in a written document."

Such musings, however, are unlikely to persuade presidents or their speechwriters to forgo this extraordinary opportunity to speak to the people directly. Moreover, Americans value these spectacles, watching the state of the union message in large numbers, even though the advent of cable television has given them the option of tuning out. From this spectacle, Michael Nelson insists, might come a useful civics lesson, a rare opportunity in today's fractious politics for the modern executive to extend the sacrament celebrated by inaugural addresses to governance:

> When the president walks into that room and people are waiting to shake his hands on both sides of the aisle, there is something quite wonderful about that, affirming the unifying value of the presidency. Then during the speech, some people cheer and some people show their displeasure, but they're all there in that same room, and they leave on good terms. I think there's something there that tells us that we can have raucous partisanship within the framework of a political system in which people deeply believe and are interested.

Indeed, the state of the union spectacle may appeal to the public because there is, as speechwriter Clark Judge suggests, "an element of sport about American politics as well as an element of camaraderie." Perhaps the rhetorical spectacle highlights how modern presidential politics, for all its faults, combines the suspense of sports with the colorful array of characters found in great literature.

Managing Speechwriting: The Modern Presidency and the Speechwriting Staff

For all the spectacle of modern presidential rhetoric, speechwriting entails important managerial imperatives. Since Warren Harding hired Judson Welliver to be the first presidential speechwriter, White House rhetoric has been a collaborative effort. Whether presidents, as may have been the case with Harding, recognize their own shortcomings as wordsmiths or whether they simply acknowledge that modern presidential politics—now involving according to Clinton speechwriter Don Baer between 400 and 500 speeches per year—make it humanly impossible for presidents to produce their own addresses, the speechwriter has become indispensable to the contemporary executive office. At the same time, speechwriters are part of a large and elaborate White House staff—the presidential institution—that poses a dilemma for contemporary executives. "A tension pervades the relationship between the president as an individual and the presidency as an institution," Andrew Rudalevige writes in his chapter on crisis speeches and other landmark addresses. But, he continues, "presidents can help themselves by attending to the institution." Rudalevige suggests, in fact, that effectively binding the rhetorical and administrative presidencies will help keep presidential speeches from descending into meaningless spectacles. "Presidents can frame issues in their favor," he argues, "by setting the agenda within their administration, gathering information and translating it into policy decisions."

More to the point, Rudalevige urges that "wordsmithing" be coordinated with policymaking. Such collaboration occurred naturally during the Truman administration, before a specialized speechwriting staff was formed. This natural integration may have contributed to the success of Truman's 1947 landmark speech pronouncing the Truman Doctrine. Facing an isolationist, Republican-dominated Congress, the president not only consulted widely with his staff, but also sought the counsel of congressional leaders. The advice of GOP Senate Foreign Relations Committee chair Arthur Vandenberg that Truman would first have to "scare the hell out of the country" if he hoped to persuade Congress to pass his program of emergency aid to Greece and Turkey was particularly germane. "The seeds of totalitarian regimes are nurtured by misery and want. They spread and grow in the evil soil of poverty and strife," Truman told a joint session of Congress and a national radio audience. "They reach their full growth when the hope of a people for a better life has died. We must keep that hope alive. The free peoples of the world look to us for support in maintaining their freedoms." As Samuel Kernell has pointed out, neither elite nor public opinion immediately supported Truman. But the speech ultimately set the tone of elite debate, journalistic coverage, and congressional deliberation. Within a few months, Truman's proposals to aid Greece and Turkey became law, and his more comprehensive Marshall Plan of postwar economic assistance to Europe would be enacted.[15]

The integration of speechwriting and policymaking became more complicated once speechwriters were organized into a specialized unit of White House staff. Paradoxically, Rudalevige observes, the formal designation of certain staff members as speechwriters went hand in hand with "the diminution of their status." They found themselves in competition with other ambitious members of the White House staff, as well as with cabinet members and pollsters. Under Gerald Ford, even remarks delivered at a Christmas party for the White House press corps required approval from eight different staff units. Nonetheless, Rudalevige insists that making speechwriters happy is not always important in formulating presidential rhetoric. Lest speeches be relegated to pure rhetoric, he argues, they ought to run the White House and cabinet gauntlet. Yet Peter Robinson, who crafted words for Reagan, observes that speechwriters play a critical part in initiating policy action: "In the Reagan White House, there were domestic policy councils and foreign policy councils. All of that was taking place. All of that was producing good paper. All of that was chugging toward the president. But quite often . . . the final decision or the final framing did not take place until there was a speech on the schedule, and a deadline, and you *had* to do it."

Perhaps speechwriters often find themselves at a strategic advantage in the speech-drafting gauntlet because their job—putting words in their boss's mouth—fosters close personal ties with the president. Obama's foreign policy speechwriter, Ben Rhodes, virtually stalked the president to figure out how he expresses ideas and policies. Rhodes spent nearly two years listening to the audios of every Obama campaign event and poring over interview transcripts to get a sense of how the president speaks. "He really understands the president's voice," notes senior Obama advisor David Axelrod. "They've got a great mind-meld on these issues." Indeed, Rhodes has made it his business to know Obama's foreign policy positions as well as any of his top advisors do. With that knowledge, he has emerged as the only member of Obama's six-person speechwriting team who doubles as a policy advisor, a role he dabbled in during the campaign. Rhodes has an open invitation to attend national security meetings, where he often pipes up to say, "Hey, I know he's going to want to talk about this." His job, Rhodes says, is "making sure that we're just running that Obama thread through everything that he says on foreign policy." That thread is usually some version of the themes Obama has touched on since the campaign: multilateral engagement, renewing American leadership abroad, and talking to adversaries.[16]

Many speechwriters in this volume testify to having a similar mind-meld with the president. Peter Robinson's arresting story of how he crafted and Ronald Reagan delivered the famous "Mr. Gorbachev, tear down this wall" speech reveals how those words survived a bitter struggle in which the State Department drafted an alternative address that sought "to strangle the speechwriter's draft." In the end, with the help of chief speechwriter Tony Dolan, Robinson's version prevailed, mainly because "by that point in my career in the White House, I had Ronald Reagan living in my head. When I was in Berlin, I very explicitly was looking for items that *he* would find arresting, looking for comments that *he* would want to adapt and deliver." Similarly, Carter speechwriter Patrick Anderson crafted words that he knew his boss would want to utter in his acceptance speech at the 1976 Democratic convention. As Anderson makes clear, the personal bond between president and speechwriter is sealed in words that express ideas, even if seemingly impractical, that they share. "There was a paragraph on peace, and the final sentence says, 'We will pray for peace, and we will work for peace until we have removed from all nations for all time the threat of nuclear destruction,'" Anderson testified. "I wrote that. I believe it. I'd like to see it happen. Carter would like to see it happen. It didn't happen. It's pure rhetoric. He wasn't going to disarm or anything. But I think people like to hear that sort of inspirational ideal. There were a lot of lines in all the best speeches that are much more what you wish for than what is likely to happen." Or, as Reagan's Berlin Wall speech suggests, sometimes what a president and speechwriter wish for happens.

And yet, the personal relationship between president and speechwriter may contribute to the "extraordinary isolation" that plagues the modern presidency.[17] The rhetorical and administrative powers the office has accrued over the years have freed it from the constraints traditionally imposed by political parties and enabled the White House to forge direct ties to the public over the heads of Congress. This development can isolate the president and his advisors and leave them at the mercy of a volatile political environment. As Rudalevige shows, Carter's famous 1979 "crisis of confidence" speech dramatically demonstrated the pathologies of a mountaintop approach to governing. Although Carter never used the term "malaise," the press, taking their cues from White House pollster Patrick Caddell, branded it with that label. Caddell had convinced the president that a speech probing the deep roots of Americans' distrust of government would enhance his moral standing. With the help of speechwriters Gordon Stewart and Hendrik Hertzberg, Carter crafted an address that he hoped would connect the nation's fractious politics and public estrangement with the energy crisis. Carter speechwriter Walter Shapiro notes in Chapter 9 that "the speech itself was, overnight, quite effective. . . . The response of the talking heads was good." But some members of the press, unaccustomed to the spectacle of a president "scolding his fellow citizens . . . like a . . . pastor with a profligate flock," found parts of the address "awkward and uncomfortable."[18] Moreover, Carter's actions a few days later bespoke his own crisis of confidence: he asked all his cabinet members to resign, but only accepted the resignations of those who were at odds with his inner circle of Georgians.

In the end, the American people came to regard Carter as a wayward leader who had lost touch with them. Rudalevige attributes Carter's debacle to poor management—he did not integrate rhetoric and policy—and bad decisions. Yet Carter's problems were also a symptom of an underlying disease: the excessive personalization of presidential politics that has plagued all recent administrations. No matter how well managed, the rhetorical presidency is unlikely to establish the president as the direct representative of the people.

Rhetoric and American Democracy

The dialogue between presidential scholars and speechwriters in this volume sheds light on the rhetorical presidency's effect on public deliberation and accountability while also raising questions about whether the American people pay attention to the words that speechwriters craft and presidents deliver. Paradoxically, as Paul Quirk has noted, political scientists criticize presidential appeals for public support both for undermining public deliberation *and* for being ineffective.[19] Tulis's book embodies both of these criticisms. On the one hand, Tulis argues that presidential appeals to public opinion have grown so routine as to foster a plebiscitary politics that both denigrates Congress's responsibility for making laws and appeals to the emotions rather than the reason of the public. On the other hand, citing examples such as Woodrow Wilson's campaign for the League of Nations and Lyndon Johnson's call for a War on Poverty, he argues that presidential appeals often fail. Indeed, as Dunn Tenpas and Rudalevige point out in this volume, there is very little evidence that presidential speeches have a significant influence on public opinion.[20]

The "hatred" that speechwriters like Khachigian express for the state of the union address suggests that presidential rhetoric can both denigrate self-government and be ineffective. These speeches, as well as the landmark addresses that Rudalevige appraises, have become national spectacles that substitute stagecraft for substance. As Miroff has argued, presidential spectacles promote "gesture over accomplishment and appearance over fact." Such political theater also damages the public because it "obfuscates presidential activity, undermines executive accountability, and encourages passivity on the part of citizens."[21]

And yet, if presidents, who are certainly attuned to public opinion, rarely change it, why do they spend so much time trying? As Dunn Tenpas points out, the state of the union address is no longer a stand-alone event but, rather, represents a key juncture in a "permanent campaign." Beginning with Clinton, state of the union messages have been followed by "rollouts" that send presidents barnstorming around the country to promote important elements of the speech. George W. Bush surpassed Clinton in his post-state of the union travels; Bush traipsed about the country for several weeks after his 2005 address in a failed effort to pass his Social Security reform package. Obama has taken the permanent campaign to still new heights. His first major address to the nation in February 2009 seemed almost routine in the wake of his constant communications with the public through late-night television; press conferences; e-mail; and the first White House deployment of "social" media such as Facebook, YouTube, and Twitter. Indeed, as president, Obama has sought to transform his elaborate 2008 grassroots campaign apparatus into a permanent institution, Organizing for America, with the hope of advancing his agenda and laying the groundwork for his reelection.[22]

Presidential rhetoric, now joined to a permanent campaign, is likely to remain a central feature of the executive office. Although the benefits of public appeals have seldom registered in surveys, presidents, with the encouragement of speechwriters, believe that communicating with the citizenry serves their political and policy objectives. Truman's 1947 address urging support for Greece and Turkey did not significantly increase anti-Communist sentiment among the public, but by shaping media analysis and congressional debate it critically advanced a new foreign policy doctrine. Moreover, presidents may be less interested in changing public opinion than they are in mobilizing supporters from the base of their parties. George W. Bush and his chief strategist, Karl Rove, for example, focused less on appeals to swing voters and independents than to Republicans. Similarly, the Obama administration, although giving much lip service to nonpartisanship, has been especially adept at mobilizing new voters who are likely to support the Democratic Party and the president's reform program.[23] Effective mobilization of such supporters might be critical in a public policy debate, even though the effect on mass opinion is relatively modest. As Quirk notes, "on a single issue, an actual vote change of say, 1 voter in 300 would have strong implications for the incentives of a member of Congress."[24]

Finally, pace Tulis, presidential rhetoric appears to be important in cultivating civic attachments. The framers of the Constitution did not clearly spell out this responsibility. In fact, following John Locke and David Hume, they placed more faith in institutional arrangements—a complex blend of checks and balances—than in presidential rhetoric to protect the rights sanctified by the Declaration of Independence. The framers especially feared that popular presidential leadership would encourage demagogy rather than civic education. To guard against the dangers of an elected despotism, the framers lodged the office in a constitutional framework, juxtaposing its power with that of the judiciary and legislature. As Dunn Tenpas suggests, they did their work well. "Try as they might," her chapter concludes about the work of presidents and their speechwriters, "the hyper-public presidency cannot overcome the inherent obstacles in our political system."

The hope that the president would contribute to civil religion was expressed most clearly by certain Anti-Federalists, who opposed the Constitution. Although most Anti-Federalists were hostile to the very idea of forming a strong executive, some expressed support for a president who would play a critical, if not the principal, part in fostering a sense of unity in a large and diverse society. As the "Federal Farmer" put it, "In every large collection of people there must be a 'first man,'" a "visible point serving as a common centre in the government, towards which to draw their eyes and attachments."[25] As the discussion of inaugural addresses in this volume shows, presidents since Washington have embraced the role of first citizen. With the development of the modern presidency in the twentieth and twenty-first centuries, the executive office has increasingly come to be viewed as a critical agent of national unity, an antidote to the tendency of individual men and women to become, as Tocqueville feared they might, confined to their own tiny private universe, consisting of themselves and their immediate circle of friends and family.[26] Clinton speechwriter Don Baer referred to this responsibility or burden of modern presidential leadership when discussing the state of the union address.

> In a nation and in a world that is moving so quickly and in which people are distracted so much, to have that one communal moment a year when the country comes together is one of the reasons why the length of these speeches doesn't matter anymore. The country actually craves it. We learned that our audience grew the longer the president went on, even though it filled me with shame that I would put him out there and he was going to go on for so long. . . . I would offer [that major presidential addresses are] a national catechism, tailored to the historical moment that the nation faces at any given point.

Lincoln's oratory best exemplifies how presidential rhetoric can become a national catechism. His two greatest speeches—the Gettysburg Address and the second inaugural—reveal that rhetoric can transcend temporal and partisan bounds. The fiery Massachusetts senator Charles Sumner, who long had thought Lincoln was too slow to act against slavery, granted in his 1865 eulogy of the slain president that his rhetoric, especially the Gettysburg Address, would immortalize him. "That speech . . . now sanctified by the martyrdom of its author is a monumental act. In the modesty of his nature [Lincoln] said 'the world will little note nor long remember what we say here; but it can never forget what they did here.' He was mistaken. The world noted at once what he said, and will never cease to remember it. The battle itself was less important than the speech."[27]

Of course, Lincoln's words, inscribed as they are on his memorial, set unrealistic expectations for presidents and speechwriters. Khachigian read all the inaugurals in preparing to craft Reagan's first one. After reading Lincoln's second, he notes in Chapter 7, "I should have stopped there and turned the assignment over to someone else. It is so dramatically poetic and excruciatingly well written; you can't come up to that standard." Yet presidents have frequently invoked Lincoln in their inaugural addresses, perhaps none more so than Barack Obama. As president-elect, Obama studied, and instructed his head speechwriter, Jon Favreau, to carefully examine Lincoln's first inaugural. After taking the oath of office on the same Bible that Lincoln had used, the new president expressed sentiments that clearly were inspired by the closing words of the 1861 inaugural address, which appealed to the "better angels of our nature." Obama said, "We remain a young nation, but in the words of Scripture, the time has come to set aside childish things. The time has come to reaffirm our enduring spirit; to choose our better history; to carry forward that precious gift, that noble idea, passed on from generation to generation: the God-given promise that all are equal, all are free, and all deserve a chance to pursue their full measure of happiness."[28]

Contemporary scholarship on presidential oratory rarely considers its important contribution to the country's values. More problematic, political scientists and historians writing about the rhetorical presidency tend to confound the art of public persuasion with plebiscitary politics. Tulis's depiction of the modern presidency suggests that executives have come to speak to the public routinely and without a prudential understanding of the executive's duty to educate, not simply to arouse, popular opinion. His distinction between the "traditional" and "modern" presidency overlooks the populist rhetoric that pervaded nineteenth-century politics, which was grounded in a highly decentralized and intensely mobilized mass party system. More to the point, a critical examination of popular leadership requires that a distinction be drawn between rhetoric, which is essential to democratic leadership, and plebiscitary politics, which denigrates it. Through rhetoric, as Thomas Pangle has observed, "the wisdom that is politically possible and the consent that is politically necessary are combined and elevated, under the somewhat distant guidance of philosophy."[29]

Although American political history offers many examples of shameless populism—indeed, some of the speechwriters in this volume admit to some questionable pandering—it also has witnessed presidential speeches that reflect the "distant guidance of philosophy." Some important examples of modern executives speaking perspicaciously include Roosevelt's 1941 state of the union address (the Four Freedoms address), John F. Kennedy's 1961 inaugural address, Lyndon Johnson's "We Shall Overcome" speech (delivered to a joint session of Congress on March 15, 1965), both of Ronald Reagan's inaugural addresses, and George W. Bush's post-9/11 speech to a joint session of Congress on September 20, 2001. Each of these speeches invoked the core principles of American politics, and each attempted to explain the meaning of the Declaration of Independence and the Constitution in the political circumstances the country faced at the time. Obama, both in his inaugural address and in speeches that he gave during the early days of his presidency, spoke eloquently to the American creed.

Perhaps the greatest danger to American democracy is not demagogy but the trivialization of presidential communication. Effective presidential orators such as Lincoln, Roosevelt, and Kennedy understood that their rhetoric would become less influential if they did not pick their opportunities to speak to the public carefully. As FDR put it to Ray Stannard Baker, Woodrow Wilson's biographer, who in 1935 urged Roosevelt to place the same emphasis on "vision" that his Democratic predecessor had,

> You are absolutely right about the response this country gives to vision and profound moral purpose that I can only assure you of my hearty concurrence and my constant desire to make that appeal . . . I know at the same time that you will be sympathetic to the point of view that the public psychology and, for that matter, individual psychology, cannot, because of human weakness, be attuned to a constant repetition of the highest note on the scale.[30]

Responsible presidential leadership, Roosevelt understood, has to combine principled rhetoric with solid accomplishments.

Since Reagan, however, presidents and their speechwriters, even though they understood the limits of rhetoric, have felt it important to carry on a constant conversation with the American people. To the traditional array of formal addresses have been added weekly radio addresses, televised press conferences, and, most recently, full deployment of the Internet. The permanent campaign has not only blurred the line between elections and governing but also undermined the concept of responsible democratic leadership.

Leaders in a democracy, Tocqueville observed, are sorely tempted to flatter the people as "too superior to the weakness of human nature to lose the command of their temper for an instant." In treating the people as their masters, in assuring them that "they have all the virtues without having acquired them," democratic leaders inevitably deprive themselves of honor; "by sacrificing their opinions, they prostitute themselves."[31]

In the final analysis, the critical task of speechwriters is to encourage presidents to be true to their opinions and to help make these opinions effective in upholding the core principles of American politics. This does not mean that presidents should ignore public opinion polls or the exigencies of practical politics. As Martin Medhurst observes in Chapter 2, presidential wordsmiths "must not let high-mindedness spill over into idealism, self-righteousness, and being perceived as so dedicated to principle that [the presidential candidate or president] loses touch with the electorate. . . . It is precisely to prevent those sorts of problems that [speechwriters] appeal to common sense." The task of those who write and deliver presidential rhetoric, then, is not to lecture the American people ex cathedra about the immorality of "rights-talk"; instead, they must encourage their fellow citizens to engage in the nation's long-standing debate about the true meaning of rights. Now, as always, the vitality of American democracy depends on popular and partisan presidential leadership that can perform the conventional yet spectacular task of giving new meaning to the proposition that a nation of individuals can pursue happiness with dignity and responsibility. This requires, however, that presidents understand not only how to address the country but also when to maintain a dignified silence.

Notes

1. Jeffrey Tulis, *The Rhetorical Presidency* (Princeton, N.J.: Princeton University Press, 1987).

2. Samuel Kernell, *Going Public: New Strategies of Presidential Leadership*, 3rd ed. (Washington, D.C.: CQ Press, 1997), 106. Kernell suggests that presidential appeals for popular support now overshadow more traditional methods of seeking influence, especially bargaining.

3. Remarks of President Barack Obama on the Economy, Georgetown University, Washington, D.C., April 14, 2009, http://www.whitehouse.gov/the_press_office/Remarks-by-the-President-on-the-Economy-at-Georgetown-University/.

4. Charles Krauthammer, "Rhetoric Meets Reality," http://www.realclearpolitics.com/articles/2009/07/24/why_obamacare_is_sinking_97598.html.

5. James Abram Garfield, Inaugural Address, March 4, 1881, http://millercenter .org/scripps/archive/speeches/detail/3559.

6. C. Van Woodward, *Reunion and Reaction: The Compromise of 1877 and the End of Reconstruction* (Boston: Little, Brown, 1966).

7. Dwight D. Eisenhower, Inaugural Address, January 20, 1953, http://www .presidency.ucsb.edu/ws/index.php?pid=9600.

8. "Franklin D. Roosevelt's First Inaugural Address," in *The Evolving Presidency: Addresses, Cases, Essays, Letters, Reports, Resolutions, Transcripts, and Other Landmark Documents, 1787–1998*, ed. Michael Nelson (Washington, D.C.: CQ Press, 1999), 106–112.

9. Ibid.

10. *New York Times*, March 5, 1933, 3.

11. Ronald Reagan, Inaugural Address, March 4, 1985, http://www.presidency.ucsb .edu/ws/index.php?pid=38688.

12. Sidney M. Milkis, "Franklin D. Roosevelt, Progressivism, and the Limits of Popular Leadership," in *Speaking to the People: The Rhetorical Presidency in Historical Perspective*, ed. Richard J. Ellis (Amherst: University of Massachusetts Press, 1998), 184–187.

13. Ronald Reagan, Remarks Accepting the Presidential Nomination, Republican National Convention, August 23, 1984, Dallas, Texas, http://www.4president.org/ speeches/reagan1984convention.htm.

14. Bruce Miroff, "The Presidential Spectacle," in *The Presidency and the Political System*, 8th ed., ed. Michael Nelson (Washington, D.C.: CQ Press, 2006), 256.

15. Harry Truman's address before a joint session of Congress, March 12, 1947, http:// avalon.law.yale.edu/20th_century/trudoc.asp; Kernell, *Going Public*, 25–26.

16. Carol Lee, "Obama Foreign Policy Speech Writer: Ben Rhodes," *Politico*, May 18, 2009, http://www.politico.com/news/stories/0509/22588.html.

17. The term "extraordinary isolation" is Woodrow Wilson's. See Wilson, *Constitutional Government in the United States* (New York: Columbia University Press, 1908), 69.

18. Patrick Caddell, "Of Crisis and Opportunity," April 23, 1979, "Memoranda: President Carter 1/10/79-4/23/79 [CF,O/A 519]," Box 40, Jody Powell Files, Jimmy Carter Library, Atlanta, Georgia; "The Scramble Starts," editorial, *Los Angeles Times*, July 17, 1979. For other examples of the press's response to the speech, see Robert Shogan, "Carter Returns to Moralistic Themes," ibid.; "Winning Neither Confidence nor More Oil," editorial, *Chicago Tribune*, July 17, 1979; "Riding Casually to War," editorial, *New York Times*, July 17, 1979; "President Carter's Directive," editorial, *Boston Globe*, July 17, 1979.

19. Paul Quirk, "When the President Speaks, How Do the People Respond?" *Critical Review* 19, nos. 2–3 (2007): 427–446, my emphasis.

20. George Edwards, examining the Reagan and Clinton administrations, concluded that the president's appeals generally fell on "deaf ears." Edwards, *On Deaf Ears: The Limits of the Bully Pulpit* (New Haven, Conn.: Yale University Press, 2003).

21. Miroff, "Presidential Spectacle," 280.

22. Sidney M. Milkis and Jesse H. Rhodes, "Barack Obama, the Democratic Party, and the Future of the 'New' American Party System," *Forum* 7, no. 1 (2009), http://www.bepress.com/forum/vol7/iss1/art7/.

23. Sidney M. Milkis and Jesse H. Rhodes, "George W. Bush, the Republican Party and the 'New' American Party System," *Perspectives on Politics* 5, no. 3 (September 2007): 461–487; and Milkis and Rhodes, "Barack Obama, the Democratic Party, and the Future of the 'New' American Party System."

24. Quirk, "When the President Speaks," 432.

25. *The Complete Anti-Federalist*, ed. with commentary and notes by Herbert J. Storing (Chicago: University of Chicago Press, 1981), 2: 310.

26. Alexis de Tocqueville, *Democracy in America*, eds. Harvey C. Mansfield and Delba Winthrop (Chicago and London: University of Chicago Press, 2000), 482–484, 606–617.

27. Charles Sumner, *Promises of the Declaration of Independence* (Boston: Tichnor and Fields, 1865), 18, 40.

28. Barack Obama, Inaugural Address, January 20, 2009, http://www.presidency.ucsb.edu/ws/index.php?pid-44.

29. Thomas Pangle, *The Ennobling of Democracy* (Baltimore, Md.: Johns Hopkins University Press, 1992), 129.

30. Franklin D. Roosevelt to Ray Stannard Baker, March 20, 1935, President's Personal File 1820, Roosevelt Papers, Franklin D. Roosevelt Library, Hyde Park, New York.

31. Tocqueville, *Democracy in America*, 246.

Contributors

Patrick Anderson, who was Jimmy Carter's chief speechwriter during the 1976 presidential campaign, also worked as a writer in the Kennedy, Johnson, and Clinton administrations. He has published nine novels and four books of nonfiction, including *Electing Jimmy Carter* (LSU, 1994). He lives in Washington, D.C., and is a book columnist for the *Washington Post*.

Don Baer was President William Clinton's chief speechwriter from 1994 to 1995 and the White House Director of Strategic Planning and Communications from 1995 to 1997. Formerly he was a national political writer for *U.S. News & World Report*, and he has been a senior media executive for Discovery Communications. He is currently Worldwide Vice Chairman of Strategic Communications for the firm Burson-Marsteller. He lives in Washington, D.C.

J. Terry Edmonds is Associate Vice President and Editorial Director in the office of the president at Columbia University. He served as chief speechwriter for President William Clinton from August 1999 until the president's last day in office in January 2001. Edmonds also served as a chief speechwriter during Senator John Kerry's 2004 presidential campaign and has written for a number of other corporate, nonprofit, and public policy clients.

Lee Huebner is the Airlie Professor in the School of Media and Public Affairs at The George Washington University and was director of that school from 2006 to 2009. He taught earlier at Northwestern University and served as interim president at the American University of Paris. From 1979 to 1993 he was publisher and CEO of the *International Herald Tribune*. A founder and former president of the Ripon Society, a Republican research organization, he received his Ph.D. in history from Harvard University and went from there to the White House Writing and Research staff under President Richard Nixon.

Charles O. Jones is Professor Emeritus of Political Science, University of Wisconsin-Madison, and a Non-Resident Senior Fellow at the Brookings Institution and the University of Virginia's Miller Center of Public Affairs. A former president of the American Political Science Association and editor of the *American Political Science Review*, he has published several books on the presidency: *The Trusteeship Presidency* (LSU, 1988), *Passages to the Presidency* (Brookings, 1998), *Clinton and Congress* (Oklahoma, 1999), *The Presidency in a Separated System* (Brookings, 2005), and *The American Presidency* (Oxford, 2007).

Clark Judge served as speechwriter and Special Assistant to both President Ronald Reagan and Vice President George Bush. He joined President Reagan's speechwriting staff in 1986 and remained with Mr. Reagan through the end of his term. A member of the Moscow Summit speechwriting team, he was the lead writer for the Toronto Economic Summit in 1988 and helped shape the White House approach to the 1988 presidential campaign. Today, as Managing Director of the White House Writers Group, he provides strategic communications counsel to clients around the world. His byline has appeared in numerous publications, including the *Wall Street Journal* and the *Financial Times*.

Kenneth Khachigian is Senior Partner in the Los Angeles and Orange County law offices of Brownstein/Hyatt/Farber/Schreck. He served as Special Consultant to the President, chief speechwriter, and senior political aide to Ronald Reagan and as speechwriter and Deputy Special Assistant to President Richard Nixon. He has participated in nine presidential campaigns, including six at a senior level, and as senior strategic and political adviser to California governors George Deukmejian and Pete Wilson. He earned his Juris Doctor degree at Columbia University.

Martin J. Medhurst is Distinguished Professor of Rhetoric and Communication, and Professor of Political Science, at Baylor University. He has taught at the University of California-Davis and at Texas A&M University. He is the author or editor of thirteen books, including *Presidential Speechwriting* (Texas A&M, 2003), *The Prospect of Presidential Rhetoric* (Texas A&M, 2008), *Before the Rhetorical Presidency* (Texas A&M, 2008), and *Words of a Century: The Top 100 American Speeches, 1900–1999* (Oxford, 2009).

Sidney M. Milkis is the White Burkett Miller Professor of the Department of Politics at the University of Virginia and Assistant Director for Academic Programs at the university's Miller Center of Public Affairs. His books include *The President and the Parties* (Oxford, 1993); *Political Parties and Constitutional Government* (Johns Hopkins, 1999); *Presidential Greatness* (Kansas, 2000) with Marc Landy; *The American Presidency: Origins and Development, 1776–2007*, 5th edition (CQ, 2007) with Michael Nelson; and, most recently, *Theodore Roosevelt, the Progressive Party, and the Transformation of American Democracy* (Kansas, 2009).

Michael Nelson is the Fulmer Professor of Political Science at Rhodes College and a Non-Resident Senior Fellow of the Miller Center of Public Affairs at the University of Virginia. His books include *Presidents, Politics, and Policy*, with Erwin C. Hargrove (1984); *The American Presidency: Origins and Development, 1776–2007* (2007), 5th edition, with Sidney M. Milkis (2007); *How the South Joined the Gambling Nation: The Politics of State Policy Innovation*, with John Lyman Mason (2007); *The Elections of 2008* (2009); and *The Presidency and the Political System*, 9th edition (2010).

Raymond Price headed the writing staff in the Nixon White House and helped President Nixon with several of his post-presidency books. He also authored his own retrospective, entitled *With Nixon* (Viking, 1977). He had previously been on the editorial staffs of *Collier's* and *Life* magazines and was the last editorial page editor of the *New York Herald Tribune*. He resides in New York City.

Russell L. Riley chairs the Presidential Oral History Program at the University of Virginia's Miller Center of Public Affairs. He has taught at Georgetown and the University of Pennsylvania and was an academic program director at the Salzburg Seminar in American Studies in Austria. He is the author of *The Presidency and the Politics of Racial Inequality* (Columbia, 1999) and editor of *Bridging the Constitutional Divide* (Texas A&M, 2010).

Peter Robinson, a former speechwriter for President Ronald Reagan, is a Fellow at the Hoover Institution, the public policy center at Stanford. He is the author of three books, including, most recently, *How Ronald Reagan Changed My Life* (ReganBooks, 2003); the host of *Uncommon Knowledge*, the

Hoover Institution's public affairs interview program; and the editor of the *Hoover Digest*. A trustee of Dartmouth College, Robinson sits on the boards of the United States Commodities Fund and Silent Cal Productions. He is working on a book about the Cold War.

Andrew Rudalevige is Walter E. Beach '56 Chair of Political Science at Dickinson College and former director of Dickinson's Humanities Program in the United Kingdom. He is the author of *Managing the President's Program* (Princeton, 2002) and *The New Imperial Presidency* (Michigan, 2006), and recently coedited *The George W. Bush Legacy* (CQ Press, 2008). He earned his Ph.D. at Harvard University and in a prior life worked in state and local politics in Massachusetts.

Walter Shapiro, since leaving the Carter White House, has covered the last eight presidential campaigns as a columnist and a reporter. He is currently a columnist for Politics Daily, a political Web site launched by AOL in mid-2009. Along the way, he has been on the staff of Salon.com, *USA Today*, *Esquire*, *Time*, *Newsweek*, and the *Washington Post*. He also wrote a book on the 2004 presidential campaign entitled *One-Car Caravan: On the Road with the 2004 Democrats before America Tunes In* (PublicAffairs, 2003).

Kathryn Dunn Tenpas is the Director of the University of Pennsylvania's Washington Semester Program, adjunct professor in the Department of Political Science, and a Non-Resident Senior Fellow at the Brookings Institution. Her primary field is the presidency with a special interest in White House staffing, presidential travel, polling, and reelection campaigns. She has written *Presidents as Candidates* (Routledge, 2003) and has published numerous articles in the *Journal of Politics*, *Public Opinion Quarterly*, *Political Science Quarterly*, the *Brookings Review*, and *Presidential Studies Quarterly*.

Index